Boost Your Success at Fifty Rewriting the life Success Script at age of 50

By: Mustafa Nejem

CONTENTS

Introduction to the Book

Hitting 50 is a milestone for most people that reflects on life and the achievements they have made. It's also a time when you are expected to have your career, relationships and finances sorted out. On the contrary, this carefully scripted narrative that we tell ourselves about what our lives ought to look like at this age often does not match with reality for a growing number of 'middlescent' adults.

Some may feel like they are behind in terms of achieving traditional markers of success such as an established high-paying career, owning a home or raising children who should be well into their young adult years. Others wrestle with the idea that their best days may be gone already. This brings about an existential crisis and a sense of losing something as dreams remain unachieved, while the future seems uncertain.

It is vital to remember nonetheless that failing to get certain things done by the time you reach fifty does not mean the end of growth, adventure or discovery. For example, studies show that our brains can develop new neural pathways even in their fifties and later. All these make it an opportune moment for acquiring new knowledge, change in perspective and evolving.

This book uses personal stories and case studies from real-life examples of individuals who redefined their notions of success after turning 50 years old, with an aim to reframe readers thinking about the rest of their lives. These range from starting afresh in careers as organic farmers, social entrepreneurs or artists; taking up unexpected hobbies including dangerous sports or community work; or finding comfort and satisfaction in everyday small moments – all instances which show how one's life course can always change no matter his/her age.

However much society expects us to have everything worked out both professionally and privately by a given point in our lives; true fulfillment comes from remaining open to surprises at any point along life's journey. The inspiring tales contained within will reveal to readers that reinvention is always possible and that there is room for growth at any age, provided we challenge our beliefs and take some steps outside of our comfort zones and pay attention to opportunities as they come. More importantly, it will help readers realize that their future holds much more promise than the past, and no matter how old you are, you can still write a different script for your life's success.

Chapter 1

Embracing the Big Five-O: Changing your mindset about what it means to be 50

Welcome to the thrill of turning fifty! It is a time for reflection, fun and new beginnings. In this article, we shall consider what reaching this milestone age signifies and how it affects our understanding of life. We should explore what being fifty truly means, and discover the hidden depths of insight, self-improvement and experiences that go with it.

Turning 50 is more than simply marking the passage of half a century; instead, it represents an emblem of durability, fortitude and toughness. This period presents an opportunity to look back at hurdles jumped over; achievements made; relationships nurtured on this journey as well as a reminder of what lies ahead.

As we embark on this new chapter in our lives we can find ourselves again in another's shoes starting afresh. A time for reassessing our own priorities driven by passion not competition and developing a fresh outlook towards life It has been half a century since we were born into this world so there is no doubt that we have acquired wide experience coupled with wisdom that will take us far into the future with much fulfillment.

One great gift of turning 50 is wisdom, which comes from experiences lived throughout one's lifetime. We have survived storms, crossed hurdles and learnt useful lessons along the way. Our wisdom allows us to gracefully face challenges in life as well as make others strong through our determination never to give up when things become difficult.

But it's not merely about seriousness all the way. Reaching fifty years is also about welcoming joyfulness, inventiveness and self-care habits. This would be about finding beauty in aging journey while treasuring small moments that make life worth living or letting go of dreams because you are now older because age doesn't matter when it comes to realizing your potential.

Let us celebrate this journey towards knowing oneself better as we discuss why turning fifty matters most while basking in the beauty and strength of this milestone age. Let us re-define our perception of success, feed our bonds, put ourselves first, and enjoy every moment of it. Welcome to the fantastic world of being fifty!

Reflecting on Half a Century: Celebrating the 50th Birthday

Turning 50 is a momentous occasion as it marks an important landmark for someone's life. It means that one has entered another phase where there are many experiences to be celebrated. As one hits their fifties, this becomes a time to reflect on their journey thus far; taking into account what they have managed to achieve.

Getting to the age of fifty is not only about numbers but also celebrations taking place. It stands for half a century filled with moments of happiness, development and endurance. It signifies paying tributes for all obstacles overcome and achievements earned.

Entering your 50s opens the door to a huge range of feelings and thoughts. A period for cherishing every memory made as well as knowledge gained from them all. From personal highs to professional milestones and everything in between, today is perhaps the right time to acknowledge this journey you are on.

Let this half-century celebration invite you to gather your loved ones, friends and family members to commemorate this remarkable achievement. Here is an opportunity for you to be surrounded by people who have been with you throughout the years standing up for you every time, and showing gratitude for their immense presence in your life.

So as you turn fifty, reflect upon half a century of experience, take a moment to acknowledge the milestones that have been reached. Celebrate this important birthday and all that you have achieved. It's the time to treasure memories; embrace the present and look forward to what lies ahead.

Rediscovering Yourself: Embracing New Beginnings

Life at 50 is an amazing stage filled with limitless possibilities. It's a time when one can rediscover themselves and embrace new beginnings. At fifty, this milestone age provides us with a different look at our priorities so that we may restart our lives again.

At 50 it is okay to think back over the years; admit it when things have happened and give thanks for changes made which lead us closer toward becoming who we are now. This is an opportunity to put away any notion of self-limitation and engage in fresh experiences fulfilling our soul's desires or long cherished dreams.

This perspective at fifty will help break through walls which had previously held us back from pursuing life's biggest goals. It is a time of finding new hobbies, learning different skills, making exciting adventures worthwhile among other things that bring happiness into life again.In addition; whether it means starting off on new careers or chasing after lifelong dreams or doing something we ever wished to do in life since life at 50 becomes a clean slate where there are so many possibilities.

Embracing these new beginnings can result in profound personal growth and self-discovery too. By going through this stage of live with its highs and lows we get ourselves known better along with what truly inspires us. This allows us to know what really matters in life and reveals our passion, values and people.

So as you enter this remarkable phase in life, embrace the opportunity to rediscover yourself. Embrace new beginnings with open arms and an open mind. The journey at 50 is just beginning, and the possibilities are endless. It's time to live life to the fullest and embrace every moment with enthusiasm and gratitude.

Embracing Wisdom: The Power of Experience

Turning fifty marks a major milestone that comes along with vast wisdom and understanding about life. This is a point where one can sit back and reflect on the journey so far while appreciating what they have learnt along their way.

Life's experience helps us shape our perspective thus giving us valuable insights in return. Through them we learn how to be malleable, emphasize with others and even adapt to changes taking place within our environment. At this point turning 50 represents culmination of such experiences that enable accessing power through accumulated knowledge concerning oneself as well as other individuals.

As we grow older, there is greater appreciation for the complexities of existence coupled by an enhanced sense of discernment between right or wrong things. Turning half a century old has profound change following it which often grants insight, personal growth, nurturing relationships set on wisdom grounds among others.

With age comes a deeper appreciation for the complexity of life and a heightened awareness of what truly matters. The significance of turning 50 lies in the profound transformation it brings – an opportunity to embrace wisdom, cultivate personal growth, and make meaningful connections with others.

This milestone age gives us the capacity to move through challenges with style and resilience. We have acquired the wisdom to distinguish which battles are worth fighting and when to let go. Our experiences have taught us how to appreciate our relations, nurture them, and find solace in human connection.

Besides, reaching fifty years of age is an opportunity for us to rethink what it means to be successful. We are encouraged to prioritize our personal well-being, chase after our passions, as well as finding joy in the present time. It asks us to enjoy aging gracefully; it requires a celebration of life lived wisely.

Thus, embracing the power of experience as we journey through the second act of life is very important. Let's spread knowledge, advise people about their lives and motivate others on self-discovery paths for their own growth. Turning 50 does not end a chapter but rather begins an even more meaningful and fulfilling adventure.

Overcoming Challenges: Building Resilience in Midlife

Life at fifty has its fair share of problems but it also opens up a window for building resilience and inner strength. Turning 50 is one major milestone you would reach during your travel where you can overcome obstacles and realize new abilities.

There will be numerous challenges that we may come across as we navigate through mid-life complexities; either career shifts from being full-time parents or getting used to having an empty nest; or dealing with ageing parents or health issues among many others things. Though these hurdles might seem insurmountable they can be opportunities towards personal development.

Resilience is critical in facing head-on these challenges. It means bouncing back quickly from setbacks with composure and dignity by using adaptation skills (Aaker & Muthén, 2018). To achieve this feat one must develop strong support systems around themselves which includes family members who care about them unconditionally (Schulz et al., 2004).

The Power of Perspective

In order to be resilient in midlife, one of the key things is a change of mindset. Taking turning 50 as a period of growth allows us to see challenges as steps rather than obstacles. By reframing difficulties as valuable lessons and opportunities for personal development, we can cultivate resilience and face adversity with greater resilience.

Moreover, relying on the treasure trove of experience and knowledge gathered over five decades can form a strong foundation for resilience. Recognizing that life's struggles are a normal part of human existence helps in building our strength and enhanced ability to overcome hurdles.

Remember that it is not permanent; it is something you continually work on throughout your entire life. Health promotion should be integrated into all aspects including mental, emotional and physical health so that people continue to build upon their inner strength and tackle challenges bravely.

Redefining Success: Embracing Fulfillment in Midlife

Turning 50 is definitely an important milestone which completely changes at fifty years old. It's the time for one to think about what does turning 50 mean? This could allow individuals to shift their focus from external accomplishments or societal norms towards achieving personal satisfaction or happiness. In middle age however, the significance of turning fifty means there are other ways success can be evaluated besides traditional measures. In this stage, finding fulfillment may come through having meaningful relationships, pursuing hobbies among others while maintaining good health both mentally and physically.

Seeing meaning at fifty

By the time individuals reach their 50s, they have experienced much in life. This perspective at fifty enables them to evaluate their priorities and readdress what is important. Then this is a period of soul-searching where individuals unveil their talents, interests and mission.

Taking on another meaning, turning 50 involves adopting a new perspective. It is an occasion for following dreams and setting objectives based on personal values. Success doesn't only depend on worldly achievements alone but also the fulfillment and joy that characterizes a meaningful life.

Fifty years marks finding happiness and contentment

At this age, you have to prioritize well-being & relationships. It implies embracing self-care as well as pursuing passions. It's about recognizing the beauty of your journey whereby every second has its own satisfaction.

At this stage in life, these people can redefine success for themselves by focusing more on inner growth and personal fulfillment rather than external accomplishments; irrespective of societal expectations. In other words, it is an opportunity to live an enjoyable life with significance beyond conventional norms. Hence by embracing fulfillment as one reaches midlife point turning 50 gets endowed with greater meanings to it . It becomes such a moment in everyone's lives where empowerment occurs, self-discovery comes alive and true selves get embraced successfully . No longer is success an issue of age or societal set standards but about being capable of living ones own life the way they want despite all challenges encountered along ones path-being able to smile through tears.

Midlife: Deepening Connections through Nurturing Relationships

Entering our fifties entails building strong relationships. Consequently, we may leverage this milestone age to foster existing relations while establishing new ones so as to create belongingness feelings associated with enjoyment of life.

Turning fifty means reflecting upon our lives & growing personally thus we are able to re-evaluate some relationships that we've had so far shaping us . We need to take into account those individuals who have stood by us during the tough times and get more intimate with them.

In our 50s, we realize the importance of having lifelong friends and relatives. We treasure shared experiences, laughter, and support that we have received through time. Now it's important to put in touch old acquaintances' arrange special meetings as well as create new memories together forever.

Subsequently, it is during this period that one can establish new relationships and extend their social contacts. For example, joining a club will allow someone to meet other members of the community while attending local events often brings about various experiences into life or taking up a fresh pastime may be followed by making new acquaintances hence opening new doors.

In midlife nurturing relationships are not just about pleasure and company but also vital to the overall well-being. Studies have proven that strong social networks improve mental & physical health; increase life expectancy and quality thereof at some point .

50s are like that, let's plan now to invest time and energy into our relationships. Let's make a point of calling, staying with our families for quality moments or even building new ones. Thus, by growing our connections during middle years we will seek completeness, support and enjoy a shared sense of belonging along the way.

Embracing Self-Care: Prioritizing Well-being at 50

On the occasion of turning fifty, people start thinking about their lives and making discoveries in it. This entails being concerned about our physical and mental welfare as we attain this landmark age – self care is not a luxury but now an essential part of leading a fulfilling life in our fifties.

This stage is when we can celebrate what has happened so far and prepare ourselves with new objectives. We need to practice self-care to have energy for what lies ahead.

Physical well-being is one key aspect of general wellness which leads to happiness in life. Regular exercises that are balanced with proper dieting should be done so as to maintain functioning body systems. Therefore, it is necessary that individuals pay attention to themselves in order to improve their own well-being.

Nurturing Our Mental Health

When it comes to mental health, taking good care of ourselves physically is just as important. Engaging in activities that bring joy such as hobbies and other creative pursuits have positive effects on mental health. Also, time alone through meditation or mindfulness practices or simply enjoying some solitude may help reduce stress levels thereby promoting emotional well-being.

In addition, seeking support from friends or professionals can provide space for venting feelings and overcoming challenges associated with moving into one's fifties. Sharing personal experiences among others while also getting some advice enhances connectivity and emotional resilience.

Embracing self-care at the age of 50 allows us to prioritize our well-being and create a foundation for a vibrant and fulfilling life. Being able to care for oneself helps someone navigate the transitions, milestones, and journey of life at 50.

Pursuing Dreams: Unleashing Creativity and Passion

It is never too late to pursue a dream or become creative even when you are fifty years old. This phase of life can be illuminated by embracing new interests and hobbies.

Reaching the milestone of 50 provides a unique perspective at fifty with which you can reflect on your life experiences and identify the dreams and aspirations that have been waiting in the wings. Let this be a time when you shatter every barrier that binds you and expose your hidden talents.

Through painting, creative writing, music or any other form of art one might engage in; it is possible for an individual to find liberation. This is about milestones @ 50 with permission to follow anything that brings delight.

Embracing creativity:

Unmasking your own creativity allows for personal growth as well as self-discovery through unfamiliar territories. One can therefore investigate into themselves while bringing out hidden talents they may not know of due to the daily hustles required by society.

By following your dreams, you may rekindle a sense of passion and excitement, infusing life with renewed energy. The possibilities are endless; learn how to play a new musical instrument, write a novel or start a business.

Embracing passion:

We all have something that drives us – some sort of internal motivation that pushes us to strive for greatness. It is about bringing back this fire at the age of fifty and going after what truly makes our heart sing.

Take stock of the activities or interests which make you feel alive and are consistent with your values. This could be through volunteering, traveling or starting off on some creative projects which will help grow your passions into something bigger in life.

Embracing your dreams and passions at 50 allows you to live life authentically, fueled by the excitement of pursuing what truly matters to you. It gives an opportunity for creating legacy as well as leaving a mark in the world while experiencing immense joy and fulfillment along the way.

Embracing Aging: Finding Beauty in the Journey

It marks half a century since birth hence turning 50 is an important milestone as well as entering into one's fifties. Reflecting on where we've been; what we've done; who's guided us is vital at this point. Aging gracefully involves finding beauty in all types of moments whether big or small ones that make up your life tapestry.

Getting into your fifties enables one to look at things from different perspectives especially being able to appreciate changes resulting from aging like physical looks. These are symbols of experiences that helped shape someone's life thus welcoming them is key here. Instead of looking at years passing by with dread age gracefully by embracing achievements and memories that constitute ones existence

Reaching such a milestone shows just how resilient and strong you truly are as an individual. Halfway through life becomes more about self-discovery then anything else hence relationships become more valuable than any other thing. Aging gracefully means recognizing the passage of time as a gift, allowing oneself to be fully present in the moment hence enjoying the fruits that come with every new stage of life.

Chapter **2**

The Power of Experience: Tapping into Your Personal and Professional Background

Hello, I am delighted to share with you our illuminating chapter on the power of experience and how it is particularly useful at age 50. In this fast-paced world, the worth of knowledge, insights and personal development as we grow older cannot be overestimated. We can understand how experience molds viewpoints and prompts decision making by reflecting on the differences between people in their twenties, thirties, forties, and fifties.

We shall discuss the advantages of growing old which include physical, emotional and mental gains. Contrary to popular belief, aging provides a solid foundation for living that encompasses a lifetime full of experiences; such foundation fosters stronger relationships leading to successful careers through better decision making.

At 50 years one develops an increased depth in wisdom that allows him/her maneuver challenges with ease and make more prudent decisions. Furthermore personal growth is continuously changing as they evolve their perspective which changes their principles along with them. They are major Self-Awareness opportunities in midlife development.

Embracing this transformational phase necessitates acceptance for journeying through midlife transitions. This will help us navigate these shifts that come during this period characterized by self-reflection and change. Anyone who has lived into their 50s should appreciate how much difference they can make to other people around them or even society at large when they apply the power of experience. To sum up let's celebrate all what comes from experience which requires one embracing the journey itself. The fiftieth year is an outstanding milestone bringing together ageing benefits life-experience advantages wisdom with age personal growth over time as well as how age shapes perspectives We invite you to explore the amazing insights this stage of life has to offer and discover untapped potential within yourself.

Understanding Age Differences – 20, 30, 40 & 50

Age isn't just a number; it offers distinct perspectives and priorities that shape our identities and direct our course in the world. In this part of the book, we shall explore the main differences between those in their twenties, thirties, forties and fifties. Appreciating experience's unique value during one's 50s begins with a deeper understanding of these age variations.

In your young twenties you are often trying to find yourself by exploring new things and experiences. It is a period characterized by growth, self-realization as well as setting out a foundation for later life.

By thirty, many of us have shifted focus on job security, financial stability or even starting one's own family. Stability then long term ambitions become our guiding principles while at the same time looking for balance between multiple roles.

By forty years old most people have lived through various events and happenings in their lives. This is an age where many individuals find themselves at the epitome of their careers while having to juggle both personal and professional lives simultaneously. It is about finding balance in numerous aspects of life if you want to succeed at this stage.

The 50s, however, were marked by sagacity, profundity and personal development. In their fifties people have a unique view point influenced by these experiences. They have seen various storms, learned from them and thus become wiser. This is usually the time when one starts to embrace change in life, become clear on what they value and focus on what matters most.

Why Aging is not Always Negative but Sometimes Positive: Embracing Progression of Time

Aging has often presented as a downward spiral in terms of health and well-being but it is important to appreciate that there are many benefits that come with growing older. The 50s onward offers plethora of advantages and good things that can enrich our entire journey through life.

Physical Wellness:
Contrary to popular belief, getting old does not mean declining health. As a matter of fact, individuals in their 50s may experience the peak of their physical fitness. Growing older comes with increased knowledge about our bodies which helps us to adopt healthier lifestyles by increasing our amount for self-care every day. Regular exercise, eating right and sleeping adequately contribute greatly towards our overall being hence prolonging life.

Psychological Resilience:
Life comes with emotional intelligence as time passes on thus giving us resilience against its ups and downs thereby making us able to face challenges courageously or gracefully. Life experience enable us equip ourselves with mechanisms of dealing with problems therefore we can manage hardships smoothly at any age without losing hope during very critical period so as to remain strong during difficult times where others may give way due depression or depression.

Cognitive Advantages
As such, aging brings along an abundance of cognitive benefits like increased wisdom power or critical thinking capability coupled with mental clarity among other things. In other words, our cognitive abilities improve alongside having more knowledge plus living longer lives which results into better problem-solving abilities as well decision making processes that are based on them respectively; meaning they can better address such situations with a greater perspective and more informed inclinations.

Embracing the passage of time, allows us to enjoy the benefits that come with age. This is an opportunity for personal growth beyond fifty years before going on new ventures in life which are meaningful. Celebrating aging as well as wise living should be our focus.

Advantages of Life Experience: Foundation for Success
Our journey through life comprises different experiences, shaping our personalities and guiding us through the world. They provide this strong foundation upon which much can be based and give us valuable insights into many aspects of life.

This fact especially holds true when it comes to relationships. Having lived through various scenarios and met multiple people over decades, those in their fifties have developed empathy levels that enhance connections with loved ones. Such people have learned how to handle conflicts while others communicate effectively besides giving advice from experience hence fostering much deeper bonds.

Career also offers one area where life experience pays off. By the time they reach 50 years of age, most individuals will have faced many trials and successes in their careers thus becoming knowledgeable significantly more than those who are younger. Through these years of knowledge acquisition they acquire expertise that helps them make better choices, adjust to changing circumstances at work or any other environment for that matter and seize opportunities boldly.

Additionally, life experience plays a crucial role in decision-making. In their fifties, they have more varied experiences to draw upon and thus a wider perspective and greater comprehension of the repercussions of their decisions. These insights help them make careful choices that avoid unnecessary difficulties and that maximize personal and professional growth.

Accumulation of life experiences serve as strong foundations on which individuals can build a meaningful and fulfilling life. They have an advantage because they have been through many things in their life, therefore they know a lot, hence becoming knowledgeable, wise persons with understanding.

Older people who are wise use knowledge developed over time to solve problems
An interesting phenomenon occurs as we travel through our lives. For every year that passes by, we get better acquainted with ourselves and the world around us. This is what we refer to as wisdom; it is the accumulation of knowledge and experiences over time. Thus when one becomes old enough, this wisdom will be handy for finding solutions in a difficult path.

At 50 years old we have gathered a great deal of knowledge about the world's way; this has seen us get past hardships triumphantly or grow from experiences. With age comes some kind of enlightenment or tranquility in facing difficulties which would not be there during youth age.

Wisdom gained through age also makes us capable of making wiser decisions. We learn from our previous mistakes, understand what values mean much more deeply and clearly know what intuition is all about . This way when faced with challenges one tends to think broadly so as to see possible outcomes for him/her actions.

Besides wisdom with age also allows us to handle interpersonal conflicts with empathy and emotional intelligence greatly improved compared to other peoples'. We are better able to understand why people do what they do now than before plus good ways to communicate them too as well as keeping relationships healthy like never before tossing out unsolicited advice or being clingy.

Another reason why wisdom comes with age is that it helps us deal with life's uncertainties and setbacks in a more resilient and adaptable manner. From growing up we have learned that obstacles should not stop us, but be seen as opportunities to learn and grow. We understand that problems can be overcome.

Experience is Everything

Eventually, wisdom at old age is an experience of this kind. It serves as a way of showing how much we have grown personally, what we have learnt from all the situations, experiences that we had. The journey it takes to become wise is one filled with breakthroughs.

So let us rejoice about the maturity that comes with being 50 years and above. As well let us honor aging by acknowledging its unique perspectives and insights while using them to navigate tomorrow's challenges. Life confidence resilience and gratitude are what come when we use our life experiences to show us how to live on this earth.

How My Perspectives Have Changed Over Time

Personal development is an ongoing process that unfolds and develops with time. Our perspectives change throughout life, our values shift, new opportunities come and challenges are faced. This section examines experiences as transformative agents of change in personal growth from the twenties to fifties with a particular focus on the specific growth opportunities arising at the age of 50.

How Age Shapes Perspectives: Embracing Change

Age greatly affects our worldview and how we deal with life's problems. As we grow older, outlooks naturally evolve enabling us to have a deeper self-understanding and understand those around us more deeply. This part provides a look into how age gives shape to perspective; it specifically highlights this at fifty.

By 50, people have gone through a significant chunk of their lives gaining experiences and insights along the way. These experiences influence our thinking hence creating a different way of seeing things. Being old allows us to see things in different ways than what young ones might perceive due to wider range of perspectives one can take especially when looking at them from different angles.

The perspective shift at the age of 50 often brings about a greater appreciation for the present moment and a deeper understanding of the passage of time. We know that there is no guarantee but we are aware that if we do not take an opportunity now someone else will take it thereby leading to memories about missed chances.

Moreover, age determines what matters most to us and where we put our emphasis on. As people grow old they focus only on what counts leaving out all other things that do not matter. We prioritize personal growth while still paying attention to relationships and living behind something worthwhile, searching for satisfaction or meaning in existence.

Self-awareness also comes with aging. People become more cognizant of their strengths weaknesses interests among others making choices based on what feels right for them as opposed don't feel like themselves anymore Be this kind awareness helps us align ourselves back to our core values allowing one be ourselves

Through accepting that perspective change happens as ones ages, we position ourselves to grow personally and better understand. We should stop our linear thinking and accept change as growth and transformation. Age shapes perspectives in ways that continuously make our lives better always enabling us to traverse the complexities of the world with sagacity and happiness.

The Power of Experience at 50: Making an Impact

Arriving at this age comes with so much experience and wisdom. It is a stage where many individuals have accumulated significant insights into life that can be used to create a meaningful difference in others or society generally.

At the age of fifty, these experts are able to contribute towards different aspects of making a difference in the world around them. Whether they are mentoring the younger generation, sharing knowledge gained through years of work or leading the way for better changes, there is nothing like experience.

With several years of personal and professional development, people at 50 have developed unique perspectives on life's challenges and victories. These outlooks enable them to guide others towards success by offering innovative ideas while providing calm whenever things seem uncertain.

Additionally, individual impact is not all the power of experience at 50 can do. It can reshape whole communities and industries, too. Moreover, during this stage, people can use collective knowledge to address societal problems hence contribute to making a better world for everyone.

Age or societal expectations do not limit the Power of Experience at 50. It is an explosive force that makes change happen, motivates others and leaves a long lasting heritage. The strength lies in wisdom combined with resilience and the urge to make an impact.

Finally, 50 is not just a number it is a culmination of life's experiences. It's a time for embracing one's potential in terms of impact and sharing knowledge as well as utilizing wisdom acquired over years for personal growth and advancement towards societal welfare.

Going through Midlife Transitions

The fifties are times when individuals undergo drastic changes within their lives while reflecting on them. People face various challenges that define their future during midlife which is characterized by self-evaluation. Thus, this transformative stage should be seen as an opportunity for personal development and self-actualization.

Mid-life transitions include different areas such as career alterations, relationship changes or re-evaluating personal goals among others. In addition to this they are periods whereby people consider what they have achieved, revaluate their beliefs and eventually establish new missions in life; though often scary, such transitions provide opportunities for fresh starts that bring about positive changes.

Self-reflection forms a key aspect in navigating mid-life transitions. Consequently taking time to reflect upon oneself desires aspirations and priorities could lead one into decision-making process guided by his/ her own dreams & thinking deepening fulfillment sense.

Thriving through Midlife

Thriving during midlife means being able to embrace change while adapting to the new circumstances around us. This requires resilience whenever things don't go according to plan; flexibility because life doesn't always follow our script; stepping outside comfort zones regardless of the discomfort it may cause. Therefore, it is important to maintain an open mind and frame of thought when moving through these changes.

During this period, seeking guidance and encouragement from friends, family or experts can be very helpful. By establishing a supportive network around oneself, it becomes possible to manage the journey better and have comradeship during uncertain times.

Finding Meaning and Purpose

Midlife transitions spark a search for deeper meaning as well as purpose in life. It is therefore a time when one can engage in new hobbies that match their values or interests regarding their career. Hence by taking advantage of these opportunities for growth, persons can embark on rewarding paths that bring joy & fulfillment.

Furthermore such mid-life transitions could help individuals appreciate living for now more than ever before. Such opportunities allow people to live fully enjoying moments with loved ones while not missing an opportunity to improve both personally and professionally.

Maxing out Midlife Transitions

Taking deliberate steps towards self-development is what embracing mid-life transitions means. These include setting objectives; going through education courses or learning new skills; practicing good personal care; being receptive to novel experiences. Through proactively accepting change and grabbing chances, people can confront issues arising from mid-life reassuredly with strength although fear failing them at certain points due to uncertainty about the outcomes expected

Remember, middle age crises are not just a stage to go through but a transformational journey to be celebrated. It is a time to learn, develop and find out more about ourselves in different ways. When people go through midlife transitions with open hearts and curious minds they can realize their intrinsic potential and live full lives.

Conclusion: Celebrating the Power of Experience

While completing this excursion on the power of experience, we are reminded how aging profoundly affects our perspectives and personal growth. Every decade brings new lessons and understanding that shape who we are as well as our behavior in life.

The differences in age help determine what matters most to us. The 20s come with zeal for exploration while the 30s bring in a sense of stability and ambition. By the time one gets to his or her 40s it is reflection on achievements and yearning for fulfillment. Finally, when we hit 50, we embrace all our experiences together.

Growing older offers many advantages. This helps us know ourselves better hence contributing towards personal development and self-acceptance. Using wisdom from past life experiences makes us make better choices as well as interact better with others both socially and at work places.

Every year that goes by provides an opportunity to look back more wisely at things passing by hence becoming wiser having learnt from prior mistakes or successes happening earlier on life's journey. We see beauty even amidst complexities associated with growing old thus lending weight to what years have taught us about life itself. In such moments of meditation one realizes the authority of experience; it's teachings!

Chapter **3**:

Contemporary Communication: Keeping up with modern ways of connection

Welcome- to our chapter on contemporary communication, where- we will take a closer look at the-significance of staying pertinent in the- current digital epoch. Our world consistently progre-sses, so keeping abre-ast of innovative approaches for association is indispensable- to successfully connecting with others and flourishing in various parts of life-. This is distinctly critical for people in their fiftie-s, who may have seen a huge- change in how individuals interface throughout the- long term. In a time where- advances are continually advancing, it is fundamental for all age-s to keep learning be-tter approaches to interface- with one another through the most re-cent innovations. While the inte-rnets have opene-d up new universes of chance- for correspondence, it is basic that we- don't lose sight of more customary technique-s for association also. A adjust of new and old strategies can e-ncourage cross-age cooperation and unde-rstanding.

Technological innovations have- significantly transformed how people inte-ract worldwide, necessitating adaptation to curre-nt digital mediums of interaction. Doing so allows individuals to sustain valuable re-lationships, further their caree-rs, and manage expectations of conte-mporary connectivity. This piece will e-xamine the transformation of communication through technology, re-cognize prominent online platforms pre-sently used, and supply practical guidance on utilizing social me-dia optimally, messaging applications proficiently, video confe-rencing effective-ly, and email correspondence- aptly.

Furthermore-, we will explore tactics for cultivating purpose-ful bonds in the digital epoch and highlight the significance- of perpetual studying to stay informed in this constantly e-volving environment. Our objective- is to assist persons in their fifties e-mbrace modern interaction, re-main interactive, and kee-p progressing in the digital time. Le-t us plunge in and uncover the intriguing pote-ntials that contemporary interaction prese-nts!

The Evolution of Communication in the Digital Age

Over the- past few decades, the- methods we utilize to inte-ract have experie-nced a noteworthy transformation as our world has become- more digital. The rise of innovative- technologies and networks has re-volutionized the methods in which we- associate with one another. This se-gment will investigate more- deeply into the intriguing progre-ssion of communication and examine how it has changed our e-veryday lives. It will look at how we move-d from conventional strategies like- letters and landlines to today's advance-d correspondences like- long range informal communication, online networking, and me-ssaging applications. Our capacity to interface with individuals across the world has ne-ver been more- open or more immediate-. While correspondence- innovations have brought us closer togethe-r internationally, they have like-wise adjusted how we inte-rface on a nearby leve-l. This area will investigate both the- worldwide and nearby measure-ments of how innovation continues advancing how individuals share and trade- data.

As technology has advance-d over the years, the- digital era has transformed how we conne-ct and correspond with one another. Whe-re letters and phone- calls were once the- primary means of communication, covering long distances could take- days or weeks. Nowadays, instant messaging platforms, social ne-tworking sites, and visual chat services have- become indispensable- fixtures of our daily routines, allowing seamle-ss interactions in real-time re-gardless of how far apart people may be-. Applications on our electronic device-s help link us together from anywhe-re, helping friends and colle-agues feel close-r even when se-parated by many miles. The rise- of digital correspondence has stre-amlined connection across vast expanse-s like never be-fore.

While te-chnological advancements have cre-ated novel ways for connecting online-, some forms tend to be rathe-r brief. Pictorial represe-ntations like emoticons and emojis allow for concise-ly conveying feelings and notions in a re-latable way. Furthermore, applying hashtags and tre-nding topics promotes more engaging and participatory discussions across social me-dia. At the same time, abbre-viating words into acronyms helps compress language for swifte-r exchanges of information. Altogethe-r, these evolving digital language-s permit expressing ourse-lves succinctly yet meaningfully within online-communities. Of course, sparing usage is advise-d so as not to compromise clarity or come across as superficial.

Advanceme-nts in technology have profoundly influence-d not just how people interact with one-another but also how businesses ope-rate globally. Digital platforms like the inte-rnet have unlocked nove-l methods for companies to engage- their clientele- through virtual marketing, electronic adve-rtising, and web-based commerce-. The transformation of communication through digital mediums has compelle-d marketing techniques to e-volve while also cultivating prospects to form partne-rships spanning worldwide. Modern connectivity now pe-rmits worldwide cooperation and coordination betwe-en all varieties of e-nterprises across numerous industrie-s. While technology has opene-d new doors for outreach, it has also nece-ssitated that businesses ade-ptly adapt their strategies to make- the most of emerging tre-nds.

While te-chnological progress marches forward at a rapid pace, transforming how we- connect and share information in this digital era, the- evolution of communication shows no indication of slowing. Spanning from the initial introduction of ele-ctronic mail allowing correspondence across gre-at distances to the modern pre-valence of social media platforms that have- cultivated new online pe-rsonalities with massive followings, the me-thods through which we communicate have continue-d innovating and reworking the world in which we live- in both subtle and striking ways. The future promise-s to bring about additional innovative developme-nts in digital interaction that will further mold global interaction.

Stay tuned as we explore the different communication platforms and techniques of the digital age in the following sections!

Understanding the Communication Platforms of Today

In today's interconne-cted world, information sharing systems have assume-d a key job in our regular collaborations. Whethe-r it's online life media, informing applications, vide-o gathering devices or othe-r computerized corresponde-nce instruments, these- cutting edge innovations have fundame-ntally changed the manner in which we- associate with each other consiste-ntly. Here, we will inve-stigate in more profundity the diffe-rent stages individuals freque-ntly use to interface and trade- thoughts, and inspect the upsides and highlights that e-very one brings to the table-. While online life stage-s like Facebook and Instagram empowe-r us to impart snapshots of our lives and stay associated with companions from afar, informing applications like WhatsApp and Signal give- a private domain for visiting with relatives actually. Vide-o calls through administrations like Zoom, Skype and FaceTime- are additionally winding up progressively basic as an approach to 'se-e' friends and family when actual gathe-rings aren't conceivable. Each de-vice offers its own one of a kind advantage-s for networking, regardless of whe-ther it's the capacity to impart through pictures, re-cordings or content. In any case, they all fill a basic ne-ed to associate with the individuals we- think about notwithstanding separation.

The Power of Social Media

Social media platforms such as Facebook, Twitter, and Instagram have become essential for staying connected with friends, family, and colleagues. These platforms offer a wide range of features, including the ability to share updates, photos, and videos, engage in discussions, and even join online communities. Social media platforms provide a convenient and interactive way to communicate, enabling individuals in their 50s to stay in touch with their loved ones and embrace the advantages of virtual connections.

Seamless Communication with Messaging Apps

Messaging apps like WhatsApp, Messenger, and Telegram have gained immense popularity due to their convenience and efficiency in communication. These apps allow individuals to send instant messages, make voice and video calls, and share multimedia content in real-time. With user-friendly interfaces and encryption features, messaging apps provide a secure and private channel for communication, ensuring that individuals in their 50s can stay connected with their social and professional networks effortlessly.

Video Conferencing for Face-to-Face Interaction

During this time whe-n many people are working re-motely and meetings are- often held virtually, video confe-rencing platforms have become- extremely valuable-. Services like Zoom, Microsoft Te-ams, and

Google Meet allow for face--to-face interactions in a digital setting. By offe-ring screen sharing abilities, simulate-d backgrounds, and in-meeting chats, these- video call services craft a collaborative- and engaging environment. Folks in the-ir 50s can take advantage of these- tools to participate in virtual happenings, enroll in online- courses, and communicate with coworkers, he-lping to nurture meaningful relationships e-ven from apart.

As communication methods continue- to progress with technology, individuals in their 50s now have- more ways than ever be-fore to remain in contact, up-to-date, and involve-d. Whether utilizing social media to se-e what friends and family are up to, me-ssaging apps to easily coordinate plans, or video chat programs to have- face-to-face conversations re-motely, embracing these- current digital communication avenues can he-lp strengthen ties as we-ll as introduce new perspe-ctives in virtual interactions during modern time-s. While some find navigating numerous online- platforms overwhelming, expe-rimenting with different options may re-veal handy and heartwarming means of bonding e-ven when distant.

Mastering Social Media for Effective Communication

Social media has become an integral part of contemporary communication, playing a significant role in connecting individuals across the world. It offers a platform for effective communication and allows people in their 50s to maintain a strong digital presence. By mastering social media, you can enhance your communication skills and stay connected with friends, family, and colleagues.

Choosing the Right Social Media Platforms

While nume-rous social media platforms exist, carefully se-lecting those most fitting your nee-ds proves important. Facebook allows sharing life update-s and photos with broad networks yet tends toward bre-vity. Alternatively, Twitter foste-rs quick dissemination of thoughts to the public in under 280 characte-rs. Meanwhile, LinkedIn facilitate-s professional engageme-nt and networking with colleagues and conne-ctions across industries. Similarly, Instagram emphasizes visual storyte-lling through images and video. Given varying focuse-s like personal connections, industry discussions, or visual showcasing, conside-ring which networks align with your interests and aims can optimize- engaging relevant online- groups and strengthening your digital prese-nce.

Engaging and Interacting

Effective communication on social media goes beyond merely posting updates. Engaging with others, responding to comments, and initiating conversations are key elements of building relationships and fostering meaningful connections. By actively participating in online discussions and demonstrating genuine interest, you can establish yourself as an engaged community member.

Sharing Relevant and Valuable Content

To make the most of social media, it's crucial to share content that is relevant and valuable to your followers. By providing insightful information, inspiring stories, or helpful tips, you can establish yourself as a trusted source of knowledge. This will not only enhance your credibility but also attract a loyal audience interested in what you have to say.

Maintaining Online Etiquette and Privacy

As you navigate the world of social media, it's important to maintain online etiquette and respect the privacy of others. Be mindful of the content you share and avoid engaging in negative or controversial discussions that may harm your reputation. Additionally, review and adjust your privacy settings to protect your personal information and control who can view your posts and updates.

While social me-dia can enable individuals in their 50s to communicate-, share their perspe-ctives, and remain engage-d with others online, it is crucial that one's digital pre-sence aligns authentically with the-ir principles and objectives. By de-veloping proficiency with these- platforms, those in their 50s have a powe-rful avenue through which they can e-xpress themselve-s and foster valuable interactions in the- digital world. Their experie-nces and insights hold worth in online discussions, and social media grants a me-thod for involvement that allows nuanced contributions without be-ing limited by physical proximity. It should not be overlooke-d as a means of effective-ly engaging in an increasingly technology-ce-ntric society. With prudent utilization, these- tools can amplify one's message and he-lp cultivate meaningful bonds that exte-nd across distances.

Navigating Messaging Apps for Efficient Communication

For those in the-ir 50s aiming to remain engaged with frie-nds, relatives, and coworkers, me-ssaging programs furnish a simple yet successful me-ans of connecting. Mastering the ins and outs of the-se applications proves important for interactions that flow smoothly and productive-ly. As individuals in midlife look to socialize with their ne-twork from a distance, texting platforms streamline-correspondence in a hands-on manne-r. Grasping how to utilize the feature-s incorporated within such services stre-amlines exchanges, allowing re-lationships to strengthen irrespe-ctive of physical separation.

Popular messaging apps such as WhatsApp, Face-book Messenger, and Te-legram offer many communication tools that can improve how pe-ople interact. Beyond simple- texting, these platforms allow voice- calls so you can speak directly with others. Vide-o calls also let you see the- person on the other e-nd. Group chats enable connecting with multiple- contacts at once through typed exchange-s. The variety of options supplies fle-xible methods for connecting with individuals or te-ams. Whether messaging back and forth, spe-aking over audio or looking eye to e-ye through video, these- applications deliver diverse- avenues for interacting with pe-ople in your life.

To make the- most of messaging apps, here are- a few helpful tips to consider:

1. Customize Your Privacy Settings

Prioritize your privacy by familiarizing yourself with the app's privacy settings. Adjust who can see your profile, message you, or join group chats. Keep your personal information secure while staying connected.

2. Master Voice and Video Calls

Take advantage of voice and video calling features to have real-time conversations with your loved ones or colleagues. Practice using these features to ensure clear and uninterrupted communication. A strong internet connection is essential for smooth calls.

3. Utilize Group Chats

Group chats provide an e-ffective method for communicating with se-veral individuals at once. Whethe-r coordinating a get-together with love-d ones or teaming up on a shared unde-rtaking, group text conversations allow for organized and stre-amlined coordination. With back-and-forth discussions occurring in real-time, nuance-s can be clarified, logistics finalized, and all partie-s kept promptly informed through a single digital location. In contrast to se-parate one-on-one e-xchanges that risk disjointed or repe-titive details, the communal aspe-ct of group chats fosters cohesion among membe-rs and moves plans smoothly

4. Stay Organized with Folders or Labels

If you use se-veral different me-ssaging programs or participate in many conversations across various platforms, think about arranging them into organize-d categories to help you swiftly find particular discussions and ke-ep your apps free of e-xcessive disorder. Pe-rhaps you could establish folders or apply labels to divide- your various chats into logical groups such as family, friends, coworkers or projects so that the- correct threads are only a click away whe-n needed while- everything else- remains neatly stored until re-ferenced once- more. This simple approach can transform a complex we-b of overlapping exchanges into a tidy syste-m that streamlines locating targete-d interactions while reducing visual chaos within the- interface of your communication applications

5. Embrace Emojis and Stickers

Add a personalized touch to your messages by using emojis and stickers. Express emotions and convey your message with more depth and fun. Emojis and stickers can help make your conversations engaging and enjoyable.

While me-ssaging apps provide a convenient way for individuals in the-ir 50s to stay socially engaged with friends and family, it is important that conve-rsations through these digital channels are- purposeful and meaningful. These- platforms can help people in the-ir 50s efficiently share important update-s and organise their schedule-s remotely. Howeve-r, there is a risk that exce-ssive time spent on me-ssaging may come at the expe-nse of in-person interactions which are- deeply important for overall we-ll-being. It is best if messaging supple-ments real-world connections, rathe-r than replacing them. Furthermore-, digital conversations should encourage thought-provoking discussions and bonding ove-r shared interests, joke-s and stories, rather than superficial e-xchanges. Harnessing messaging apps to foste-r quality interactions may better se-rve the objective- of enjoying technology's

Embracing Video Conferencing for Face-to-Face Interaction

In today's digital world, video conferencing has become an essential tool for facilitating face-to-face interaction, regardless of geographical barriers. With the ability to see and hear each other in real-time, virtual meetings through video conferencing platforms have revolutionized the way we connect and collaborate.

There- are a few key be-nefits to utilizing video confere-ncing technology. Firstly, it allows for a more personal and e-ngaging method of communication compared to solely re-lying on audio calls or messages. By having the ability to se-e facial expressions and body language- through video, participants in a conference- are able to have more- meaningful and authentic interactions that be-tter resemble- what would occur in traditional in-person meetings. This he-lps foster stronger connections be-tween those communicating re-motely. Rather than just hearing a voice-, being able to observe- subtle non-verbal cues through vide-o can aid understanding and make discussions fee-l more natural. The visual ele-ment aids conveying information and nuances that may be- lost with audio alone. Overall, video confe-rencing provides a personable- experience- that makes remote conve-rsations feel lively and atte-ntive in a similar manner to interacting face- to face.

Furthermore-, video conferencing doe-s away with the necessity for trave-ling over long distances, saving both time and financial re-sources. Whether it's for busine-ss gatherings, professional growth sessions, or conne-cting with cherished individuals, digital mee-tings by means of video confere-ncing programs guarantee a helpful and productive- approach to associating with others. Video confere-ncing spares travel costs and voyaging time, making it simple-r to join colleagues and partners re-motely for gatherings without leaving work or home-. It permits proficient and individual associations without requiring physical ne-arness, bringing convenience- to a wide range of corresponde-nce needs.

While it is crucial to optimize- your video conferencing se-tup, do not forget simple courtesy. Conne-ct from a quiet space with dece-nt lighting, but also smile warmly and make eye- contact. Speak clearly yet calmly into your microphone- so others can hear you well. Te-st audio and camera beforehand so as not to waste- minutes troubleshooting. Yet also liste-n actively to others rather than fussing with se-ttings. A stable connection helps, but more- valuable is showing full presence- to your fellow participants. Together you can make- the most of virtual meetings through both te-chnology and compassion.

When conve-rsing in virtual meetings, be sure- to sustain eye contact by gazing into the came-ra rather than the display. This helps cultivate- a sense of intimacy and involveme-nt with the other attende-es. Furthermore, willingly take- part in discussions by posing inquiries and concentrating attentive-ly to guarantee fruitful interaction.

Video confe-rencing enables you to inte-ract with colleagues, friends, and love-d ones in a personal manner e-ven when apart geographically. Through virtual face--to-face meetings, you can e-xperience the- perks of real-time communication from afar while- maintaining important relationships. Both professional confere-nces and casual video chats allow for engaging discussions that foste-r understanding betwee-n participants. By embracing this technology, one can take- advantage of digital connectivity to nurture me-aningful bonds throughout different circumstances. Whe-ther discussing work matters or catching up with companions over virtual coffe-e, leveraging vide-o platforms ensures interactions re-tain their significance despite- any distances involved.

Enhancing Email Communication in the Digital Era

Today in our digital world, email continue-s to serve as an important means of conne-cting with others in personal and work contexts. As pe-ople in their 50s maneuve-r the changing communication environment, it is crucial the-y strengthen their e-mail abilities to adjust to the evolving ne-eds of the digital era. While- email stays a useful method of conne-cting, different options for interacting have- emerged ove-r time. It is beneficial for those- in their 50s to thoughtfully consider expanding the- ways they engage with othe-rs online to remain effe-ctively linked through a variety of ave-nues. Though email retains re-levance, diversifying approache-s to communication can help foster rich interactions suitable- for a modern, technology-cente-red society.

To ensure- efficient messaging and e-ffective email communication, the-re are a few tactics that can be- utilized. Primarily, organizing emails into folders and imple-menting filters can assist in managing the flood of me-ssages and preserving an organize-d inbox. Categorizing emails based on significance-, undertaking, or sender can stre-amline interaction and make ce-rtain significant messages aren't disre-garded. Keeping your inbox organize-d through filing emails into pertinent folde-rs helps reduce clutte-r so you can focus on high priority messages. You may also consider applying filte-rs that automatically file emails from certain se-nders or containing specific keywords. This targe-ted approach to email manageme-nt helps simplify communication and keeps you on top of what matte-rs most.

Furthermore-, when crafting emails, it is crucial to maintain professionalism and clarity. Cle-ar subject lines and concise me-ssages allow recipients to unde-rstand the purpose of the e-mail at a glance.

Breaking up longer me-ssages into shorter paragraphs and utilizing bullet points or numbe-red lists can make the conte-nt easier to digest and re-ad. Providing a brief yet clear summary upfront will he-lp recipients understand the- intent effective-ly. While brevity is good, ensuring sufficie-nt context is also important for comprehension. Striking a balance- between concise-ness and comprehensive-ness will help craft message-s that engage recipie-nts.

Prompt response-s to emails are crucial in today's fast-paced digital e-nvironment. People anticipate-hearing back relatively soon afte-r sending a message, so it's important to routine-ly check your inbox and address urgent corre-spondence without delay. Carving out brie-f periods several time-s a day dedicated solely to parsing through, re-plying to, and otherwise dealing with accumulate-d emails helps to efficie-ntly process the steady stre-am of communications without feeling bombarded. Prioritizing tasks and corre-spondence flagged as time--sensitive assists in kee-ping workflow orderly and ensuring timely re-sponses to colleagues, clie-nts, and others needing a quick re-ply. Regularly designated inte-rvals for email maintenance ke-eps incoming messages from piling up too high to e-asily manage all at once and helps corre-spondents know when to expe-ct a response.

While e-mail is commonly used for basic communication, taking advantage of additional feature-s can help streamline workflows and e-nsure consistent messaging. Tools such as e-mail templates allow users to quickly ge-nerate personalize-d messages with company boilerplate- text already included, saving valuable- time compared to composing each e-mail from scratch. Autoresponders automatically gene-rate replies like- out-of-office notifications when the re-cipient is away, keeping clie-nts and colleagues informed. Signature- blocks append contact details and other standard information to the-end of messages, maintaining a profe-ssional identity across all correspondence-. Making use of capabilities beyond me-rely writing and sending message-s can notably upgrade productivity and quality when corresponding through e-mail. Getting acquainted with the various options provide-d in today's platforms improves the email e-xperience ove-rall.

To wrap things up, people- in their 50s are able to boost the-ir emailing abilities in the digital pe-riod by utilizing helpful tactics for instance organizing their me-ssages neatly, kee-ping an expert deme-anor, giving well-timed replie-s, and making the most of the attributes acce-ssible on email programs. Doing this allows them to e-asily handle the demands of conte-mporary interaction and guarantee productive-correspondence in the-ir individual and expert connections. While- email continues to be a valuable-tool, maintaining a balance and avoiding being tied to constant communication is also important. Taking bre-aks and prioritizing face-to-face time re-mains beneficial.

Building Meaningful Relationships in the Digital Age

In today's digital age, me-aningful relationships have taken on an alte-red form. As individuals traverse the- virtual world of modern correspondence-, it is pivotal to recognize how to cultivate and nourish associations in this digital pe-riod. While technological advances have- shifted how we interact, ge-nuine human bonding remains significant. To foster unde-rstanding between pe-ople in a remote e-nvironment requires e-ffort to personalize exchange-s and thoughtfully acknowledge others' pe-rspectives. Though scree-ns now separate many encounte-rs, focusing on empathy, active listening, and showing inte-rest in another's expe-riences can still bring individuals togethe-r across distances.

Contemporary communication me-thods profoundly influence how relationships form and de-velop today. Though technology allows for constant connectivity across any distance-, bringing people closer on the- surface, it also presents ne-w issues in truly connecting with one anothe-r. However, if utilized strate-gically, virtual interactions have the capability to be- just as personally rewarding as direct conve-rsations. While electronic corre-spondence facilitates contact in a conve-nient manner, more atte-ntion must be paid to the quality of engage-ment to derive fulfillme-nt from exclusively digital dialogue. With aware-ness and effort, meaningful bonds can still blossom without physical proximity through virtual channe-ls, but this outcome requires inte-ntionality and presence rathe-r than passive participation. If both parties make unde-rstanding each other a priority over cursory update-s and aim to listen with empathy, relationships may flourish inde-pendently

While te-chnology allows for easy connections across distances, foste-ring meaningful relationships online re-quires awareness and e-ffort. A few approaches can help stre-ngthen bonds even whe-n not in-person. Firstly, prioritize quality over quantity by de-dicating focused time for undivided conve-rsations. Ask thoughtful questions and offer full attention whe-n communicating. Secondly, share vulnerable- experience-s to cultivate trust. Revealing aspe-cts

1. Authenticity and Empathy

While digital re-lationships rely on sincerity - it is important to prese-nt your authentic self when inte-racting with others virtually. Taking the time to unde-rstand different perspe-ctives can also aid in building rapport online, as considering anothe-r's point of view helps promote compassion. Virtual conne-ctions thrive when we bring our ge-nuine selves to conve-rsations and seek to understand varie-d experience-s.

2. Active Listening

When inte-racting in a digital setting, being an attentive- listener takes on incre-ased significance. It is crucial to pay close atte-ntion to subtle hints, variations in tone, and emotions conve-yed when conversing re-motely. By focusing on these nuance-d details during virtual communications, your comprehension will be- strengthened and the- individual you are engaging with will fee-l your genuine intere-st in what they have to say. While te-chnology can facilitate connection, active liste-ning helps ensure rich unde-rstanding despite the lack of in-pe-rson cues.

3. Quality Engagement

While virtual conne-ctions can occur easily through casual interactions on apps and media, me-aningful relationships necessitate- more proactive engage-ment. Rather than idly scrolling, consider contributing thoughtful fe-edback and starting discussions aligned with your passions. Leave- considerate comments promoting furthe-r dialogue. Reach out to acquaintances to stre-ngthen bonds and learn more about share-d interests. Participate in conve-rsations with attentiveness, bringing a willingne-ss to understand others and be unde-rstood. Through such interactive efforts, digital re-lationships have potential to flourish beyond surface--level exchange-s into truly enriching connections.

4. Virtual Coffee Chats

While face-to-face interactions may not always be possible, you can still recreate the experience virtually. Schedule "virtual coffee chats" or video calls with friends, family, or colleagues to catch up and deepen your connections.

5. Join Online Communities

Find online communities or forums that align with your interests or hobbies. Engage with like-minded individuals, share your experiences, and contribute to discussions. This allows you to connect with people who share your passions and build relationships around common interests.

By impleme-nting relationship-building strategies online-, you can cultivate significant bonds even from a distance-. Bear in mind that virtual interactions have the- capability to be every bit as re-warding and enriching as face-to-face one-s, provided they are handle-d deliberately and since-rely. Take advantage of the- possibilities that modern communication mediums afford us to de-epen your remote- relationships with purposefulness and ge-nuineness.

Lifelong Learning: Continuing to Evolve in Contemporary Communication

In today's fast-paced digital world, life-long learning has become vital for continuing to be- applicable and adjusting to the consistently e-volving communication environment. For individuals in their 50s, it is e-xtremely important to adopt a mindset of growth and look for possibilitie-s for persistent learning so as to skillfully handle- modern communication. Communication methods are transforming at an acce-lerated pace pre-sently, necessitating that pe-ople of all ages actively ke-ep developing the-ir competencies and knowle-dge. While it may be a challe-nge to learn new skills or adapt to modifications late-r in life, maintaining an open attitude towards continuous se-lf-improvement can assist persons in the-ir 50s to smoothly interact using current technologie-s and techniques. Pursuing opportunities to e-xpand one's learning helps e-nsure they stay engage-d with alterations in how people conne-ct and collaborate.

While continual le-arning allows individuals to remain aware of eme-rging developments, te-chnologies, and platforms increasingly integral to mode-rn connection and correspondence-, focusing on particular areas can strengthen proficie-ncy. Prioritizing familiarity with evolving social media, expe-rtise with instant messaging applications, adoption of video chat utilitie-s, and refinement of e-mail practices ensures flue-ncy with predominant means of interaction. Howe-ver, further investigation may re-veal supplemental ave-nues worthy of study to maintain relevancy within e-ver- changing communication landscapes.

Luckily, various tools and technique-s exist to assist people in the-ir journey for continuous learning. Online classe-s, seminars, and instruction guides can delive-r helpful understandings and applicable information. Additionally, ke-eping in contact with experts in your fie-ld, participating in pertinent communities, and going to skill-building se-ssions can encourage relationship-forming chance-s and make the sharing of new ide-as easier. IN CASE knowledge- exchange is a crucial part of lifelong le-arning, yet connecting with others can also le-ad to discovering new prospects.

By committing themse-lves to continual education as they e-nter their fifth decade-, individuals in their 50s can persist in deve-loping their contemporary communication abilities, guarante-eing they remain informe-d of new trends, pertine-nt to current circumstances, and efficacious in both the-ir personal and work collaborations. While one may fe-el less inclined to le-arn as time passes, maintaining an openne-ss to learn about emerging communication style-s, platforms, and best practices is integral to associating succe-ssfully with all generations. Whethe-r learning occurs through formal courses, indepe-ndent research, or e-xposure in day-to-day life, reinve-st

Chapter 4

The Digital Leap: Staying relevant in an ever-evolving tech landscape

While te-chnology continues advancing rapidly, gaining proficiency in evolving digital syste-ms is important for career progress and se-lf-improvement eve-n after age 50. Remaining knowle-dgeable about current te-chnological trends helps sustain rele-vance during a time when the- job market demands tech-savvy applicants. Acquiring and sharpe-ning skills for in-demand technologies, though challe-nging, can assist those over 50 to adapt successfully to shifts in the- digital world.

Here- are some strategie-s to consider when see-king to stay competitive in the quickly shifting te-ch field. We'll examine- skills necessary to progress within your pre-sent position or investigate fre-sh possibilities. this section offers pe-rspectives on navigating the continuously e-volving tech sector. Whethe-r aiming to refine talents for your curre-nt job or scout new prospects, focusing on versatility, continual le-arning and strong soft abilities can support maintaining relevancy. While- technical expertise- remains important, also prioritizing collaboration, effective- communication and problem-solving often distinguishes candidate-s. Commit to regularly updating knowledge of late-st tools, trends and best practices. Look for opportunitie-s to enhance existing qualifications, whe-ther through formal education, vocational training or indepe-ndent study. Networking proves additionally valuable-, as relationships frequently le-ad to insights about new openings or guidance for care-er paths. With dedication to self-improve-ment and awareness of industry change-s, you can effectively chart your route- through an unpredictable

From embracing the digital age and assessing your tech skills to identifying gaps, leveraging your experience, and overcoming ageism, we've got you covered. We'll also share tips for work-life integration and show you how to future-proof your tech skills to ensure long-term success.

If you're pre-pared to take the digital plunge- and remain applicable in an constantly transforming technological e-nvironment at 50 and above, let's jump right in. The- online world is continually evolving at a rapid pace, so ke-eping your skills up to date will be crucial. We-'ll explore some concre-te steps you can take to boost your proficie-ncy with new tools and platforms, helping you to adapt smoothly as industry trends change-. I'll also provide some tips for maintaining a growth mindset and a willingne-ss to

Embracing the Digital Age

As the rate- of technological progress continues to acce-lerate, maintaining familiarity with innovations after age- 50 is crucial for navigating an increasingly digital society. By making an effort to e-xplore new tech tre-nds as they emerge-, older individuals can better adapt to te-chnical developments and maintain e-ngaging relationships in our technology-centric world. From communication tools that facilitate- interaction across distances to ente-rtainment platforms that deliver stimulating conte-nt, embracing changes in the re-alm of computers and mobile device-s empowers older adults to active-ly participate in a culture now heavily shape-d by online connectivity. While the- pace of change introduces ongoing challe-nges, an openness to le-arning about the latest tech can he-lp those over 50 seamle-ssly integrate useful ne-w tools and resources into daily activities, allowing me-aningful involvement eve-n as advancements rede-fine modern life.

While it's important for those- over 50 to be aware of e-merging technologies, focusing on solutions that dire-ctly enhance daily life is most valuable-. Mobile phones, for example-, can strengthen connections to family and community. Acce-ssible apps allow video chats or message- sharing on the go. Home device-s too provide benefits - voice- assistants simplify tasks, security systems offer pe-ace of mind, and smart appliances automate routine-s. Rather than adopting all trends, discerning use-ful innovations tailored to individual needs and inte-rests optimizes quality of life. Staying informe-d aids choosing technologies purposefully to e-nrich experience-, from leisure pursuits to wellne-ss, in ways respecting users' pre-ferences.

While te-chnological progress delivers re-markable benefits, ke-eping pace with constant changes can prove- difficult for individuals less acquainted with innovative de-vices. That is why it is crucial for older persons to pursue- direction and assistance when e-ngaging with modern tools. Resources e-xist to help seniors fee-l at ease exploring the- digital sphere, whethe-r classes introducing new tech, online-guides demonstrating functionality, or one-on-one- help addressing individual querie-s. Working to understand rather than avoiding unfamiliar systems e-mpowers self-sufficiency today and tomorrow.

Additionally, staying connected is crucial for older adults in the digital age. From communicating with loved ones through video calls to accessing online resources for health and wellness, technology offers a wealth of opportunities for seniors to remain connected to their communities and lead fulfilling lives. While e-mbracing the advantages of technology doe-sn't necessitate an imme-diate and total alteration of your lifestyle-, thoughtfully integrating useful innovations into your regular routine- can help you more convenie-ntly maintain important relationships and access helpful re-sources. Discovering the appropriate- equilibrium takes some e-xperimentation to dete-rmine what degree- of involvement optimally compleme-nts your particular needs and prefe-rences without being ove-rly disruptive.

Here- are some specific te-chniques and abilities that can help pe-ople over 50 adjust to and move through the- consistently changing advanced world. We will give- helpful tips, assets, and expe-riences on how to remain aware- of current advances in innovation, welcome- innovation patterns for more seasone-d grown-ups, and undoubtedly explore me-chanical headways as a senior. A portion of the proce-dures incorporate kee-ping yourself refreshe-d on new advances through online asse-ts and preparing, finding how innovations can help in day by day tasks and exe-rcises, and connecting with more youthful age- relatives on how to utilize ne-w gadgets. While new advance-ments keep showing up, taking baby ste-ps and focusing on profitable applications can encourage adjustme-nt without an excess of perple-xity. Reach out to local area focuses and instructional classe-s on offer to enable you to fe-el more good in the advance-d condition and exploit openings it brings.

Assessing Your Tech Skills

While te-chnologies continue advancing rapidly, taking stock of your existing digital abilitie-s as someone over 50 can he-lp you adapt and evolve with the changing time-s. Gaining further proficiency in various technologie-s is significant for maintaining competitiveness and significance- in today's digital environment. As an individual in the late-r stages of life, assessing your curre-nt tech talents allows recognizing any are-as for improvement. Enhancing technical lite-racy permits continuing to contribute and engage- in a world that grows increasingly reliant on digital tools on a regular basis.

When e-valuating your technical abilities, it is best to be-gin by pinpointing the spots where you fe-el less assured or informe-d. Are there de-finite innovations or devices that you battle- with? Are there ide-as or terms that are unfamiliar? Taking note of the-se regions will assist you with prioritizing your studying and progress. Pe-rhaps you find it harder to keep up with ne-w programming languages or struggle more with syste-m administration tasks. It could also be the case that ne-tworking concepts or cybersecurity be-st practices are less cle-ar. By recognizing these particular te-chnical areas needing improve-ment, you can focus your efforts on learning more- about the topics you understand the le-ast. Doing so will aid in strengthening your overall te-chnical skills set.

Once you have identified the areas for improvement, explore the abundance of resources available to enhance your tech skills. Online tutorials, webinars, and e-learning platforms offer convenient and accessible ways to learn and practice new technologies. Additionally, consider enrolling in courses or workshops specifically designed for older adults to ensure a comfortable learning environment.

Don't be afraid to ask for help or seek guidance from tech-savvy friends, family members, or colleagues. They can offer valuable insights, share their experiences, and provide support as you navigate the world of technology.

Staying knowledge-able about changing technologies afte-r the age of fifty nece-ssitates a continuous endeavor to le-arn new concepts, adapt to innovations, and sustain inquisitivene-ss over time. By making the e-volution of one's technical abilities a routine- undertaking and embracing each ste-p of strengthening skills, one will discove-r that proficiency with devices and programs can se-rve as a formidable instrument for both individual and care-er developme-nt. While mastering eve-ry nuance of tech may not happen imme-diately, remaining dedicate-d to gradually building familiarity through persistent curiosity allows useful applications of innovation to re-main accessible in eve-ryday circumstances.

Identifying Technology Gaps

As someone- over the age of 50, it is critically important to pinpoint any te-chnological deficiencies you might posse-ss in order to remain current in the- technology sector. Realizing the- places where e-nhancement could be be-neficial is the initial phase towards narrowing those- deficiencies and maintaining pace- with technological developme-nts as a more experie-nced individual. While it's natural for anybody to have ce-rtain technical areas that could use stre-ngthening as fields progress rapidly, be-ing aware of one's own is key to addre-ssing them appropriately. Whethe-r it involves updating skills on commonly used software programs or ge-tting familiarized with new platforms ente-ring the workplace, taking stock of one's te-chnical aptitudes periodically is a sensible- way to safeguard against obsolescence- in a digital age.

To identify te-chnology gaps, begin by taking stock of your existing technical abilitie-s and understanding. Critically examine your compe-tence in realms like- digital literacy, programming dialects, programming applications, and deve-loping innovations. Reflect on the spe-cific specialized abilities that are- sought after in your area of work or industry. It is important to carefully asse-ss where you exce-l and where you may nee-d additional learning in order to fully equip yourse-lf with the tools and knowledge ne-cessary to keep up with the- evolving technological landscape of your occupation.

Recognizing technology gaps:

When e-xamining your work or personal responsibilities, se-arch for duties or issues where- technology creates obstacle-s to effectivene-ss or output. Detect regions whe-re you sense le-ss at ease or informed contraste-d with your associates. Stay mindful of patterns and moveme-nts in the tech area that you may not be- acquainted with, and consider ways you can improve your unde-rstanding and skills to more fully participate in the digitally-focuse-d present.

Bridge the gaps:

When you've- pinpointed where your te-chnology skills can improve, it's time to start addressing those- weak spots. Begin searching for le-arning prospects and materials tailored to your distinct re-quirements. Online classe-s, seminars transmitted over the- internet, and instructional videos can furnish be-neficial information and coaching. Become part of te-chnology communities and professional relationships to link up with spe-cialists who can deliver recomme-ndations and assistance as you work on upgrading your abilities. These- digital options present straightforward ways to enhance- your understanding and gain fresh insights from others. While- advancing your expertise take-s commitment, focusing on interactive opportunitie-s that suit your schedule and priorities he-lps you advance efficiently.

If you prefer a more structured approach, consider enrolling in a tech education program or attending workshops that focus on the specific skills you need to develop. Additionally, don't hesitate to reach out to colleagues or mentors who can provide mentorship and share their expertise.

Kee-p in mind that maintaining proficiency with technological deve-lopments after the age- of 50 necessitates a constant commitme-nt to self-education. Welcoming life-long learning and flexibility when innovations re-quire modifications will help ensure- that you confidently traverse te-chnological shifts as a senior, allowing you to stay competitive as the- digital world continuously evolves. By recognizing any de-ficiencies in your technical abilitie-s and actively endeavouring to re-medy such shortcomings, you can work to narrow technology gaps and thus sustain your capability to capably navigate advance-ments, even as fre-sh developments re-gularly emerge.

Lifelong Learning for Tech Success

Within today's swiftly evolving te-ch sector, keeping up to date- and competitive is imperative-, irrespective of age-. For individuals over 50, it is crucial to adjust to technological changes and pe-rsistently educate one-self to stay pertinent in this digital e-ra. While the tech world advance-s at a swift pace, maintaining curiosity and an enthusiasm to learn can he-lp people of all ages fe-el less intimidated by te-chnology shifts. Making an effort to understand new syste-ms, whether through online tutorials, community classe-s or peer guidance, allows individuals to le-verage innovations rather than fe-eling excluded by the-m. Adapting skills to the modern workplace doe-s not require becoming an e-xpert overnight but does ne-cessitate an openne-ss to adapt. Continuous learning, even on topics outside- one's primary expertise-

Staying up to date with e-volving technologies later in one-'s career not only enable-s continued advancement, but is inte-gral to thriving professionally. By maintaining familiarity with technical deve-lopments after the age- of 50, individuals can broaden their abilities, re-inforce their rele-vance in the workplace, and capitalize- on fresh prospects. While adapting to change- becomes more difficult with time-, cultivating new tech-relate-d expertise afte-r 50 grants access to new possibilities and he-lps ensure enduring e-mployability.

While ke-eping up with the rapid changes in te-chnology is challenging, continuous learning at any age allows one- to adapt and remain a valuable asset in the-ir career. To stay competitive- past 50 in the tech industry require-s embracing learning as a lifelong proce-ss. By keeping an open mind and de-dicating time to gaining fresh skills and knowledge-, one can maintain relevance- despite the fie-ld's constant evolution. Updating competencie-s through ongoing education keeps worke-rs equipped to handle ne-w difficulties and offer meaningful contributions, e-ven as innovations emerge-. Whether learning happe-ns through formal coursework, self-study, or on-the-job training, making le-arning a priority is key to longevity in this fast-paced domain.

There are various strategies that can help you stay current in tech after 50. One effective approach is to enroll in online courses, webinars, and workshops that focus on technology and its applications. These resources provide valuable insights, industry knowledge, and practical skills that can help you adapt to technology changes and stay competitive.

While maintaining profe-ssional connections and participating in networks is important for ongoing education, it is e-qually valuable to diversify one's le-arning outside of such standard forums. Interacting with associations of similar minds and attending se-ctor events offers introductions to nove-l concepts, developing te-ndencies, and new angle-s through peer interplay. It in addition allows for te-amwork and communal dissemination of familiarity. However, ve-nturing beyond routine circles can spark cre-ative thinking through unforesee-n partnerships and exposures to alte-rnative industries.

Exploring mentorship programs is anothe-r effective way to stay up-to-date- and competitive in your field. Through such programs, e-xperienced me-ntors can offer invaluable guidance and support by sharing le-ssons learned from their own care-ers. With a mentor, you gain insight into how best to navigate- the constantly shifting technological landscape. A me-ntor would be able to advise you on upcoming tre-nds, highlight new skills to develop, and caution against pote-ntial pitfalls. Their vast experie-nces navigating industry changes can help you do so more- smoothly. Reaching out to a mentor provides acce-ss to practical strategies

It is important to continuously refine- your technical abilities and remain aware- of industry developments as ke-y aspects of adapting to technological changes afte-r the age of fifty. By committing to ongoing self-e-ducation and maintaining an outlook focused on potential for growth, you can stay rele-vant in technology fields at fifty years of age- and later, gaining access to fresh prospe-cts and difficulties presente-d by the digital era. Remaining up to date- with changes and open to expanding your unde-rstanding allows workers over fifty to roll with technological wave-s rather than be swept aside- by them.

Seeking Tech Support and Resources

While advancing age- often means slowing down, kee-ping your mind engaged is crucial as one age-s. As individuals pass 50 years of age, navigating new te-chnologies can seem daunting ye-t remaining informed on changes is important. Fortunate-ly, many helpful resources e-xist to assist those wishing to expand their knowle-dge of technology and comprehe-nd evolving innovations. Websites, instruction manuals, community colle-ge courses, and senior ce-nters frequently provide- classes tailored for older adults se-eking to cultivate familiarity with device-s, programs, and online safety measure-s. By taking advantage of learning opportunities provide-d in one's community, an individual over the halfway mark of life- can continue learning new skills and staying me-ntally agile.

Starting out, you may wish to contact technical support e-xperts or specialists who can help you compre-hend and work out any technology-linked proble-ms you may come across. Whether it's figuring out how to utilize- a new gadget or overcoming an programming issue-, looking for specialist direction can spare you time- and annoyance. These spe-cialists have broad preparing managing a wide scope- of gadgets and programming issues and can walk you through fixes and arrange-ments effortlessly. The-y'll clarify issues in basic terms and give you ste-p-by-step headings to take care- of even the most muddle-d issues without stress. On the off chance- that you run into an issue you can't settle all alone-, don't hesitate to get some- answers from the pros - they're- there to enable- you to utilize your innovation effective-ly and productively.

Furthermore-, there are se-veral digital platforms and online communities cre-ated specifically to address the- technical needs of olde-r adults. These website-s provide beneficial tutorial vide-os, discussion forums, and question-and-answer sections allowing use-rs to inquire about issues they face- and obtain guidance from others who have e-ncountered comparable difficultie-s. The tutorial videos demonstrate- how to perform common tasks step-by-step, making it e-asier for seniors to understand. The- forums foster engageme-nt among members facing similar struggles. Through posting inquirie-s and reviewing response-s from peers, individuals can troubleshoot proble-ms together. Whethe-r you need aid with operating a ne-w device, strengthe-ning certain digital skills, or getting reacquainte-d with changing technology, these online- hubs are designed to offe-r helpful resources and a supportive- community to turn to.

Furthermore, staying current with tech trends and developments can be achieved through newsletters, blogs, and technology-focused publications. Subscribing to credible sources will help you stay informed about the latest advancements, tips, and tricks, ensuring you are always in the loop.

While ke-eping up with ever-changing te-chnology can feel daunting, having a growth mindset and taking small ste-ps forward each day allows continual learning well into our se-nior years. A variety of helpful re-sources exist to smooth this journey, from online- tutorials and patient family members to local classe-s offering guidance. See-king assistance when confronting unfamiliar terrain pre-vents any one roadblock from halting progress e-ntirely. Together, a willingne-ss to learn new skills and utilize available- support systems empowers us to fe-el comfortable and confident e-ngaging with technology throughout life's later chapte-rs. This enables full participation in today's digital world, connecting with love-d ones near and far as well as acce-ss to services, ente-rtainment and information.

Building a Professional Network

While maintaining compe-titiveness and kee-ping abreast of updates is important for all in the te-ch field regardless of age-, those over 50 can espe-cially benefit from actively building profe-ssional connections. Creating meaningful re-lationships with colleagues, thought leade-rs within the industry, and potential mentors can significantly boost care-er opportunities later in life-. Through establishing such rapport, an individual gains exposure to fre-sh perspectives and insights that younge-r contacts may discuss, remains aware of eme-rging trends, and cultivates advisors who can offer guidance-. interactions may also prompt introductions to new projects or role-s fitting one's skills. Meanwhile, othe-rs find value in a senior worker's vast e-xperience and willingne-ss to impart hard-earned wisdom. By devoting e-ffort to networking, an individual positioned well for continue-d professional growth

While ne-tworking provides many advantages, such as possible job prospe-cts, information about different industries, and use-ful guidance, it is important not to overexte-nd yourself. Cultivating relationships takes e-ffort over time. Focus first on strengthe-ning your existing connections by demonstrating inte-rest in their work and sharing rele-vant updates from your own experie-nces. Look for organic ways to learn from others, such as asking re-spectful questions during casual conversations. In this way, you can e-xpand your circle of contacts gradually through thoughtful engageme-nt, increasing your exposure to ne-w developments, pe-rspectives, and chances to contribute- your own insights wherever the-y may help.

To effe-ctively establish a successful ne-twork, you should initially attend sector associated gathe-rings like conference-s, workshops and occasions. These eve-nts offer prospects to connect with othe-r professionals working in similar roles, swap thoughts on industry trends and difficultie-s, and potentially lay the groundwork for future collaborative- relationships. In addition, exploring online communitie-s and forums pertinent to your specialize-d field can help broaden your profe-ssional network, where you can participate- in discussions on pertinent topics, reque-st guidance from more expe-rienced colleague-s, and share your own knowledge and vie-wpoints. Taking these initial steps can he-lp cultivate beneficial profe-ssional connections and relationships over the- long term that may potentially assist with future care-er progression or opportunities.

While conne-cting with others professionally, it is crucial to genuine-ly engage with eve-ry individual you meet, as well as e-xhibit an eagerness to gain knowle-dge from their expe-riences. Be e-nergetic in starting discussions and cultivating bonds. Recall, ne-tworking should not just focus on obtaining for yourself, but additionally giving to others. Provide he-lp, contribute your understandings, and encourage- those within your professional connections.

Networking Tips:

While atte-nding industry events and confere-nces provides opportunities to ne-twork with other professionals in your field, it is also worthwhile- considering less conventional ave-nues. Look locally for relevant me-etupsConnecting with online- forums and communities allows you to interact with professionals in your are-a of expertise. The-se virtual gatherings provide opportunitie-s to ask questions of and learn from others with spe-cialized knowledge and e-xperience. You can gain he-lpful advice, newWhile maintaining ope-n communication is important, thoughtfully consider others' comfort leve-ls before striking up conversations. Warmly gre-et those you encounte-r to foster welcoming interactions

You can offer assistance, share- useful insights, and lend helpful support to the- contacts in your network. Provide guidance orWhile maintaining a pre-sence on professional ne-tworking platforms is important, it is best to remain active in mode-ration. Posting updates too frequently could diminish the-irTo reap the- greatest advantages, consiste-ntly grow and differentiate your ne-twork by connecting with a variety people- from diverse backgrounds. Broadening your circle-s allows you to gain new perspective-s

Staying competitive-, current, and aware of new de-velopments in technology is ke-y to having a successful and fulfilling career e-ven after 50 years of age- in the tech sector. Cultivating re-lationships with other professionals through industry eve-nts and online communities allows you to learn about e-merging trends, gain valuable insights from colle-agues' experie-nces, and find opportunities to demonstrate- your ongoing skills and passions. By continuously engaging with your network, you can clarify how your expe-rtise remains applicable in an e-volving field, clarify where additional training could unlock ne-w areas of growth, and clarify how mentoring others may furthe-r your own learning. An active network supports ongoing compe-titiveness through fresh pe-rspectives and connections that re-inforce

Leveraging Experience and Transferable Skills

Your wealth of e-xperience and transfe-rable skills acquired over de-cades in the tech fie-ld represent invaluable- assets that can help you remain compe-titive and adapt to ongoing technology changes as some-one over 50. By capitalizing on your distinct strengths, such as de-ep expertise- built over a long career spe-nt navigating previous industry transformations, you are well-positione-d to successfully navigate the constantly e-volving tech landscape and kee-p yourself well-verse-d in ongoing developments. Your unde-rstanding of challenges faced and solutions applie-d during earlier periods of disruption can offe-r valuable insights when adjusting to new de-velopments. With strategic e-mphasis on continually honing transferable skills that maintain rele-vance across multiple eras of te-ch evolution, in addition to enthusiasm for ongoing learning, you maintain strong pote-ntial to sustain a meaningful role in the industry throughout dynamic pe-riods of transition.

One way to highlight your experience is by showcasing your successful track record and highlighting specific projects or achievements that demonstrate your expertise. This will not only demonstrate your capabilities to potential employers or clients but also show your ability to adapt to technology changes. Additionally, your transferable skills can play a significant role in staying current in tech after 50. Transferable skills are those that can be applied across various roles or industries. For example, skills like problem-solving, communication, leadership, and adaptability are highly valued in the tech field. Emphasize these skills in your resume, cover letter, and interviews to showcase your versatility and ability to excel in the tech industry.

Furthermore-, remaining updated in technology afte-r 50 necessitates an e-agerness to persiste-ntly learn and increase your skillse-t. Realize the significance- of continuous learning and search for possibilities to broade-n your understanding and stay current with deve-loping technology patterns. Online le-ssons, workshops, industry gatherings, and professional qualifications can assist you in obtaining new abilitie-s and showcase your dedication to staying competitive-. While it is important to expand your knowledge- through these avenue-s, it is also essential not to overload yourse-lf. Slow and steady improvement through mode-rate exploration of new tre-nds and occasional lessons is a sustainable approach for lifelong le-arning.

Staying connecte-d with others in your field proves highly be-neficial. Cultivating robust professional relationships grants e-ntry to helpful assets, guidance, and pote-ntial employment. Make e-fforts to participate in sector expos, e-nlist with business affiliations, and engage in online- circles to broaden your contacts and kee-p abreast with evolving industry patterns. Your ne-twork serves as a valuable re-source for knowledge, advice-, and opportunities that may otherwise re-main unseen. Interacting with othe-rs with similar interests dee-pens understanding of deve-loping innovations and shifting market needs.

Ultimately, by capitalizing on your past e-xperience and applicable- abilities, consistently furthering your e-ducation, and establishing a robust professional community, you are able- to stay competitive in technology e-ven at fifty years of age or more-. Welcome the chance-s that engineering pre-sents, adjust to its developme-nts, and highlight your distinctive advantages to stay rele-vant in the tech domain. While te-chnology will progress in unexpecte-d ways, your dedication to learning new skills, sharing knowle-dge with colleagues, and applying your dive-rse talents across industries can he-lp sustain a fruitful career well into the- future. Though change is inevitable-, focusing on self-improvement and collaboration e-nsures ongoing contributions to the field re-gardless of advancing years.

Balancing Work and Personal Life

As someone- over 50 working with technlogy, achieving equilibrium betwe-en professional and personal re-sponsibilities can be an ende-avor. Neverthele-ss, preserving equilibrium is paramount for ke-eping technical abilities sharp, staying abre-ast of developments in the- domain of your work, and retaining competitivene-ss. While juggling job duties and personal commitme-nts isn't facile, dedicating time to e-ach ensures continuing rele-vance and satisfaction in both domains.

An efficie-nt tactic for balancing job and private life is to prioritize your time- and establish boundaries. Decide- your most efficient hours and dedicate- them to concentrated work, while- also ensuring to schedule time- for personal activities and unwinding. Doing so will assist you in maintaining a balanced inte-gration of work and life.

Prioritizing tasks and allocating responsibilitie-s wisely is crucial for sustaining your work-life balance. Ge-t in the habit of delegating dutie-s to colleagues who are capable- of handling them. Establish attainable goals and kee-p stakeholders informed about your capacity so work doe-s not pile up. Maintaining open communication about availabilities he-lps team members unde-rstand your limitations. Doing so prevents you from overcommitting your time- and leaves room for non-work commitments that are- meaningful to you outside your job.

Furthermore-, maintaining organization and effectivene-ss is crucial. Make the most of productivity tools and technologie-s that can assist you in streamlining your work processes and saving time-. This will enable you to complete- duties more efficie-ntly, permitting space for individual intere-sts.

While e-stablishing clear boundaries betwe-en work and personal life is important, it is not always e-asy to fully disengage from one's care-er even during off-hours. Taking occasional bre-aks from emails and calls related to your job can he-lp you recharge without work-relate-d stresses intruding on leisure- time. However, the- demands of employment may at time-s necessitate re-sponding to missions outside standard working periods. A balanced mode-ration is key to preserving we-llness - disconnecting where- feasible but also recognizing re-alities of certain roles. Prioritizing se-lf-care yet responding re-asonably as needed can support maintaining work satisfaction along with me-ntal and emotional health over the- long term.

Lastly, don't forget to make time for self-care and personal development. Engage in activities that bring you joy and rejuvenation, whether it's pursuing a hobby, exercising, or spending quality time with loved ones. By nurturing your well-being, you will not only enhance your overall satisfaction but also boost your productivity in the tech industry.

While striving to maintain e-xpertise in eve-r-evolving tech fields re-quires dedication, properly balancing care-er responsibilities with pe-rsonal well-being helps sustain long-te-rm success. Thoughtfully scheduling time for work, family, and se-lf-care helps preve-nt burnout. Communicating clear expectations re-garding availability sets healthy boundaries. Making he-alth a priority supports both professional growth and relationships. With careful planning and fle-xibility, technical professionals can deve-lop rewarding careers and full live-s even as industries rapidly change-.

Overcoming Ageism and Stereotypes

In today's swiftly transforming tech se-ctor, individuals over 50 regularly encounte-r the intimidating obstacle of ageism and pre-conceived notions. Howeve-r, it is vital to acknowledge that age alone- does not determine- one's capability to adjust to technological deve-lopments or remain competitive- in their area of expe-rtise. While some may assume- that older workers lack the aptitude- to learn new skills, expe-rience can provide valuable- perspective and wisdom gaine-d over decades. Additionally, many te-chnical abilities translate well re-gardless of age. With dedication to continual le-arning, willingness to embrace change-, and perseverance- against prejudice, expe-rienced professionals posse-ss untapped potential to stay rele-vant through periods of disruption.

With decade-s of living, those over 50 have accumulate-d a treasure trove of le-ssons learned and issues solve-d that could prove invaluable to addressing mode-rn challenges in technology. While- youth brings energy and novel ide-as, advanced age includes the- benefits of perspe-ctive and judgement hone-d through personal and societal changes ove-r multiple decades. By e-mphasizing the depth of understanding and proble-m-solving abilities gained through a long caree-r spent overcoming obstacles, the- digital world could tap into a source of insight otherwise ove-rlooked due to superficial biase-s regarding age. Highlighting the unique- expertise accumulate-d through serious life expe-riences can help dispe-l outdated stereotype-s that wisdom comes only with youth, redirecting focus to the- true content of character and qualifications of individuals, re-gardless of years.

While it is important to re-main proactive in adapting to ever-e-volving technological changes, demonstrating fle-xibility and capability, more experie-nced professionals can showcase that maturity ne-ed not equate to obsole-scence. By making an effort to re-adily accept emerging innovations, olde-r workers have the opportunity to illustrate- that the passage of time doe-s not necessarily rende-r one dated or uncompetitive-.

Furthermore-, getting involved within the te-chnology field through networking and finding support can aid in dismantling biases associate-d with age. Forming associations with peers, atte-nding sector occasions, and taking part in online communities can e-ncourage cooperative e-ffort and supply possibilities for improvement and le-arning. Connecting with others working in similar domains allows sharing of skills and knowledge-, as well as bringing diverse vie-wpoints and experience-s. Making an effort to participate can help gain e-xposure to new ideas and ke-ep updated with latest tre-nds, thereby furthering one-'s learning and expertise-. While age may differ, a common inte-rest in the domain serve-s as a basis for productive interactions and growth.

In conclusion, moving past preconce-ived notions regarding age and ste-reotypes is critical for individuals over the- age of fifty to succeed in the- technology sector. By emphasizing the- distinctive worth they bring, adjusting to technological e-volutions, and cultivating a robust professional community, seniors can traverse- the tech realm with assurance- and carry on offering impactful contributions. While change can be- difficult, an open and understanding environme-nt allows people of all backgrounds to share the-ir talents.

Future-Proofing Your Tech Skills

Staying knowledge-able with innovations in technology is exce-ptionally significant as an individual more than 50 years old. The continually progre-ssing realm of tech prese-nts a wealth of chances for more se-asoned grown-ups to instruct themselve-s, keep deve-loping, and keep in contact. By making your advanced abilitie-s ready for what's to come, you can confidently e-xplore the computerize-d time and welcome the- most recent improveme-nts with adaptability and interest. The e-ndless openings that innovation brings permits the- more seasoned e-ra to keep participating and associated with frie-nds and family, regardless of separation. While- keeping up with each ne-w gadget or application can appear to be an ove-rwhelming assignment, focusing on core compute-r abilities and reliably refre-shing your learning gives stable ground to ke-ep developing alongside- advances at your own particular pace.

There- are a few important technology tre-nds designed specifically for olde-r adults that can help future-proof your later ye-ars. Wearable health tracke-rs allow you to monitor your vitals from your wrist, providing peace of mind. Meanwhile-, smart home devices allow you to control lights, the-rmostats, locks and more through voice commands or a mobile app, making tasks e-asier. From remote patie-nt monitoring to fall detection alarms, innovations in connecte-d caregiving offer safety and inde-pendence. Exploring options such as the-se empowers you to be-nefit from advancing tech solutions tailored for se-niors, conveniently enhancing daily life- while you age. Staying informed on such de-velopments allows you to leve-rage technology's full potential.

To ensure you remain relevant in the tech industry, continuous learning is essential. Embrace online courses, workshops, and tutorials to expand your knowledge and acquire new skills. Platforms like Coursera, LinkedIn Learning, and Udemy offer a wealth of resources to assist you in enhancing your tech literacy. By continuously updating your skillset, you can adapt to technology changes and confidently navigate the digital landscape.

Connecting with othe-rs interested in te-chnology can offer useful help and pe-rspectives. Joining groups cente-red around tech, going to technology confe-rences, or participating in online discussions allows building re-lationships with people facing similar challenge-s. Through cooperating and exchanging ideas, you gain important knowle-dge and remain inspired in constantly updating your te-chnical abilities. Working with a community of peers and advisors provide-s encouragement on the-path of always improving skills to match changes in the industry.

Chapter 5

Social Media Savvy: Navigating online platforms for personal branding

Welcome to the world of personal branding in the digital age! In today's interconnected world, social media has become a powerful tool for building and enhancing your personal brand. Navigating the vast landscape of online platforms can be overwhelming, but fear not – we're here to guide you through it. Whether you're an aspiring entrepreneur, a creative professional, or simply someone looking to showcase their talents, understanding how to leverage social media is essential for establishing an authentic and compelling online presence. In this section, we will delve into the intricacies of personal branding, provide tips and strategies for navigating popular social media platforms, and equip you with the knowledge to build a strong and consistent online presence.

Let us be-gin investigating the intriguing realm of se-lf-branding on online social networks. Through working togethe-r, we'll liberate the- aptitude of these platforms to e-nrich your personal image, associate with your aime-d gathering, and position yourself as a thoughtful pionee-r in your field. These ne-tworks give us a stage to gently ye-t productively get the word out about our gifts, inte-rests, and experie-nces. By making a steady posting plan and associating with applicable clie-nt bunches, we can demonstrate- our mastery and manufacture trust, driving intere-sted parties to get to know us supe-rior. This personal brand administration will assist us with perceiving ope-n doors to team up with others and advance our profe-ssion or business objectives. The-re's a entire unive-rse of potential before- us - I'm energized to he-lp you investigate!

Understanding Personal Branding

Nowadays in our digital world, crafting an individual brand has become- crucial for professionals hoping to differentiate- themselves and be- noticed in an overflowing arena. It e-ntails thoughtfully forming and managing an authentic online identity that pre-cisely displays your qualities, talents, and how you wish to be- viewed by others. Whe-ther you realize it or not, you alre-ady have a brand - it's up to you how you shape and promote it. Your online- representation should highlight your distinctive-skills, experience-, and personality to attract the type of opportunitie-s and interactions that are the be-st fit. While branding takes ongoing effort, taking control of your digital image- can pay dividends in advancing your goals and career in re-levant ways.

Why is Personal Branding Important?

While pe-rsonal branding does involve crafting an impressive- resume and memorable- tagline, it goes much dee-per than surface ele-ments. Developing a authe-ntic and distinctive identity within your field is ke-y. Such a well-defined pe-rsonal brand can help you discover new prospe-cts, establish trustworthiness, and garner a loyal group of supporte-rs. Though the process, one se-eks to distinguish themselve-s from competitors by clarifying what makes them unique-ly qualified through small details and nuanced e-xperiences rathe-r than vague generalitie-s.

Tips for Developing a Strong Personal Brand Online

Here- is a minimally expanded text with an inte-rmediate depth and purpose- to clarify:

There are a fe-w things to keep in mind when looking to de-velop a strong personal brand online. Focus first on craft Define Your Brand Identity: Start by identifying your unique strengths, values, and passions. This will form the foundation of your personal brand and guide your messaging across all online platforms.It is important to establish a cohe-rent visual persona that matches your pe-rsonal brand when presenting yourse-lf online. Select a limite-d color palette, typeface-s, and graphic elements that capture- the essence- of who you are and what you represe-nt. Apply these visual components consiste-ntly across all of your digital profiles and materials so viewe-rs instantly recognize your unique visual signature-. A unified visual identity helps audie-nces easily identify you and your work, and re-inforces your brand values each time- they encounter your online- presence. While- simplicity is key, subtle variations can help avoid monotony and ke-ep your design fee-ling fresh. The goal is to choose visuals thatShowcase Your Expertise: Position yourself as an authority in your field by sharing valuable insights, knowledge, and industry updates. Publish articles, create videos, or conduct webinars to showcase your expertise. Engage active-ly with your target audience: Cultivating re-lationships with those you seek to re-ach is pivotal for effectively re-presenting yourself profe-ssionally. Reply thoughtfully to feedback, comme-nce discussions in a welcoming manner, and contribute- regularly to industry dialogues to portray yourself as an acce-ssible and well-informed individual. Though inte-ractions, demonstrate your passion and expe-rtise while learning from othe-rs, strengthening your personal brand through mutually-be-neficial connections. Connecting with influe-ntial people in your field who can e-ndorse and broadcast your individual brand is a smart strategy. Look for opportunities to te-am up with industry leaders on tasks, attend gathe-rings together, or partner on e-fforts that strengthen how trustworthy you see-m and help more people- discover your work. Experts in a given are-a often have sizeable- audiences and collaborating can introduce your contributions and pe-rspective to fresh e-yes. Pursuing interactions and joint initiatives with such figure-s spreads awareness of your name- and talents to those beyond your dire-ct network. Continuously Learn and Evolve: Personal branding is an ongoing process. Stay up to date with industry trends and adapt your strategies accordingly. Always be open to learning and improving your personal brand.

Impleme-nting these personal branding sugge-stions can help craft a compelling online image- that connects with your intended followe-rs and aids your career ambitions. While some- ideas may require minor e-ffort, thoughtfully applying even a few can progre-ssively develop a digital profile- highlighting your unique strengths and value. Whe-ther highlighting relevant qualifications, cultivating use-ful connections, or sharing insightful perspective-s, a balanced branding approach tailored to your particular field allows prospe-cts to better understand how you may support the-ir specific needs.

Leveraging Social Media Platforms

Social media platforms supply a capable- route to feature your e-xceptional abilities and talents re-garding individual branding. By utilizing the proper tactics, you're able- to harness these platforms succe-ssfully to cultivate a powerful personal brand that conne-cts with your planned target audience-. These destinations pe-rmit you to exhibit examples of your work, give- bits of knowledge, and interface- with people who may be ke-en on your gifts. On the off chance that done- capably, web-based media can assist you with de-veloping trust and support for what makes you exce-ptional, subsequently building your notoriety as an e-xpert in your field. While it take-s some investment initially to make- quality substance and fabricate a following, concentrating on applicable-, important substance that adds worth for others will pay bene-fits over the long haul as you assemble- a network of individuals keen on your particular spe-cialty.

Each social media platform provide-s a distinct collection of capabilities and tools, making it crucial to comprehe-nd how to move around and make the most of what e-ach has to offer. It's important to take the time- to explore the various options available- on each network so you can bette-r determine whe-re and how to focus your efforts. Whethe-r it's sharing updates, engaging with followers, or promoting your brand, re-cognizing the strengths of each individual platform will he-lp you optimize your approach and connect with the right audie-nce.

Let's e-xamine a few prevale-nt social media platforms more closely and inve-stigate recommendations on capitalizing on the-m productively for individual branding. Whether asse-ssing Facebook, Instagram, LinkedIn or Twitter, focusing conte-nt on pertinent intere-sts while engaging with others in a conside-rate manner can strengthe-n an online presence- over the long term. Tailoring update-s appropriately across networks and maintaining consistency in voice- and messaging helps establish cre-dibility.

1. Instagram

Instagram is a visual medium that pe-rmits folks to showcase their inventive-ness and construct a visually interesting private- model. With its concentrate on prime- quality photographs and engaging visible content mate-rial, Instagram offers a super chance to spotlight your skills, passions, and non-public fashion. Utilize- related hashtags, captioning that engage-s your target market, and photographs that seize- attention to entice your vie-wers and construct a robust on-line identity. Whilst constructing your pre-sence on Instagram, reme-mber to upload content material re-gularly to maintain folks engaged and share snapshot from nume-rous aspects of your existence- to provide perception into who you're-. Be certain that your captions upload context and which me-ans to the photos you percentage- to help tell your tale.

2. LinkedIn

LinkedIn provide-s a valuable space for caree-r-oriented networking and re-putation cultivation. Users can highlight their qualifications, connect with othe-rs in similar occupations, and craft a public persona emphasizing strengths and know-how. Optimizing your profile-, routinely engaging with industry discussions, and spotlighting past work can help e-stablish yourself as a reliable re-source in your domain. Connecting with others se-eking to share knowledge- or collaborate on projects aids professional de-velopment. While ne-tworking is emphasized, demonstrating accomplishme-nts and continually adding to competencies stre-ngthens recognition as a contributor.

3. Twitter

Twitter provide-s an avenue for real-time- discussions and speedy updates, allowing you to inte-ract with your followers and exhibit your character. Use- Twitter to distribute worthwhile pe-rspectives, sector ne-ws flashes, and important communications with the people- who pursue you. Be certain your Twitte-r profile precisely mirrors your individual brand and ke-ep a steady tone throughout your twe-ets.

4. YouTube

YouTube provides an excellent opportunity to showcase your expertise through video content. Create engaging and informative videos related to your niche, share tutorials, and provide valuable insights to build a loyal audience. Optimize your video titles, descriptions, and tags to increase discoverability and actively engage with your viewers through comments and discussions.

It is esse-ntial to keep in mind that eve-ry social media platform has its own particular target audience- and goal, so you must shape your material and involveme-nt techniques fittingly for eve-ry one. By comprehending the- qualities and subtleties that make- each network unique, you can proficie-ntly utilize them to advance your own image- and associate with more individuals. Differe-nt stages regularly draw in various kinds of clients, so it pays to conce-ntrate your substance for eve-ry stage's normal client instead of re-using a similar substance crosswise over stage-s. This permits you to interface with crowds on an incre-asingly customized and applicable leve-l. Remembering how to amplify the- one of a kind characteristics of each stage- can assist you with accomplishing more noteworthy openne-ss and developing your impact.

Building a Consistent Online Presence

Building and sustaining consistency is vital for e-ffective personal branding online-. Here, we will e-xamine strategies for crafting a uniform and cohe-sive brand persona across multiple social me-dia sites. Developing a unifie-d image through a steady voice and visual style- helps earn trust and reliability with your vie-wers. While consistency is ke-y, some variation keeps things inte-resting. Mix longer, more comple-x sentences with brie-f, witty ones. Provide clarification on core points but also include- relevant example-s. Focus on your viewers' nee-ds rather than just information delivery. A consiste-nt yet nuanced approach across platforms helps conne-ct with people in an authentic way.

A fundamental tactic for cultivating a ste-ady online presence- involves applying consistent branding ele-ments like an instantly identifiable- logo, color scheme, and visual appearance-. Employing recognizable branding traits assists in solidifying your brand identity and making it re-adily recognizable across platforms. Some ke-y branding components to maintain consistency include your logo always appe-aring in the same spot, utilizing your brand colors throughout all visuals, and kee-ping a uniform design style for ele-ments like images, buttons, and he-adings. Consistency with branding allows your audience to quickly associate- specific imagery or styles with your company, he-lping you become more me-morable as people e-ncounter your internet pre-sence in differe-nt locations.

Moreove-r, maintaining consistency in your tone of voice and ke-y messages across various social media platforms like- Facebook, Instagram and LinkedIn is critical. By kee-ping your brand's voice uniform when creating posts for diffe-rent networks, you can provide a cohe-sive experie-nce that helps cultivate community and re-sonate with your target audience-. Whether crafting visual content for Instagram or writing longe-r form updates for LinkedIn, retaining a similar tone- that aligns with your overall branding strategy allows your messaging to flow cohe-rently no matter where- a person engages with your conte-nt online. This united front is important for building recognition of your e-xpertise and values as pe-rceived by clients and followe-rs.

Establishing a consistent posting routine- is important for keeping audience-s engaged with your brand over the- long run. While the specific sche-dule may vary depending on your targe-t audience and goals, sele-cting a frequency such as wee-kly or monthly and sticking to it allows your followers to rely on fresh conte-nt appearing at predictable inte-rvals. Whether you post once a we-ek or a few times pe-r month, maintaining this predictable cadence- demonstrates your commitment to re-gularly providing value. It also gives reade-rs a reason to check in with your brand that isn't depe-ndent on any one post. While the- topics and types of content you share can vary, knowing ne-w insights and information will consistently emerge- on your set dates helps ke-ep your audience inve-sted. A steady stream of valuable- discussions, tips

To optimize your online- presence for purpose-s of establishing your brand identity, it is crucial to consistently inte-ract with your target audience. Be- sure to reply to comments and me-ssages promptly in order to appear e-ngaged and attentive to fe-edback. Additionally, actively join rele-vant discussions within your industry sphere to position yourself as an authoritative- yet approachable voice. This pe-rsonalized participation helps make your brand se-em more genuine- and human while strengthening bonds with the- people you aim to reach.

While e-stablishing a continuous online presence- requires dedication and work, the- outcomes prove to be worthwhile-. By employing these tactics thoughtfully and ste-adily over time, you can reinforce- your individual image and differentiate- yourself amidst the many voices online-. From crafting a clear message to sharing consiste-nt, quality content, focus on gradually developing your brand to attract and e-ngage your ideal audience-. Interact respectfully with othe-rs in your industry as well, as relationships and reputation carry we-ight online. Though competition abounds, small steps e-ach day can lead to meaningful progress if approache-d with patience and care.

Crafting Compelling Content

Creating compe-lling content is an important aspect of personal branding that can substantially influe-nce how your brand is perceive-d online. Developing pie-ces that genuinely inte-rest your intended re-aders through relatable subje-cts and clear explanations is central to cultivating a powe-rful personal brand identity. Here-, we will look at impactful methods for crafting material that grabs atte-ntion and authentically portrays your brand.

To create captivating content, it's important to understand the interests and preferences of your target audience. Conducting thorough research and leveraging insights from social media analytics can help you gain valuable insights into what your audience wants to see and engage with. By identifying their pain points, aspirations, and interests, you can tailor your content to meet their needs and establish a genuine connection.

Telling an impactful story is one- of the best ways to truly capture your audie-nce's attention through content. Storie-s have an amazing ability to stir emotions, help pe-ople feel unde-rstood, and leave a mark. By adding storytelling e-lements into what you share, your conte-nt will stick with people more and have- more meaning. You could recount parts of your own e-xperience to make- your brand seem real. Te-lling quick motivational tales or describing how certain clie-nts succeeded can motivate- and teach others. Detailing how a custome-r or patient overcame challe-nges through your solution shows the value you offe-r. Weaving in these kinds of narrative-s helps form a bond and makes your message- more heartfelt than just facts alone-. Whether openly re-flecting on your journey, briefly inspiring with succe-ss stories, or giving case studies, incorporating some- story elements e-ngages people be-tter than a straightforward pitch alone.

While visual e-lements such as images, vide-os, and graphics have grown more prominent across digital platforms, the-ir inclusion must thoughtfully align with both one's overarching brand and intende-d viewers. Consider that high-quality visual additions can stre-ngthen the attraction of your material while- simultaneously drawing focus to your personal image. Ne-vertheless, e-nsure all content - whethe-r written, seen or he-ard - consistently reflects your de-fined brand and resonates with your pre-ferred reade-rs. Create material that appe-als visually yet harmonizes with who you aim to repre-sent through a unified identity acce-ssible across all mediums.

Finally, be consistent in your content creation efforts. Developing a content calendar and sticking to a regular posting schedule can help you maintain a steady flow of content and engage your audience consistently. By providing valuable and relevant content on a regular basis, you can position yourself as an authority in your niche and gain the trust and loyalty of your followers.

In the following portion, we- will explore approaches for involving with your vie-wers and cultivating purposeful communications on social media ne-tworks. Some tactics we will consider involve- posting intriguing content on a routine basis to maintain engage-ment, asking open-ende-d questions to spark discussion, and responding helpfully to comme-nts and messages to build rapport. While social platforms can facilitate- superficial interactions, applying these- kinds of techniques may help you form de-eper

Engaging with Your Audience

Building a successful personal brand goes beyond creating compelling content; it also involves actively engaging with your audience on social media. By fostering meaningful connections and interactions, you can establish yourself as an authority in your industry and build a community of loyal followers.

While re-sponding rapidly to feedback exhibits that you acknowle-dge and appreciate your audie-nce's involvement, it is also important not to fe-el pressured to instantly re-act to every message-. Addressing inquiries, issues, or e-xpressions of encourageme-nt in a well-timed manner he-lps demonstrate consideration for pe-ople's input. While swift response-s can strengthen bonds of interaction and trust, not e-veryone is available around the- clock. Replying when you have the- time and mental space to offe-r a thoughtful answer is often prefe-rable to hasty or superficial replie-s. Making a genuine effort to e-ngage with followers at a reasonable- pace shows valuing their contributions without coming across as reactive-. Whether acknowledging que-stions, dealing with complaints respectfully, or e-xpressing gratitude for support, meaningful e-ngagement on your own schedule- fosters healthier re-lationships than constant availability suggests.

Utilize social media features such as polls, surveys, and interactive content to encourage your audience to participate and share their opinions. By involving them in the conversation, you not only gain valuable insights but also make them feel invested in your brand.

Engaging your audience- through thoughtful discussion is another effective- means of connecting with your reade-rs. Pose intriguing questions that stimulate critical thinking on pe-rtinent issues. Inquire about the-ir perspective on pote-ntial new approaches or service-s in order to gain valuable insights. Spark interactive- dialogues surrounding relevant industry the-mes. By cultivating exchange of ide-as in this manner, you foster a sense- of fellowship and establish yourself as a de-pendable source of information. While- interaction enriches unde-rstanding from varied viewpoints, stay attentive- to diverse opinions to maintain respe-ct and open-mindedness.

Connecting with your targe-t market involves being live-ly in distributing their content and exhibiting gratitude- for their backing. By redistributing customer-made- substance, including confirmations from clients, or giving open acknowle-dgments not just approves your supporters howe-ver in addition fortifies the association among your image- and your devotees. It is critical to de-monstrate your crowd that you regard what they share- and that you need to help spre-ad their message. A basic approach to do this is by occasionally re-tweeting, quoting, or sharing posts made by your supporte-rs covering your image. This permits your supporte-rs to feel heard while- likewise arriving at more e-xtensive crowds. Additionally including a couple of individual words of thanks or praise- for your crowd's commitment can go far towards building trust and responsibility.

Remember, consistency is crucial when it comes to audience engagement. Regularly post valuable and relatable content, be responsive, and actively participate in industry conversations. By consistently showing up and engaging with your audience, you can deepen their connection to your brand and foster long-lasting relationships.

Monitoring Your Brand Reputation

Deve-loping a robust personal brand demands continuous vigilance and ade-pt handling of your online image. Here-, we will inspect fundamental instrume-nts and tactics to help you proactively track your brand reputation and cope- with any detrimental remarks or asse-ssments that may surface. While maintaining your online- presence, it is wise- to routinely monitor search engine-s and social networks for mentions of your name. Take- note of both positive and negative- feedback to bette-r understand how others perce-ive you. Should criticisms arise, address the-m respectfully and thoughtfully rather than be-coming defensive. Turning a ne-gative into a positive learning e-xperience can bolste-r your reputation in the long run. Staying active and e-ngaged online also provides opportunitie-s to accentuate your qualifications and expe-rtise. Consistently showcase your work and value-s to keep cultivating trust within your network.

Utilize Online Reputation Management Tools

Monitoring your brand reputation across various online platforms can be challenging without the right tools. Thankfully, there are several online reputation management tools available that can simplify the process. These tools enable you to track mentions of your name or brand, monitor social media conversations, and gather valuable insights about your online reputation.

Brandwatch and Google Ale-rts are two helpful reputation manage-ment tools that allow monitoring of a brand across online channels. Brandwatch offe-rs robust social listening functionality to track and analyze discussions relate-d to your company on various social media platforms. This gives insights into customer se-ntiment and how the public perce-ives your brand. Another option is Google Ale-rts, which provides notifications when your brand is refe-renced on various website-s like news articles, blogs, and social me-dia. Though more basic than Brandwatch, Google Alerts is conve-nient for getting a gene-ral sense of where- your brand is mentioned online. Both tools provide- visibility into brand conversations and mentions occurring across the inte-rnet, helping with issues manage-ment and protecting organizational reputation.

Respond Promptly and Professionally

Within contemporary socie-ty, it has become very important to re-act rapidly and appropriately to any adverse re-marks or evaluations encountere-d on networking platforms. Addressing issues and se-ttling troubles promptly shows your dedication to client fulfillme-nt and can assist with reducing the impact of negative- viewpoints. While it's significant for organizations to react de-ftly to criticism online, it's additionally basic to do as such courteously and productively. By taking a conside-rate, understanding way to fee-dback, one can turn negative asse-ssments into openings for change that fortify the- client experie-nce. A mindful reaction acknowledge-s both positive and negative input with appre-ciation, investigating how administrations could be enhance-d moving forward. This builds trust and shows clients their assessme-nts were paid attention to.

When re-sponding to negative fee-dback, it is best to stay composed and considerate-. Clarify any misunderstandings politely, and acknowledge- valid criticisms gracefully. Reacting defe-nsively will likely only make the- situation worse

Stay relaxe-d and collected, stee-ring clear of protective or challe-nging terminology. Remain peace-ful and composed while clarifying any misunderstandings to re-duce tension.While addre-ssing their concerns, make an e-ffort to understand the situation from their pe-rspective. Acknowledge- their frustration in a calm, sympathetic manner to he-lp diffuse tensions. Ask respe-ctful questions thatIf nee-ded, express re-gret for any misunderstanding and propose a me-thod to remedy their issue-s or pacify their worries. Suggest an ide-a for assuaging their concerns or resolving difficultie-s respectfully.If nee-ded, continue the discussion in a more- private setting to find a tailored solution in a le-ss public manner.

Regularly Monitor Review Sites and Social Media

Review sites and social media platforms are popular channels for individuals to voice their opinions and experiences. Monitoring these platforms can provide valuable insights into how your brand is perceived by the public and allow you to identify and address any potential reputation issues.

It is wise to configure- notices or updates for evaluation locations like- Yelp, Google Revie-ws, or TripAdvisor, guaranteeing that you are quickly cautione-d of any new surveys. Furthermore-, closely screen your online- media records to remain e-ducated about any discussions or refere-nces identified with your image-. By setting up notices, you can react rapidly to any re-cent surveys and address any clie-nt issues or worries right away. Scree-ning online media permits you to partake- in discussions with clients and supporters, while like-wise keeping an e-ye out for any negative re-marks. This close observing of client input and online- media will permit you to consistently e-nhance and refine your administrations or ite-ms dependent on re-al client input. Prompt reaction to input through surveys or online- media talks can assist you with building trust and consistency with your objective- market.

By taking a proactive and atte-ntive approach on social media, you will be able- to sustain a favorable brand reputation and handle any critical comme-nts before situations dete-riorate further. It is important to regularly monitor your profile-s and actively engage with followe-rs to demonstrate your commitment to custome-r service. Addressing issue-s promptly shows that you value people's opinions and want to re-solve concerns, which fosters goodwill. Re-sponding respectfully to dissatisfied use-rs can also prevent

Take Advantage of Positive Feedback

Tracking your brand's reputation is not only important for re-sponding to unfavorable reviews—you should also acknowle-dge and take advantage of positive- feedback. If clients post favorable- reviews or discuss pleasant inte-ractions, show appreciation and interact with them to cultivate- devoted brand supporters. Whe-n people share positive- experience-s, it's a chance to thank them for the fe-edback and potentially start a dialogue. This allows you to furthe-r understand what aspects of your business or products the-y value most. It may also give them a way to he-lp spread the word and fee-l invested in your success. Le-veraging positive revie-ws presents an opportunity to foster goodwill and stre-ngthen relationships with satisfied custome-rs.

Acknowledging positive- reviews and fee-dback is a gracious way to show gratitude for support from customers and fans. Thanking those who have- shared enthusiastic reactions to your products or se-rvices on social media or retaile-r websites inspires othe-rs to express their own satisfaction. Re-sponding to compliments demonstrates that you value- customers' input and prioritize building relationships. This e-ngagement helps e-stablish your brand as one focused on forging connections with clie-nts through respectful interaction. Illustrating appre-ciation for satisfied patrons in turn encourages additional constructive- comments from those who witness the- exchanges, strengthe-ning your reputation and credibility among a wider audie-nce through word-of-mouth recommendation.

Ultimately, care-fully tracking your brand image is an essential aspe-ct of curating your online personal brand. By leve-raging the appropriate resource-s, replying quickly and respectfully, and active-ly checking evaluations and social networks, you can succe-ssfully govern your online reputation and pre-serve a positive brand pe-rception. Whether re-acting to positive or negative re-views on sites detailing pe-rsonal experience-s, or engaging constructively in social media conve-rsations, consistently demonstrating your dedication to custome-r satisfaction and quality work will reinforce your credibility and trustworthine-ss over time. With diligence- and good faith, even occasional missteps ne-ed not define your broade-r reputation if addressed re-spectfully.

Analytics and Measurement

When it come-s to personal branding on social media, kee-ping track of how your efforts are rece-ived is important for consistent progress and re-finement. The statistics available- provide useful understandings into what strate-gies are working well and what could use- adjustment, aiding informed choices ge-ared towards strengthening your pe-rsonal brand over time. Gauging engage-ment and reach across platforms shows where- attention is highest or lowest, so atte-ntion can be focused accordingly. Ongoing assessme-nt creates opportunity for boosting effe-ctiveness by building on approaches that attract inte-rest while reworking those- attracting less interaction. With measure-ment as a guide, brands continuously optimize to re-sonate more compellingly with inte-nded audiences.

Understanding the Importance of Analytics

Analytics grant you the ability to monitor pivotal be-nchmarks and assess the productivity of your social media marke-ting for personal branding. By examining evide-nce like involveme-nt rates, scope, and conversions, you can achie-ve important understandings into your audience-'s behaviors and inclinations. This information permits you to refine- your substance, customize your message-s, and maximize your procedures for pre-ferable outcomes. Howe-ver, it is important to remembe-r that analytics only show correlations, not causes, so testing strate-gies is still necessary to de-termine the most e-ffective approaches.

Key Analytics for Personal Branding

A few e-ssential indicators to focus on when evaluating the- effectivene-ss of your personal brand building efforts include we-b traffic and engagement me-trics, thought leadership recognition, and care-er or business opportunities ge-nerated. Some factors to track include- your website's visit counts and traffic sources to unde-rstand audience growth. Social media followe-r counts and engagement rate-s on different platforms provide insight into your influe-nce.

1. Reach and Impre-ssions: These basic metrics give- insight into the extent your conte-nt is being seen and share-d across social media. They indicate how many use-rs may have encountere-d your message, whethe-r they engaged or not. Tracking re-ach and impressions over time can he-lp clarify if your online presence- is growing, and which platforms or types of content see-m to spread furthest in your target audie-nce's networks.

2. While me-asuring likes, comments, shares, and othe-r forms of engagement can he-lp provide insight into how well your content conne-cts with followers, it is important to remembe-r that forming meaningful relationships is the true- goal. Content that provokes thoughtful discussion and inspires re-aders to learn more can build strong conne-ctions, even if raw engage-ment metrics are not the- highest. Focus first on crafting messages that value- your audience and provide ge-nuine value. High engage-ment often follows when pe-ople feel unde-rstood and that their time investme-nt will benefit them in some- way. Quality interactions where re-aders

feel he-ard, rather than just seen, he-lp establish the bonds of trust that strengthe-n your personal brand over the long run.

3. Conversion Rates: Tracking the number of conversions, such as clicks to your website or email sign-ups, helps you evaluate the effectiveness of your call-to-action and the overall impact of your personal branding efforts.
4. Audience Demographics: Understanding your audience demographics, such as age, location, and interests, allows you to tailor your content and strategies to better target and engage with your ideal audience.

Effectively Measuring Success

When measuring the success of your personal branding strategies, it's essential to set clear objectives and define relevant key performance indicators (KPIs) based on your goals. Regularly reviewing and analyzing your analytics data will help you identify trends, spot opportunities for improvement, and make informed decisions to enhance your personal brand.

Conclusion

Analytics offer me-aningful understandings into how adequately your individual brand atte-mpts on interpersonal organizations are pe-rforming. By checking central estimations and bre-aking down information, you can settle on choices guide-d by factual proof to enhance your procedure-s and upgrade your total individual brand. Stay tuned for the following are-a, where we will inve-stigate the significance of ke-eping in front of patterns as far as individual branding. By investigating basic insights like- commitment, reaches, and adhe-rents, you can concentrate your e-ndeavors on the procedure-s that produce the best outcome-s. This permits you to consistently upgrade how you e-xhibit yourself online and remain applicable-. The following area will give more- setting on ongoing patterns and how to adjust to kee-p your image fresh.

Staying Ahead of Trends

As the world of social me-dia and digital marketing continues to rapidly transform, kee-ping abreast of emerging patte-rns is pivotal for preserving a robust personal image- online. By adopting the most up-to-date social me-dia branding tactics and digital branding methods, people have- the ability to lift their interne-t profile and position themselve-s as sector influencers. Some- strategies to consider involve- experimenting with ne-w visual content styles on platforms like Instagram and Linke-dIn, engaging with followers by asking questions to spark discussions, consiste-ntly publishing useful information and insights relevant to your fie-ld through blogs or videos, and partnering with compleme-ntary brands or individuals for mutually-beneficial promotional campaigns. While digital landscape-s evolve at an expe-dited pace, maintaining adaptability and creativity he-lps individuals customized tailored approaches to highlight e-xpertise and stay connecte-d with their target audience-s.

While monitoring social me-dia platforms remains essential for tracking shifting tre-nds, focusing too heavily on constant changes could distract from cultivating meaningful conne-ctions. Taking occasional breaks from scan updates allows one to conte-mplate how best utilizing new fe-atures might enhance e-ngaging with their authentic intere-sts and values. Rather than fee-ling compelled adapting persona pure-ly due reaction, thoughtful consideration which update-s naturally align personal passions offers sustainable approach le-veraging technological progression be-nefit relationships.

While maintaining aware-ness of emerging digital marke-ting patterns is important, it is essential to ide-ntify opportunities for growth. Both leveraging cutting-e-dge technologies and e-xperimenting with novel conte-nt designs allow for outreach to intende-d groups in purposeful manners. Whethe-r utilizing latest devices, inve-stigating unusual formation of materials, or accessing rising networks, taking proactive- steps in adopting electronic branding tactics can se-t people separate- from their rivals and aid in relating to aimed crowds substantially.

Furthermore-, engaging with the online community and active-ly taking part in pertinent discussions can provide important advantage-s. By joining industry-focused groups on social media, participating in forums on topic-rele-vant websites, and cooperating with notable- influencers, people- can obtain precious understanding into deve-loping patterns and position themselve-s as influential thinkers in their are-a of expertise. Inte-racting with others intereste-d in similar specializations presents opportunitie-s to exchange perspe-ctives, acquire knowledge- from experience-d individuals, and strengthen one's own profe-ssional network. While observing ongoing conve-rsations, an individual may also detect problems to addre-ss or ideas to contribute that could help push the-ir field forward. Actively repre-senting one's profession online- hence allows gaining insights that facilitate profe-ssional growth and leadership through collaborative participation.

Chapter 6

Rediscovering Creativity: Picking up old hobbies or starting new ones

Welcome to our chapter on rediscovering creativity and embracing the joy of hobbies at 50! Whether you're looking to pick up old hobbies or embark on new ones, this section is filled with inspiring ideas and practical tips tailored to those in their prime years. Engaging in hobbies at 50 brings countless benefits, from enhancing mental well-being to forming new connections with like-minded individuals. Let's explore the world of hobbies for 50-year-olds and discover a range of hobby ideas perfect for older adults.

Embracing the Joy of Hobbies at 50

Reaching the- landmark age of 50 is a notable achieve-ment that provides a special chance- to take pleasure in le-isurely interests and pastime-s. Pursuing hobbies not only delivers tre-mendous satisfaction but also aids complete fulfillme-nt and wellness. As people- in their peak years, folks should inve-stigate an ample assortment of re-creational activities and enjoyable- interests that can bring enthusiasm and me-aning to their days. Whether it's discove-ring a new skill, reconnecting with nature-, volunteering your time or e-xploring your creative side, making the- effort to indulge in hobbies and fun pursuits is good for both your me-ntal and physical health during this phase of life.

While the- recreational choices available- to 50-year-olds are plentiful and wide--ranging, some activities may suit certain individuals more- than others based on personal inte-rests and abilities. In addition to more cre-atively oriented pastime-s involving art mediums like painting, writing, and ceramics work, options e-xist for those seeking to stay physically active- through nature expeditions like- hiking, rounds of golf out on the course, or various styles of dancing done- either alone or with a partne-r. Whether one's proclivitie-s lean towards pursuits allowing artistic expression or alte-rnatives permitting cardiovascular exe-rtion in a scenic outdoor setting or social setting, this stage- of life continues to make room for hobby-drive-n engagement and e-njoyment.

Cultivating an outdoor garden can pre-sent a rewarding hobby for those in middle- age. Whether growing ve-getables, fruits, or flowers, de-veloping a beautiful plot of land outside one-'s home allows for a feeling of achie-vement each time- new life eme-rges. Spending time imme-rsed in nature, observing plants grow unde-r one's care, brings a sense- of calm. One comes to understand nurturing re-lationships as seeds are sown, te-nder leaves and blooms e-merge. Gardening offe-rs relaxation through activities like we-eding, pruning, and enjoying the se-renity of the natural world at a leisure-ly pace. Beyond visual delights, garde-ning also benefits health as fre-sh air and mild exercise re-duce stress. For those se-eking an engaging and fulfilling pastime, cultivating one-'s green thumb prese-nts quality time surrounded by life, color, and tranquility.

Puzzles and game-s that challenge the mind, such as che-ss, crosswords, and Sudoku, can provide entertainme-nt alongside cognitive bene-fits for those seeking me-ntal stimulation. Engaging in these types of activitie-s helps keep the- brain active and sharpens problem-solving skills. Che-ss requires strategizing se-veral moves in advance and thinking tactically. It e-xercises planning and logic. Solving crosswords and Sudoku involves applying re-asoning abilities to decipher clue-s and discern patterns. Both activities give- the mind a enjoyable workout that may he-lp preserve cognitive- function. While providing a engaging pastime, puzzle-s and games that activate differe-nt areas of thinking show promise for enhancing me-ntal agility.

Exploring culinary pursuits like cooking or baking can be- a fun way to express your creative- side while enjoying tasty home--cooked meals. The kitche-n serves as a place whe-re you can experime-nt with different recipe-s and ingredients to discover your own style- in the kitchen. Whethe-r you're testing new flavors or le-arning techniques, time spe-nt in the kitchen allows you to expre-ss yourself through food. You have the fre-edom to be inventive- with what you create. Trying your hand at recipe-s outside your comfort zone can lead to surprising re-sults. The process of meal pre-paration becomes an engaging activity be-yond just eating to survive. It cultiv

Discovering and engaging in recreational activities for 50-year-olds not only provides an outlet for personal growth and self-expression, but it also offers opportunities for social connections. Joining hobby clubs, attending workshops, or participating in group activities can lead to new friendships and a sense of belonging.

Embracing the joy of hobbies at 50 is a celebration of life's possibilities and a reminder that there is no age limit to pursuing one's passions. So, whether it's picking up an old hobby or venturing into uncharted territory, there are countless fun hobbies awaiting middle-aged adults to explore and savor.

The Power of Rediscovering Old Hobbies

Revisiting old pastime-s can be a nostalgic and rewarding expe-rience. For those re-aching their peak years at 50, e-ngaging with pursuits you appreciated in times past might strongly re-kindle your enthusiasm and provide a fe-eling of familiarity. Rediscovering a hobby from your youth may transport you back to simple-r times and remind you of why you were- initially attracted to that activity. While tastes and inte-rests often change throughout life-, reconnecting with an old hobby can sometime-s refresh your perspe-ctive and help you find rene-wed purpose and enjoyme-nt. Such nostalgic reflections of pursuits from decade-s past may stimulate creative ide-as for adapting beloved activities to your curre-nt stage of life, allowing you to appreciate- old friends in new ways.

At this stage of life, you have accumulated a wealth of experiences and memories. Picking up old hobbies can transport you back to cherished moments and help you reconnect with your true self. Whether it's dusting off your old guitar and strumming some chords or dusting off your sewing machine to create beautiful garments, the joy and satisfaction of reigniting your past hobbies is unparalleled.

Furthermore-, by rediscovering old passions you have the- potential for inner deve-lopment and self-manifestation. It pe-rmits you to contact your imaginative part, improving your general prospe-rity and giving a sound outlet for self-disclosure. Taking an inte-rest in exercise-s that once brought you tremendous joy can he-lp lessen pressure-, build certainty, and advance a fee-ling of significance and heading. While re-connecting with past interests has advantage-s, it is additionally essential to consistently atte-mpt new things and develop as an individual.

Rediscove-ring old hobbies you once enjoye-d can provide uplifting emotional and mental advantage-s while also enhancing your physical well-be-ing. Activities like gardening allow you to spe-nd time outside tending to plants and flowe-rs, keeping your body active through various motions involve-d in cultivation. Dancing is a fun way to stay lively, as different dance- styles encourage move-ment that exercise-s your muscles and joints. Playing sports provides health pe-rks as well, whether it's a casual game- of basketball with friends or solo tennis practice-, motion helps your cardiovascular system. These- pursuits that reignite your intere-sts from the past support a more robust lifestyle- by maintaining activity levels, finesse- for physical tasks, and general fitness, contributing to we-llness in a balanced manner.

Rediscove-ring past passions provides benefits, as you re-tain knowledge from initial expe-riences. Skills only nee-d refinement, rathe-r than starting from scratch. Familiarity expedites progre-ss, enabling enjoyment at a re-laxed pace through visible e-nhancements. What was once a hobby re-mains, with room for enhanced technique-s and expertise. Though time- away, memories sustain foundations for rene-wed activities to unfold with ease-. Rekindling sparks enjoyment through challe-nges just beyond current capabilitie-s.

While introspe-ction on past passions can be illuminating, one must also thoughtfully consider how to re-alistically incorporate nostalgic hobbies amid prese-nt responsibilities. Reach out to truste-d companions and like-minded souls within online circle-s seeking their pe-rspective on judiciously blending fond me-mories with modern commitments. Unite-d in shared interests, pe-rhaps others can lend pragmatic proposals on gradually rekindling e-mbers of former fascinations within life's conte-mporary constraints.

Remember, it doesn't matter how much time has passed since you last pursued your hobbies. The joy and fulfillment they bring are timeless. So, dust off your paintbrushes, lace up your hiking boots, or pick up that novel you've always wanted to write. The power of rediscovering old hobbies can rejuvenate your soul and enrich your life in ways you never thought possible.

Starting Fresh: New Hobby Ideas for Older Adults

Reaching the- halfway point of your life is a great opportunity to try new things and ste-p outside your comfort zone. At 50, your caree-r and responsibilities may have se-ttled into a routine, leaving space- to discover interests you've- not had time for previously. Taking up hobbies at this stage- can reinvigorate your days with enthusiasm and a se-nse of purpose. Do you long to expre-ss yourself artistically or stay active physically? The choice-s for enjoyable pastimes suite-d to mature adults are plentiful. Le-t me share a few options worth conside-ring that may spark your curiosity:

Creative Pursuits:

1. Painting: Unleash your artistic side and express yourself through colors and strokes.
2. Writing: Dive into the world of storytelling, memoirs, or poetry and let your imagination soar.
3. Photography: Capture moments and explore the world through the lens of a camera.

Physical Activities:

- Hiking: Embarking on scenic trails allows one- to discover nature's wonders through bre-athtaking hikes. Wandering gently grade-d paths provides the opportunity to appreciate-spectacular surroundings while enjoying light e-xercise in a stress-fre-e setting
- Gardening: Cultivate your green thumb and create a tranquil oasis in your backyard.

While golf provide-s a relaxing escape amidst tranquil surroundings on the- course, focusing on refining your swing technique- and shotmaking strategy can aid your improvement at the- sport. Taking time to analyze your past rounds may reve-al tactical adjustments which could lower your scores going forward, such

These are just a few examples of the wide range of hobbies available for older adults. Remember, the key is to choose activities that bring you joy and a sense of satisfaction. So, embark on this new chapter of your life, explore your interests, and start a hobby that will enrich your days and contribute to your overall well-being.

Benefits of Pursuing Hobbies Later in Life

Exploring the manifold advantage-s of taking up pastimes in later years can e-nrich your life considerably. Partaking in hobbies not only introduce-s delight and meaning, but also has bene-ficially influences various ele-ments of wellness for e-lders. Some of the pe-rks include reducing stress, boosting cognitive- function, furnishing an outlet for self-expre-ssion, strengthening social connections, and sparking a re-newed sense- of purpose. Whether it be- learning a musical instrument, embarking on do-it-yourse-lf projects, volunteering your time- and talents, or rediscovering childhood passions, discove-ring new hobbies as an older adult can

Mental Health and Cognitive Function

Engaging in hobbies and pastime-s provides a myriad of psychological benefits. Pursuits like- tackling puzzles, mastering a new musical instrume-nt, or creative ende-avors activate the mind, heighte-ning remembrance, focus, and proble-m-solving skills. These activities e-xercise the brain by challe-nging it to learn new skills, think strategically, and apply re-asoning abilities. Whether choosing up a nove-l interest or carrying on with existing one-s, integrating hobbies into one's routine- supports mental wellness and cognitive- function through intellectual stimulation.

Physical Well-being

Engaging in hobbies that e-ntail physical exertion, like garde-ning or dancing, can aid in sustaining and enhancing general physical condition. Routine- physical activity supports cardiovascular fitness, reinforces muscle-s, and enhances flexibility, assisting more- experience-d individuals remain dynamic and autonomous. Gardening nece-ssitates activities like digging, planting, wate-ring and weeding which exe-rcise the body. Dancing is a social activity that allows one to move- to music in a enjoyable manner, ke-eping both the body and mind active. Re-gular physical pursuits, whether leisure-ly or more labor intensive, can be-nefit seniors by helping the-m perform everyday tasks and re-main independent for longe-r.

Social Connections

Pursuing hobbies provides an opportunity to connect with like-minded individuals, fostering new friendships and social connections. Whether joining a hobby group or participating in community events, engaging with others who share your interests enhances your social support network and reduces feelings of isolation.

Emotional Well-being

Hobbies offe-r an imaginative outlet and a means of e-motional articulation. They furnish a technique to unwind, le-ssen pressure, and e-nhance state of mind. Taking an intere-st in pleasurable exe-rcises can build self-este-em, certainty, and by and large e-motional prosperity. Hobbies give a re-prieve from regular day to day e-xistence stresse-s and permit individuals to center around some-thing they appreciate. The-y can help discharge pressure- and deliver dopamine and se-rotonin, chemical substances that upgrade state- of mind. Hobbies additionally give a phase to be-come more acquainted with yourse-lf and discover new abilities and abilitie-s. Associating with an enthusiasm can give a fee-ling of achievement and satisfaction, upgrading ce-rtainty.

By embracing hobbies later in life, you can reap these benefits while discovering new passions and exploring exciting avenues of self-expression. Whether it's painting, hiking, cooking, or playing an instrument, finding the right hobby can enhance your life in countless ways.

Overcoming Challenges and Limitations

As you embark on your hobbies at 50, it's important to acknowledge that age may bring certain challenges and limitations. However, it should never discourage you from pursuing your passions and interests. With the right mindset and practical strategies, you can overcome these obstacles and adapt activities to suit your abilities.

One common challenge that older individuals may face is physical limitations. It's essential to listen to your body and choose hobbies that align with your physical capabilities. If you have mobility issues, consider low-impact activities like yoga or swimming. Alternatively, if you prefer more vigorous pursuits, consult with a healthcare professional to ensure your safety.

While cognitive- changes that occur with aging can potentially hinder pursuits e-njoyed earlier in life-, engaging your mind remains important. If noticing decline-s in recollection or focus, contemplate-pastimes stimulating brain function, such as puzzles, crosswords or learning a ne-w instrument. Partaking in activities exe-rcising cognition may help preserve- mental skills and offer pleasing challe-nges to the mind. Some options to e-xplore could be joining a local community education program, starting a daily journal or taking up drawing - finding ways suitable- for your interests to kee-p sparking creativity and curiosity.

Adapting and Modifying Hobbies

While adapting hobbie-s can help work around physical limitations, it is important to listen to your body and not push yourself too hard. Garde-ning is a wonderful hobby that provides both mental and physical be-nefits, but bending and knee-ling for extended pe-riods may cause strain or discomfort for some. Fortunately, the-re are modifications like e-levated planters and raise-d beds that allow you to enjoy outdoor cultivation while minimizing stre-nuous motions. Arthritis can pose challenges for hobbie-s requiring dexterity. Broad brushstroke-s or handbuilding with clay offer creative outle-ts for those with joint issues by relying more- on overall arm and hand movements rathe-r than small, precise ones. Finding activitie-s aligned with your current abilities is ke-y so that hobbies add joy instead of additional pain or limitations. With some adjustme-nts and the right selection, inte-rests need not be- abandoned or outgrown as bodies change ove-r time.

Furthermore, seeking support and assistance can make a significant difference in overcoming challenges. Connect with local community centers or organizations that offer resources and workshops tailored to older adults. By joining these groups, you can learn from experienced hobbyists and gain valuable insights on adapting activities.

Remember, age should not deter you from pursuing hobbies that bring you joy and fulfillment. Embrace the notion that hobbies are meant to be enjoyed and adapted to suit your circumstances. With a positive attitude and practical adaptations, you can overcome challenges and continue to engage in your favorite pastimes well into your prime years.

Connecting with Like-Minded Individuals

Engaging in hobbies at 50 opens up a whole new world of connections with like-minded individuals who share your interests and passions. Whether you enjoy outdoor activities, arts and crafts, or intellectual pursuits, there are plenty of opportunities to connect with others who are also seeking meaningful recreational activities.

To start, consider joining local clubs or community organizations that cater to your specific hobbies. Many communities have groups dedicated to hiking, cycling, photography, gardening, and more. These clubs often organize regular outings, workshops, and events where you can meet fellow enthusiasts and make lasting friendships.

Online Communities

Online communities are another fantastic way to connect with like-minded individuals from the comfort of your own home. There are numerous forums, social media groups, and hobby-specific websites that bring people together based on shared interests.

By joining these online communities, you can engage in discussions, share tips and advice, and even collaborate on projects with people from all over the world. It's a convenient way to expand your network and find support from those who understand your passion.

Additionally, you can explore platforms like Meetup, which offers the opportunity to find local groups and events tailored to your hobbies and recreational interests. With Meetup, you can easily connect with people in your area who are looking to form social connections through shared activities.

Connecting with othe-rs who share your interests allows you to e-nhance your enjoyment of hobbie-s while gaining a support system. It provides an opportunity to de-velop meaningful relationships and a se-nse of belonging by becoming part of a community with othe-rs passionate about similar activities. Finding individuals with comparable e-nthusiasms lets you experie-nce hobbies on a dee-per level through share-d understanding.

Incorporating Hobbies into Everyday Life

As we progre-ss through the diverse phase-s of life, it is vital that we discover instance-s of pleasure and significance in our re-gular daily habits. For more seasoned grown-ups, incorporating inte-rests into everyday life- can be an excelle-nt approach to cultivate and nourish individual passions. Regardless of whe-ther you're rediscove-ring an old enthusiasm or investigating new side- interest thoughts, consolidating these- exercises into your re-gular routine can essentially upgrade- your general personal satisfaction and we-llbeing. These activitie-s can give aged people- a feeling of purpose and achie-vement, while additionally ke-eping up their psychological and actual wellne-ss. Hobbies permit more se-asoned grown-ups to keep le-arning new abilities and kee-p their minds dynamic. While certain day by day tasks may turn out to be- progressively troublesome- with age, discovering intere-sts that intrigue you can counteract fee-lings of seclusion and melancholy. Additionally, good hobbies give- more seasoned grown-ups a chance- to interface with others who impart similar inte-rests, subsequently e-xpanding their social life also.

When it comes to incorporating hobbies into your everyday life, finding the right balance is key. Remember that hobbies should be enjoyable and not add unnecessary stress to your already busy schedule. Here are some practical tips to help you make the most of your free time:

Create a Hobby Schedule

Set aside dedicated time each week to indulge in your hobbies. By creating a schedule, you ensure that you prioritize these activities and make them a non-negotiable part of your routine. It can be as little as 30 minutes a day or a few hours each weekend, whatever works best for your lifestyle.

Combine Hobbies with Other Tasks

Look for opportunities to incorporate your hobbies into other daily tasks. For example, if you enjoy listening to audiobooks, you can combine that with your daily walk or workout session. If gardening is your passion, consider growing herbs or small plants in your kitchen or balcony, making it a part of your cooking routine.

Share and Involve Others

Sharing your hobbies with othe-rs allows you to socially engage with friends, family or coworke-rs around mutual interests. You might organize re-gular get-togethers or e-nroll in clubs and communities focused on your pastimes to me-et people with similar passions. Pursuing hobbie-s alongside others enhance-s the experie-nce while cultivating meaningful re-lationships. Whether holding periodic hobby me-etups or joining a club, engaging togethe-r in activities gives you an opportunity to bond over share-d interests in a way that brings you closer.

Be Flexible and Adaptive

While life- can bring unexpected turns that may alte-r your priorities at times, try to maintain flexibility within your hobby routine-. Be willing to adapt your schedule as ne-eded to accommodate change-s. The objective is to find time- for enjoyable activities without fe-eling overburdene-d. When demands arise, conside-r shortening sessions or reducing fre-quency to better balance- obligations. Pursue interests, ye-t do so at a sustainable pace suited to your e-volving circumstances.

Stay Curious and Explore New Areas

Keep an open mind and embrace new opportunities to expand your horizons. Don't be afraid to explore new hobby ideas that pique your interest. Consider taking up a workshop or class to learn something new. This not only adds variety to your hobbies but also stimulates your mind and keeps you engaged. Incorporating hobbies into your daily routine is a powerful way to bring joy and fulfillment into your life. By setting aside time for activities that you enjoy, you prioritize self-care and personal growth. So, let your hobbies become an integral part of your everyday life, and embrace the sense of satisfaction that comes from pursuing your passions.

Cultivating a Growth Mindset

While pursuing fre-sh interests or reviving past passions late-r in life, maintaining a growth attitude is indispensable-. It is common to question one's abilities whe-n branching out into unfamiliar domains. However, with a few important tactics, individuals can surpass se-lf-uncertainty and relish the proce-ss of lifelong studying and self-improveme-nt. Cultivating new skills or rekindling dormant talents afte-r 50 requires an openne-ss to learn through mistakes and perse-vere in the face- of setbacks. With patience and pe-rsistence, one can ste-adily expand their comfort zone and re-ach higher levels of compe-tency. The rewards lie- not just in achieving mastery but in the pe-rsonal enrichment that stems from ste-pping beyond perceive-d limitations.

Embrace Challenges and Set Realistic Goals

As you begin your hobby journey at 50, it's important to embrace challenges and set realistic goals for yourself. Understand that progress takes time and effort, and that setbacks or mistakes are an integral part of the learning process. By adopting a growth mindset, you allow yourself the freedom to make mistakes and learn from them, ultimately enhancing your skills and knowledge in your chosen activities.

Develop a Positive Attitude

While positive- thinking aligns with nurturing a growth attitude, concentrating solely on pe-rceived constraints often re-stricts potential. A wiser approach emphasize-s inherent talents and abilitie-s, accepting change as a lifelong journe-y. No matter one's years, fre-sh opportunities continually arise to enrich live-s through newly acquired skills. Advanced age- also brings deepening insight and le-arned perspective-s, offering much to share within cherishe-d pastimes. Therefore-, regard experie-nce as a gift that, when shared, cultivate-s community and joy.

Seek Opportunities for Learning and Improvement

Actively seek opportunities to expand your knowledge and improve your skills in your chosen hobby. Engage in workshops, classes, or online tutorials specifically designed for individuals in their prime years. Surround yourself with mentors or like-minded individuals who can offer guidance and support in your hobby journey. Remember, the learning process is ongoing, and by continuously seeking growth, you'll be amazed at how far you can progress.

Embrace the Joy of Exploration

Starting hobbies at 50 opens up a world of possibilities, allowing you to explore new interests and passions. Embrace the joy of exploration and try activities you've always been curious about. Allow yourself to step out of your comfort zone and discover new hobbies that ignite your curiosity and bring you fulfillment. Cultivate a sense of adventure and approach your hobbies with an open mind and a willingness to learn.

By cultivating a growth mindset, you'll find that starting hobbies at 50 is not just about the activity itself, but also about personal development, self-discovery, and creating new connections with others who share your interests. Embrace the journey and enjoy the many rewards that come with pursuing your passions at this exciting stage of life.

Making the Most of Your Prime Years

As you enter your prime years, it's the perfect time to explore fun hobbies and recreational activities that bring joy and fulfillment to your life. Engaging in hobbies not only provides an avenue for self-expression but also enhances your overall well-being. Whether you're rediscovering old passions or trying something new, there are plenty of exciting options for middle-aged adults.

One of the benefits of pursuing hobbies at this stage of life is the opportunity to pursue activities that you may have put on hold due to various commitments. Now, you can fully immerse yourself in activities that genuinely interest you without the pressure of work or raising a family. From painting and photography to cooking and gardening, the choices are endless!

Participating in recreational activities is not only a great way to relax and unwind but also a chance to connect with like-minded individuals. Joining clubs or groups centered around your favorite hobbies allows you to meet new people and build meaningful social connections. Whether it's a book club, hiking group, or arts and crafts class, these shared experiences foster a sense of belonging and camaraderie.

Embracing hobbies during your prime years is about more than just having fun; it's about investing in yourself and prioritizing your well-being. So go ahead and explore new passions, revisit forgotten hobbies, and make the most of this exciting phase of your life. Engage in fun recreational activities that bring you joy and create memories that will last a lifetime.

Chapter **7**

Emotional Intelligence at its Peak:
Understanding and harnessing emotional wisdom

Welcome to our comprehensive guide on emotional intelligence at 50! In this section, we will explore the fascinating world of emotional intelligence (EI) and its immense benefits, particularly for individuals who are in their 50s. Life at this stage is filled with unique challenges and opportunities, and developing emotional intelligence can be a game-changer.

Emotional intelligence is the ability to understand, manage, and effectively express emotions, both in ourselves and others. It involves developing key skills such as self-awareness, empathy, emotional regulation, and effective communication. By harnessing emotional wisdom, individuals can enhance their relationships, make better decisions, and improve their overall well-being.

Whether you're seeking personal growth or aiming for professional success, emotional intelligence at 50 can be a powerful tool. By actively developing these skills, you can navigate midlife challenges with grace and resilience. Our aim is to provide you with practical insights, techniques, and resources to foster emotional intelligence and integrate it into your everyday life.

Join us on this journey as we uncover the transformative potential of emotional intelligence and unlock the key to personal and professional success at 50. Let's dive in and embark on this exciting exploration of understanding and harnessing emotional wisdom for a rewarding life ahead.

What is Emotional Intelligence?

Emotional intelligence is a set of skills and abilities that allows individuals to understand, manage, and express their emotions effectively. It encompasses self-awareness, empathy, emotional regulation, and interpersonal skills, all of which contribute to personal growth and well-being.

For individuals in their 50s, active-ly cultivating emotional intelligence- abilities becomes progre-ssively crucial. It is a transformative journey that e-mpowers individuals to expertly handle- the intricacies of midlife with re-silience and insight. By refining the-se talents, people- can strengthen their re-lationships, make wiser choices, and fe-el higher gratification in all parts of life. While- honing emotional intelligence- allows for navigation of life's complexities, the-re remains an incomplete- understanding of the journey's full impacts.

At its core, emotional intelligence equips individuals with the tools to recognize and regulate their emotions, understand the emotions of others, and forge meaningful connections. This self-awareness and empathetic understanding are vital for navigating the interpersonal challenges that often arise in midlife.

Through emotional intelligence development at 50, individuals can cultivate a deeper understanding of themselves and others, enhancing their ability to communicate effectively, resolve conflicts, and build strong, supportive relationships. By fostering emotional intelligence skills, individuals can create a solid foundation for personal growth and success in various domains, including career, family, and personal well-being.

The Benefits of Emotional Intelligence at 50

Emotional intelligence is a valuable asset for individuals who are 50 years old and above. By developing emotional intelligence skills, they can experience numerous benefits in various aspects of their lives.

Enhanced Relationships

One of the key benefits of emotional intelligence is its ability to improve relationships. Individuals with high emotional intelligence are better equipped to understand and empathize with others, which fosters stronger connections and deeper bonds. They can effectively navigate conflicts, communicate openly, and build harmonious relationships with family, friends, colleagues, and partners.

Improved Decision-Making Skills

Emotional intelligence also plays a significant role in enhancing decision-making abilities. People who possess emotional intelligence are better able to manage and regulate their emotions, allowing them to think more clearly and rationally when faced with important choices. This enables them to make sound decisions that align with their values and goals, leading to greater satisfaction and fulfillment in life.

Overall Well-Being

Emotional intelligence contributes to overall well-being by promoting better self-awareness, self-care, and stress management. Individuals with developed emotional intelligence can effectively recognize and manage their own emotions, leading to reduced stress levels and enhanced mental and emotional health. They are more resilient in the face of challenges and are better equipped to maintain a positive mindset, leading to a greater sense of well-being and contentment.

As individuals reach the age of 50 and beyond, investing in emotional intelligence becomes increasingly important for a fulfilling and successful life. By harnessing emotional wisdom and cultivating emotional intelligence skills, individuals can enjoy the benefits of improved relationships, enhanced decision-making, and overall well-being.

Understanding Emotional Intelligence in Midlife

Developing emotional intelligence is a lifelong journey that holds special significance during midlife. As individuals reach the age of 50, they often face unique challenges and opportunities for personal growth and self-reflection. In this section, we will explore the importance of emotional intelligence at 50 and provide guidance on assessing your own emotional intelligence.

Self-awareness is a crucial aspect of emotional intelligence. It involves understanding and recognizing your own emotions, strengths, and limitations. By being aware of your emotional reactions and patterns, you can gain valuable insights into your behavior and make conscious choices in managing your emotions effectively.

Examining your emotional acume-n can furnish valuable discernments into zone-s of quality and territories requiring improve-ment. By assessing the diffe-rent parts of emotional insight, for example-, self-comprehension, e-mpathy, and enthusiastic administration, you can acquire a more profound compre-hension of your general e-nthusiastic intelligence coe-fficient (EQ). There are- different instruments and appraisals acce-ssible that can help illuminate you on your qualitie-s and shortcomings identifying with understanding and dealing with fe-elings, both your own and other individuals'. By concentrating on zone-s requiring work, for example, e-xpanding mindfulness of nonverbal communication or reacting all the- more intentionally to fee-lings, you can enhance how you interface- and cooperate with others.

Emotional Intelligence Assessment

An emotional inte-lligence assessme-nt gives you a systematic way to analyze and quantify your e-motional intelligence. The-se evaluations commonly involve answe-ring a collection of questions or hypothetical situations that prompt you to conside-r your emotional reactions. The re-sults furnish helpful criticism and provide you with a foundational grasp of your emotional inte-lligence strengths and place-s for progress. While assessme-nts can supply insight, developing emotional inte-lligence is an ongoing process of se-lf-reflection.

By understanding your emotional intelligence at 50, you can take proactive steps to enhance it further. This knowledge empowers you to focus on specific areas that can make a significant impact on your personal and professional life. It allows you to cultivate stronger relationships, make better decisions, and navigate the challenges of midlife with wisdom and resilience.

Next, we will explore practical techniques and strategies for developing emotional intelligence in individuals who are 50 years old and above, enabling you to harness the full potential of emotional wisdom.

Techniques for Developing Emotional Intelligence

For those in the-ir 50s and beyond, cultivating emotional intellige-nce is profoundly important. It equips individuals to face life-'s obstacles with poise and self-knowle-dge, to foster meaningful conne-ctions, and to continue their personal journe-y. Some practical methods to bolster e-motional skills include listening attentive-ly, reflecting on fee-lings before reacting, and e-mbracing change through fresh perspe-ctives. Pausing to understand others and acknowle-dge how experie-nces shape viewpoints also nurture-s insight. With application and empathy, emotional intellige-nce contributes to well-be-ing, compassion, and fulfillness in later life.

1. Cultivate Empathy:

Empathy allows one to grasp and e-xperience anothe-r person's emotions and point of view. Try placing yourse-lf in another's position by envisioning their circumstance-s and genuinely hearing the-ir perspective without judgme-nt. Respond with kindness, care, and conce-rn for their situation. Additionally, involvement in volunte-er or community service opportunitie-s can cultivate empathy through interaction with dive-rse individuals and appreciation for diverse- experience-s.

2. Master Emotional Regulation:

Emotional regulation involves managing and expressing emotions in a healthy and balanced way. Recognize and acknowledge your emotions, and develop techniques to regulate them effectively. Meditation, deep breathing exercises, and journaling can be valuable tools in this journey.

3. Enhance Communication Skills:

Effective communication is a cornerstone of emotional intelligence. Practice active listening, clear expression, and assertiveness to promote open and honest communication. Seek feedback from others to improve your communication skills continually.

4. Practice Self-Reflection:

Allocate time for self-reflection to gain a deeper understanding of your emotions, thoughts, and behaviors. Identify patterns, triggers, and areas for growth. Consider keeping a daily journal or engaging in activities like mindfulness to foster self-awareness.

5. Seek Feedback and Coaching:

Ask for feedback from trusted friends, family members, or mentors to gain insights into how you may be perceived by others. Consider working with an emotional intelligence coach who can provide guidance and support in your journey towards self-improvement.

By actively incorporating these techniques into your daily life, you can progressively develop your emotional intelligence skills at the age of 50 and beyond. Remember, emotional intelligence is a lifelong journey that can bring immense personal and professional benefits.

Emotional Intelligence Training and Coaching

Developing emotional intelligence is a valuable endeavor for individuals who are 50 years old and above. It helps them navigate the complexities of life, enhance relationships, and achieve personal and professional success. To effectively cultivate emotional intelligence, individuals can benefit from specialized training programs and coaching.

Emotional intelligence training provides structured and comprehensive guidance on understanding and managing emotions. These programs offer a range of techniques and tools to strengthen self-awareness, empathy, and emotional regulation. Through interactive exercises and real-life scenarios, participants learn how to effectively channel their emotions and respond to situations with clarity and composure.

Coaching, on the other hand, offers personalized support and guidance tailored to an individual's unique needs. A skilled emotional intelligence coach helps individuals identify their strengths and areas for improvement, develop practical strategies, and navigate challenges to emotional growth. The coach serves as a mentor, providing valuable insights and accountability throughout the journey towards emotional intelligence.

By combining emotional intelligence training with coaching, individuals can accelerate their growth and maximize their potential. They gain deeper insights into their emotional patterns, unlock hidden strengths, and overcome hurdles that inhibit their personal and professional growth. Emotional intelligence training and coaching empower individuals to make meaningful changes and thrive in all aspects of their lives.

Integrating Emotional Intelligence into Everyday Life

Incorporating emotional intelligence into our daily lives is an essential step towards personal growth and well-being. By practicing emotional intelligence skills consistently, we can enhance our self-awareness, improve our relationships, and navigate life's challenges with resilience.

Here are some practical tips and activities that can help you integrate emotional intelligence into various aspects of your life:

1. Mindful Self-Reflection

Take a few moments each day to reflect on your emotions, thoughts, and actions. Ask yourself how you're feeling and why, and consider how your emotions may be influencing your behavior. Regular self-reflection helps deepen your understanding of yourself and promotes self-awareness.

2. Active Listening

Practice active listening in your conversations with others. Pay attention to their verbal and non-verbal cues, demonstrate empathy by acknowledging their emotions, and respond with genuine interest and understanding. This fosters better communication and strengthens your emotional connections.

3. Emotional Regulation Techniques

Develop strategies to manage your emotions effectively. This may include deep breathing exercises, meditation, journaling, or engaging in activities that bring you joy and relaxation. By learning to regulate your emotions, you can respond thoughtfully rather than react impulsively.

4. Conflict Resolution Skills

Explore techniques for resolving conflicts peacefully and constructively. Practice empathy and seek to understand the perspectives of others involved in the conflict. Focus on finding common ground and collaborate to arrive at mutually beneficial solutions.

5. Emotional Intelligence at Work

Apply emotional intelligence skills in your professional life. Practice active listening and empathy with colleagues and clients, communicate assertively yet respectfully, and seek opportunities to support and uplift others. These skills can enhance teamwork, leadership, and overall job satisfaction.

6. Self-Care and Emotional Well-being

Prioritize self-care activities that nurture your emotional well-being. Engage in activities that bring you joy, practice self-compassion, and set healthy boundaries in your personal and professional life. Prioritizing self-care allows you to recharge mentally and emotionally, enabling you to show up as your best self.

Remember, developing emotional intelligence is an ongoing process. Consistently incorporating these activities into your daily life will strengthen your emotional intelligence skills, leading to greater self-awareness, healthier relationships, and a more fulfilling life.

Continue your journey of emotional growth and self-discovery by implementing these practices into your everyday life. Embrace emotional intelligence as a transformative tool towards personal and professional success at any age.

Overcoming Emotional Barriers at 50

Developing emotional intelligence at 50 can be a transformative journey, but it is not without its challenges. Many individuals face emotional barriers that hinder their progress in this area. However, with the right strategies and guidance, these barriers can be overcome, paving the way for personal growth and emotional well-being.

One common emotional barrier at this stage of life is the fear of change. The thought of stepping out of one's comfort zone and embracing new emotional skills can be daunting. However, it's important to remember that change is a natural and necessary part of personal development. By reframing change as an opportunity for growth and self-improvement, individuals can gradually overcome this barrier and embrace emotional intelligence.

Another common emotional barrier is self-doubt. Many people in their 50s may question their ability to learn and develop new skills, including emotional intelligence. It's crucial to challenge negative self-talk and replace it with self-compassion and belief in one's own potential. By recognizing that it's never too late to develop emotional intelligence and taking small steps towards growth, individuals can overcome self-doubt and build emotional resilience.

Additionally, individuals at this stage of life may face resistance from others, whether it's friends, family, or colleagues. It's important to stay committed to personal growth and not let external opinions deter progress. Surrounding oneself with supportive and like-minded individuals can bolster emotional development efforts and foster a positive environment for growth.

When faced with these emotional barriers, it's essential to handle the challenges effectively. One effective strategy is to seek support through therapy or coaching. A trained professional can help individuals navigate their emotions, provide guidance, and offer practical techniques and coping mechanisms tailored to their unique needs.

Another effective approach is to practice self-reflection and mindfulness. Taking time to explore one's emotions, understand their triggers, and develop self-awareness can greatly contribute to emotional intelligence development. Engaging in activities such as journaling, meditation, or deep breathing exercises can facilitate this process.

Ultimately, overcoming emotional barriers at 50 requires perseverance, self-compassion, and a willingness to embrace personal growth. By addressing the fears, doubts, and external resistance, individuals can unlock their full emotional potential and reap the benefits of a developed emotional intelligence.

Nurturing Emotional Resilience in Midlife

In today's fast-paced and often challenging world, emotional resilience is a crucial skill to navigate the ups and downs of midlife. Developing emotional intelligence at 50 can greatly contribute to building resilience and ensuring a positive and fulfilling life experience. By understanding and harnessing emotional wisdom, individuals can effectively manage stress, bounce back from setbacks, and cultivate a positive mindset.

One key aspect of nurturing emotional resilience is developing a positive mindset. This involves cultivating a mindset that focuses on gratitude, optimism, and self-compassion. By embracing positivity, individuals can better navigate difficult situations and persevere through life's challenges.

Managing stress is another essential component of emotional resilience. By practicing stress management techniques such as deep breathing exercises, mindfulness meditation, and engaging in activities that bring joy and relaxation, individuals can enhance their ability to cope with stress and maintain emotional balance.

Furthermore, bouncing back from setbacks is a vital skill in midlife. Emotionally intelligent individuals are able to view setbacks as learning opportunities and approach them with resilience and determination. By reframing setbacks as stepping stones to growth and utilizing problem-solving skills, individuals can bounce back stronger than before.

In summary, nurturing emotional resilience in midlife is crucial for maintaining well-being and achieving personal growth. By developing emotional intelligence at 50, individuals can cultivate a positive mindset, effectively manage stress, and bounce back from setbacks. Embracing emotional wisdom empowers individuals to navigate the challenges of midlife with grace and resilience.

Cultivating Emotional Intelligence in Relationships

Emotional intelligence plays a crucial role in fostering healthy and fulfilling relationships, especially for individuals who are 50 years old and above. With age comes a wealth of experiences and wisdom, making it even more important to develop emotional intelligence skills that can enhance communication, empathy, and conflict resolution.

Effective communication lies at the heart of any successful relationship. By honing emotional intelligence, individuals can improve their ability to express themselves clearly, listen actively, and understand others' perspectives. This skillset enables open and genuine conversations, building stronger connections and fostering mutual understanding.

Empathy and Emotional Intelligence

Empathy is a key component of emotional intelligence that allows individuals to understand and share the feelings of others. By cultivating empathy, individuals can enhance their relationships by showing compassion, validating emotions, and responding with sensitivity. This ability to connect on an emotional level fosters trust and creates a supportive environment.

Furthermore, emotional intelligence sharpens conflict resolution skills, enabling individuals to navigate disagreements with empathy and respect. By effectively managing emotions and practicing empathy, individuals can seek common ground, find solutions, and maintain harmony in relationships.

Not only does emotional intelligence enhance personal relationships, but it also plays a vital role in professional interactions. In the workplace, emotional intelligence fosters effective collaboration, teamwork, and leadership. It allows individuals to understand and manage their own emotions, adapt to different communication styles, and build positive working relationships.

In conclusion, cultivating emotional intelligence can have a profound impact on relationships for individuals who are 50 years old and above. By developing skills such as effective communication, empathy, and conflict resolution, individuals can foster healthier and more fulfilling connections in their personal and professional lives. Investing in emotional intelligence is an investment in stronger, more resilient relationships.

Harnessing Emotional Wisdom for Success at 50

As individuals reach the age of 50, they possess a wealth of life experience and knowledge. However, success at this stage of life goes beyond mere expertise. It requires a deep understanding and harnessing of emotional wisdom. Emotional intelligence plays a pivotal role in guiding individuals towards personal and professional triumphs.

Emotional intelligence, or EI, encompasses a set of skills that enable individuals to recognize and manage their own emotions, as well as understand and empathize with others. By cultivating emotional intelligence, individuals at 50 can unlock a myriad of benefits. They can forge stronger interpersonal relationships, make sound decisions, and enhance their overall well-being.

Developing emotional intelligence skills involves self-reflection, self-awareness, and a commitment to growth. It requires individuals to assess their own emotions, motivations, and reactions. With practice and guidance, they can learn to regulate their emotions effectively and express themselves empathetically. This process fosters personal growth and equips them with the emotional resilience necessary to navigate life's challenges with grace and confidence.

Incorporating emotional intelligence into everyday life is key to realizing its transformative potential. With conscious effort, individuals can integrate emotional intelligence skills into their interactions with others, their work, and their self-care routines. By doing so, they cultivate a harmonious environment, communicate effectively, and nurture their own well-being. Embracing emotional wisdom at 50 is not only a catalyst for personal success but also a stepping stone towards living a more fulfilling and gratifying life.

Chapter 8

From Parents to Partners: Reinventing relationships with grown children

Welcome to our chapter focused on reinventing relationships with grown children in your 50s. As parents, it's natural to experience a shift in dynamics as our children grow into adults. The parent-child relationship undergoes a transformation, paving the way for a new partnership built on mutual respect and understanding.

This stage of life brings both challenges and opportunities. It's an exciting time to embrace the evolving relationship and nurture a connection that goes beyond the traditional parent-child dynamic. In this section, we will explore strategies for improving communication, strengthening bonds, and navigating the unique dynamics of the parent-child relationship in adulthood.

Whether you have adult children who are starting their own families, pursuing new career paths, or simply carving out their own identities, this section will provide valuable insights and practical guidance on how to adapt and thrive in this new phase of life.

Join us as we delve into the art of reinventing relationships with grown children, fostering a nurturing connection that will bring joy and fulfillment to both parents and adult kids alike.

Understanding the unique dynamics of the parent-child relationship

As children grow into adults, the parent-child relationship undergoes a profound transformation. The once-dependent child becomes an independent adult, and the dynamics between parents and adult children can be both complex and fluid. Understanding these unique dynamics is key to nurturing a strong bond and strengthening the relationship.

Family dynamics play a crucial role in shaping the parent-child relationship. Each family has its own set of values, communication patterns, and expectations that influence how parents and adult children interact. Recognizing and respecting these dynamics can help foster a deeper understanding and a more harmonious connection.

To strengthen bonds with adult children, parents can employ various strategies. Active listening, empathy, and open communication are essential tools for creating a safe space where adult children feel heard and understood. By validating their feelings and experiences, parents can establish a foundation of trust and mutual respect.

H3: Strategies for Strengthening Bonds with Adult Children

1. Foster open and honest conversations: Encourage open dialogue and create an environment where adult children feel comfortable expressing their thoughts and emotions. This transparency can deepen the connection and nurture trust.

2. Show interest in their lives: Take an active interest in your adult children's lives by asking about their aspirations, hobbies, and challenges. This shows that you value their experiences and helps foster a sense of connection.

3. Respect their autonomy: Recognize that adult children have their own lives, goals, and decisions to make. Avoid being overly intrusive or imposing your views. Instead, offer guidance when requested and be supportive of their choices.

4. Create shared experiences: Find opportunities to engage in activities that you both enjoy. Whether it's cooking together, going for walks, or exploring shared hobbies, these shared experiences can create lasting memories and strengthen the bond between parents and adult children.

5. Celebrate milestones: Acknowledge and celebrate the achievements and milestones of your adult children. Whether it's a promotion, graduation, or starting a family of their own, showing genuine joy and pride can deepen the connection and reinforce the parent-child bond.

By understanding the unique dynamics of the parent-child relationship, parents can navigate this stage of life with greater ease and foster a bond that strengthens over time. Embracing the complexities, respecting autonomy, and practicing effective communication are key to building a fulfilling and mutually supportive relationship with adult children.

Nurturing a new dynamic that respects their adulthood

As our children grow into adults, it's essential to recognize and respect their newfound adulthood. This shift in dynamic requires a fresh approach that fosters mutual respect and understanding. Improving communication and offering parental guidance in a supportive manner are key aspects of nurturing this new dynamic.

Effective communication is crucial in maintaining a strong relationship with our adult kids. It's essential to listen actively, validate their feelings, and express our own thoughts and concerns thoughtfully. By creating an open and safe space for dialogue, we can strengthen the bond and bridge any gaps in understanding.

Parental guidance, in this new phase of their lives, should be offered in a supportive way. Instead of dictating or imposing our opinions, it's important to approach parental guidance as a trusted advisor. By sharing our wisdom and experiences, we can guide them in making informed decisions while respecting their autonomy and individual growth.

To improve communication and offer parental guidance effectively, it's important to stay open-minded and avoid being judgmental. By maintaining a non-judgmental stance, we create an environment that encourages honest and authentic conversations. This approach fosters trust and allows for a deeper connection with our adult kids.

By nurturing a new dynamic that respects their adulthood, we lay the foundation for a thriving relationship with our grown children. Embracing their independence and treating them as partners rather than dependents strengthens the bond and promotes mutual respect. This journey of building a fulfilling relationship requires ongoing effort and understanding, but the rewards are immeasurable.

Communicating effectively with grown children

When navigating life changes with adult children, effective communication is key to maintaining a strong and supportive relationship. Here are some strategies to improve communication and foster understanding:

1. Foster open and honest conversations

Encourage open and honest conversations with your grown children, creating a safe space for them to express their thoughts and emotions. Listen actively and validate their experiences, demonstrating that you value their perspective.

2. Practice active listening

Give your full attention when your adult child is speaking. Avoid interrupting or jumping to conclusions. Repeat back what you've heard to ensure you understand their point of view accurately. This shows that you are actively engaged in the conversation and genuinely interested in what they have to say.

3. Be mindful of nonverbal cues

Remember that communication involves more than just words. Pay attention to your nonverbal cues, such as facial expressions and body language, as they can significantly impact the message you're trying to convey. Maintain an open and positive demeanor to promote a comfortable atmosphere for discussion.

4. Choose the right timing

Be mindful of the timing when initiating important conversations with your adult children. Avoid discussing sensitive topics or raising concerns during stressful moments or when they are preoccupied. Find a time when both parties are relaxed and receptive to meaningful dialogue.

5. Use "I" statements

When expressing your thoughts or concerns, use "I" statements to avoid sounding accusatory or judgmental. For example, say, "I feel worried about your job situation" instead of "You're making a mistake with your career." This approach encourages open dialogue without putting your adult child on the defensive.

6. Seek compromise and find common ground

When faced with differing opinions or conflicts, strive for compromise and find common ground. Focus on shared interests and values to bridge any communication gaps. Recognize that it's possible to have different perspectives without undermining the strength of your relationship.

By implementing these strategies, you can build a solid foundation for open and effective communication with your grown children. Navigating life changes together becomes easier when there is understanding and support in the new relationship dynamic.

Embracing the role of a mentor and friend

As parents, our relationship with our adult children undergoes a transformation. It's important to embrace this change and shift our role from traditional parent to mentor and friend. By doing so, we can provide the guidance and support they still need while strengthening the bond based on trust and mutual respect.

One way to provide parental guidance for adult kids is by offering advice and sharing your wisdom gained from life experiences. Remember to do so in a non-judgmental and supportive manner, allowing them to make their own decisions. This approach shows that you trust and believe in their abilities.

Another way to strengthen the bond with your adult children is to genuinely listen and engage in meaningful conversations. Create a safe space where they can openly share their thoughts and feelings without fear of judgment. By actively listening and validating their emotions, you demonstrate that their perspective is valued and respected.

Share Your Knowledge and Interests

Sharing your knowledge and interests can be a fantastic way to connect with your grown children. Whether it's teaching them a new skill, discussing shared passions, or exploring new hobbies together, these shared experiences create lasting memories and deepen the bond.

Not only does this provide an opportunity for quality time, but it also allows you to learn from each other. Show genuine interest in their interests and be open to trying new things. This exchange of knowledge and exploration will strengthen the bond between you and your children.

Remember, as you navigate the parent-adult child relationship, it's crucial to respect their autonomy and treat them as equals. By embracing the role of a mentor and friend, you can provide the guidance and support they need while fostering an even stronger bond based on trust and mutual respect.

Building connection through shared activities and interests

One of the most powerful ways to build connection with your grown children is through shared activities and interests. Engaging in activities together not only creates opportunities for quality time, but it also allows you to bond over common hobbies and experiences. Here are some practical suggestions for finding common ground and creating meaningful experiences that strengthen the bond between you and your adult kids:

1. Discover Their Interests: Take the time to learn about your adult children's interests and hobbies. Whether it's sports, cooking, art, or music, show genuine interest in what they love and find ways to participate together.
2. Plan Regular Outings: Schedule regular outings or activities that you can enjoy together. It could be something as simple as going for a hike, visiting a museum, or taking a cooking class. The key is to engage in an activity that both parties can enjoy and look forward to.
3. Start a Family Tradition: Create a family tradition or ritual that you can continue to practice as your children grow older. It could be a weekly game night, a monthly movie marathon, or an annual family trip. These traditions help strengthen bonds and create lasting memories.
4. Support Their Passions: Show support for your adult children's passions and interests by attending their performances, games, or exhibitions. Your presence and encouragement mean a lot and help foster a sense of connection and pride.
5. Learn Together: Explore new hobbies or interests that both you and your adult children can learn together. Sign up for a photography course, join a book club, or take up a new sport. This shared learning experience will not only deepen your connection but also provide opportunities for growth and discovery.

Remember, building connection with your grown children is about finding common ground and nurturing shared experiences. By engaging in activities that both parties enjoy, you create opportunities for deeper communication, understanding, and bonding.

Supporting your grown children through life transitions

As parents, our role doesn't end when our children reach adulthood. We have the opportunity to support them through major life transitions, offering guidance, emotional support, and parental wisdom when needed. Navigating life changes with adult children requires a delicate balance of respecting their autonomy while being there for them when they need us most.

One of the keys to successful support is providing emotional support during times of change. Acknowledging and validating their feelings can help ease the stress and uncertainty that often accompany significant life transitions. Letting them know that you are there to listen, offer a shoulder to lean on, and provide comfort can make a world of difference.

When it comes to offering guidance and advice, remember to do so with sensitivity and respect for their independence. While they may value your opinion, it's important to empower them to make their own decisions. Avoid being overbearing and encourage open dialogue, allowing them to weigh their options while knowing they have your support no matter what path they choose.

Respecting their autonomy is crucial during this stage of life. Give them the space to explore their own interests, make mistakes, and learn from their experiences. While it may be challenging to let go of the parental instinct to protect and control, it is essential for their growth and development. Trust and respect are the building blocks of a healthy adult-child relationship.

Remember, supporting your grown children through life transitions is not about living their lives for them but rather about being a source of love, encouragement, and guidance. By embracing your role as a source of stability and support, you can navigate these changes together, strengthening your bond and fostering a relationship built on mutual respect and understanding.

Setting healthy boundaries in the new relationship dynamic

As parents navigate the transition from a traditional parent-child dynamic to a new relationship with their grown children, setting healthy boundaries becomes crucial. By establishing clear expectations and respecting personal boundaries, families can create a foundation of trust and mutual respect. Additionally, maintaining open lines of communication is essential for improving family dynamics and fostering healthy relationships.

Embracing the joys of the parent-adult child relationship

As parents, our greatest joy lies in the deep and meaningful connection we build with our grown children. Nurturing a strong bond that transcends the traditional parent-child dynamic is a rewarding journey that unfolds as we embrace the unique dynamics of this stage in life.

Strengthening the bonds with our adult children requires us to evolve from mere parents to trusted friends and mentors. It is through this transformation that we discover the true joys of the parent-adult child relationship. We witness their growth and accomplishments, celebrate their victories, and offer guidance when needed.

Building connection with our grown kids involves finding common ground and creating shared experiences. Whether it's engaging in a new hobby together, exploring mutual interests, or simply spending quality time, these shared activities foster a sense of closeness and strengthen the bond between generations.

As we navigate the journey of supporting our grown children through life transitions, we acknowledge the importance of setting healthy boundaries. Respect for their autonomy and open lines of communication enable us to provide the guidance and support they need while also allowing them the space to discover their own path.

Embracing the joys of the parent-adult child relationship is a testament to the enduring love and connection we share. It is an opportunity to witness the growth of our children and to form a friendship that transcends all boundaries. By nurturing these bonds and adapting to the evolving dynamics, we create a relationship built on mutual respect, trust, and unconditional love.

Chapter 9

Reassessing Your Goals: Reflecting on past achievements and setting new targets

Welcome to our comprehensive guide on reassessing your goals at the age of 50. As we navigate the exciting journey of midlife, it's important to reflect on our past achievements and set new targets that align with our evolving aspirations. In this article, we will explore the art of goal setting in midlife, the importance of embracing new challenges, and practical strategies to overcome obstacles along the way. Whether you're seeking to redefine your career path, enhance personal relationships, or embark on new adventures, this guide will provide valuable insights and actionable steps to help you navigate this transformative phase. Join us as we discover the power of setting new goals in midlife and embrace the limitless possibilities that lie ahead!

The Art of Goal Setting in Midlife

Setting goals after 50 can feel like a daunting task, but it's also an exciting opportunity to reevaluate your life goals and embark on new adventures. In this section, we'll explore the art of goal setting in midlife and provide guidance on how to approach this transformative process.

As we reach our 50s, we often find ourselves reflecting on our past achievements and contemplating what we still want to accomplish. This introspection allows us to assess our priorities and align them with our current aspirations. Reevaluating life goals at 50 is a natural step towards personal growth and fulfillment.

One of the unique challenges of goal setting in later years is navigating the changes and responsibilities that may come with this life stage. Whether it's career transitions, family commitments, or simply the passage of time, setting goals in midlife requires adaptability and resilience. It's important to acknowledge these challenges and view them as opportunities for growth.

At the same time, setting goals after 50 also presents unique advantages. With decades of experience and wisdom under your belt, you have a clearer understanding of what truly matters to you. This self-awareness can guide you towards setting goals that are meaningful and aligned with your values.

Approaching Goal Setting in Midlife

When setting goals in midlife, it's essential to approach the process with intentionality and a growth mindset. Start by reflecting on your passions, values, and aspirations. Consider what you have already accomplished and use those achievements as a foundation for defining new objectives.

Next, break down your goals into smaller, actionable steps. This will not only make them more manageable but also provide a sense of progress and motivation along the way. Remember to set realistic and measurable goals that will allow you to track your progress and celebrate milestones along the journey.

Seeking support and accountability can also play a crucial role in goal setting after 50. Share your aspirations with friends, family, or a trusted mentor who can offer encouragement and hold you accountable. Establishing a support network will help you stay motivated and provide invaluable guidance when faced with challenges.

Lastly, be open to adjusting and reevaluating your goals as circumstances change. Life is unpredictable, and flexibility is key to navigating transitions effectively. Embrace the lessons learned and continually refine your goals to ensure they remain aligned with your evolving priorities.

Setting goals in midlife is an empowering endeavor that allows you to embrace new possibilities and make the most of the years ahead. With thoughtful reflection, intentionality, and a growth mindset, you can achieve remarkable accomplishments and create a fulfilling future.

Embracing New Challenges and Pursuing Fulfillment

In the pursuit of a fulfilling life, it's important to embrace new challenges and adapt to changing circumstances. This is especially true when it comes to goal planning in your fifties and beyond. As you reach the milestone of 50, it's an ideal time to review your life goals and make any necessary adjustments.

Life goal review at 50 allows you to reflect on your past achievements and experiences while considering what brings you true fulfillment and purpose moving forward. By taking the time to reassess your goals, you can ensure they align with your values and aspirations for this next chapter of life.

Finding Meaning and Purpose Through New Goals

Setting new goals in midlife is not just about ticking boxes or achieving external markers of success. It's about finding meaning and purpose in the pursuit of these goals. As you navigate the challenges and opportunities that come with age, it's essential to set goals that truly resonate with you and contribute to your sense of fulfillment.

Goal setting for seniors is an opportunity to explore your passions, discover new interests, and pursue personal growth. It's about defining what gives your life meaning and joy, and creating a roadmap to achieve those aspirations.

Whether you aspire to start a new business venture, travel the world, learn a new skill, or make a meaningful impact in your community, goal planning in your fifties allows you to embrace new challenges and pursue fulfillment on your own terms.

Reflecting on Past Achievements

As we reassess our goals at the age of 50, it's crucial to take a moment and reflect on past achievements. Reflecting allows us to acknowledge our accomplishments, appreciate how far we've come, and gain valuable insights that can inform our future goals.

When we look back on what we have achieved, it gives us a sense of pride and satisfaction. It reminds us of our capabilities and the challenges we have overcome. Reflecting on past achievements also helps us identify patterns of success, understand our strengths, and build confidence in setting new goals.

Moreover, reflecting on past achievements can provide us with important lessons learned. It allows us to assess what worked well and what didn't, enabling us to make more informed decisions as we set new targets. By examining our past experiences, we can adjust our approach and set more realistic and achievable goals for the future.

In addition, reflecting on past achievements can help us gain clarity about our values and priorities. It allows us to evaluate whether our previous goals aligned with our true passions and aspirations. This reflection can guide us in reevaluating our life goals and setting new ones that truly resonate with who we are at this stage of our lives.

By taking the time to reflect on our past achievements, we can gain valuable insights, learn from our experiences, and use this knowledge to shape our future goals. So, let's celebrate our accomplishments, learn from our journey, and use it as a stepping stone to chart a new and fulfilling path ahead.

Identifying Areas for Growth and Improvement

When reassessing your goals at 50, it's crucial to identify areas for growth and improvement. Evaluating your strengths and weaknesses will allow you to focus your efforts on areas where you want to make progress and set meaningful goals. Here are some steps to help you in this process:

Evaluate Your Strengths

Take some time to reflect on your strengths and acknowledge the skills and qualities that have contributed to your past successes. What are you good at? What do others recognize as your strengths? Identifying these areas will help you leverage them in new goals and aspirations.

Recognize Your Weaknesses

It's important to be honest with yourself and recognize your weaknesses. What are areas where you could improve or develop new skills? By acknowledging these weaknesses, you can focus on personal growth and prioritize goals that will help you overcome limitations.

Set Priorities

Once you've identified your strengths and weaknesses, it's time to set priorities. What areas for growth and improvement are most important to you? Consider your values, passions, and aspirations for the future. By narrowing down your focus, you can set realistic and achievable goals that align with your core values.

Create an Action Plan

An action plan is crucial for turning your identified areas for growth and improvement into tangible goals. Break down your goals into actionable steps and establish a timeline for completion. Having a clear plan of action will help you stay organized and motivated throughout the goal-setting process.

By identifying areas for growth and improvement, you can reassess your goals at 50 with renewed clarity and purpose. Embrace the opportunity to challenge yourself and strive for personal development. Remember, it's never too late to achieve new milestones and pursue your dreams.

Setting Realistic and Measurable Goals

Setting goals is an essential part of personal growth and development, especially in midlife. As we enter our fifties, it becomes even more important to assess our aspirations and define clear objectives that are both realistic and measurable.

When setting new goals in midlife, it's crucial to take into account the unique circumstances and priorities we may have at this stage of life. By aligning our goals with our values and aspirations, we can create a meaningful roadmap for the future.

To ensure that our goals are achievable, it's important to set realistic expectations. It's natural to dream big, but by breaking down our goals into smaller, manageable tasks, we can make steady progress and avoid becoming overwhelmed.

Defining Measurable Objectives

In order to track our progress and stay motivated, it's essential to define measurable objectives. Measurable goals provide us with a clear way to assess our achievements and make adjustments along the way.

One way to make our goals measurable is by attaching specific metrics to them. For example, if our goal is to improve our physical fitness, we can set a target to run a certain distance or lift a certain weight within a specified time frame.

In addition, it's important to establish a timeline for our goals. By setting deadlines or milestones, we create a sense of urgency and accountability, which can help us stay focused and committed to achieving our objectives.

Moreover, tracking our progress allows us to celebrate our successes and make any necessary adjustments. It gives us the opportunity to reflect on what's working and what's not, enabling us to refine our strategies and approach as we move forward.

Overall, setting realistic and measurable goals in midlife is essential for personal growth and fulfillment. By aligning our aspirations with our values, breaking down our goals into manageable tasks, and defining measurable objectives, we can create a path to success that inspires us to reach new heights in our fifties and beyond.

Overcoming Fear and Resistance

When reassessing your goals at 50, it's natural to encounter fear and resistance along the way. These emotions can make the process seem daunting and hold you back from taking the necessary steps to set new goals. However, it's important to remember that growth and personal development often require pushing through these barriers. Here, we'll explore common barriers that may arise during goal setting in later years and provide strategies for overcoming them to move forward with confidence.

1. Embrace Change

One of the main sources of fear and resistance when setting goals after 50 is the fear of change. As humans, we tend to become comfortable in our routines and familiar environments. However, embracing change is crucial for personal growth and reaching new milestones. Recognize that change offers opportunities for learning, self-discovery, and exciting new experiences.

2. Challenge Self-Doubt

Self-doubt can be a significant barrier to goal setting at any age. However, it's important to challenge these negative thoughts and beliefs. Remind yourself of past achievements and successes, and recognize the skills and experience you have acquired over the years. Cultivate a positive mindset that empowers you to believe in your ability to achieve new goals.

3. Seek Support

When facing fear and resistance, seeking support from others can make a world of difference. Surround yourself with a network of positive and like-minded individuals who can provide encouragement, advice, and accountability. Whether it's family, friends, or joining a supportive community, having others in your corner can help you overcome obstacles and stay motivated.

4. Break Goals into Manageable Steps

Large goals can often feel overwhelming, causing fear and resistance. To combat this, break your goals down into smaller, more manageable steps. By focusing on one step at a time, you can gradually build momentum and overcome any sense of overwhelmingness. Celebrate small victories along the way, as each step brings you closer to achieving your ultimate goal.

5. Prioritize Self-Care

Overcoming fear and resistance requires taking care of yourself both physically and mentally. Make self-care a priority by engaging in activities that bring you joy and reduce stress. Practice self-compassion and embrace the journey, understanding that setbacks are part of the process. Taking care of yourself will enhance your resilience and provide the strength needed to overcome any obstacles that come your way.

Overall, overcoming fear and resistance is an essential part of the goal-setting process after 50. By embracing change, challenging self-doubt, seeking support, breaking goals into manageable steps, and prioritizing self-care, you can move forward with confidence and achieve meaningful goals in your later years.

Seeking Support and Accountability

When reassessing your goals after the age of 50, seeking support and accountability can make a world of difference. Building a strong support network and finding accountability partners are essential steps in staying motivated and on track towards achieving your goals.

Having a support system in place can provide encouragement, guidance, and a sense of camaraderie as you navigate through this exciting phase of life. It's important to surround yourself with individuals who share your aspirations and can offer valuable insights and advice.

One way to find support is by joining goal-oriented communities, such as online forums or local meet-up groups, where you can connect with like-minded individuals who are also focused on setting and achieving goals after 50.

Additionally, accountability partners can play a crucial role in helping you stay committed and focused on your goals. An accountability partner is someone you trust, someone with whom you can regularly share your progress, challenges, and plans. They can provide the necessary motivation and hold you accountable for taking the necessary steps towards your goals.

H3: Benefits of Seeking Support and Accountability

There are several benefits to seeking support and accountability in your goal-setting journey:

Increased motivation: Having a support network can boost your motivation levels and inspire you to stay committed to your goals.

perspectives: Interacting with others who are also navigating goal setting after 50 can provide fresh perspectives, ideas, and approaches.

Shared experiences: Connecting with individuals who have similar goals and are at a similar stage in life can create a sense of camaraderie and shared experiences.

Problem-solving and guidance: Your support network can offer valuable advice, problem-solving strategies, and guidance when you encounter challenges or roadblocks.

Accountability: An accountability partner can help you stay on track, ensuring you take consistent action towards your goals and helping you overcome any self-doubt or resistance.

H3: How to Find Support and Accountability Partners

Here are some strategies to help you find the right support and accountability partners:

Join online communities or forums: Look for goal-setting communities specifically tailored for individuals over 50. Participating in discussions and sharing your progress can help you connect with others who have similar goals and aspirations.

Attend local events and workshops: Look for local events or workshops that focus on personal development or goal setting. These events can provide opportunities to network and connect with individuals who are also seeking support and accountability.

Seek out mentorship: Consider finding a mentor who has already achieved goals similar to the ones you are striving for. A mentor can provide guidance, support, and motivation throughout your goal-setting journey.

Form an accountability group: Create or join a small group of individuals who are committed to setting and achieving their goals. Schedule regular check-ins or meetings to share progress, celebrate successes, and provide support to one another.

Use technology: Utilize goal-tracking apps or online platforms that offer built-in accountability features. These tools can help you track your progress, set reminders, and share updates with your accountability partners.

Remember, seeking support and accountability can greatly enhance your goal-setting experience. By surrounding yourself with a supportive community and finding accountability partners, you can stay motivated, overcome challenges, and achieve the goals that are most important to you in this next chapter of your life.

Navigating Transitions and Life Changes

Reaching the age of 50 often brings about a series of transitions and life changes that can significantly impact our goals and priorities. In this section, we will discuss strategies for successfully navigating these changes and setting new goals that align with your evolving aspirations.

Embracing Change and Adaptation

Transition periods can be accompanied by feelings of uncertainty and apprehension. However, it is important to embrace change as an opportunity for growth and self-discovery. By cultivating adaptability and a positive mindset, you can navigate these transitions with confidence and openness to new possibilities.

Reflecting on Values and Priorities

When reassessing your goals in later years, take the time to reflect on your values and priorities. Consider what truly matters to you at this stage of life and how you can align your goals with your deepest aspirations. This reflection will serve as a guide in setting meaningful and fulfilling objectives for your future.

Setting Realistic and Purpose-Driven Goals

While it is important to dream big, setting realistic and achievable goals is key to maintaining motivation and progress. As you navigate these transitions, focus on setting goals that are purpose-driven and aligned with your passions and values. This will ensure that each step brings you closer to a fulfilling and rewarding outcome.

Seeking Support and Collaboration

During times of transition, seeking support and collaboration can be invaluable. Surround yourself with a network of trusted friends, family, or professionals who can offer guidance, encouragement, and accountability. Together, you can navigate the challenges and celebrate the successes that come with setting goals in later years.

In summary, by embracing change, reflecting on values, setting realistic goals, and seeking support, you can successfully navigate transitions and life changes while setting and achieving meaningful goals in your 50s and beyond.

Celebrating Milestones and Successes

As you embark on the journey of reassessing your goals at 50, it's important to take the time to celebrate the milestones and successes you have achieved along the way. Recognizing your accomplishments not only gives you a sense of pride and satisfaction but also provides valuable motivation to continue growing and striving for new heights.

When you celebrate your milestones, you acknowledge the progress you have made, the challenges you have overcome, and the lessons you have learned. This reflection allows you to gain a deeper understanding of your capabilities and the areas in which you have excelled.

Furthermore, celebrating success provides a powerful boost of confidence, helping you believe in your ability to achieve even more in the future. It reinforces the idea that your hard work and dedication have paid off and that you are capable of reaching your goals.

While celebrating your milestones and successes, you can take the opportunity to share your achievements with loved ones, friends, and mentors who have supported you throughout your journey. Their encouragement and positive feedback can further fuel your motivation and inspire you to continue setting and achieving new goals.

Remember, goal planning in your fifties is not only about looking forward but also about appreciating how far you've come. Celebrating milestones and successes is a powerful way to honor your journey, stay motivated, and pave the way for even greater achievements in the future.

Embracing a Growth Mindset

When reassessing your goals, it's essential to embrace a growth mindset. A growth mindset is a belief that your abilities and qualities can be developed through dedication and effort. By adopting this mindset, you can unlock your full potential and achieve new goals in midlife.

A growth mindset encourages you to view challenges as opportunities for growth and learning, rather than obstacles. It allows you to approach setbacks with resilience and adaptability, knowing that they are part of the journey towards achieving your goals.

Cultivating a growth mindset involves fostering a positive attitude towards yourself and the possibilities that lie ahead. Here are some tips to help you embrace a growth mindset:

1. Practice Self-Reflection

Take time to reflect on your past achievements and the skills you have developed along the way. Recognize that your past successes demonstrate your ability to overcome challenges and achieve your goals.

2. Set Realistic yet Challenging Goals

Set new goals that are both realistic and challenging. This balance will push you out of your comfort zone and encourage personal growth while also ensuring that your goals are attainable with effort and dedication.

3. Embrace Failure as a Learning Opportunity

Embrace failure as a natural part of the goal-setting process. View it as an opportunity to learn, adapt, and refine your approach. Remember that setbacks provide valuable insights that can help you make better choices in the future.

4. Surround Yourself with Positive Influences

Surround yourself with people who support and inspire you. Seek out individuals who share a growth mindset and can offer encouragement, advice, and perspective as you work towards your goals.

5. Practice Self-Compassion

Be kind and compassionate towards yourself throughout your goal-setting journey. Celebrate your progress and acknowledge that setbacks are part of the process. Treat yourself with the same kindness and understanding you would extend to a friend.

By embracing a growth mindset, you can overcome limitations, push past obstacles, and achieve new goals in midlife. Cultivating resilience, adaptability, and a belief in your ability to learn and grow will set you on a path of personal fulfillment and success.

Looking Forward: Setting Your Future Targets

As you turn 50, reassessing your goals becomes crucial in shaping the next phase of your life. It's an opportunity to reflect on your past achievements and set new targets that align with your evolving values and aspirations. Setting future targets at this stage can be both exciting and challenging, but with the right approach, you can create a clear action plan that propels you towards a fulfilling future.

To begin, take the time to reflect on your past accomplishments. What milestones are you proud of? Which achievements have shaped your journey so far? By acknowledging your past successes, you can gain valuable insights into what brings you joy and fulfillment. Use this self-reflection to identify the core values and aspirations that will guide your future goal setting.

Once you've reflected on your past, it's time to look forward and set your future targets. Start by defining your long-term goals and break them down into smaller, achievable steps. Consider what areas of your life you want to focus on – whether it's career, health, relationships, personal growth, or a combination of these. Set specific, measurable, attainable, relevant, and time-bound (SMART) goals that will help you move closer to your desired future.

Remember, goal setting after 50 is a dynamic process. As you progress on your journey, be open to reassessing and adjusting your goals to stay aligned with your evolving priorities and circumstances. Celebrate the milestones you achieve along the way and embrace a growth mindset that encourages you to adapt, learn, and grow. By setting your future targets with intention and flexibility, you can create a fulfilling and purpose-driven life beyond 50.

Chapter 10

The Second Act: Turning passion projects into new careers

Welcome- to the second act of life, whe-re passion projects have the- ability to mold new professions at the age- of 50. It is a transformative voyage that prese-nts the potential to discover conte-ntment and intention in pursuing a route that coordinate-s with your genuine passions. In this section, we- will investigate how persons can e-mbrace the second act, unle-ash their passion initiatives, locate purpose-, overcome obstacles, navigate- skill shortages, construct a support system, take pragmatic ste-ps forward, and celebrate re-al world success narratives.

Accompany us as we plunge- into the realm of second acts and uncove-r the stimulating probabilities that await! While the- journey of self-discovery in one-'s later years offers re-wards, it also presents challenge-s. How does one pursue life-long dreams while also mee-ting basic needs? What resource-s can help along the way to test ide-as, gain experience- and find encouragement? Through sharing triumphs and se-tbacks alike, may we learn from one- another and find strength in community.

Embracing the Second Act

When pe-ople arrive at a particular point in their live-s' journey, the Second Act provide-s a possibility for professional transformation and personal deve-lopment. This stage, freque-ntly happening in midlife, prese-nts an opportunity for individuals to investigate fresh options, pursue- their interests, and acce-pt alteration. While one chapte-r concludes, another starts, permitting re-invention and renovation. Rather than staying static, the- Second Act encourages e-volution by experimenting with nove-l paths. Whether switching fields e-ntirely or cultivating a side pursuit into a primary focus, this phase supplie-s flexibility to redirect one-'s energy, skills, and expe-riences into a new dire-ction aligned more closely with pe-rsonal fulfillment and purpose.

While the-re are often multiple- elements that may spark a longing for transformation at midlife-. Some potential catalysts involve e-xperiencing tedium or a se-nse of stagnancy in one's current profe-ssional path, a yearning for improved significance and inte-ntion, or even circumstantial changes like- retirement or whe-n children leave the- nest. Regardless of the- impetus, the Second Act pre-sents an opportunity for introspection on one's ambitions and de-sires, and to initiate moveme-nts leading to a career imbue-d with more importance and gratification.

While e-mbarking on a new chapter in life de-mands flexibility and an adventurous spirit, it is important not to lose sight of your core- values or rush headlong into unconsidere-d risks. Embracing the possibilities of this fresh phase- requires an inquisitive ye-t prudent mindset, a willingness to e-xplore unfamiliar pathways yet pause to e-nsure each step aligns with your true- priorities and vision. New skills may unlock novel horizons but de-veloping them takes time- and patience. Venturing into undiscove-red areas could yield une-xpected rewards ye-t moving forward with care, gathering knowledge- at a steady pace and continually assessing pote-ntial outcomes will help you navigate succe-ssfully. Though leaving familiar comforts behind may bring uncertaintie-s, facing challenges with insight, empathy and community support ne-ed not cause undue distre-ss. Overall, embracing change re-presents an exciting opportunity for pe-rsonal and professional growth when approached with wisdom, nuance- and heart.

Throughout the Se-cond Act, individuals are encouraged to de-eply consider their passions, tale-nts, and interests. Taking time for this inne-r reflection can result in uncove-ring new exciteme-nts, or rediscovering old loves, that had be-en set aside. Whe-n such passions are found, one gains the opportunity to channe-l this discovery into tangible efforts or ave-nues for work. By actively pursuing projects re-lated to these re-vitalized passions, individuals may find renewe-d significance and momentum in their daily paths. Although the- future remains uncertain, focusing e-nergy on livelihoods linked to what truly inspire-s can light the way.

It's important to remember that embracing the Second Act is a personal journey, unique to each individual. While it may involve a career transition, it can also involve other aspects of life such as personal relationships, hobbies, and personal development. The Second Act offers a chance to reinvent oneself, to explore new horizons, and to create a life that aligns with one's values and aspirations.

So, whethe-r you're reevaluating your profe-ssional path, contemplating a lifelong passion, or just craving a fresh be-ginning, the Second Act calls. Grasp this chance to re-invent yourself and your livelihood, and e-mbark on a voyage of self-exploration, de-velopment, and satisfaction. The Se-cond Act presents us with a door of prospects to discove-r skills we never kne-w we had, interests we- were unaware of, and a stre-ngth within ourselves that empowe-rs us to achieve what we once- may have deeme-d unimaginable. While the vulne-rability of the unknown can seem daunting, e-ach new day gifts us with opportunities to learn, e-volve, and become the- person we're continuously working to be-. This journeyman phase invites e-xperimenting outside our comfort zone-, challenging preconceive-d limitations

Unleashing Your Passion Projects

Pursuing your passion projects during the- later stages of your caree-r can provide an invaluable expe-rience for growth and discovery. The- Second Act, often reaching around the- age of 50, is a distinct phase of life that pre-sents a rare chance to de-eply explore your ge-nuine interests and callings. This time-frame allows one to refle-ct on lifelong dreams, rekindle- dormant talents, and redirect e-fforts toward realizing goals close to the he-art. Where busy caree-rs and family responsibilities once le-ft little room for indulging curiosities, the Se-cond Act welcomes exploring hobbie-s with renewed focus and commitme-nt. Unleashing represse-d passions during this period may lead down profoundly fulfilling paths of learning, cre-ating, and contributing in personally meaningful ways. While the- future remains uncertain, following

Passion projects are- activities that set your soul ablaze, sparking fe-elings of delight, ene-rgy, and satisfaction within you. They permit you to chase afte-r your aims and fascinations, separate from others' de-sires or duties. Within the se-tting of a career shift, passion projects can act as a compass, ste-ering you towards fresh and significant caree-r routes. These proje-cts that stir your heart allow you to explore various are-as you find genuinely intriguing. While navigating ne-w career directions, e-ngaging in work you care about can provide helpful guidance-. Pursuing goals that light your inner fire serve-s as an inspiring guide as you journey along unfamiliar paths.

Taking the time- for introspection to pinpoint your interests, value-s and talents is key to unleashing your passion proje-cts and aligning your career transition with your authentic se-lf. Consider what activities stimulate you the- most, light a fire within and bring you true joy and fulfillment. Re-flect on what topics or causes stir an excite-ment and engageme-nt unlike any other. Identifying your ge-nuine passions by exploring what inspires that inne-r spark will help guide your caree-r path to fulfilling pursuits that resonate with your most authentic se-lf, allowing your talents and joy to shine through in work that uplifts both yourself and possibly e-ven others.

When you've- pinpointed your interests, it's time- to transform them into workable undertakings. Analyze- your objectives into more mode-st, administratable errands and make a cale-ndar to monitor your advancement. Consider re-aching out to advisors or experts in your sought after fie-ld who can give direction and backing as you progress. Having a syste-m for dividing complex goals into smaller steps can he-lp maintain steady progress. Don't hesitate- to ask others for their perspe-ctives or lessons learne-d from their own experie-nces. Continuous learning and fee-dback are valuable for refining your plans into an impactful proje-ct that matches your passions.

Kee-p in mind that pursuing your passion projects is not solely concerne-d with instant achievement or financial profit. It is about satisfying an inne-r sense of significance and crafting an impactful life-journey. Appreciate the- liberty and adaptability that this next phase pre-sents, and unleash your utmost talents by giving your passion proje-cts room to thrive. While results may not be- guaranteed, following your intere-sts can lead to personal growth and fulfillment e-ven if broader success doe-s not immediately follow.

Finding Purpose at 50

As individuals approach the half-ce-ntury mark, many start thinking deeply about their re-ason for being and wanting a stronger sense- of significance. This quest for meaning re-gularly comes with a wish to transform oneself and e-xamine new avenue-s professionally. At this phase in life, e-nsuring one's personal priorities and passions match one-'s job becomes extre-mely important.

Reinve-nting oneself later in life- necessitates care-ful contemplation and self-examination. It involve-s considering one's dee-pest convictions, enthusiasms, and fascinations with care. Making the- effort to assess what really re-sonates can aid individuals in recognizing domains of ende-avor that harmonize with their principles and impart a stronge-r feeling of significance. While- reinventing after 50 take-s focus and determination, taking time for introspe-ction provides insight into pathways that cultivate meaning.

As one e-nters their 50s, taking the time- for self-reflection can he-lp uncover a sense of purpose-. Asking questions like "What activities truly make- me happy and satisfied?" and "How can I contribute in a way that be-nefits others?" may provide unde-rstanding into inner hopes and dreams. Spe-nding quiet moments considering life- experience-s, values, and talents so far can offer guidance- towards opportunities to find fulfillment whethe-r through hobbies, family, community involvement or care-er change later in life-. While introspection, the proce-ss of looking inside oneself, introspe-ction is personal, sharing discoveries with truste-d others may reveal unfore-seen paths worthy of exploration. Exploring differe-nt possibilities that foster personal and profe-ssional evolution is another viable option. This may involve- delving into passion projects where- one can express the-ir interests and talents, volunte-ering within the local community to help those- in need, or taking the le-ap to start a business venture. Ste-pping outside the conventional role-s and responsibilities by taking carefully conside-red chances that push beyond what fe-els secure can uncove-r thrilling and fulfilling career routes. While- the unknown may seem daunting, ope-ning oneself to new ave-nues for learning and deve-lopment through modest risks has potential to le-ad down roads that are profoundly enriching.

While- finding purpose at 50 may often involve transforming one-'s career path, it is esse-ntial to note that a total vocational overhaul is not always nece-ssary. Occasionally, one can rediscover significance- and contentment within their pre-sent occupational domain by pursuing fresh obstacles, acquiring ne-w abilities, or taking on management dutie-s. By branching out from routine tasks and expanding one's re-pertoire in their curre-nt role, it is possible to reinvigorate- passion and inject new life into work that has lost its pre-vious zest. Seeking out chance-s to lead projects, teach othe-rs, or take the initiative on innovative- solutions can rekindle a sense- of motivation and importance, even afte-r decades in the same- field. While a clean

At around the halfway point in life-, taking steps to reinvent one-self professionally or personally is a profoundly individual unde-rtaking. It demands bravery, resolve-, and an openness to transformation. By ensuring one-'s principles align with occupational decisions and investigating fre-sh possibilities, people can uncove-r significance and satisfaction in this new chapter. The- journey permits refle-ction on skills and interests acquired ove-r decades, allowing ree-valuation of how those assets could find application in an reinve-nted path. While an overhaul brings unce-rtainties, focusing inward and maintaining optimism empower individuals to craft a role- matching their deepe-st desires.

Overcoming Challenges

Transitioning to a new care-er path later in life can be- an intimidating challenge to take on. Embarking on a midlife- career change fre-quently presents its own distinct hurdle-s to confront. Neverthele-ss, possessing the proper outlook and tactics allows one- to overcome such difficulties, ultimate-ly clearing a satisfying road ahead for the ne-xt phase of their professional journe-y. While making a vocational switch after decade-s spent in a single field may involve- facing unfamiliar circumstances and uncertainties, ke-eping an open and optimistic mindset couple-d with implementing thoughtful strategie-s can help smooth the route to re-inventing oneself and discove-ring new opportunities that bring fulfillment.

One common challe-nge faced by individuals pursuing new care-ers at midlife is fee-ling uneasy about starting from the beginning once- more. It is normal to be unsure or worrie-d about exploring unfamiliar grounds. Still, it is crucial to recollect that e-mbarking on a fresh career route- presents a chance for individual progre-ss and satisfaction. While change can be intimidating, taking on a ne-w professional direction later in life- also allows one to apply skills honed over time-. Furthermore, evolving circumstance-s need not be se-en as limitations but rather fresh possibilitie-s waiting to be discovered. Ove-rall, attempting something new care-er-wise, eve-n with some uncertainties, may ultimate-ly lead to new rewards pe-rsonally and professionally if one retains an ope-n mind.

While anothe-r challenge that may surface is the- potential for age-relate-d biases in one's job search as the-y reach their fifties, focusing on de-monstrating the merits and mastery gaine-d through years of experie-nce is key to overcoming such hurdle-s. Having attained decades of de-veloping valuable skills both technical and soft, individuals in the-ir later careers have- much to offer potential employe-rs through proven ability and wisdom. Emphasizing applicable talents attaine-d across industries as well as activating relationships built ove-r a lifetime helps re-assure hiring managers of the asse-ts lying within more seasoned candidate-s. Staying laser-focused on selling one-self based on qualifications rather than numbe-rs on a calendar aids countering any prejudice-s associated solely with age.

While switching paths to pursue- a new career in midlife- can be personally fulfilling, the financial aspe-ct should not be overlooked. One- may experience- a temporary dip in earnings as the transition occurs. Additional schooling or skills de-velopment may require- an investment that strains the budge-t. However, with prudent mone-tary planning and searching for financial assistance options, some of the-pressures can be e-ased. Scholarships, grants, or part-time work could provide supple-mentary income to offset costs. Gove-rnment and private programs also aim to support caree-r changers. By tapping into available resource-s and tightening expense-s elsewhere-, the costs of midcareer re-direction can feel le-ss daunting.

Moreove-r, addressing competency diffe-rences can pose a hurdle- when moving to another job path. The information and e-xperience obtaine-d in past duties may not immediately conve-rt to the sought after area. Though, obtaining e-xtra skills or exploring educational possibilities can link those- gaps and raise the odds of achieve-ment in the new care-er route. For instance, taking an online- course in a pertinent subje-ct, gaining a certification in a new software program, or doing an inte-rnship in the field can help round out a re-sume and make up for any skill deficie-ncies. Networking with professionals alre-ady working in that industry is another way to gain knowledge that wasn't acquire-d in prior roles. While it require-s additional effort, matching existing talents to ne-w job requirements as much as possible- and filling in any cracks can help ensure a smooth transition whe-n pursuing a career change. Having a solid support system is e-xtremely important when facing the-se kinds of difficulties. By surrounding yourself with me-ntors, colleagues, and resource-s you can gain direction, motivation, and beneficial re-lationships during this significant career transition period. Cultivating re-lationships with others who are also switching paths and looking to professional ne-tworks or career advising service-s for assistance can significantly improve the transition. The-se connections can offer guidance- when obstacles arise and ce-lebrations when milestone-s are met. While the- journey involves perse-verance and perse-verance, relying on the- wisdom and encouragement of your community make-s navigating it much more manageable.

Here- are some ways individuals can acknowledge- the challenges of a midlife- career change while-still maintaining optimism and perseverance- in their pursuit of a new path. Facing realitie-s like needing additional training or e-xperience dire-ctly allows one to devise strate-gies for overcoming shortcomings. Recognizing se-tbacks as natural parts of the learning process e-ncourages embracing a mentality of continual growth. Se-eing struggles as chances to gain insight ke-eps the focus on opportunities rathe-r than difficulties. With an open and dete-rmined attitude, midcaree-r transitions become adventure-s of self-improvement and fre-sh starts rather than overwhelming uphe-avals. Understanding the dynamic nature of profe-ssional reinvention empowe-rs people to welcome- changes and conquer hurdles along the-ir evolving journey.

Navigating Skill Gaps and Education

When conside-ring embarking on a midlife caree-r transition by venturing into new opportunities, you may commonly face- competency differe-nces that want addressing. Obtaining the e-ssential talents and wisdom can significantly boost your probabilities of accomplishme-nt in the next chapter. While- the journey of upskilling won't be smooth, de-dicated efforts in learning ne-w tools can help you make the most of fre-sh beginnings. Focus on areas that fascinate you rathe-r than perceived gaps - your inte-rests are more like-ly to nurture fulfillment long-term. Though change- invariably involves uncertainties, having an ope-n and curious mindset may smooth the way towards growth.

While e-xploring new career opportunitie-s is important, it's also worthwhile examining existing skillse-ts that could be enhanced or applie-d in different ways. Rele-vant training, whether through formal education or informal options, allows one- to build upon current strengths and explore-complementary areas of inte-rest. Many institutions and online learning platforms now provide-versatile programming tailored for those- seeking caree-r changes or upgrades later in life-. Courses, seminars and certification programs ofte-n allow blending work with study, permitting focused skill de-velopment to occur around existing re-sponsibilities. Consider surveying available- local and digital options to uncover surprising alignments betwe-en past experie-nce and emerging role-s, as continuing to learn may reveal unfore-seen pathways worth investigating furthe-r.

While linking with e-xperts in your preferre-d area can offer important enlighte-nment into the abilities and le-arning essential, going past direct associations can promote- more profound comprehension. Associations, gathe-rings, and online networks give chance-s to meet individuals with diverse-experience-s and perspectives who can addre-ss inquiries, impart experie-nces, and help with see-ing the more exte-nsive photo. Associating with others working in a comparative fie-ld allows trading of thoughts and opens entryways to potential ope-n doors. By broadening your system through dynamic contribution instead of dormant me-mbership, you raise your profile while- picking up profound bits of knowledge into industry patterns and difficultie-s. What's more, the individuals you mee-t can turn into a wellspring of guiding in your vocation journey or eve-n help with future business. While- gaining from others, you likewise offe-r your singular

While de-termining the abilities ne-cessary to gain, don't neglect the- portable abilities you prese-ntly have. Your past experie-nces and proficiency can be important re-sources in your fresh caree-r path. Spend some time e-valuating your present skill set and re-cognize regions where- you can make the most of your existing le-arning. For example, consider the- various responsibilities you've had in e-arlier roles and how certain te-chniques like communication, problem-solving or te-amwork could be useful in a new fie-ld. Likewise, refle-ct on any hobbies or interests that have- developed transfe-rable soft skills. Leveraging cross-applicable- strengths can help smoothen the- transition to a different profession and boost your chance-s of standing out to potential employers.

Staying knowledge-able on the most rece-nt changes and advancements in your are-a of expertise is pivotal for continue-d achievement. The- world is consistently progressing, so make sure- to keep yourself we-ll-informed on new ideas, te-chniques, and technologies shaping your industry. Commit to continuously de-veloping your abilities and perspe-ctives over time. Look for chance-s to refine existing tale-nts and acquire new skills all through your professional journe-y. Do not hesitate to adapt as circumstances re-quire. This persistent willingne-ss to learn and grow will serve you we-ll whether starting anew or forging ahe-ad in your current path.

Building a Support Network

While a midlife- career change provide-s an opportunity for personal and professional growth, shifting directions at this stage- can also bring difficulties. One important aspect that notably impacts how smoothly the- transition unfolds involves developing a robust syste-m of support. Whether it's family, friends, me-ntors or colleagues, cultivating a network of individuals to offe-r guidance, feedback and e-ncouragement throughout the proce-ss can significantly aid in navigating challenges and boost chances of achie-ving your goals. Reaching out to those investe-d in your well-being and tapping into their wisdom and pe-rspectives makes tackling obstacle-s and setbacks more manageable-. Likewise, their validation and optimism he-lps sustain motivation on discouraging days. Building community is key to weathering the- ups and downs of reinventing yourself and your path at midlife-.

When reinventing oneself at 50, it's essential to surround yourself with mentors, peers, and resources who can offer guidance, share experiences, and provide much-needed encouragement. Having a support network can help you navigate the uncertainties and setbacks that may arise during your Second Act.

One way to build a support network is by seeking out mentors who have successfully transitioned into new careers themselves. These individuals can offer valuable insights, advice, and strategies based on their own experiences. Look for professionals in your desired field or industry who are willing to share their knowledge and expertise.

Connecting with me-ntors who have already navigated care-er transitions can offer invaluable guidance- and advice drawn from personal expe-rience. Howeve-r, speaking with peers curre-ntly undergoing similar journeys may provide anothe-r important perspective. Fe-llow travelers in this phase of profe-ssional reinvention can relate- to the feelings of unce-rtainty and offer mutual encourageme-nt. By joining networks, online groups, or local gatherings of individuals e-mbarking on new chapters, you gain access to a community of comrade-s likewise charting fresh paths. Exchanging insights and support with those- navigating congruent second acts may alleviate- doubts through shared understanding.

Resource-s such as career coaches, industry-spe-cific forums, and online courses can offer invaluable- assistance in establishing your support system. The-se types of resource-s can furnish you with extra direction, educational prospe-cts, and entrée to a more e-xtensive system of profe-ssionals in your selected are-a of work. Career coaches can offe-r targeted advice and fe-edback that facilitates your professional growth. Industry-spe-cific forums connect you with networks of establishe-d specialists within your field who can provide me-ntorship. Online courses suppleme-nt your learning with virtual classroom settings and material that de-epen your understanding of tre-nds and best practices. Tapping into seve-ral avenues of support broadens your le-arning opportunities and exposure that aids advancing your care-er path.

As you move forward in your care-er journey, it is important to cultivate strong re-lationships that can provide assistance during both opportunistic and difficult times. While- leaning on others for guidance can e-ase setbacks, equally significant is le-nding your own support. Offering a listening ear and sharing both triumphs and struggle-s with your network fosters meaningful conne-ctions. Through this exchange, you help e-stablish a community of mutual uplift and motivation. No one succeeds alone-, so contribute your experie-nces generously to de-epen your relationships and e-mpower others facing transitions of their own. Toge-ther, a circle of understanding and e-ncouragement makes the- path ahead less daunting for all.

Deve-loping a system of guidance during your midlife care-er change is crucial for your future accomplishme-nt. The advice, inspiration, and important relationships you e-stablish through your support community can offer the drive and backing ne-cessary to enthusiastically accept your ne-xt stage of professional deve-lopment and thrive in your fresh job dire-ction. While altering caree-r paths at a later phase of life pre-sents challenges, cultivating a circle- of individuals dedicated to helping you achie-ve your objectives make-s confronting those obstacles more manage-able. Surrounding yourself with people- invested in your success he-lps boost confidence and provides diffe-rent viewpoints for overcoming issue-s that arise throughout the transition. Their e-ncouragement also makes e-mbracing changes feel le-ss daunting and alone. The network you build for yourse-lf during this process proves invaluable for both profe-ssional and emotional support in acclimating to a new caree-r path.

Taking Practical Steps Forward

While pursuing a passion as a ne-w career path require-s dedication, taking gradual, well-considere-d steps can help ensure- success. Transitioning fields demands balancing e-nthusiasm with pragmatic planning. The following suggestions aim to provide strate-gic guidance for clarifying objectives and making ste-ady progress towards them:

1. Set Clear Goals

Reaching a ne-w career path first require-s establishing distinct and accomplishable objective-s. Carefully consider your aspirations and what you aim to realize- in this next phase. Then de-compose your goals into more manageable-, specific actions that you can continuously work on implementing. Whe-ther its improving certain skills through additional education or training, stre-ngthening professional connections, or gaining re-levant experie-nce through volunteer work, de-fining incremental steps will he-lp keep you motivated and progre-ssing steadily toward your overarching aims.

2. Create an Action Plan

Deve-loping an action plan is important for clearly defining your steps from initial passion proje-ct to ultimate career change- goal. Within the plan, specify the e-xact tasks and checkpoints you need to accomplish along the- journey. Prioritize the various dutie-s and create a schedule- that syncs with your desired timeframe- for transitioning careers. Some ke-y things to include are rese-arch tasks to further explore your ne-w field of interest, skills to stre-ngthen, potential contacts to network with, and mile-stones to mark your progress. Refe-r back to the plan regularly to stay on track while allowing fle-xibility if unexpected de-lays occur. With a well-structured action plan, your pathway to a new care-er can be smoother and more- achievable.

3. Stay Motivated

Making a caree-r shift can undoubtedly be difficult, though kee-ping an optimistic mentality is crucial for achieveme-nt. You would benefit from associating with encouraging individuals, including re-liable confidants, advisors with expertise-, and helpful materials. Be sure- to acknowledge eve-n minor triumphs as you progress to preserve- your enthusiasm and continue moving forward steadily. While-changes can be daunting, focusing on positivity and drawing inspiration from others paving similar paths make-s navigating transitions far more manageable.

4. Research and Learn

Take the time to research your desired career field and industry trends. Stay updated with the latest developments and technologies relevant to your passion projects and new career. Invest in continuous learning and skill-building to enhance your chances of success.

5. Network and Seek Support

Establishing a robust support system plays an indispe-nsable role during caree-r changes. Reach out to others in your inte-nded area who share similar aspirations to gle-an fresh perspective-s and recommendations. Identify me-ntors capable of coaching you through each phase and furnishing pre-cious contacts within the industry. Their expe-rtise and introductions can streamline your se-arch and help you make informed choice-s at critical junctions. Do not hesitate to tap various avenue-s to widen your circle, as each ne-w acquaintance holds potential to directly or indire-ctly advance your goals. What may start as casual exchanges could blossom into e-nduring alliances empowering you throughout your journe-y.

Taking practical steps forward toward your goals ne-cessitates commitment and pe-rsistence. Establishing unambiguous objective-s, crafting a plan of action, maintaining inspiration, investigating and gaining knowledge, and cultivating a circle- of assistance can convert your pursuits of passion into a gratifying new profe-ssional path. Progress requires dilige-nce in numerous small efforts sustaine-d over time rather than one- grand achievement. With targe-ted efforts each day or we-ek focused on your objective-s, support from others, and openness to continual le-arning, steady advancement be-comes possible.

Celebrating Success Stories

Here- are some inspiring accounts that shed light on how courage-ous individuals embarked on fresh ne-w careers at the halfway mark of life-. Their journeys exe-mplify that pursing dreams and interests late-r in life remains emine-ntly attainable. In fact, such bold career switche-s after fifty can foster immense- personal evolution and professional de-velopment. Consider the- story of one man who transitioned from a long caree-r in finance to follow his true passion for photography. Discovering photography late-r in life reignited his drive- for constant learning and creative e-xpression. Or another who left a stable- government job to start an artisanal bakery, finding une-xpected fulfillment in sharing handcrafte-d breads with the local community. Their succe-ss stories provide living proof that our goals and intere-sts at midlife deserve- brave pursuit, with potential to lead down re-warding new paths.

One such success story is Jane Thompson, who left her corporate job in finance to pursue her lifelong passion for gardening. At 50, she enrolled in horticulture classes and gained hands-on experience in local botanical gardens. Today, Jane runs her own thriving landscaping business and finds immense joy and fulfillment in creating beautiful outdoor spaces for her clients.

Another inspiring example is Mark Johnson, who decided to follow his passion for writing and storytelling after spending years in the insurance industry. At 52, Mark published his first novel, which became a bestseller and kickstarted his career as an author. His dedication and perseverance to pursue his dreams at 50 have not only brought him personal satisfaction but also critical acclaim in the literary world.

While the-se inspiring stories highlight how achieving succe-ss later in life should not be hinde-red by one's age, pursuing ne-w passions and career paths during what is known as the "Se-cond Act" period provides an important opportunity for personal and profe-ssional reinvention. The storie-s demonstrate the transformative- power of embracing change afte-r decades spent in pre-vious roles or industries. By taking risks and following intere-sts, individuals are able to craft dee-ply meaningful and engaging new chapte-rs that enrich both their own lives as we-ll as the lives of those around the-m. Rather than viewing age as a limitation, the- "Second Act" can be a rele-ase into fresh possibilities and a re-minder that personal growth has no endpoint. Through ope-nness to exploration and change, e-ven major life transitions later in life- result in unforesee-n fulfillment and reward.

In the next section, we'll explore the future prospects and trends of the Second Act, reflecting on the changing landscape of work and the evolving opportunities that await those seeking midlife career changes.

The Future of the Second Act

As we look ahe-ad to the future, the Se-cond Act holds great promise for individuals wishing to explore-new career paths during midlife-. With the evolving nature of work and shifting de-mographics in society, this transformative journey of care-er reinvention is be-coming more relevant and achie-vable for people now than e-ver before. While- the road ahead may bring challenge-s and uncertainties with changing caree-rs later in life, the Se-cond Act also brings fresh opportunities to apply skills and expe-riences gained ove-r the years in novel ways that can be- personally fulfilling and make worthwhile contributions for othe-rs. For those willing to adapt and evolve with changing time-s, midlife career transitions through the- Second Act concept may prove a stimulating ne-w phase of professional deve-lopment and growth.

One of the- crucial tendencies we-'re bound to observe is an amplifie-d concentration on individual completion and intention in vocation se-lections. An increasing number of pe-ople are understanding that it's ne-ver past due to chase afte-r their interests and locate- significance in their work. The Se-cond Act grants the possibility to redeve-lop yourself, draw on untouched gifts, and embrace- new obstacles with excite-ment and enthusiasm. While change- can seem daunting, having the courage- to walk new paths often leads to pe-rsonal growth and rewards that enhance both our care-ers and lives. By reconside-ring what truly inspires us at this stage, we ope-n doors to growth that reinvigorates our daily efforts.

Furthermore-, technological enhanceme-nts and the ascent of far off work have diminishe-d the topographical restrictions relate-d with beginning another vocation stage. Pe-ople presently have- the flexibility to investigate- an extensive varie-ty of profession openings and profit by deve-loping chances paying little hee-d to where they live-. This worldwide open door to investigate- new roads empowers substantially more- self-sufficiency and adaptability in planning one's e-xpert way. While earlie-r eras may have felt bound to stay ne-ar home, the computerize-d upset has evacuated those- hindrances and permits us all to spread our wings re-gardless of where we- set down foundations. With the capacity to associate and work from pre-tty much anyplace, the sky is the limit for what we- can accomplish at this next phase of our professions.

While socie-ty progresses in acknowledging the- insight and knowledge attained through ye-ars, a developing respe-ct exists for the particular abilities and e-xposures persons contribute at the-ir stage of life post their primary care-er. Corporations and groups are progressive-ly embracing diversity and incorporation, ene-rgetically searching for individuals who have e-mbarked on an occupation transformation midway through their professional journe-y. This change in outlook clears a path for enhance-d approval and aid for those pursuing fresh vocations at fifty or later. The-re remains more work to be- done, but positive moveme-nt in recognizing life's richness that come-s from varied experie-nces at different phase-s of life can help create- new opportunities for personal and profe-ssional fulfillment even in one-'s later years.

Chapter **11**

Retirement Planning: Beyond The basics, to a lively retirement

Welcome to our comprehensive guide on retirement planning at 50. As you approach this significant milestone, it's crucial to go beyond the basics and create a vibrant and secure retirement. In this section, we will explore essential strategies, saving tips, investment advice, and income planning techniques specifically tailored to individuals in their 50s.

Preparing financially for re-tirement nece-ssitates more than guarantee-ing adequate savings. It involves e-stablishing distinct aims, making prudent investment choice-s, and welcoming an energe-tic and rewarding retireme-nt life. Regardless of whe-ther you envision exploring globally, spe-nding time with loved ones, or pursuing ne-w interests, a well-de-vised retireme-nt plan will assist you in accomplishing those desires. While- it is essential to consider accumulation suffice-nt assets for life after full-time-employment, equally significant is giving thought to how you want to spe-nd your time in retireme-nt and making choices now that lead toward fulfilling that vision later. Care-ful planning at this stage regarding both money and goals can smooth your transition to a life-style of leisure pursuits rathe-r than work obligations and help you enjoy a fruitful, active re-tirement for many years.

Throughout this section, se-veral important retireme-nt-related subjects will be- explored such as setting goals for your golde-n years, approaches to conserve- funds for the future, investme-nt vehicles to examine-, developing a retire-ment income strategy, he-althcare matters to ponder, and the- advantages of working with a financial expert. We-'ll look at defining what you hope to accomplish in retire-ment and saving tactics to employ now so you're financially pre-pared later in life. Various inve-stment opportunities will be inspe-cted including commonplace options for building your nest e-gg. Devising a retireme-nt cash flow plan involves deciding how much you can afford to withdraw each ye-ar from your savings.

Through the re-mainder of this piece, you will gain unde-rstanding and self-assurance to direct your re-tirement preparation ve-nture and appreciate an animate-d and secure future. Le-t us plunge in! By the end, you will have- a better idea of whe-re to start planning for your retireme-nt years. While retire-ment seems far off, it's important to start planning and saving e-arly. Understanding a few basic concepts can he-lp put you on the right track to ensure your re-tirement years are- comfortable. We'll discuss some of the- key factors to consider like e-stimating your expenses, taking advantage- of employer sponsored plans, and inve-sting for

Setting Retirement Goals for a Bright Future

As you reach the- age of 50, retireme-nt planning takes on greater significance-. It is essential to establish distinct re-tirement objective-s that will direct you towards a radiant and fulfilling next chapter. Re-tirement aims act as the corne-rstone of your monetary and way of life plans, pe-rmitting you to synchronize your dreams with your financial capacities. Some- key points to consider encompass life-style prefere-nces in retireme-nt, like travel plans, hobbies, spe-nding priorities and health care ne-eds. Carefully revie-wing finances and determining targe-ted retireme-nt income will help ensure- a smooth transition to your retirement ye-ars. Maintaining flexibility within plans also allows for unexpecte-d changes in expense-s or circumstances. Preparing strategically now can he-lp reduce stress and support e-njoying your later years to the fulle-st.

When conte-mplating your retirement obje-ctives, take into account the diffe-rent facets of your life that you wish to e-mphasize. This could incorporate taking trips, pursuing pastimes, de-voting more time with loved one-s, or even beginning a little- venture. By imagining the re-tirement lifestyle- you want, you can establish aims that mirror your own special wants and motivations. Some aspe-cts to reflect on include how fre-quently you hope to travel, what hobbie-s pique your interest, how much involve-ment you want with family, or if starting a business is important. Considering priorite-s can assist in saving appropriately and aid establishing a retire-ment plan tailored to your vision.

To ensure that your retirement goals are achievable, it is essential to assess your financial situation and evaluate how much you need to save. Conducting a thorough analysis of your current expenses, anticipated healthcare costs, and any potential sources of income, such as Social Security, will help you determine the financial resources required to support your goals.

Setting e-xplicit, quantifiable, attainable, applicable, and time--restricted (SMART) goals is a powerful strate-gy. For instance, a clear retire-ment objective may involve- amassing $500,000 in retirement cost savings inside- the following 15 years. This focused goal offe-rs a distinct target, a time period, and a quantifiable- final result. Achieving this type of obje-ctive requires consiste-nt effort over an exte-nded time frame, like- contributing a planned amount to retireme-nt accounts each month. Breaking a large financial goal into smalle-r steps makes steady progre-ss feel more manage-able and helps ensure- the goal remains a priority. Regularly re-viewing progress and making adjustments as ne-eded can help maximize- the chances of realizing the- objective within the allotte-d window. SMART goals are most effective- when integrated into an ove-rall financial plan and aligned with a person's priorities and available- resources.

It's important to kee-p in mind that retirement planning should re-main flexible, as your objective-s may transform as the years pass. As you move close-r to retiring, consistently re-e-xamine and alter your aims to guarantee- they correspond with any alterations in your circumstance-s. For instance, you may decide late-r in life that you want to spend more time- with your grandchildren instead of exte-nded travel. Or, an unexpe-cted major health issue could influe-nce how you envision your retire-ment. Continuing to review your re-tirement vision allows you to adapt your savings approach and timeline-s accordingly. While retireme-nt may seem far off today, taking some time- now and then to reflect on any shifts will he-lp smooth your transition to that next life stage.

Setting re-alistic yet aspirational retireme-nt goals that resonate with your personal prioritie-s and fit within your financial capabilities allows you to embark on a purposeful journe-y towards a bright future filled with security and fulfillme-nt in your later years. Consider what truly matte-rs most to you as you envision your retireme-nt lifestyle then thoughtfully asse-ss your current savings and projected e-xpenses to establish a plan that motivate-s without overwhelming. With diligent ye-t balanced efforts to optimize your situation ste-p-by-step over the e-nsuing years, you can work towards making your retireme-nt

Saving Strategies for a Solid Financial Foundation

As you approach retire-ment age, ensuring your financial se-curity in your later years nece-ssitates employing judicious saving strategie-s that will construct a sturdy financial foundation to rely upon. By adopting these prude-nt retirement saving re-commendations, you can make certain a ple-asant and stable retireme-nt. Some key things to focus on include incre-asing contributions to your retirement funds whe-never possible, e-ven if just small incremental incre-ases annually, paying down debts to reduce- monthly expenses during re-tirement, diversifying your re-tirement investme-nts across different asset classe-s to minimize risk to your savings, and reevaluating your inve-stment allocations periodically to make sure- they still align with your goals, risk tolerance, and time-line to retireme-nt. Careful planning and disciplined saving can go a long way in positioning yourself for a re-tirement you can truly enjoy without worrying about

1. Budgeting

Creating a budge-t is vital for taking control of your finances. Carefully analyze your spe-nding in different categorie-s like housing, food, transportation, and entertainme-nt to see where- you can reduce costs. Also dete-rmine your earnings and nece-ssary expenditures to de-vote a consistent amount each pay pe-riod towards long-term savings. Retireme-nt planning should start early, so dedicate a fe-asible portion of income on a monthly basis to retire-ment investments. With discipline-d budgeting, you have the powe-r to systematically put aside funds for your golden ye-ars while living within your means today.

2. Maximize Contributions

Make the most of your retirement accounts by maximizing your contributions. If you're 50 or older, take advantage of catch-up provisions that allow you to contribute additional funds. Whether it's your 401(k), IRA, or any other retirement account, increasing your contributions can significantly boost your savings.

3. Diversify Your Investments

While thinking about re-tirement, diversifying your inve-stment profile is extre-mely important. Contemplate incorporating stocks, bonds, and additional prope-rty types to distribute your danger and conce-ivably accomplish higher returns. Speak with a mone-tary consultant to build up an venture procedure- that coordinates with your objectives and dange-r limit. Consider a blend of deve-lopment situated and low danger ve-ntures. Stocks can offer higher re-turns yet convey more unpre-dictability contrasted with bonds or reserve- funds. Bonds are lower hazard yet re-gularly offer bring down returns over the- long haul. Incorporate worldwide business se-ctors as well to support your portfolio. Remembe-r your retirement time- span and withdrawal procedure, adjusting your speculation ble-nd as you move nearer to re-tirement. Continuously audit and alter your proce-dure as your circumstance changes afte-r some time.

4. Automate Savings

While it may be- tempting to dip into your savings for everyday e-xpenses, resist that urge- by setting up automatic transfers each pay pe-riod. Having funds from your paycheck or bank account transferred dire-ctly into retirement plans like- 401(k)s or IRAs ensures consistent savings without the- need to reme-mber manual contributions each month. Automating your contributions remove-s the decision-making aspect and guarante-es that a portion of your income supports your future financial se-curity, even on busy wee-ks when saving may slip your mind. Small, regular amounts deposite-d automatically really add up over the long run. Don't risk losing out on valuable- compound interest or employe-r matching contributions that come from disciplined, habitual saving. Make saving for re-tirement effortle-ss by signing up for automated transfers today.

5. Minimize Expenses

There- are a few approaches you may take- to help lower your costs and set aside- more funds for your golden years. Think about downsizing to a smalle-r home if your current reside-nce is more space than you truly ne-ed, which could help reduce- your monthly housing expenses. Also e-xamine your discretionary spending to se-e where cuts could be- made, such as canceling unused subscriptions, me-mberships, or streaming service-s. Search for methods to conserve- on everyday outlays like food and utility bills as we-ll. Switching to LED light bulbs, lowering your thermostat a few de-grees in winter/raising it a fe-w in summer, and meal planning are some- examples. While e-ach individual adjustment may seem minor, the- cumulative impact of multiple modest modifications can re-sult in worthwhile savings added to your retire-ment kitty over the long haul.</

There- are several prude-nt approaches you can take to construct a robust financial base and guarante-e a comfortable retire-ment. It's recommende-d to begin retireme-nt saving early in your career so your funds have- time to accrue intere-st and growth over many decades. While- it's important to set aside retire-ment assets consistently, e-ven small regular contributions can make a big diffe-rence if maintained dilige-ntly for years. Speaking with a financial consultant can also help optimize- your retirement strate-gy at age 50. They may provide advice- on appropriate investment allocations or savings targe-ts tailored to your unique goals and timeline-. With strategic planning and discipline over the- long-haul, you can help support yourself confidently once- you decide to stop working.

Investing for Long-Term Growth and Stability

Making prudent financial choice-s is essential for accumulating assets and producing re-venue during one's se-nior years. As people ne-ar their fifth decade of life-, it becomes increasingly vital to make- tactical monetary moves that equalize- prospects for profits with security. Here-, we will investigate se-veral investment possibilitie-s appropriate for retireme-nt planning at age fifty. Some choices to conside-r include diversified stock and bond mutual funds, which can offe-r long-term growth while balancing risk, as well as guarante-ed income annuities, which provide- steady cash flow. Be sure to care-fully research any potential inve-stment and spread funds across a variety of options to he-lp maximize returns while minimizing volatility ove-r the coming decades prior to re-tirement. Consulting a financial advisor can also help craft a strate-gic plan tailored to individual priorities, timeline-, and risk tolerance.

Stocks

When planning for re-tirement, many investors conside-r stocks as they can offer rewarding re-turns in the long run. Owning shares in well-e-stablished businesses that have- a history of steadily increasing their profits ye-ar after year allows you to bene-fit from their success over de-cades. These firms have- proven they can navigate diffe-rent economic climates, giving your mone-y growth potential. However, to re-duce your vulnerability to any single company's pe-rformance, it is wise to spread your stock inve-stments across different industrie-s and sectors. Diversifying in this manner he-lps provide protection if one are-a of the stock market decline-s, lessening the impact on your total re-turns. While including stocks in a retireme-nt portfolio offers upside, mixing in a variety of asse-ts helps ensure your ne-st egg weathers ine-vitable market fluctuations

Bonds

Bonds offer a more conservative investment option for individuals planning their retirement. They provide fixed income and can help stabilize a portfolio. Consider diversifying your bond holdings by investing in different types, such as government bonds, corporate bonds, or municipal bonds.

Real Estate

Owning real e-state can be a smart choice for re-tirees see-king both long-term growth and a consistent reve-nue stream. Rental prope-rties allow investors to collect monthly re-nt checks that can supplement the-ir income in retireme-nt. Even after accounting for maintenance- costs and property management fe-es, rental income is re-latively stable compared to inve-stment returns that can fluctuate in the- stock market. Additionally, the value of re-al properties has gene-rally risen over decade-s, so land and buildings hold the possibility for appreciating significantly in worth. Real e-state investment trusts, or REITs, function similarly by pooling mone-y from many investors to purchase income-ge-nerating commercial real e-state and mortgages. REIT shareholde-rs then gain a share of the re-ntal profits generated. The- steady cash flows from rent collections as we-ll as the potential for rising property value-s in the

Diversification

Spreading inve-stments across multiple asset cate-gories like stocks, bonds, and real e-state is crucial for controlling hazard and maximizing profits. By dispersing investme-nts among numerous asset types, the- influence of any single inve-stment's performance is de-creased. Thinking about mee-ting with a monetary consultant to devise a dive-rsified profile that coordinates with your re-tirement objective-s. Remember, investing for retirement at 50 requires careful consideration of your risk tolerance, time horizon, and financial goals. It's advisable to seek retirement investment advice from a qualified professional to ensure your portfolio is aligned with your specific needs and circumstances.

Creating a Retirement Income Plan

Preparing for re-tirement is an esse-ntial move toward guaranteeing mone-tary security and inner sere-nity in your golden years. As you draw closer to turning 50, it turns out to be- progressively critical to plan an exhaustive- pay stream intend to fund your favored way of life- and cover your costs. There are- a few key components to conside-r while planning for retireme-nt. It is significant to figure the entire- measure of cash you will require- to support yourself every ye-ar taking into account elements like- duty on retirement income-, medical coverage costs, cost of living incre-ases and other anticipated costs. You should like-wise survey your current inve-stment funds and retireme-nt records to survey what measure- of cash you presently have put away and what you have- to spare more to accomplish your target. Furthe-rmore, you have to choose the- wellsprings of retireme-nt pay like government re-tirement plans, individual retire-ment records or continued compe-nsation. Having a nitty gritty arrangement assists you with settling

Retirement income planning involves various strategies and considerations that can help you make the most of your accumulated savings and investments. One key element is the utilization of annuities, which provide a guaranteed income stream throughout your retirement. Annuities can offer the peace of mind of a fixed income, regardless of market fluctuations.

There- are several important factors to conside-r when structuring your Social Security income during re-tirement. Taking the time- to learn the ins and outs of the program will he-lp you choose the most advantageous age- to begin collecting bene-fits. By strategizing wisely, you can maximize your monthly Social Se-curity payments. This can assist in supporting the retire-ment lifestyle you e-nvision. Some key decisions impacting your be-nefits include whethe-r to claim early at a reduced amount or de-lay receipt for higher life-time payouts. Thorough research on the-se options allows for an informed sele-ction tailored to your individual priorities and financial circumstances in re-tirement.

To dete-rmine a balanced withdrawal rate from your re-tirement funds that will allow your savings to endure- throughout your senior years, it is important to thoughtfully consider both your anticipate-d lifetime as well as e-xpected medical e-xpenses. Calculating a careful e-xtraction level means strate-gically balancing the amounts withdrawn to guarantee your re-serves will continue providing for ne-cessary costs even late- into retirement. Factors like- your projected lifespan and pote-ntial healthcare bills must be we-ighed to establish a sustainable pace- of distributions that will not outpace returns, leaving too little- behind over time. A me-asured approach accounting for variables like life-expectancy and future me-dical costs can help secure a withdrawal me-thodology maintaining resources for as long as nee-ded after caree-r conclusion.

See-king guidance from a knowledgeable- financial advisor experience-d in retirement planning can prove- extremely valuable- during this significant life stage. They are- able to thoroughly evaluate your curre-nt economic circumstances, align your retire-ment objectives with your e-arnings opportunities, and custom-craft a retireme-nt earnings plan uniquely suited to fully addre-ss your unique needs and dre-ams. A specialist retireme-nt advisor can offer perceptive- insight into how best to strategize your savings and inve-stments to generate- sufficient income to cover your e-ssential living costs as well as any desire-d pursuits once you stop working. Their expe-rtise assists with constructing a practical strategy for transitioning to retire-d life with confidence your financial re-quirements will reliably be-satisfied.

It is important to kee-p in mind that preparing for retireme-nt income involves an ongoing process that may ne-cessitate alterations as ye-ars pass. As your situation evolves, it is imperative- to reevaluate and modify your plan suitably to pre-serve financial stability and adjust to new aims or difficultie-s that could develop. Your nee-ds and resources are unlike-ly to remain static, so periodic revie-w and refinement of your re-tirement strategy can he-lp ensure it continues se-rving you well as life brings changes. Factors like- health events, family status shifts, e-conomic variations, and shifting priorities are best addre-ssed proactively through timely plan update-s.

Healthcare Considerations for Retirees

As people- approach the half-century mark in their life-, careful thought must be given to planning for re-tirement, espe-cially when it comes to future he-althcare needs. With age- often comes greate-r requirements for me-dical care, so having a well-deve-loped strategy is vital. A few important e-lements to refle-ct on include focusing first on how to cover rising costs for care. Me-dical expenses have- a way of multiplying in our later decades, the-refore wisely allocating savings spe-cifically earmarked for such nee-ds proves prudent. Evaluate curre-nt and projected insurance situations too, taking into account how policie-s may change or costs increase ove-r time. Consult professionals knowledge-able about options for supplemental cove-rage if gaps appear. Additionally, assess one-'s overall health and any pree-xisting conditions requiring ongoing treatment. Fore-thought given to accessing nee-ded services, doctors and facilitie-s as years advance ensure-s the best quality of

Medicare Enrollment

Understanding Me-dicare and enrolling at the right time- is crucial for retirees' he-althcare planning. Medicare offe-rs indispensable healthcare- coverage for those ove-r 65 and some disabled individuals. It's critical to comprehe-nd the eligibility standards, enrollme-nt windows, and coverage choices acce-ssible. There are- a few sorts of Medicare, including Part A for hospital care- and Part B for doctor's visits and preventive care-. Part D gives prescription drug coverage-. It's vital to enroll during Initial Enrollment Period around age- 65 to abstain from paying late charges later on. Individuals may like-wise enroll in Medicare- Advantage plans, otherwise calle-d Part C, which are oversee-n by private insurance organizations approved by Me-dicare and regularly incorporate Part A, Part B, and re-gularly Part D. These plans freque-ntly have monthly premiums howeve-r may have lower out-of-pocket costs. The- choices can be confusing so it's prudent to counse-l a Medicare guide or counse-lor to choose the protection de-sign that best suits one's particular nee-ds and spending limit. Proper planning is fundamental for e-nsuring suitable healthcare is acce-ssible during retireme-nt.</

Long-Term Care Insurance

While se-curing long-term care insurance is wise- to safeguard against depleting re-tirement funds on unexpe-cted medical costs, deciding what type- is best warrants careful assessme-nt. Placing funds into long-term care insurance provide-s financial protection should assisted living, nursing home care-, or in-home health service-s become nee-ded in the future. By thoroughly re-searching options, one can identify policie-s suiting their likely care ne-eds and budget. Quality long-term care- policies ease worrie-s over how to afford care down the road, allowing re-tirement to be e-njoyed without that concern in the background. Though an important conside-ration, selecting the right long-te-rm care coverage take-s due diligence.

Managing Healthcare Expenses

When re-aching retirement, prope-rly handling medical costs grows increasingly vital. It's crucial to comprehe-nd diverse healthcare- expenditures, like- premiums, deductibles, co-payme-nts, and prescription medication prices. Care-fully investigating and contrasting health insurance policie-s, exploring assistance programs, and planning a budget for me-dical costs can assist guarantee you have ade-quate financial means to satisfy your healthcare- necessities succe-ssfully and economically.

By taking the time- to thoroughly evaluate factors involving your healthcare- situation and blending relevant aspe-cts into your retirement strate-gy, you can help shield your medical we-llness as well as fiscal soundness. Doing so pe-rmits savoring a safe and lively time of re-tirement free- from excessive worrie-s concerning future costs.

Embracing an Active and Fulfilling Retirement Lifestyle

When ne-aring the age of 50, effe-ctive retireme-nt planning involves more than finances alone-. The goal should be crafting a lifestyle- after career that re-mains lively, purposeful, and involves social inte-raction. After decades de-dicating yourself to your work, it's important to make the most of your fre-e time by partaking in activities you find re-warding and connecting with others. Whethe-r pursuing longstanding interests, exploring ne-w hobbies, traveling, voluntee-ring or spending quality moments with loved one-s, thoughtful preparation now can help ensure- you feel engage-d and energized during this upcoming phase-.

One key aspect of an enriching retirement is pursuing hobbies. Whether it's painting, gardening, cooking, or playing a musical instrument, indulging in activities that bring you joy can provide a sense of purpose and fulfillment. Hobbies not only keep your mind engaged but also help you connect with like-minded individuals who share your interests.

Voluntee-ring is an excellent way to re-main active and connected during re-tirement. Lending a hand to the- community not only helps others but also enhance-s your own well-being. Whethe-r guiding up-and-coming professionals or assisting local nonprofit organizations, there are- endless opportunities to cre-ate positive change and e-stablish an enduring legacy. You could share your e-xpertise by advising small businesse-s or teaching elderly re-sidents new skills. Offering your time- to lead after-school programs allows youth to gain knowledge- from someone with life e-xperience. Le-nding a hand with environmental projects or me-al delivery service-s for those in need pe-rmits contributing to important causes. Volunteering pre-sents a rewarding means to spe-nd extra hours with purpose.

Maintaining good mental and physical health is crucial for enjoying a vibrant retirement. Regular exercise, such as walking, swimming, or yoga, helps keep your body fit and your mind sharp. Additionally, engaging in activities that challenge you intellectually, such as reading, puzzles, or learning a new language, can contribute to cognitive well-being.

In retire-ment, you gain precious time to nourish and re-inforce relationships with loved one-s. Making meaningful memories with family and frie-nds through get-togethers, trips away, or casual chats ove-r coffee can be profoundly satisfying source-s of happiness. Think about contributing to social organizations or neighborhood committee-s to broaden your circle and deve-lop fresh bonds. Spending quality moments with the- people closest to you, from multige-nerational relatives to long-time-companions, allows deeper appre-ciation of the connections that enrich our live-s. Whether sharing adventure-s, swapping stories, or providing support through good and challenging periods, strong re-lationships are what ultimately matter most. Che-rish the opportunity retireme-nt presents to invest in those- who matter most through both everyday inte-ractions and special experie-nces you share side by side-.

Lastly, remember to prioritize self-care and relaxation in your retirement lifestyle. Take time for yourself to recharge and rejuvenate. Whether it's through meditation, spa treatments, or simply indulging in a favorite hobby, make self-care a regular part of your routine. Retirement is the perfect time to finally put yourself first and embrace a balanced and fulfilling lifestyle.

Seeking Professional Retirement Planning Services

As individuals near the- golden years of retire-ment, strategizing for this next phase- of life can feel intimidating give-n its financial and lifestyle implications. Planning for one's se-nior years need not be- a lonely endeavor, howe-ver. Seeking guidance- from retirement e-xperts can help simplify what may otherwise- seem an overwhe-lming process. A financial advisor can work closely with individuals to clarify goals and outline customize-d strategies for maintaining well-be-ing in retirement. The-y may assess factors like life e-xpectancy, health nee-ds, housing decisions and desired activitie-s to construct a comprehensive ye-t flexible plan. Partnering with such profe-ssionals leaves room for adjustments along the- way and alleviates worries of financial inse-curity down the road.

Retire-ment planning involves many complex conside-rations regarding finances, health care-, living situations, and leisure activities. Expe-rienced financial advisors can offer invaluable- assistance navigating these intricacie-s for those reaching age 50. The-y possess comprehensive- understanding of the industry accumulated from ye-ars of guidance provided to clients. Financial advisors are- trained to analyze clients' spe-cific goals, assets, income sources, anticipate-d expenses, risk tole-rance, and time horizon to tailor a customized strate-gy. This personalized approach aims to optimize how savings and inve-stments are structured and withdrawals are- scheduled to sustain a client's de-sired lifestyle throughout the-ir retirement ye-ars. While do-it-yourself online tools may provide- a starting point, the expertise- of a dedicated financial advisor can help make- retirement planning a le-ss daunting process with their insights ensuring a more- secure financial future.

Here- is a moderately expande-d version of the input text with an inte-rmediate depth and purpose- to clarify:

Working with a retirement planning profe-ssional allows individuals to take advantage of numerous he-lpful services. A planner can assist with asse-ssing one's current financial situation and projecte-d retirement ne-eds. They will analyze factors like- your savings, investments, expe-cted social security and pension be-nefits, healthcare costs, and de-sired retirement.

1. When planning for retirement, it is crucial to asse-ss your goals and determine the- steps neede-d to achieve them. A financial advisor can assist with this important proce-ss, helping you evaluate your dre-ams and desires for retire-ment. They will work closely with you to unde-rstand what you hope to accomplish in your later years, whe-ther it be exte-nsive global travel, starting a new busine-ss venture, or simply relaxing at home-. From there, an advisor can customize a strate-gic plan to match your specific aspirations. Different goals will re-quire varying levels of savings, so a tailore-d strategy is key. By clarifying your objective-s and devising solutions, an advisor ensures you make- informed decisions to reach your re-tirement vision. Their guidance- eliminates

2. Investment portfolio management: Professionals can offer expert advice on investment options that are suitable for individuals in their 50s. They can provide insights on asset allocation, diversification, and rebalancing strategies to ensure long-term growth and stability.

3. Creating a strate-gic retirement income- plan involves factoring in the various reve-nue streams that will be acce-ssible during those post-employme-nt years, like Social Security, pe-nsion plans if accessible, and returns from inve-stments. Financial consultants can assist develop a compre-hensive strategy that combine-s these sources to ge-nerate a steady flow of funds for living e-xpenses. They'll provide- guidance on optimizing Social Security advantages by de-termining the proper claiming age-. Advisors also establish withdrawal rates from investme-nt accounts that balance current nee-ds with maintaining principal for decades of retire-ment. By considering all accessible- income sources and crafting a balanced plan, individuals can approach re-tirement with confidence- that basic living costs are covered.

4. Tax-efficient strategies: Professionals can identify tax-saving opportunities and develop strategies to minimize tax liabilities during retirement. They can offer advice on tax-efficient investment vehicles and asset allocation techniques.

When pre-paring for retirement, it is important to conside-r future healthcare ne-eds and costs. Services that focus on long-te-rm planning can provide useful guidance on issue-s like Medicare e-nrollment and long-term care insurance-. These types of me-dical expenses are- difficult to foresee and save- for, but having a plan in place makes a significant differe-nce. An advisor can help walk through options for managing health cove-rage as you age. They may discuss things like- supplemental insurance that pairs with Me-dicare, or long-term care policie-s that can help fund assisted living or nursing home care- if needed. By thinking ahe-ad to potential medical situations in retire-ment, you can feel more- secure knowing steps have- been

See-king guidance from professional financial advisors can greatly boost one-'s odds of enjoying a comfortable and secure- retirement. An advisor is able- to analyze an individual's unique circumstances, such as income-, assets, expense-s, health, and long-term goals, and deve-lop a customized strategy accordingly. They can re-commend the most suitable savings and inve-stment approaches to accumulate sufficie-nt funds for retirement ne-eds over time. Rathe-r than navigating retirement pre-paration independently, an advisor's e-xpertise helps simplify comple-x financial matters and eases anxie-ties. Their ongoing support and monitoring helps e-nsure retiree-s do not stray from their personalized blue-print as life circumstances or the e-conomic landscape changes. For those se-eking reassurance that the-ir retirement plans re-main on the right track even as ye-ars pass, the personalized insight and ove-rsight of a financial professional provides valuable pe-ace of mind.

As we look ahe-ad to the next section, we- will delve into the diffe-rent components involved in le-ading an engaged and rewarding re-tired life. While finance-s are crucial, it is equally important to take into account othe-r factors that can contribute to an active and secure- retirement e-xperience. Some- of these ele-ments include continuing to learn ne-w skills and pursue hobbies and intere-sts, maintaining social connections through community involvement or volunte-ering, and focusing on physical and mental well-be-ing through activities such as travel, exe-rcise, or lifelong learning. Prope-r planning in these diverse- yet complementary domains can he-lp support a lively and fulfilling retireme-nt journey.

Enjoying a Lively and Secure Retirement

By the time- you reach your late forties, pre-paring for retirement should be- a top priority to ensure you have a stimulating and re-warding next chapter. Throughout this piece-, we have examine-d several tactics and factors that are important to conte-mplate as you map out your retireme-nt plan at this phase of your life. While re-tirement may see-m far away, taking a moderate look at your finances, savings, and goals for your se-nior years can help bring clarity and calmness. Conside-ring options like contributing more to your 401(k) or IRA, downsizing expe-nses, or working a few extra ye-ars are steps worth exploring now to be-nefit your future self. Navigating re-tirement planning become-s clearer when broke-n into smaller intermediate- objectives rather than an ove-rwhelming distant deadline.

One important le-sson highlighted is actively directing your mone-tary matters. By establishing unambiguous retire-ment aims and constructing a stable fiscal base via e-fficient savings tactics, you can make sure a ple-asant retirement living. Maximize- additions to retirement re-cords and benefit from catch-up arrangeme-nts uniquely intended for pe-rsons in their fifties. It is significant to freque-ntly reassess your funds and adapt your methodologie-s as essential. Maintaining a balanced budge-t allows you to set aside more for your late-r years. The catch-up provisions give a valuable-chance to bolster your retire-ment reserve-s before stopping work. Organizing finances with a long te-rm view in mind can go far in securing contentme-nt in retirement.

Aligning your retire-ment goals with your core principles and what re-ally matters most to you is equally important. Be sure- to factor in non-monetary eleme-nts, like sustaining an energe-tic and rewarding retireme-nt experience-. Pursue pastimes you enjoy, look for volunte-ering roles that ene-rgize you, and place high importance on your e-motional and physical well-being. Embrace the- chances that retireme-nt presents and nurture a fe-eling of significance and satisfaction.

While re-tirement planning poses difficultie-s, meeting with financial expe-rts can significantly assist your process. Advisors offer skilled knowle-dge and customized strategie-s to help you maximize your retire-ment funds and make prudent choice-s. Their counsel can guarantee- that you develop a holistic retire-ment plan addressing your unique ne-eds, priorities, and goals. Factors like life-span projections, healthcare costs, inflation rate-s, and taxes necessitate- comprehensive planning. Working with a profe-ssional provides peace of mind knowing all aspe-cts are considered. Don't he-sitate to rely on an advisor's expe-rience and insights for important retire-ment decisions.

Chapter **12**

Personal Peace: Strategies for stress reduction and inner serenity

We e-xtend a warm Welcome to our de-tailed guide on attaining inner pe-ace and diminishing anxiety in your 50s. This phase of living fre-quently presents with distinct te-sts and sources of pressure, ye-t it's never too late to e-mphasize your wellness and nurture- inner tranquility. Here, we- will investigate helpful approache-s and mindfulness techniques spe-cially adapted for older adults. This stage ofte-n requires adjusting to changes in your body, care-er and relationships while facing unce-rtainties about the future. Howe-ver, practicing gratitude, embracing e-ach moment and focusing on personal growth can help promote- greater calm and happiness. Simple- techniques like de-ep breathing, journaling and staying active in hobbie-s you find meaningful are easy ways to re-duce stress. Spending time- with supportive people, he-lping others or exploring your creativity and spirituality also nourish inne-r contentment. While ne-w stresses may arise, applying the-se strategies can foste-r improved coping and serenity within.

Life in your 50s can be a time of reflection, transition, and personal growth. It's crucial to incorporate self-care practices that promote stress reduction and inner peace. By adopting a holistic approach to well-being, you can create a solid foundation for a fulfilling and harmonious life.

Throughout this section, we- will explore a variety of te-chniques and methods that can help you e-ffectively manage the- pressures of daily living and discover inne-r peace. Whethe-r it's mindfulness meditation, expre-ssing gratitude, or other approaches, e-ach tactic aims to reduce stress and promote- overall health and happiness. While- some emphasize quie-t reflection, others involve- actively focusing on life's blessings. Colle-ctively, they offer re-search-backed means for calming the- mind and body, boosting resilience, and appre-ciating life's simpler pleasure-s—which in turn can aid in confronting challenges from a place of re-stored balance. While re-gularly practicing even a few can e-nhance wellness, combining diffe-rent strategies may provide- the most benefit by targe-ting stress from numerous angles. I hope- the following recommendations provide- you with practical yet powerful tools for cultivating greate-r calm and contentment where-ver your journey leads.

Come along with us on this voyage- of self-learning and empowe-rment as we investigate- the influential technique-s for decreasing anxiety and achie-ving inner stillness in your fifties. Le-t us embark on a road of self-care and mindfulne-ss, making each and every day a stage- towards accomplishing the peace and calm you me-rit. We will analyze practical approaches to re-duce daily stressors and promote ove-rall well-being. Through discussion and activities, we- will explore methods to tame- racing thoughts and cultivate acceptance. Make- self-reflection a priority by carving out time- for journaling, meditation, or relaxing hobbies. Small adjustme-nts can lead to improved sere-nity so you fully enjoy this phase of life.

Understanding the Impact of Stress in Your 50s

As individuals ente-r their 50s, they regularly e-ncounter distinct tests and stressors that can e-ssentially influence the-ir actual and psychological wellbeing. Dealing with pre-ssure in center life- turns out to be progressively critical for ke-eping up general prospe-rity and accomplishing an inward feeling of sere-nity. A portion of the difficulties incorporate juggling family and care-er responsibilities, caring for aging pare-nts, facing physical changes that come with getting olde-r, and coping with uncertainties about the future-. It is important during this phase of life to adopt stress-busting te-chniques like engaging in re-gular exercise, pursuing hobbie-s, spending time with friends, practicing de-ep breathing, and getting ade-quate sleep. Surrounding one-self with a strong support system and maintaining a positive outlook can also he-lp make this transition easier. While- some stress is inevitable-,

At around mid-care-er, strain can originate from numerous places, for e-xample work progressions, money re-lated worries, relationship e-lements, and wellbe-ing issues. The aggregate- weight of these worry cre-ators can take a toll on both the psyche and body, prompting e-xpanded powerlessne-ss to uneasiness, gloom, and differe-nt wellbeing issues. It is along the-se lines exce-ptionally essential to create- viable anxiety administration procedure-s to relieve the-se impacts and keep ourse-lves sound, both actually and rationally amid a bustling time where- numerous changes might be happe-ning simultaneously. Some basic yet succe-ssful methods incorporate meditation, e-xercise, getting e-nough rest, spending quality time with love-d ones and prioritizing personal well-be-ing. While juggling multiple demands, it is important we- make conscious efforts to lower stre-ss levels in a balanced manner.

While e-ntering their fifth decade-, taking a proactive approach to handling stress through various technique-s can help reduce strain's harmful e-ffects on well-being. Some- strategies involve discove-ring outlets to release- feelings in positive ways, e-mbracing relaxing activities, and nurturing an optimistic outlook. Stress manage-ment need not be- reactive—impleme-nting practices in your 50s to deal with pressure-'s challenges can bene-fit your health and happiness. Finding balance through dive-rse stress-reducing strate-gies tailored to your nee-ds promotes resilience- against life's demands.

Emotional well-be-ing plays a vital role in effective-ly handling stress during midlife. When pe-ople recognize and communicate- how they feel in constructive- ways, they can stop sentiments from e-scalating and influencing their psychological soundness. This can be- accomplished through exercise-s, for example, kee-ping a journal where one re-cords their considerations and fee-lings, conversing with a dependable- companion or advisor who will listen empathetically, or associating in imaginative- outlets that engage se-lf-articulation, for example, composing, drawing, photography, music or moveme-nt. Making space for reflection and e-xpression gives urgent he-lp in overseeing life-'s difficulties.

In addition, integrating re-laxation methods into everyday sche-dules is extreme-ly important for handling pressure productively. De-ep breathing workouts, guided image-ry, stepwise muscle re-laxation, and being present-minde-d practices are a few te-chniques that can be incorporated. Engaging in pastime-s that endorse relaxation and se-lf-care, for example yoga, re-flection, or devoting time to inte-rests, can moreover offe-r much-required pressure- alleviation.

Remaining hope-ful through appreciation and reframing self-doubtful ide-as can assist persons maintain resiliency and handle- pressure in midlife. Noticing mome-nts of thankfulness, exercising se-lf-kindness, and centering on the- favorable parts of existence- can meaningfully affect overall we-ll-being and nurture a sentime-nt of inner calm. While focusing on gratitude, compassion, and positivity he-lps cope with challenges, it is also important to acknowle-dge and process difficult emotions in a he-althy way. Continuing to cultivate relationships, pursue me-aningful activities, and practice self-care- can further support one's mental he-alth during this transitional phase.

While the- 50s can be a stressful time of life- as responsibilities increase- and health concerns may arise, imple-menting stress-relie-ving practices can help you navigate this de-cade with more calmness and e-quilibrium. By learning about how stress physically affects your body and mind during this stage-, as well as discovering technique-s to manage pressure and te-nsion, you can cultivate inner peace- even when face-d with challenges. Some strate-gies like dee-p breathing, relaxing activities, social support, and maintaining a he-althy lifestyle can aid in kee-ping stress response in che-ck. Balancing duties with self-care allows for gre-ater ease and composure- during this transitional phase. With an understanding of stress's

The Holistic Approach to Stress Relief

In today's fast-paced world, whe-re many are pulled in multiple- directions, having methods to reduce-stress is extreme-ly important, particularly for those further along in age. A holistic way to re-lieve pressure- acknowledges the close- relationship betwee-n one's thoughts, physical health, and soul, enabling pe-ople to handle things causing strain from various perspe-ctives and attain a feeling of compre-hensive wellne-ss. Whether it be carving out time- for meditation, embarking on a walk outdoors, or spending mome-nts with loved ones, addressing stre-ss from mental, physical, and spiritual avenues can support re-taining balance even whe-n juggling responsibilities see-ms never-ending.

There- are several re-laxation techniques that can be incorporate-d into one's daily routine to help promote- an overall sense of we-ll-being and calm. These me-thods span from simple deep bre-athing exercises, whe-re one consciously focuses on inhaling and e-xhaling in a slow, controlled manner, to more involve-d practices like guided image-ry and progressive muscle re-laxation. Guided imagery involves visualizing pe-aceful or relaxing scene-s in one's mind to help distract from stresse-s or worries. Progressive muscle- relaxation works to reduce physical te-nsion by systematically tensing and relaxing diffe-rent muscle groups throughout the body. Me-ditation is another integral relaxation te-chnique that can be done daily. By taking e-ven just a few minutes e-ach day to sit quietly and either focus on one-'s breathing or repeat a calming mantra, individuals give- their mind and body an opportunity to unwind. Making a conscious effort through various relaxation me-thods to decompress both physically and mentally has be-en shown to lower stress le-vels while cultivating inner se-renity. Overall, intentionally re-laxing helps counteract the we-ar and tear that stress brings by promoting

While maintaining ove-rall life balance is esse-ntial in managing stress levels and boosting whole--person wellness, ce-rtain targeted efforts also provide- benefits. Scheduling time- for physical activity, smart nutrition, and adequate rest he-lps recharge our bodies. Pursuing passions through hobbie-s, bonding with others, and spending moments amidst nature-'s peace lift our spirits. Making room for self-care- and things that bring purpose aids in achieving equilibrium and fulfillme-nt.

While taking a compre-hensive strategy to alle-viate stress can help grownups proactive-ly control and decrease anxie-ty levels, which subseque-ntly advances general physical and psychological we-llbeing. Integrating relaxation me-thods and embracing a adjusted way of life are- pivotal advances towards accomplishing inner sere-nity and appreciating a more quiet and fulfilling pre-sence. Some prove-n approaches include yoga, meditation, de-ep breathing exe-rcises, spending time with love-d ones or in nature, kee-ping a gratitude journal, and scaling back on responsibilities whe-n needed. Howe-ver, it is also important to acknowledge that some- stress is part of daily life and can often motivate- us to manage our time well and tackle- challenges. The ke-y is distinguishing excessive worry from occasional pre-ssure and having tools ready to lower te-nsion during high-demand times.

Mindfulness Meditation for Inner Serenity

Mindfulness meditation is a powerful practice that can bring about inner peace and serenity, particularly for older adults. By cultivating a state of awareness and non-judgmental presence, mindfulness meditation enables individuals to manage stress effectively and find calm amidst life's challenges.

While the-re are differe-nt mindfulness meditation methods for se-niors, many focus on self-kindness, noticing physical sensations, and conce-ntrating solely on the prese-nt. Techniques are de-signed to cultivate understanding and care- for oneself, helping olde-r individuals tune into bodily feelings without judgme-nt. They also aim to anchor attention firmly in the now, a strate-gy shown to reduce stress and boost we-ll-being in aging adults. Mindfulness has proven be-nefits for the elde-rly population, and tailored practices provide a ge-ntle way to appreciate e-ach moment as it occurs.

Body Scan Meditation

The body scan me-ditation is a commonly used mindfulness technique- for older adults. This practice involves slowly and care-fully shifting one's focus of attention through differe-nt areas of the physical body, from the top of the- head all the way down to the toe-s. By bringing gentle awarene-ss to each body part, one at a time, te-nsions can be noticed and observe-d without criticism. This allows an individual to develop a richer aware-ness of their embodie-d experience-. As each area is acknowledge-d in a non-judgmental manner, a dee-per sense of conne-ction to the physical self can eme-rge. The body scan also promotes re-laxation by encouraging a state of calm prese-nce within. Although it involves systematically che-cking in with various regions, this exercise- need not be rushe-d. Allowing sensations to simply be noticed at a re-laxed pace can help cultivate- stillness from the inside out.

Let me- provide you with some additional context and de-tails to help clarify how to incorporate body scan meditation into your daily practice-. Find a peaceful location where- you won't be disturbed, somewhe-re you can sit or lay comfortably. Once settle-d, take a few dee-p breaths to help relax your body and calm your mind. Bring an ope-n and curious awareness to how your entire- physical form feels in this prese-nt moment. Beginning with the top of your he-ad, direct non-judgmental attention throughout your body slowly making your way down, noticing any place-s of tightness, pressure or strain. Allow any se-nsations, whether pleasant or unple-asant, to simply be without attaching stories or resisting what is. As te-nsions arise, gently breathe- into tight areas, visualizing each exhalation re-leasing and relaxing those place-s of discomfort. Continue scanning your entire body in this patie-nt, compassionate manner before- finally redirecting focus back to the natural rhythm of your bre-ath flowing in and out.

Loving-Kindness Meditation

Practicing loving-kindness me-ditation is another way mindfulness can cultivate inne-r peace. This technique- involves channeling positive thoughts and care- towards yourself as well as others. By consciously foste-ring emotions of affection, bene-volence, and wishing well, loving-kindne-ss meditation nourishes a perce-ption of interdepende-nce while decre-asing feelings of tension. It prompts se-nding hopes for health, joy, and security to yourse-lf at first. Then it expands that goodwill in widening circle-s—to loved ones, acquaintances, ne-utral parties, difficult people, and finally all be-ings. Regular sessions may strengthe-n your capacity for empathy and compassion, helping you expe-rience life's stre-sses with more ease-.

Incorporating loving-kindness me-ditation into your daily routine can help cultivate compassion. Ge-t comfortable and let your eye-s gently close. Start by silently re-peating phrases like "May I be- happy. May I be healthy. May I be safe-. May I live with ease," wishing yourse-lf well-being. As you continue, broade-n your wishes of kindness to include those- close to you, saying "May my family be happy. May my friends be- healthy." Widen your circle of loving-kindne-ss further, wishing "May all living beings be safe-. May all find ease." With each re-petition, envision sending fe-elings of care, warmth and goodwill radiating outward from your heart to e-ach individual or group. This simple practice can help ge-nerate greate-r care, understanding and goodwill both within yourself and for othe-rs each day.

Incorporating mindfulness me-ditation into your daily routine provides a path to inner calm and e-ffective stress manage-ment. Practices like body scans or loving-kindne-ss meditations furnish useful technique-s for nurturing peace and stillness. Appre-ciate how mindfulness can strengthe-n your well-being by reducing inne-r turmoil. Simple yet impactful exe-rcises done regularly, such as focuse-d breathing, can gradually lessen me-ntal noise so you experie-nce life's moments with gre-ater ease. While- changes take time, a daily de-dication to presence he-lps smooth difficult emotions that may otherwise fe-el overwhelming. Discove-r serenity within by opening to e-ach moment as it is, without clinging to what was or reaching for what is yet to be-.

Practicing Gratitude and Positive Thinking

While e-ntering one's 50s, taking time e-ach day to appreciate life's ble-ssings and adopting an outlook focused on strengths rather than struggle-s can profoundly impact well-being. Choosing to see- challenges as opportunities for growth rathe-r than difficulties to avoid, and reflecting on gratitude- for relationships, health and simple ple-asures can reframe pe-rspective in a manner that facilitate-s resilience whe-n facing inevitable stresse-s. This practice of mindfulness fosters optimism which se-rves to strengthen re-solve when navigating life's curve-balls, enabling one to carry on with dete-rmination despite difficulties while- retaining joy in each new day.

The Power of Gratitude

Expressing appre-ciation for what you have is a meaningful habit that can redire-ct your attention from problems to bene-fits in your daily experience-. By sincerely recognizing and valuing the- gifts and favorable moments, you can educate- your thoughts to notice the attractivene-ss and prosperity that encompasses you. Gratitude- helps you understand that while challe-nges occur, there is simultane-ously much to feel thankful for - health, love-d ones, opportunities, or simply being alive-. Maintaining a perspective focuse-d on life's blessings, rather than only trouble-s, nourishes well-being and optimism. Though issue-s will always arise, cultivating gratefulness balance-s awareness of difficulties with aware-ness of life's richness.

Begin practicing gratitude- by maintaining a journal where you record thre-e things daily that you feel appre-ciative for. Jot down small pleasures, acts of thoughtfulne-ss from others, or simply express thanks for your we-ll-being and family members. De-veloping gratitude as a routine will initiate- your brain to instinctively search for favorable aspe-cts of each day. While negative-s sometimes surface unbidde-n, consciously focusing on positives trains your thoughts in a healthier dire-ction. Simple yet sincere- lists of thankfulness offer perspe-ctive and lift moods without effort. Gratitude soothe-s and satisfies deepe-r than fleeting pleasure-s; like nourishing food, it sustains.

The Strength of Positive Thinking

Positive thinking doe-s not mean denying the pote-ntial problems or hardships that may come your way. It is about changing the way you vie-w challenges by focusing on opportunities and answe-rs instead of dwelling on obstacles. Whe-n your perspective be-comes one of optimism, you empowe-r yourself to be more adaptable- to life's ups and downs. This resilience- helps lower your stress le-vels since an optimistic mind is prepare-d to deal with troubles in a calm manner. With a positive- outlook, you take better care- of your mental health by boosting your mood and reducing fe-elings of anxiety. Overall, shifting to thinking favorably about your circumstance-s greatly enhances your we-ll-being and quality of life.

Practicing positive affirmations is one- technique that can be quite- effective. Positive- affirmations involve stating encouraging phrases or mantras to yourse-lf each day. For instance, you may say "I have the- ability to deal with any obstacles life pre-sents" or "I opt to concentrate on the- good aspects in every sce-nario." By routinely reinforcing optimistic ideas, you can re-educate your mind to notice the-chances and potential solutions available e-ven when facing difficulties. Re-peating uplifting statements daily he-lps reshape how you view challe-nges and allows you to focus on solutions instead of only problems. With a pe-rspective emphasizing abilitie-s over limitations, you empower yourse-lf to handle what comes your way.

Embracing a Positive Mindset

In addition to expre-ssing gratitude and self-affirmation, there- are alternative approache-s to fostering an optimistic frame of mind. Consider surrounding yourse-lf with uplifting influences, such as cherishing quality time- with family and friends who empower and e-ncourage you. Engage in hobbies, pastime-s, and pursuits that fill your spirit with delight and satisfaction. Make an effort to e-ngage with people and participate- in things that bring more lightness to your life. While- it is important to acknowledge difficulties, focusing on positivity has be-nefits for your well-being and outlook. Finding activitie-s you find genuinely fulfilling helps promote- a balanced perspective-.

Additionally, practicing mindfulness and being present in the moment can help you let go of negative thoughts and worries about the future. Take time each day to engage in activities that calm and center you, such as meditation, deep breathing exercises, or gentle yoga.

While achie-ving inner tranquility in your later years is a life-long endeavor, cultivating an attitude of thankfulne-ss and maintaining an optimistic outlook can equip you to travel through life's highs and lows with e-legance and calm. Appreciating the- simple pleasures while- acknowledging difficulties, yet focusing on future- hopes, may smooth your path as age brings changes. Continue-d efforts to foster calm self-re-flection and care for your well-be-ing can support peace within, allowing you to savor each mome-nt and meeting of each ne-w day.

Nurturing Self-Care and Self-Compassion

As we age- into our 50s and beyond, it is crucial that we make time- to care for both our physical and mental wellbe-ing. When our lives become- busy with responsibilities to others, it can be- all too easy to neglect our own ne-eds. However, taking the- steps to manage stress and stay e-motionally balanced offers enormous be-nefits. Simple practices like- deep breathing, journaling, spe-nding time outdoors in nature, and surrounding ourselve-s with uplifting company can work wonders. Make these-nourishing activities a non-negotiable part of your routine-. Schedule time for re-flection each day, if only for a few minute-s, to cultivate inner peace- and perspective. Expre-ssing gratitude for life's blessings, howe-ver small, is another habit that pays immense- dividends. Seeking he-lp from others should stress overwhe-lm also shows wisdom. By nourishing our spirit as diligently as we do our bodies, we- give ourselves the- best chance of enjoying he-althy and happy years ahead.

1. Prioritize Rest and Relaxation

While it is important to take- time for ourselves to re-lax and recharge our minds and bodies, e-specially during busy or stressful periods, it is also worthwhile- to consider using some of that personal time- to further our understanding of important issues. Activitie-s like reading can both relax us and e-xpose us to new ideas and pe-rspectives, helping us be-come more well-rounde-d. A soothing bath allows muscles to unwind while giving space for conte-mplation. Gentle yoga tones the- body while calming the breath and ce-ntering the mind. Finding the right balance- of relaxation and learning ensure-s we return to our commitments fe-eling refreshe-d in both body and spirit.

2. Engage in Activities That Bring You Joy

While maintaining a balance-d lifestyle is important, it is equally crucial to re-serve certain pe-riods for pursuits that uplift your spirit and satisfy your soul. Whether your bliss is found in cherishing a pastime-, communing with nature, or dedicating yourself to imaginative- undertakings, carving brief yet consiste-nt breaks for such joyous occupations can considerably bette-r your total wellness and decre-ase mental pressure-. While responsibilities must be- satisfied, neglecting activitie-s that reinvigorate your being risks sacrificing harmony. Make- sure to thoughtfully and deliberate-ly schedule sporadic yet sacre-d slots for recreations that allow your anxietie-s to freely drift away as wonder and satisfaction fill your days.

3. Practice Self-Compassion

It is important to be caring and unde-rstanding towards yourself during both good and difficult moments. Recognize- the skills you possess and goals you have achie-ved, and speak to yourself with warmth, particularly whe-n facing troublesome periods. Making se-lf-compassion a regular part of your routine can help you roll with life-'s punches more smoothly and maintain inner se-renity when stresse-s arise. While nobody is perfe-ct, focusing on your capabilities and showing yourself grace e-mpowers you to meet challe-nges with balance and resilie-nce.

4. Establish Boundaries

Learn to se-t clear limits and decline re-quests that may overburden you whe-n needed. Making your we-ll-being a high priority means avoiding overcommitting your time- and energy. By establishing limits, you can ke-ep work, family duties, and self-care- balanced in your schedule to side-step feeling worn out. Saying no re-spectfully will protect your health and allow focusing fully on re-sponsibilities rather than spreading yourse-lf too thin. Maintaining control over obligations helps sustain emotional and physical we-llness long-term.

5. Connect with Supportive People

Surrounding yourself with caring love-d ones who recognize the- need for self-care- and self-compassion can greatly aid your well-be-ing journey. Developing re-lationships with those who offer understanding, motivation, and dire-ction allows you to make looking after your own nee-ds a priority. Friends and relatives willing to liste-n without judgment provide encourage-ment during challenges. The-ir support helps you maintain focus on behaviors promoting health and happine-ss. While caring for others, do not forget to care- for yourself through the strength of a circle- invested in your balanced we-ll-being.

By nurturing self-care and self-compassion, you can effectively manage stress and cultivate inner serenity in your 50s. Remember, taking care of yourself is not selfish but rather an essential part of living a balanced and fulfilling life.

The Power of Breathing Techniques

When it comes to reducing stress and promoting inner calm, one often overlooked yet powerful technique is breathing. By incorporating specific breathing exercises into your daily routine, you can experience immediate stress relief and find a sense of inner peace.

One simple technique to try is deep belly breathing. Find a comfortable position, either sitting or lying down, and place one hand on your abdomen. Take a slow, deep breath in through your nose, feeling your abdomen rise as you fill your lungs with air. Hold the breath for a moment, and then exhale slowly through your mouth, feeling your abdomen fall as you release the air.

The 4-7-8 bre-athing technique can help calm your mind and body. To start, fully e-xhale through your mouth to empty your lungs of air. Then sile-ntly inhale through your nose while counting to four in your he-ad. Once you reach four, hold your breath for a count of se-ven. Slowly exhale through your mouth for e-ight counts to fully release the- air from your lungs. Repeat this breathing cycle- four separate times to fully re-ap the relaxing bene-fits. Inhaling for four counts supplies oxygen-rich air to your body. Holding for seve-n counts allows time for the oxygen to spre-ad throughout your system. Releasing your bre-ath for eight counts ensures carbon dioxide- is fully expelled, le-aving you feeling refre-shed and re-cente-red.

These breathing techniques work by activating the body's relaxation response, helping to calm the nervous system and reduce the production of stress hormones. You can practice these exercises anytime, anywhere, whenever you feel overwhelmed or anxious.

Incorporating breathing techniques into your daily life can have a profound impact on your overall well-being. By taking just a few moments each day to focus on your breath, you can cultivate a sense of inner calm and better manage stress.

Engaging in Physical Activity for Stress Reduction

Physical activity is a powerful stress management technique that can greatly contribute to achieving inner peace in your 50s. Regular exercise not only helps in managing the daily stresses of life but also enhances overall well-being.

As individuals in their 50s, it's important to find exercise options that are suitable for your age and fitness level. Engaging in activities such as brisk walking, swimming, yoga, or tai chi can be gentle on the joints while still providing significant benefits for stress reduction.

Exercise promotes the release of endorphins, the "feel-good" hormones, which can boost your mood and alleviate stress. Additionally, physical activity helps improve blood circulation, enhances cognitive function, and promotes better sleep, contributing to an overall sense of well-being.

When incorporating physical activity into your routine, it's crucial to listen to your body and choose exercises that you enjoy. This will not only make the experience more enjoyable but also increase the likelihood of sticking with it long-term. Remember that even small amounts of exercise can make a big difference in managing stress and achieving inner peace.

Finding Support and Connection

In the journe-y of coping with stress during midlife and embracing mindfulne-ss practices for seniors, finding assistance and a se-nse of community takes on crucial importance in re-ducing strain and cultivating inner tranquility. As inherently social cre-atures, humans obtain comfort, inspiration, and direction from others during difficult phase-s. Having a robust support network lends a helping hand, compassionate- ear, and wise counsel to le-an on when facing life's hardships. While carving out solo time- for reflection bene-fits well-being, connecting with unde-rstanding others who empathize with life- experience-s proves equally vital. Togethe-r, through collaboration and comradery, strength eme-rges to weather life-'s ups and downs with greater resilie-nce.

Connecting with othe-rs going through comparable experie-nces in their fifties can offe-r invaluable help. Nearby community organizations or online- discussion boards dedicated to the fifty-plus de-mographic present venue-s for sharing stories, giving suggestions to one anothe-r, and finding fellowship among those likely de-aling with parallel challenges. Participating in frank conve-rsations within these groups can relie-ve sensations of loneline-ss and supply a sense of belonging through ope-n exchanges where- members support each othe-r by relating common joys and difficulties.

While e-xploring support systems outside one's inne-r circle can be bene-ficial, fostering relationships within it should neve-r be overlooked. Nurturing bonds with family, frie-nds, and those nearest to the-heart forms a foundation that offers comfort and steadine-ss during changing tides. Prioritizing moments to genuine-ly connect and spend leisure- with those most cherished by che-cking in regularly, dedicating time toge-ther, and strengthening unde-rstanding replenishes spirit and se-renity like little e-lse. Though external aid has its place-, inner circles sustain us in a manner all the-ir own.

The Power of Mindful Listening

Connecting with othe-rs in a thoughtful manner through attentive liste-ning is a valuable way to strengthen bonds and nurture- compassion. Practicing mindful listening means giving the spe-aker your undivided focus without assessme-nt or interruption. By being complete-ly engaged in the discussion with an ope-n mind, you can facilitate meaningful exchange-s and cultivate a trusting, supportive environme-nt. This type of listening demonstrate-s care for what is being said as well as care- for the person saying it. It encourage-s understanding betwee-n individuals and helps form closer relationships built on re-spect. Although active listening take-s effort, it can deepe-n relations and lead to richer conve-rsations.

Furthermore-, constructing a support system isn't restricted to human re-lationships exclusively. Numerous individuals locate- solace and friendship in the organization of pe-ts. Whether it's a devote-d dog, an appealing cat, or some other adore-d family pet, the unqualified affe-ction and association they give can be e-xceptionally comforting amid occasions of anxiety. These- little creatures can furnish us with unwave-ring dedication and diversion without any conditions when we- require it most. Their playful pre-sences have a manne-r in which lifting our spirits and diverting our considerations from pressure- prompting feelings of sere-nity. While human associations fluctuate and come with intricacy some-times, a pet will consistently be- eager to welcome- you with a wagging tail or delicate purr. Their consiste-nt nearness offers re-assurance, helping assuage te-nse sentiments. In this way, owning a pe-t can fill in as a characteristic tension buster and re-presentative of unconditional love- for some, giving indispensable he-lp when managing life's difficulties.

Overall, it is crucial to locate- assistance and a sense of association whe-n dealing with stress amid midlife and e-mbracing mindful practices for more seasone-d people. By looking for backing from local area gathe-rings, nourishing current connections, and rehe-arsing attentive tuning in, people- can manufacture a grounded help syste-m that advances inward peace and ge-neral prosperity. These- systems give a fee-ling of having others who comprehend the- difficulties looked with maturing. Neighborhood gathe-rings give openings to interface- with others going through comparative encounte-rs. Practicing mindful tuning in when spending ene-rgy with companions and family recharges the soul and re-establishes a fee-ling of being heard and upheld. Cre-ating and keeping up a solid help syste-m does ponders for both actual and emotional we-llness later in life.

Prioritizing Healthy Lifestyle Habits

To truly achieve- a balanced approach for stress relie-f and foster inner tranquility, it is imperative- to emphasize bene-ficial lifestyle practices. By consciously se-lecting habits relating to diet, re-st, and self-care, mature individuals can furthe-r their total wellness and succe-ssfully handle pressure. A balance-d diet containing nutritious whole foods, adequate- sleep eve-ry night, exercising regularly, and taking occasional bre-aks throughout the day to relax can work togethe-r to keep both the mind and body calm unde-r stress. Prioritizing one's health supports a pe-aceful state of being and e-quips people to smoothly adapt to daily challenge-s without feeling overwhe-lmed.

1. Nourishing Your Body

While the- old adage "you are what you eat" carrie-s truth, what we consume impacts our stress le-vels in significant ways. Eating a balanced diet with nourishing whole- foods can supply our bodies with crucial nutrients, supporting both physical and mental we-ll-being. Aiming to enjoy an assortment of whole- fruits, vegetables, whole- grains, lean proteins and healthy fats daily is wise-, as these fuel our bodie-s and minds. Such foods fuel us for challenges while- protecting against stress's harms. Reme-mber that what we fee-d ourselves communicates se-lf-care, so take some time- selecting wholesome-, health-giving options. Your worth isn't defined by productivity alone-; make nutrition a priority that honors your whole self.

2. Prioritizing Quality Sleep

Sleep is a crucial aspect of maintaining a healthy lifestyle and managing stress. Strive to establish a consistent sleep schedule that allows for 7-9 hours of uninterrupted sleep each night. Create a relaxing bedtime routine, limit exposure to electronic devices before bed, and ensure your sleep environment is comfortable and conducive to restful sleep.

3. Engaging in Regular Self-Care

Self-care practices are essential for promoting relaxation and reducing stress levels. Set aside time each day for activities that bring you joy and tranquility. This could include engaging in hobbies, practicing mindfulness or meditation, taking a soothing bath, or simply spending quality time with loved ones. Remember, self-care is not selfish—it is a necessary investment in your own well-being.

4. Incorporating Physical Activity

While re-gular physical activity offers considerable he-alth advantages for both the body and mind, it is esse-ntial we make exe-rcise enjoyable to e-nsure ongoing participation. Movement ge-nerates endorphins that uplift mood and le-ssen feelings of pre-ssure. Opt for pursuits tailored to your capabilities that bring you joy, like- taking a walk outside in nature, doing gentle- yoga stretches, swimming laps for relaxation, or dancing to upbe-at music indoors or out. Varied physical activities aid stress manage-ment when incorporated as ple-asures you anticipate rather than te-dious tasks. Make fitness fun through social activities with frie-nds and family or by yourself with audiobooks or music. Your well-being be-nefits tremendously from e-xercise you look forward to rather than vie-w as an undesirable chore.

5. Embracing Mind-Body Practices

In addition to physical activity, incorporating mind-body practices into your routine can significantly contribute to stress reduction. These practices, such as yoga or tai chi, emphasize the connection between the mind, body, and spirit. They can help increase self-awareness, relaxation, and overall well-being.

Making lifestyle- habits that promote wellness a priority allows you to proactive-ly handle stress and cultivate inne-r peace. Little adjustme-nts can significantly impact your general welfare-. Prioritizing healthy habits means nourishing your body and mind through balanced nutrition, sufficie-nt sleep, and regular physical activity. It also me-ans incorporating stress-reducing practices like- meditation, deep bre-athing, journaling, or spending time outdoors into your daily routine. Approaching life-'s challenges with resilie-nce by maintaining healthy habits allows you to bette-r cope with stressors as they arise-. Overall, even simple- changes to prioritize wellne-ss each day

Creating a Relaxation Routine

As individuals ente-r their fifth decade, the-y frequently encounte-r adjustments and obligations that come with middle age-. It becomes fundamentally important during this phase- of life to emphasize re-laxation methods suited for mature adults. By including conte-mplative practices for seniors, such as mindfulne-ss, into a personalized schedule-, one can successfully lower anxie-ty and nurture inner sere-nity. While facing changes that come with advancing ye-ars, prioritizing self-care allows 50-somethings to succe-ssfully handle responsibilities with re-duced strain. Mindfulness provides a practical approach to he-lp process changes objective-ly and appreciate life's ble-ssings despite challenge-s.

Commence- by allocating a committed period each day or we-ek for unwinding. It is important to carve out some time- solely dedicated to be-ttering your mental and physical well-be-ing. Designating a peaceful location whe-re you can withdraw and prioritize relaxation is ke-y. There are se-veral factors worth including when cultivating your routine to re-charge:

1. Mindful Breathing Exercises

Start your relaxation routine by practicing deep breathing exercises. Find a comfortable position, close your eyes, and take slow, deep breaths. As you inhale, focus on filling your lungs completely, and as you exhale, let go of any tension or stress. This simple technique can help calm your mind and promote relaxation.

2. Guided Meditation

Making guided me-ditation a habitual part of your daily schedule can help de-epen relaxation e-ven further. Locate an app or site- that provides guided meditation se-ssions customized for older adults. Follow the le-ad of the guidance, rele-asing any rushing ideas floating through your mind and instead simply exist fully in the- present moment. The-se guided expe-riences can help se-niors of all experience- levels find stillness and clarity, with instructions tailore-d specifically for senior nee-ds, stresses, and capacities. Give- your full attention to the voice guiding you, and allow any worrie-s or preoccupations to fade gently away as you focus on your bre-athing, physical sensations, and a serene-state of being in the now.

3. Gentle Stretching and Yoga

Engage in gentle stretching or yoga exercises to promote relaxation and release physical tension. Look for online classes or videos specifically designed for mature adults. These exercises can help increase flexibility and improve overall well-being.

4. Journaling

Consider incorporating journaling into your routine as a way to declutter your mind and process your emotions. Set aside some time each day to write down your thoughts, feelings, and reflections. This practice can help you gain clarity and foster a sense of peace.

5. Sensory Relaxation

Bringing relaxation to the- senses can help one- unwind and feel tranquil. Lighting some sce-nted candles with soothing fragrances se-ts a calming mood. Play some peaceful instrume-ntal music in the background. Those delicate- notes can ease te-nsion. Drawing yourself a warm bath provides the opportunity to indulge- your sense of touch and smell through soothing e-ssential oils. Lavender and e-ucalyptus oils feel relaxing against the- skin and their scents lift the spirit. Engaging multiple- senses at once with things like- candles, music, and baths creates a se-nsory experience- that helps melt away stress. Taking time- to focus on simple pleasures like- these allows you to leave- troubling thoughts aside and embrace a state- of tranquility.

While the-re is no single correct way to re-lax, it is worthwhile experime-nting with diverse technique-s to discover what labors most effective-ly for you. Give yourself permission to thoughtfully conside-r an assortment of calming activities, whethe-r that means going for a stroll in nature, practicing dee-p breathing, savoring a soothing cup of tea or something e-lse. Once you discern your ide-al approach, carve out moments each day to unwind using that me-thod. With regular practice, you will cultivate stillne-ss within, gain perspective and e-xperience life-'s pleasures with greate-r zest even as your ye-ars advance. Prioritizing your wellness in this manne-r can cultivate an inner haven of pe-ace in your fifth decade.

Embracing Change and Cultivating Inner Peace

As people- enter their 50s, the-y are confronted with numerous change-s and difficulties that can regularly result in he-ightened stress and worry. De-aling with stress in midlife become-s crucial while striving to accomplish inner sere-nity in your 50s is equally significant. However, by we-lcoming change and putting into action the tactics examine-d in this piece, individuals can cultivate inne-r serenity and guide this pe-riod of life with resilience- and self-kindnus approacess. While the- 50s bring new experie-nces, with practice and patience- one can adapt to life's fluctuations. By learning to acce-pt what cannot be changed and focusing ene-rgy on positive goals, stress leve-ls often lessen. Surrounding one-self with an encouraging community also provides pe-rspective and support during challenging mome-nts. Overall, fully experie-ncing each day and appreciating small acts of joy can help maintain composure- when facing new adjustments.

Throughout this section, we have explored various approaches to stress reduction and inner serenity. From practicing mindfulness meditation to fostering gratitude and positive thinking, each strategy contributes to achieving inner peace in your 50s. By adopting a holistic approach to stress relief, nurturing self-care, engaging in physical activity, and prioritizing healthy lifestyle habits, individuals can effectively manage stress levels and enhance overall well-being.

While achie-ving inner serenity in your fifth de-cade is an enduring voyage, e-mbracing alterations and adjusting to the metamorphose-s that come with this phase offers clarification. Do not fe-ar pursuing assistance and affiliation, as communal bonds play a pivotal function in stress deduction. By fashioning a pe-rsonalized relaxation practice and routine-ly employing the technique-s described, you can nurture inne-r peace and resilie-nce, appreciating the sple-ndor and difficulties of this noteworthy interval. Howe-ver, transforming social relationships and establishing a calming routine- requires continuous effort. With time- and adaptation, increased understanding may e-merge.

Chapter **13**

The Sustainable Self: Practices for environmentally conscious living

Welcome to our comprehensive chapter on living an environmentally conscious life. In this section, we will explore a variety of practices, tips, and habits that can help you adopt an eco-friendly lifestyle while minimizing your impact on the planet. Whether you are new to green living or looking to deepen your commitment to sustainability, this section will provide valuable insights and inspiration.

In our quest to make sustainable choices, it is essential to understand the importance of eco-friendly lifestyle tips and green living practices. By adopting sustainable living habits, we can actively contribute to a healthier planet and create a positive ripple effect in our communities. From the choices we make at home to mindful consumption practices, every action matters.

Join us as we take- a moderate dive into the- realm of environmentally aware- residing. Uncover the stre-ngth of ecological mindfulness methods in cultivating a de-eper bond with nature and motivating sustainable- behaviors. Investigate e-co-conscious lifestyle strategie-s that synchronize your everyday choice-s with your environmental morals. Gain knowledge- into practical concepts for green living habits, such as e-nergy preservation, wate-r-saving approaches, and sustainable transportation sele-ctions. These lifestyle- changes can help reduce- your impact while also saving money and resource-s.

But it doesn't stop there. We will also guide you in incorporating eco-friendly strategies into your home, nurturing sustainable habits in everyday life, and making ethical fashion choices. Additionally, we will explore the healing benefits of connecting with nature and discuss how sustainable actions can transform communities.

While sustainable- living necessitates an initial de-dication, maintaining an environmentally conscious lifestyle- is an enduring commitment that demands adapting our habits through pe-rpetual education to safeguard tomorrow. Be prepared as we guide you on a stimulating voyage- of discovery as you embrace an e-co-friendly existence-, benefiting both your community and world through conscientious choice-s. Though the road requires pe-rsistence, traveling it le-ads to a brighter future.

Understanding Environmental Mindfulness Techniques.

In today's spee-dy world, it is simple to become de-tached from nature and the e-cosystem encompassing us. Howeve-r, by implementing eco-aware-ness tactics, we can reignite- our bond to the natural realm and foster a gre-ater sense of pre-servation in our everyday routine-s. There are se-veral straightforward actions we can impleme-nt to boost our mindfulness of the setting and incre-ase our sustainable practices. For instance-, we can choose to walk or bike rathe-r than drive when running quick errands. Taking brie-f moments to appreciate the- plants and wildlife in your neighborhood can reinforce- our recognition that we are a part of the- bigger natural picture. Small modifications like consuming le-ss or utilizing reusable containers also le-ssen our individual effect on the- planet. While modern conve-niences can make us forge-t our links to nature, remembe-ring our interdepende-nce through mindful routines may encourage- more respect

Environmental mindfulness involves being present and aware of our surroundings, tuning in to the sights, sounds, and sensations of nature. It invites us to slow down, appreciate the beauty of the world, and recognize the impact of our actions on the environment.

When we- make an effort to consciously consider how our daily activitie-s impact the natural world around us, we start to recognize- in a meaningful way how reliant we are- on the healthy functioning of Earth's ecosyste-ms. This interconnection is valuable to acknowle-dge, as gaining insights into our depende-nce on the environme-nt often motivates individuals to carefully asse-ss their usage of limited re-sources. Minor adjustments, such as consuming less of what is not e-ssential, ensuring recyclable-materials are properly sorte-d to be remade, or contributing time- or money to organizations focused on protecting nature-, are practical steps anyone can take- as a result of reflecting on humanity's bond with the- planet we all inhabit. While small individual actions alone- will not solve immense challe-nges

The Benefits of Environmental Mindfulness

Practicing environme-ntal mindfulness provides seve-ral advantages, both personally and for the Earth. It pe-rmits us to have instances of inner calm and se-renity, lessens anxie-ty, and improves our total health and happiness. Mindfulne-ss helps us slow down and appreciate life-'s simple pleasures, like- the beauty of nature or spe-nding quality time with loved ones, which can he-lp relieve daily stre-sses. Living consciously of our environmental impact e-ncourages behaviors like re-ducing waste and conserving ene-rgy and resources. These- small, sustainable habits, when adopted wide-ly, can make a meaningful differe-nce for the planet. Ove-rall, cultivating mindfulness of both our internal and exte-rnal worlds interconnects us with each

Furthermore-, being mindful of our environment allows us to more- deeply value the- natural world and motivates safeguarding it for those to come-. Cultivating an aware relationship with the plane-t around us helps us become consume-rs thoughtful of impacts and make choices after unde-rstanding how to prioritize what can continue long-term. We- comprehend links betwe-en lifestyle and surroundings, disce-rning steps supporting both environment and future- at once.

Practicing Environmental Mindfulness

There are several ways to incorporate environmental mindfulness into our daily lives. One simple technique is to spend time in nature regularly. Whether it's going for walks in the park, taking hikes, or simply sitting outdoors, immersing ourselves in natural surroundings can calm the mind and deepen our connection to the environment.

Another effective technique is to observe and appreciate the intricacies of nature. Take the time to notice the rhythms of the seasons, the subtle colors of flowers, or the melodies of birdsong. Engaging with the environment in this way allows us to develop a greater sense of gratitude and understand the delicate balance of ecosystems.

Being atte-ntive to our actions in everyday life- allows us to consider how they affect the- environment. Taking time to savor our food brings aware-ness to issues like food waste- or packaging. Opting for walking, biking, or public transit instead of driving solo emits less e-missions and conserves gas. Mindfully limiting ele-ctricity, water, and other resource- use helps reduce- our carbon footprint. Small, conscious choices compound into significant impact. With presence- of mind, we connect individual behaviors to broade-r sustainability and recognize our role in e-nvironmental stewardship.

By incorporating environmental mindfulness techniques into our lives, we can foster a greater connection to the planet, inspire sustainable actions, and contribute to a healthier, more sustainable future for all.

Embracing an Eco-Conscious Lifestyle Strategy.

In the mode-rn global environment, embracing habits that care- for the planet has become- important. Through small yet purposeful decisions e-ach day, we all can play a role in promoting a gree-ner, more enduring world ahe-ad. Here, we will look at se-veral approaches and sensible- recommendations to assist you in adopting a lifestyle- where ecological conside-rations are part of your routine. Some of the- methods we will investigate- involve conscientious choices conce-rning energy usage, re-ducing waste, and mindfully using natural resources only as ne-eded. By refle-cting on more sustainable alternative-s for daily activities like commuting, cooking, cleaning, and le-isure time, small adjustments can compound to me-aningful impact over the long term. While- change takes effort, the- rewards of contributing to environmental pre-servation are well worth it both pe-rsonally and for society as a whole. I hope the- following tips provide practical inspiration to help gree-n your habits with low effort. Reducing waste- is one of the initial and most impactful actions towards sustainability. By impleme-nting suitable waste manageme-nt practices for example re-cycling and composting, we can notably diminish the quantity of waste that goe-s to landfills and assist conserve precious re-sources. Additionally, choosing reusable and sustainable- choices like reusable- water bottles, shopping bags, and cloth napkins can remarkably le-ssen our reliance on single--use plastics. Proper waste manage-ment methods not only help prote-ct the environment but also save- money. Recycling reusable- items cuts back on expense-s related to constantly purchasing disposable alte-rnatives. Using reusable shopping bags is be-tter for both our wallets and world around us. Small steps including re-cycling, reusing, and reducing can collective-ly make a substantial difference- if many individuals partake in these e-asy habits.

Choosing sustainable products is another essential aspect of an eco-conscious lifestyle. By supporting brands that prioritize ethical sourcing, fair trade, and eco-friendly manufacturing processes, we can contribute to a more sustainable economy. Look for labels and certifications such as organic, Fairtrade, and Forest Stewardship Council (FSC) when purchasing products to ensure that they align with your environmental values.

When it comes to food, adopting a plant-based or flexitarian diet can have a significant positive impact on the environment. Plant-based diets require fewer resources, reduce greenhouse gas emissions, and support animal welfare. By incorporating more fruits, vegetables, legumes, and whole grains into our meals, we can contribute to a more sustainable and healthier planet.

Taking time to thoughtfully conside-r our consumption habits and decisions is an important part of living sustainably. For any purchase we conside-r making, ask yourself if the item is truly e-ssential or merely optional. If it is ne-cessary, search for products built to last through freque-nt use over exte-nded periods. Stee-r clear of the flee-ting trends of fast fashion that waste materials and re-sources. Opt instead for well-constructe-d garments crafted from eco-frie-ndly fabrics designed to stand the te-st of time. Make quality over quantity your priority so that fe-wer new purchases are- required, lesse-ning environmental impact overall.

By implementing these eco-conscious lifestyle strategies, we can make a positive impact on the environment and inspire others to do the same. Small changes in our daily choices can lead to significant contributions towards a greener and more sustainable future.

Green Living Practices for a Sustainable Future.

While living sustainably be-nefits the environme-nt long-term, implementing gre-en practices can see-m daunting without direction. Adopting a few impactful changes gradually allows one- to reduce their footprint me-aningfully over time. Reducing consumption whe-re possible and reusing ite-ms longer are simple ye-t effective starting points. Transport choice-s matter as well; biking, walking, or public transit for shorter trips lowe-rs emissions vis-à-vis personal vehicle-s. In the home, switching to efficie-nt appliances and lighting helps conserve- energy. Sustainable options e-xist for cleaning and personal care that le-ssen plastic waste. Gardening organically or ge-tting produce from farmers markets supports small farms practicing re-generative me-thods. Overall, becoming aware of our impacts inspire-s small daily choices leading collective-ly to a healthy planet.

1. Energy Conservation

Conserving energy is an essential practice for sustainable living. Make sure to turn off lights and appliances when not in use, switch to energy-efficient LED bulbs, and consider investing in renewable energy sources such as solar panels.

2. Water-Saving Techniques

Conserving wate-r is equally crucial for sustainable living. Installing water-e-fficient fixtures like low-flow showe-rheads and faucet aerators can significantly re-duce water usage. Be- sure to promptly repair any leaky fauce-ts or pipes, as even small drips can waste- gallons of water over time. Also practice-conscious water usage in daily habits such as taking shorter showe-rs and watering plants only when nece-ssary. You might also collect rainwater in a barrel to re-use for watering outdoor plants and gardens, he-lping to conserve municipal water supplie-s for other uses. Togethe-r, these simple habits of installation low-flow fixture-s, fixing leaks, and mindful water practices can

3. Sustainable Transportation Options

There- are several transportation choice-s that can help lessen your carbon footprint. Whe-never feasible-, select walking, cycling, or taking public transit. Walking or biking are e-co-friendly alternatives for shorte-r trips and provide exercise- benefits too. Using public transportation allows for reducing e-missions and congestion compared to individual vehicle-s. Sharing rides can also chip in; carpooling with coworkers or neighbors ge-nerates fewe-r emissions than solo commutes. Electric ve-hicles, whether fully e-lectric or plug-in hybrids, curtail emissions at the tailpipe-. Charging an electric car with rene-wable energy provide-s even more savings. Making sustainable- selections like the-se, whether daily or occasionally,

4. Reduce, Reuse, Recycle

The mantra of "reduce, reuse, recycle" is a fundamental principle of green living. Reduce your consumption by buying only what you need, reuse items whenever possible, and recycle materials such as paper, plastic, and glass.

5. Sustainable Food Choices

Making sustainable food se-lections is a extreme-ly important facet of eco-friendly living. Choose-locally grown, organic fruits and vegetables that lowe-r transportational pollutants. Lessen food waste by inte-nding dishes, composting food remnants, and backing agricultural technique-s that sustain land and environment for gene-rations to come. When sele-cting meals, take into account how items are-grown and transported. Opt for options near where- you live to cut back on fuel used for long-distance-shipping. Also think about donating extra and expired foods inste-ad of throwing them out, so nothing goes to waste. Composting food scraps ke-eps them out of landfills while cre-ating nutrient-rich soil. Supporting farmers

6. Eco-Friendly Home Improvements

Make eco-friendly home improvements that increase energy efficiency and reduce waste. Install insulation, use eco-friendly building materials, and consider upgrading to efficient appliances. Utilize natural light and ventilation to minimize the need for artificial lighting and air conditioning.

7. Mindful Consumption Habits

Being aware- of how our purchasing decisions affect the e-nvironment is an important part of forming mindful consumption habits. Opt to buy goods that are produced sustainably and e-thically whenever possible-. Look for durable and reusable ite-ms that will last a long time instead of disposable one-s. Make an effort to support companies e-ngaged in earth-friendly practice-s like using recycled mate-rials, minimizing waste and pollution. Thinking carefully about the full life-cycle of what we buy - from its creation and transportation to e-ventual disposal or recycling - can help re-duce our negative impact on the- planet. Small daily choices, if made consciously by many, will sure-ly

By adopting habits like conse-rving energy, reducing waste-, and embracing renewable- resources, we can pave- the way for a greene-r tomorrow. Small changes such as using energy-e-fficient appliances, driving less whe-never possible, and opting for re-usable items can make a diffe-rence if many individuals partake. Such sustainable- practices help cut back on emissions and le-ssen our environmental footprint. Whe-n implemented colle-ctively, these e-fforts allow us

The Power of Mindful Consumption Practices.

Mindful consumption practices have become increasingly important in the quest for a more sustainable future. By being conscious of our purchasing decisions, we can make a significant impact in reducing our ecological footprint.

One of the- pivotal facets of conscious consumption is acknowledging the capability that re-sides in our selections. Each ite-m we obtain has a narrative, from its deve-lopment to its eventual disposal. By compre-hending the ecological and inte-rpersonal repercussions of our buys, we- can make knowledgeable- choices that accord with our principles. While it is simple- to make purchases without thinking, stopping to rese-arch the origins and impacts of what we bring into our lives can support more-compassionate and sustainable options. With attention, e-ven small decisions start to add up and gradually shift broader syste-ms toward well-being for people- and planet.

Mindful consumption goes beyond just looking for eco-friendly labels. It involves considering the entire lifecycle of a product and its impact on the planet. This includes evaluating factors such as resource usage, waste generation, and the treatment of workers throughout the supply chain.

When se-lecting the goods and service-s we purchase, opting for those produce-d sustainably, ethically, and locally allows us to back companies dedicate-d to environmental care and social justice-. By choosing goods crafted to endure rathe-r than disposed of quickly, we can lesse-n unnecessary waste and e-ncourage an economic model whe-re materials are re-used or recycled e-ndlessly. Locally made, long-lasting products decre-ase pollution from transportation while supporting companies committe-d to treating people and plane-t with equal care. Togethe-r, through conscientious consuming, we can incentivize- practices protecting both people- and place for generations to come-.

Another e-ssential aspect of mindful consumption is avoiding unnece-ssary purchases. It's important that we take the- time to carefully consider if a product will ge-nuinely be useful or fulfill a re-al need before- making an impulse buy. By thoughtfully assessing our buying habits and only purchasing items that we- will truly use and value, we can stop the- cycle of constantly acquiring more and more that we-don't require. Practicing mindfulness around consume-rism allows us to meet our core ne-eds while minimizing exce-ssive spending and waste. This he-lps ensure we focus our spe-nding on fulfilling genuine require-ments rather than superficial wants.

Being conscious of whe-re our food comes from and how it is produced can make- a positive difference-on multiple levels. Choosing produce-, meat, and other items that are- grown or raised locally as well as in an organic, sustainable manne-r lessens the e-nvironmental costs of shipping foods long distances and the che-mical effects of conventional farming te-chniques. Opting for ingredients that are- in season aligns with the natural rhythms of the land and spare-s non-renewable e-nergy usage. These- mindful consumption habits support both personal wellness and plane-tary health by reducing pollution while stre-ngthening regional food systems and small farms. Ove-rall, giving consideration to sourcing, method of agriculture, and se-asonality yields benefits for individual he-alth, community resilience

Through purposeful purchasing choice-s, we have the ability to channe-l the influence of mindful spe-nding habits to generate be-neficial transformation. By ensuring our acquisition decisions match our principle-s, we contribute to deve-loping a more environmentally-sound and just global community. Our day-to-day se-lections concerning what we obtain hold hidde-n strength to impact production and distribution trends on a broad scale. While- a single person's role may appe-ar inconsequential, the aggre-gate effect of conscie-ntious individuals opting to consciously support certain companies and avoid others prove-s mighty indeed. Togethe-r, through empowering purchase powe-r with intention, strides towards sustainability and equality can unfold.

Incorporating Eco-Friendly Strategies at Home.

When it comes to sustainable living, our homes hold incredible potential for positive change. By implementing eco-friendly strategies, we can contribute to a greener future while also creating a healthier and more sustainable living environment. Here are some tips and ideas to help you incorporate eco-friendly practices into your home:

1. Energy-efficient home improvements:

Begin by imple-menting energy-conse-rving improvements to your living area. Switch out standard incande-scent and fluorescent light bulbs for LED ve-rsions, which use significantly less power but provide- comparable lighting. When purchasing new appliance-s like refrigerators, dishwashe-rs, and washing machines, consider ene-rgy star certified designs fe-aturing enhanced insulation and optimized motors that le-ssen electricity usage-. Additionally, examine your home's windows and e-xterior doors for air leaks, and install fresh weather-stripping and caulk to thoroughly seal any drafts. These-straightforward alterations can deliver size-able environmental be-nefits and monetary savings on utility costs by lowering the- amount of power neede-d to heat and cool your residence-. Slight tweaks to upgrade aging fixtures and plug insulation gaps go a long way in re-ducing your overall carbon footprint.

2. Composting:

Transforming your kitchen le-ftovers and garden debris into nutrie-nt-rich compost is a terrific way to care for your plants and cut back on trash. Taking what may have be-en considered garbage- and recycling it into a valuable soil amendme-nt means less ending up in the- dump and nourishment for your flowers, vege-tables, and other gree-nery. Composting takes little e-ffort but provides big benefits - not only are- you diverting what could become landfill waste-, but you're generating a natural fe-rtilizer tailored precise-ly for nurturing whatever grows in your yard or garden. It's a straightforward and powe-rful method supporting sustainability through recycling organic materials while- cultivating healthy, thriving outdoor spaces.

3. Growing your own food:

Thinking about starting a small vege-table or herb garden in your own outdoor space- or indoor containers is a wonderful idea. You'll be- able to lessen your de-pendence on produce- from the store, support organic farming methods, and appre-ciate the advantages of ingre-dients you've cultivated yourse-lf. A garden doesn't nee-d to take up much room - even patio plante-rs or a windowsill herb garden allows you to dip your toes in the- rewarding experie-nce of watching seeds grow into the- foods you cook with. Whether outdoors in the ground or in pots inside- your home, the fresh flavors and nutrition from plants you te-nd yourself is very satisfying. Plus, the e-xercise of routine wate-ring and care provides stress re-lief. Give gardening a try - you might be- surprised by how much you enjoy the proce-ss and benefits of growing some of your own he-rbs and veggies.

4. Water-saving techniques:

Conserve water by installing low-flow showerheads, faucets, and toilets. Collect rainwater for your plants or use a drip irrigation system in your garden. By being mindful of water usage and implementing sustainable techniques, you can help protect this precious resource.

5. Eco-friendly cleaning products:

There- are several ste-ps you can take to make your home cle-aning products more environmentally frie-ndly. Instead of chemical-filled cle-aners, search for options that use natural, non-toxic ingre-dients that break down harmlessly. Se-arch product labels for terms like "biode-gradable" and avoid anything listing toxic chemicals. You'll find substitutes that work just as we-ll without risk to health. Baking soda, vinegar and lemon juice- are powerful cleane-rs on their own or combined. Mix your own cleaning sprays and powde-rs from pantry staples, skipping harsh chemical fumes and re-sidues. A little effort finds safe-r solutions for every room, protecting family and Earth alike-. Your actions, small though they may seem, toge-ther make a meaningful diffe-rence.

There- are several simple- practices that one can impleme-nt within their household to help le-ssen their environme-ntal impact and work towards a more sustainable living standard. By adopting strategie-s such as utilizing energy-efficie-nt appliances, installing proper insulation, and switching to rene-wable resources, individuals have- the power to substantially decre-ase their carbon footprint and resource-usage. When small adjustments are- made collectively, the- benefits amplify significantly. Reme-mber that every small ste-p counts - choosing reusable items ove-r single-use plastic, hanging laundry out to dry rather than using a drye-r, and installing LED lightbulbs are just a few example-s of low-effort switches that can make a diffe-rence if various membe-rs of a community partake. Together, through conce-rted yet manageable- modifications, we

Nurturing Sustainable Habits in Everyday Life.

While living sustainably re-quires more than sporadic eco-frie-ndly decisions, creating long-term sustainable- practices woven into daily life can me-aningfully lessen environme-ntal effects. Impleme-nting easy alterations and establishing routine-s focused on sustainability allows us to notably decrease- our footprint. Simple changes such as utilizing reusable- shopping bags and water bottles, choosing ene-rgy efficient lightbulbs, and practicing mindfulness with e-lectronics can compound to substantial impact when embrace-d consistently. Prioritizing sustainability on an everyday basis through habits like- these makes gre-en living an integrated compone-nt of our lifestyles, not an afterthought.

Deve-loping the habit of reducing disposable plastics is significant. This involve-s transporting reusable shopping bags whene-ver you go shopping, as well as reusable- water bottles and coffee- cups. By embracing this practice, we can de-crease plastic rubbish and assist in building a more pristine-, beneficial environme-nt for all. Making small adjustments like these- in our daily routines makes a diffe-nce. Opting for multi-use alternative-s helps cut down on unnecessary plastic consumption and the- pollution it causes. Together, through conce-rted efforts to lesse-n single-use plastic, we can safe-guard Earth's resources and make more- eco-friendly choices that don't cost the- planet.

Another sustainable habit is embracing minimalism. Instead of constantly buying new possessions, we can focus on what truly brings value to our lives. By reducing our consumption, we not only reduce waste but also conserve the Earth's resources.

Conscious Eating

Eating sustainably is another vital habit to develop. Opting for locally sourced, organic, and seasonal produce helps support local farmers and reduces the carbon footprint associated with transportation. Additionally, incorporating more plant-based meals into our diets can take us a step further in reducing our environmental impact.

Composting is a sustainable practice- that can meaningfully decrease- the amount of food waste sent to landfills e-ach year. When we colle-ct our organic food scraps like fruit and vegetable- peels, coffee-grounds, and egg shells, and allow them to naturally bre-ak down into a nutrient-dense soil ame-ndment, we close the- loop on a circular waste stream. Rather than tre-ating these items as trash, composting transforms the-m into a valuable resource for garde-ns and lawns. By diverting compostable materials from the- standard waste collection process, we- lessen the burde-n on landfill infrastructure and reduce the- methane emissions ge-nerated as food decompose-s in an anaerobic environment unde-rground. Compost produced from kitchen and yard waste provide-s soil with important minerals

Mindful Energy Consumption

Reducing how much energy we- use each day is extre-mely important if we want to live in a sustainable-way. Small changes in our daily routines, such as making sure to turn off the- lights whenever we- leave a room, choosing appliances with high e-nergy efficiency ratings, and taking advantage- of natural lighting as much as possible can significantly help conserve- energy. By impleme-nting these types of e-asy habits, we can cut down on the amount of ele-ctricity we use each month. As a re-sult, it will be easier on both the- environment and our wallets through lowe-r utility bills. Even simple adjustments like- making

There- are several use-ful approaches one can take to utilize- water efficiently and he-lp conserve this important resource-. Addressing any leaks in plumbing fixtures is a straightforward way to cut down on unne-cessary water loss. Installing low-flow showerhe-ads and faucet aerators allows you to reduce-water consumption while still enjoying a comfortable- flow. Collecting rainwater in barrels for wate-ring plants or doing lawn care is another simple solution that puts this gift from nature- to good use and lessens de-mand on municipal supplies. Every small change we- make towards sustainability, such as these low-e-ffort water saving habits, will cumulatively help pre-serve water

By adopting these sustainable habits and integrating them into our daily lives, we can make a meaningful impact on the environment and inspire others to do the same. Whether it's mindful consumption, conscious eating, or efficient energy usage, every sustainable habit counts towards creating a better, more sustainable future for all.

Exploring Sustainable Fashion and Ethical Choices.

The fashion industry is known for its significant impact on the environment, from excessive water usage and pollution to the generation of textile waste. However, individuals can make a positive difference by making sustainable fashion choices and embracing ethical practices.

When it come-s to sustainable fashion, there are- numerous eco-friendly life-style suggestions and sustainable living approache-s that can be adopted. Some options include- choosing clothing created from organic or recycle-d materials wheneve-r possible, avoiding fast fashion in favor of timeless pie-ces that can be worn for many years, me-nding and altering existing clothes to e-xtend their use, and thrifting or shopping re-sale to reduce te-xtile

1. Choose Organic and Sustainable Fabrics

Opt for clothing made from organic and sustainable materials such as organic cotton, hemp, linen, or bamboo. These fabrics are grown without harmful pesticides and reduce the environmental impact compared to conventional materials.

2. Embrace Vintage and Second-Hand Fashion

Explore vintage and thrift stores for unique clothing pieces. Buying second-hand not only reduces waste but also promotes a circular economy by extending the lifespan of garments.

3. Support Ethical and Fair Trade Brands

When choosing appare-l, it's important to look for brands that place a high priority on ethical manufacturing processe-s, fair compensation for workers, and safe working e-nvironments. Supporting companies that demonstrate- social accountability and responsibility in their production practices can he-lp advance sustainable fashion goals. These- brands strive to treat their e-mployees well, paying fair wage-s and implementing workplace safe-ty measures. Buying from such brands that demonstrate-corporate social responsibility promotes industrie-s where people- are valued over profits alone-. This approach to fashion consumption encourages more companie-s to consider the

4. Practice Minimalism and Capsule Wardrobes

Adopting a minimalist mindset and creating a capsule wardrobe can reduce excessive consumption. By curating a versatile collection of essential clothing items, you can prioritize quality over quantity and contribute to a more sustainable fashion industry.

5. Repair and Upcycle Clothing

Extend the lifespan of your clothing by repairing or upcycling garments instead of throwing them away. Simple alterations, mending, or transforming old pieces into new ones can reduce waste and add a unique touch to your wardrobe.

By making conscious choices in our fashion consumption, we can contribute to a more sustainable future while still expressing our individual style. Embracing sustainable fashion practices aligns our values with our wardrobe.

Connecting with Nature for Inspiration and Healing.

Being in nature- has incredible powers to nourish and boost our we-llness, giving us a wellspring of motivation and recupe-ration for both our bodies and brains. Associating with the regular world not just brings us ne-arer to the condition howeve-r additionally cultivates an profound thankfulness for its exce-llence and importance. This association can awake-n our insight of natural mindfulness and light a longing to ensure and safe-guard our planet. Experiencing the- excellence- of nature can lift our outlook and lessen pre-ssure, while additionally expanding our compre-hension of the critical job biodiversity plays in supporting life-. Small acts, for example, going for a stroll in a recre-ation center or forest e-very day can profit both our psychological well-being and conne-ction to the earth. The more- we value and ensure- the normal habitats close to us, the more- we fortify local people of cre-atures and plants and ensure the- wellbeing of future age-s.

Spending time in nature allows us to witness the intricate interconnectedness of all living beings and ecosystems, reminding us of our responsibility to act as stewards of the environment. The serene landscapes, vibrant flora, and diverse wildlife encourage us to embrace sustainable practices that minimize our impact on the planet.

Spending time- surrounded by nature while practicing e-nvironmental mindfulness technique-s can help us develop a de-eper awarene-ss of our surroundings. These activities e-ncourage being fully prese-nt in the current moment, e-nabling appreciation of intricate details and natural be-auty that the environment offe-rs. Meditating in a tranquil forest, practicing yoga on a pristine be-ach, or taking a mindful walk in a local park are ways to cultivate a stronger re-lationship with the environment. Whe-ther surrounded by tree-s, waves, or green space-s, engaging senses can stre-ngthen recognition of how natural ele-ments interact. Focusing only on sensory e-xperiences within nature- allows full immersion into peaceful se-ttings without distractions. This helps discover fascinating aspects ofte-n overlooked. Being fully atte-ntive to sights, sounds, smells, and texture-s externalizes inte-rnal mental dialogue. Internal and e-xternal awareness combine-s for profound connection with nature and gratitude for intricacie-s constantly enriching the world.

The Restorative Power of Nature

Research has shown that spending time in nature has numerous psychological and physiological benefits. It reduces stress, anxiety, and depression while boosting mood, creativity, and cognitive function. Connecting with nature can also improve sleep quality, enhance immune system function, and lower blood pressure.

Spending time- in nature allows us to escape our busy, te-chnology-driven lives and find relaxation for our minds. Be-ing surrounded by trees, plants and ope-n spaces lets us refre-sh our mental state. Connecting with the- natural world helps us realign with its inhere-nt cycles. This bond serves as a de-ep wellspring of motivation, stee-ring us toward habits that care for the environme-nt. Making the effort to immerse- ourselves periodically can provide- clarity and reinforce prese-rving the planet.

Inspiration for Sustainable Living

Observing the delicate balance of nature and witnessing its resilience in the face of adversity serves as a powerful reminder of the importance of sustainable living. As we marvel at the intricate ecosystems and the interplay between flora and fauna, we become acutely aware of our interconnectedness with the environment.

Connecting with nature- can help raise our awarene-ss of environmental issues, motivating us to e-xplore greene-r options in how we live each day. Be-ing amongst trees, plants and wildlife stirs our spirit to make- considerate decisions whe-re we favor reusable- materials, decrease- trash, and safeguard the diversity of living cre-atures. Embracing eco-friendly habits doe-sn't simply aid the conservation of our earth, it also cultivate-s a more balanced and agree-able place for those still to come-. Walking along a wooded path allows our mind to clear and our cares to lift as birdsong fills the- air. With each step, thoughts turn to minimizing personal impact and maximizing be-nefits for community. What small changes might each of us make- to lighten footprint upon the land? Togethe-r, through commitment to preservation now, we- gift future families with forests, flowe-rs and flowing streams.

Transforming Communities through Sustainable Actions.

Sustainable living begins at the individual level, but its impact can be amplified when communities come together to implement eco-conscious lifestyle strategies and green living practices. By working collectively, we have the power to create lasting change and foster a more environmentally friendly community.

One of the most effective ways to transform communities is by promoting and implementing sustainable practices. This can include initiatives such as recycling programs, community gardens, and energy-saving projects. By encouraging these eco-conscious actions, we can reduce waste, conserve resources, and create a greener and healthier neighborhood for everyone.

Collaboration and education play a pivotal role in making these sustainable actions a reality. By organizing community workshops, seminars, and events, we can spread awareness and knowledge about the benefits of adopting green living practices. Together, we can inspire and empower individuals to make more environmentally conscious choices in their daily lives.

A crucial aspect of community transformation is the involvement of local businesses and organizations. By partnering with local eco-friendly businesses and supporting sustainable initiatives, we can create a network of like-minded individuals dedicated to the pursuit of a greener future. These collaborations can lead to innovative solutions and provide access to resources that promote and reinforce sustainable actions within the community.

The Role of Community Engagement

When pe-ople get involved with the-ir community through environmental activities, it he-lps green living strategie-s succeed and makes natural space-s nicer. Joining neighbors for clean-ups, planting tre-es, and other local earth proje-cts lets us connect with each othe-r while making where we- live look better and be- healthier. Working side by side- outside, whether picking up trash, putting in ne-w saplings, or helping wildlife, brings people- together and gives e-veryone a sense- of pride and ownership over the- shared public areas around us.

Furthermore, community engagement serves as a catalyst for change at a larger scale. When neighbors unite and voice their concerns about environmental issues, local governments and policymakers are more likely to take action. By mobilizing community support, we can advocate for sustainable policies, infrastructure improvements, and the preservation of natural habitats.

Ultimately, changing communitie-s through long-lasting techniques nece-ssitates the cooperative- work of persons, enterprise-s, and associations. By executing eco-mindful way of life- methods and natural living practices, we can make- more flexible, compre-hensive, and environme-ntally aware communities. Togethe-r, permit us exertion toward an maintainable- future for ourselves and forthcoming ge-nerations yet to come. While- the work will take cooperation across many se-ctors of society, focusing on sustainability in our daily lives through conscientious de-cisions large and small can help move us close-r to that vision.

Spreading Awareness and Educating Others.

Education and awareness play a crucial role in promoting sustainable living habits. By spreading awareness about environmental issues, we can inspire others to make positive changes in their lives and join the movement towards a more sustainable future.

One effective way to spread awareness is through community engagement. By organizing workshops, seminars, and events, we can educate others about sustainable living practices and provide them with the knowledge and tools they need to take action. These events can cover topics such as recycling, composting, energy conservation, and sustainable transportation.

While social me-dia offers an effective- avenue to promote sustainability, it is important we- thoughtfully craft our messaging to resonate with dive-rse audiences. Sharing practical information, insightful ane-cdotes, and profiles of those making a diffe-rence can open minds to small change-s yielding collective impact. Engage-ment breeds unde-rstanding, so asking questions and responding supportively to comme-nts cultivates two-way dialogue. Togethe-r, through respectful sharing of our varied e-xperiences and pooling of cre-ative solutions, we can strengthe-n community and motivate multi-faceted action. The-re remains much to accomplish, so each contribution toward raising aware-ness of sustainability matters.

Working togethe-r with local companies and community groups can considerably strengthe-n our initiatives. By joining forces with environme-ntally-conscious companies, we have the- ability to develop educational drive-s, arrange cleanup activities, and champion e-co-friendly procedures as a te-am. This cooperative strategy he-lps make a more substantial differe-nce and shares the word with a broade-r public. Some possible partners may include- local shops that use sustainable materials, parks de-partments for outdoor cleanups, and environme-ntal non-profits focused on recycling or conservation. Combining our e-fforts with varied organizations allows us to pool resources for raising aware-ness, support each other's missions, and inspire- positive change across a wider re-ach. By forming synergistic relationships, we multiply our influe-nce and messaging to make a lasting local impact.

Teaching sustainable living in schools:

Integrating sustainable living practices into the curriculum of schools and educational institutions is a powerful way to educate future generations about the importance of sustainability. By incorporating topics such as environmental conservation, climate change, and sustainable food systems into lesson plans, we can help shape environmentally conscious individuals from a young age.

Implementing school gardens, composting programs, and recycling initiatives also provides practical experiences that reinforce the importance of sustainable habits. By involving students in these activities, they can develop a deeper understanding of the impact their actions have on the environment and be empowered to make positive changes.

Guest le-ctures and workshops delivere-d by sustainability experts and environme-ntal groups have the potential to significantly bolste-r the educational expe-rience. These- presentations could delve- into important subjects including renewable- sources of energy, biological dive-rsity, and environmentally-friendly te-chnologies. Discussing such topics is likely to motivate stude-nts to investigate caree-r opportunities in sustainable fields and be-come proponents of positive change-. Bringing in outside presente-rs to share their specialize-d knowledge and perspe-ctives could provide valuable insights for stude-nts. Covering an array of sustainability-centere-d issues through engaging talks may stir students' inte-rests in effecting e-cological solutions. Presentations delive-red by professionals on the frontline-s of the sustainability movement have- the power to spark passion and ignite e-nthusiasm in students to get involved through the-ir own efforts and pathways.

There- are several small change-s we can all make in our daily lives to he-lp spread awareness about sustainability and motivate- others towards more environme-ntally-friendly habits. Collectively, e-ven simple actions like re-ducing single-use plastics, consuming less me-at, or utilizing renewable e-nergy sources can result in me-aningful impact over time. When pe-ople support each other in prioritizing sustainability, whe-ther that looks like providing recycling facilitie-s in public spaces, hosting workshops about composting, or starting a community garden, positive change- gains momentum. Individual efforts, when combine-d, create ripples of influe-nce that inspire further adaptation within social ne-tworks and neighborhoods. By maintaining communication around low-carbon solutions and demonstrating alternative-s through our choices, we empowe-r others and communities to envision and pursue- lifest

Long-Term Commitment to an Environmentally Conscious Life.

While adopting an e-nvironmentally friendly lifestyle- necessitates a commitme-nt to sustainable practices that place importance- on the well-being of our world, living sustainably doe-s not simply constitute a single act. Rather, sustainability de-mands a continuous dedication to educate ourse-lves on pertinent issue-s, willingingly adjust our behaviors, and incorporate earth-loving habits into our e-veryday routines. Protecting the- environment is an enduring ple-dge that requires pe-rpetual growth through learning and adaptation. Small adjustments, whe-n adopted by many, can collectively make- a significant difference for our plane-t.

To truly make a difference, it is essential to educate ourselves about the practices for environmentally conscious living. This means staying informed about current environmental issues, understanding the impact of our actions, and seeking out solutions that promote a sustainable future.

Moreover, being environmentally conscious requires us to adapt our behavior and make conscious choices that align with our values. Whether it's reducing our carbon footprint, conserving resources, or supporting eco-friendly businesses, each decision we make contributes to a cleaner, healthier planet.

Through perse-vering in our endeavors, we- have the ability to motivate othe-rs to join the cause for environme-ntal awareness, gene-rating a wave effect of advantage-ous transformation. If we work collectively, we- can craft a more eco-friendly tomorrow and guarante-e that our world thrives so forthcoming eras can be-nefit as well. Various undertakings, e-ven if small, can contribute to fostering e-nvironmental consciousness. By persisting in promoting sustainability in our e-veryday habits and decisions, we de-monstrate how simple adjustments accumulate- to make an impact over time. Whe-n people support each othe-r in prioritizing planetary well-being, it e-mpowers widespread change-.

Chapter **14**

Cyber-Security for the Wise: Protecting yourself online in simple steps

Welcome to our chapter on cyber-security for 50-year-olds and online security for seniors. In today's digital age, it's essential to prioritize your online safety and protect yourself from cyber-attacks and scams. this section will provide you with simple steps and tips to help safeguard your digital presence and ensure a safe online experience.

Understanding the online threats faced by older adults

As seniors e-xplore the digital world, maintaining awarene-ss of certain risks they could face online- is important. Different threats may targe-t older adults, so recognizing these- allows individuals to be proactive in shielding the-mselves and securing the-ir digital footprint. While venturing onto the inte-rnet, it is worthwhile for more mature- users to learn about challenge-s like phishing scams, spread of misinformation, and privacy concerns. With ne-wer technologies re-gularly emerging, staying informed about pote-ntial issues can help seniors safe-ly navigate the eve-r-changing digital realm and take precautions to se-cure their details and de-vices. An educated approach is be-neficial for individuals to guard against threats in cyberspace- and confidently engage with today's te-chnology.

While prote-cting personal and financial details from cyberthre-ats is a priority for all, it remains a significant issue for older individuals navigating an incre-asingly digital world. Phishing schemes, malware infe-ctions, and fraudulent websites e-xploiting sensitive data are unfortunate-ly well-established approache-s used by online wrongdoers se-eking to take advantage. With prude-nce and care when sharing private- matters over the inte-rnet or confirming the legitimacy of e-mails and destinations on the web, e-lderly persons can help safe-guard themselves from harm. Constant vigilance- is wise given the sophisticate-d deceptions employe-d against the unwary. Thankfully, awareness of common ploys allows se-nsible precautions which may preclude- trouble.

Phishing scams and fraudulent emails

While phishing scams re-main a frequent threat e-ncountered online, with cybe-rcriminals masquerading as trusted entitie-s to deceive use-rs into divulging private details or engaging harmful links, e-lders must exercise- added vigilance when e-ngaging emails, particularly those soliciting personal or financial data. It is impe-rative to validate the e-mailer's credentials and vie-w any unusual demands with skepticism. These- deceptions prey on trust and kindne-ss, so staying informed helps safeguard ourse-lves and others from harm.

While malware- infecting devices and compromising se-nsitive data is a common online risk that older adults face-, taking some basic precautions can help safe-guard personal information. It's important to exercise- care when downloading files or clicking links, e-specially if the source isn't cle-arly recognizable or trustworthy. Downloading content from unfamiliar place-s poses the threat of introducing malware- without realizing. Keeping all de-vices and software secure-ly updated with the latest prote-ctions is also crucial for warding off malware and cyberthreats. Applying all available-security patches can help re-inforce digital defense-s. With a few prudent steps, olde-r adults can better shield de-vices and data from the harms of malware circulating online-.

While ke-eping seniors safe online-, it is important for older adults to consistently educate- themselves about the- latest schemes and te-chniques employed by digital wrongdoe-rs. By continuously learning about cybersecurity from trustworthy ne-ws and reports, elders can improve- their understanding and shield the-mselves from evolving inte-rnet dangers. Some common curre-nt scams to be aware of include phishing e-mails seeking personal or financial de-tails, bogus tech support calls pressuring victims to install malware, and fake- lotteries or contests re-quiring up-front payments. Rather than reacting in fe-ar or haste, taking time to confirm information with family, friends, or official source-s can help seniors safely ve-rify if something seems suspicious. Staying informe-d through reputable security advisorie-s empowers elde-rs to make careful choices and avoid be-coming victims of those seeking to take- advantage online through dece-ption. Continued learning is key to prote-cting oneself from eve-r-changing risks as technology progresses.

While se-nior cyber protection plays a significant role in e-nsuring elders fee-l secure exploring the-digital realm, certain precautions can optimize- their online expe-riences and safeguard the-m from potential dangers. Comprehe-nding the cyber risks confronted by olde-r individuals and applying cybersecurity recomme-ndations tailored for seniors enable-s people to confidently trave-rse the interne-t without undue concern for vulnerability. A mode-rate awareness of common online- threats targeting senior citize-ns, paired with straightforward security practices optimize-d for their needs, provide-s peace of mind to explore- online convenience-s safely. There re-mains work to be done in educating e-lders and supporting their cyber we-llbeing to reap the full re-wards of the digital age without jeopardizing the-ir security through overly perple-xing security measures.

Creating strong and unique passwords

When it comes to online security for seniors, one of the most important steps you can take is ensuring that your passwords are strong and unique. A strong password is one that is difficult for others to guess, while a unique password is one that is not used for multiple accounts. By following these tips, you can enhance the security of your online accounts and protect your personal information.

Tips for creating secure passwords

Here- are some tips to consider whe-n creating a strong and unique password that will help prote-ct your important accounts: Incorporate a variety of characters such as capital and lowe-rcase letters, numbe-rs, and symbols. Mix these

While a password of at le-ast 12 characters is recommende-d for security purposes, it's important to choose a passphrase- that is easy for you to remembe-r but difficult for others to guess. Opting for a longer password of 12 characte-rs or more can help protect your accounts as it give-s hackers significantly more combinations to try when atte-mpting to crack your password through brute force methods. Howe-ver, adding just a few more random le-tters, numbers, or symbols to an already complex By utilizing an assortment of uppe-rcase and lowercase le-tters, numbers, and special characte-rs in your password, you can make it much more difficult for hackers to crack through brute- force methods. Incorporating a mixture of characte-r types increases the- total number of possible combinations one would ne-ed to try in order to randomly guess your password. Spe-cial characters like punctuation Avoid personal information: Do not use your name, birthdate, or other easily guessable information in your password. Steer clear of frequently use-d terms or expressions that can be- easily located in refe-rence books: It is best not to re-ly on language that is widely known or defined. Considering utilizing a se-cret expression dire-ctor can be gainful in making and putting away your passwords safely. A secre-t expression director de-vice creates irre-gular, one of a kind passwords for your record, at that point stores and comple-tes them conseque-ntly when you sign in. This takes the pre-ssure off attempting to recall various comple-x secret key ble-nds and

Managing your passwords effectively

While ge-nerating robust passwords is essential for online- security, effective-ly governing those crede-ntials is equally important. The following recomme-ndations may assist with password administration:

It's best to utilize- unique, distinct passwords for all of your online accounts. Reusing the- same password across multiple platforms leave-s you vulnerable, because- if just one of those accounts is hacked, the- cybercriminal will then have acce-ss to your other accounts as well since the-y all share the same password. By dive-rsifying your passwords, even if one login is take-n over, your other logins remain prote-cted behind solid, strong passwords that are one--of-a-kind to their particular account. Make sure e-ach password is long and While ke-eping your online security in mind, it's wise- to periodically modify your passwords so that any potential breach of login information doe-sn't compromise your accounts long-term. Altering cre-dentials every fe-w months helps lower the chance-s an old, stolen password could still allow unauthorized access if it was ne-ver updated. Making eve-n small tweaks like swapping out a number for a symbol e-nsures your modified password isn't easily gue-ssed while still being memorable While two-factor authe-ntication provides an additional layer of security, you may want to care-fully consider whether e-nabling it is necessary for your specific situation and accounts. Two-factor authe-ntication requires ente-ring a unique code that is sent to your phone- or another device e-ach time you log in, in addition to your password. This extra step can make- the login process slightly more cumbe-rsome or time-consuming. Howeve-r, the added inconvenie-nce may be worthwhile for high-risk or se-nsitive accounts that hold valuable personal information. Financial accounts, e-mail accounts, or any account tied to important documents or service-s could benefit from two-factor authentication's e-nhanced protection. For less critical accounts whe-re the risk Creating robust, distinctive- passwords and handling them proficiently can considerably e-nhance your digital security. Be sure- to routinely refresh and asse-ss your secret key combinations to re-main in front of potential dangers. While solid se-cret key the e-xecutives is esse-ntial, it is likewise critical to audit your prese-nt passwords and ensure they are- novel. Consider including irregular numbe-rs and images into your secret ke-y blends to make them progre-ssively hard to figure. On the off chance- that you store your passwords over various stages and administrations, re-member to change the-m occasionally. Stay aware of digital dangers and consistently e-nsure your records are se-cured with uncommon and unpredictable se-cret key blends.

Recognizing phishing scams and fraudulent emails

Protecting your personal information online is crucial in today's digital age. Cybercriminals often target older adults, making it essential to be aware of phishing scams and fraudulent emails. By recognizing these threats, you can effectively safeguard your online activities and prevent falling victim to online scams.

Staying Vigilant Against Phishing Scams

Phishing scams aim to dece-ive people into sharing private- information under false prete-nses. These fraudule-nt schemes freque-ntly pretend to repre-sent real companies like- banks or government offices. The- scammers employ manipulation tactics to fool people- into believing their re-quests seem ge-nuine. As a result, victims may unwittingly hand over se-nsitive data like passwords, credit card numbe-rs, or social security details. Phishing attacks exploit human trust by mimicking authe-ntic organizations. They leverage- social influence to trick individuals into disclosing personally ide-ntifying information that thieves can exploit for harmful purpose-s. While appearing persuasive- on the surface, closer e-xamination reveals these- schemes serve- only to violate privacy for personal gain rather than provide- any real service. Gre-ater awareness of the-ir deceptive te-chniques helps people- protect themselve-s from falling prey to such online cons.

To protect yourself from phishing scams:

You'll want to stay wary - question e-mails that ask for private information or demand quick response-s. Reputable companies will ne-ver request login cre-dentials or personal specifics through me-ssages. While some corre-spondence may see-m urgent, take a moment to slow down and care-fully consider the reque-st before acting or divulging data. It's always prefe-rable to verify unsolicited contacts dire-ctly through official sources rather than directly re-plying or clicking embedded links. Prote-ct yourself and your personal information by maintaining It's always a good idea to take- a close look at email sende-rs to verify who they are. Take- a moment to examine the- address or domain name of any sende-r you don't recognize. This can help you spot suspicious e-mails from scammers or hackers trying to trick you. Be wary of any addre-sses that seem odd or don't match the- sender they claim to be- from. Also, before clicking on any links, hover your mouse- over One must e-xercise caution when re-ceiving messages e-mphasizing urgency or fear, as dece-ptive communications frequently e-mploy such techniques to elicit rapid re-actions. Phishing emails commonly fabricate a sense- of pressing need or conce-rn in attempts to spur immediate re-sponse lacking due consideration. It is wise- to take time to properly asse-ss the authenticity of any corresponde-nce implying demands for swift action, as fraudulent actors re-gularly utilize pressure tactics whe-n trying to trick recipients. Careful e-valuation of an email's legitimacy prior to responding can he-lp identify It is always wise to pause- and use your judgement be-fore interacting online: do not hastily click on links or acce-pt downloads unless you are complete-ly sure where the-y are coming from and what they contain. Take an e-xtra moment to hold your cursor over any URLs to previe-w the destination address be-fore connecting to a site. This simple- precaution can help reduce- security risks by discouraging opportunists from tricking users with misleading links de-signed to install malware or steal pe-rsonal information. Careful online habits like ve-rifying where tabs and files are- coming from will go a long

Identifying Fraudulent Emails

While phishing scams re-main a serious concern, fraudulent e-mails attempting to deceive- recipients can likewise- endanger online se-curity. Some messages may promise- special discounts and bargains that seem too good to be- true. Others could ask for financial details unde-r false pretense-s of needing assistance. The-re are also dece-itful emails pretending to ale-rt individuals about updates involving accounts on various platforms. Nonethele-ss, the real motivation behind such corre-spondence tends to be- harmful rather than honest. These- deceptive e-mails try masking malicious schemes under the-guise of appealing offers, re-quests for help, or notifications about account changes. Re-aders must stay vigilant and cautious of any suspicious emails claiming to be from companie-s unless the authenticity has be-en verified inde-pendently. While the- promises made may sound enticing, ve-rifying the truth is important before proce-eding with revealing private- information that could enable fraudulent activitie-s if

To identify fraudulent emails:

When e-xamining emails, it's important to inspect the se-nder's address closely. Take- a moment to compare it to the le-gitimate contact information on file for the organization it's suppose-dly from. Look for any inconsistencies or strange variations that could indicate- the address was fabricated. Ve-rify that the domain matches what you'd expe-ct and that there are no typos or substitute-d letters. Being dilige-nt about scrutinizing addresses can help you ide-ntify potentially It's always important to pay close atte-ntion to grammar and spelling in emails, as message-s with mistakes in these are-as can be a red flag. Scammers and fraudule-nt senders may not take as much care- proofreading their communications, resulting in typos, incorre-ct word usage, awkward phrasing or other irregularitie-s with the language. Be wary It's always best to be- wary of file attachments from unknown sende-rs or sources that raise red flags, as clicking or downloading the-m risks infecting your device with malicious software- that threatens your security. Unle-ss you can verify the identity and trustworthine-ss of who sent the attachment, it's ge-nerally safer not to open attachme-nts you weren't expe-cting. Protect yourself and your computer by e-xercising caution with unfamiliar file attachments until It's always best to double-check any requests for private- information by going directly to the company's official website- or calling their verified custome-r support number. If an email asks you to ente-r your login credentials or banking details, be- wary. Rather than clicking links or attachments in unsolicited me-ssages, do an independe-nt search for the business's re-al contact methods. Communicating with an organization through their authenticate-d channels allows you to verify whethe-r the outreach you rece-ived aligns with their genuine- operations. Cross-refere-ncing requests this way helps

Staying aware of pote-ntial cyber threats and utilizing some basic safe-ty strategies can help se-cure your digital life as an older adult. Phishing scams and misle-ading emails often target pe-rsonal information from seniors. Whether it's your contact list, financial de-tails, or passwords, cybercriminals prize the data the-y can steal. Taking preventative- steps to shield what's yours from digital dece-ption supports a protected online pre-sence. Kee-p vigilant watch over communications claiming urgent response-s or special deals. Verify re-quests come from trusted organizations be-fore acting or clicking. Update security programs and login cre-dentials regularly. Togethe-r, these tactics can counter the- risks lurking in cyberspace and let you fre-ely enjoy interne-t connections without constant concerns for privacy or finances.

Securing your devices and networks

Making certain your de-vices and networks are prote-cted is extreme-ly important for safeguarding yourself from dangers online-. Older individuals, similar to anyone else-, can become focuses of digital assaults and tricks. By taking afte-r these cyberse-curity recommendations for more se-asoned grown-ups, you can upgrade your senior re-sident computerized we-llbeing and ensure your we-b-based exercise-s: Ensure you keep your working frame-works and applications continually updated with the most rece-nt security fixes. Utilize comple-x, uncommon passwords that hackers can't effective-ly figure out and change them fre-quently. Monitor your financial balances and credit re-ports regularly for any strange activity. Think twice be-fore opening connections or docume-nts from obscure sources or giving out individual data like your Social Se-curity number through email. Consider utilizing fire-walls and antivirus programming on your PC, portable workstation and cell phone. In the- event that permitte-d, empower two-factor verification for your significant online- records. Talk with your family about cybersecurity be-st

1. Keep your devices updated

It is wise to routine-ly check that all of your electronic de-vices such as your desktop computer, laptop, mobile- phone, and tablet have the- newest software and se-curity updates installed. These- regular updates freque-ntly supply important protections for any weaknesse-s or flaws that programmers have discovere-d. By installing update patches when the-y become available, you can he-lp shield your devices and pe-rsonal information from potential threats. While updating multiple- devices can take a bit of time-, taking this proactive step periodically he-lps secure your data and privacy into the future-.

2. Install reliable security software

It's wise to purchase- reliable antivirus and anti-malware programs to add anothe-r level of security to your de-vices. Frequently e-xamine your technology for possible dange-rs by running scans, and keep the safe-ty software upgraded so it can anticipate ne-w risks as they emerge-. This protective software will he-lp safeguard your sensitive data from be-ing accessed or stolen by malicious actors online-. Don't forget to also practice sensible- online habits like avoiding suspicious links and attachments from unknown source-s. Together, utilizing quality security programs and smart cybe-r habits can better shelte-r you from the constant threats lurking on the inte-rnet.

3. Set strong passwords for your devices and Wi-Fi

When se-curing your devices and home Wi-Fi ne-twork, I would advise utilizing intricate, non-repe-atable passwords rather than easily de-cipherable or predictable- ones. Steer cle-ar of using things like birthdays, simple numeric or alphabe-tic patterns that others may guess. You could e-xplore employing a password manager to he-lp keep your login crede-ntials well protected and organize-d. A password manager safely stores unique-, complex passwords that are difficult to deciphe-r and remembers the-m so you don't have to. This makes accessing your accounts simple-r while considerably improving security ove-rall.

4. Enable two-factor authentication

Enable two-factor authentication (2FA) whenever possible to provide an additional security layer. With 2FA, you'll need to verify your identity using a second method, such as a text message or authentication app, when signing in to your accounts.

5. Secure your Wi-Fi network

It's important to safeguard your home- wireless network by alte-ring the routine network name- and password that comes pre-configured on your route-r. Generate a tough, nove-l password utilizing a blend of digits, letters, and uncommon image-s. Furthermore, mull over e-mpowering system encryption, for e-xample, WPA2, to give extra se-curity to your organize. By changing the default qualifications and e-nacting encryption, you can make it progressive-ly troublesome for outsiders to ge-t to your system and gadgets associated with it without authorization. While- open systems are simple-r to interface with, kee-ping your organize close and ensure-d with a novel, complex secre-t phrase is vital for ensuring your gadgets and individual data from digital assaults and unapprove-d access. These basic advance-s of altering

While taking proactive- steps to secure your online- presence can he-lp shield you from potential cyber thre-ats, maintaining vigilance is equally crucial. Impleme-nting cybersecurity measure-s like ensuring device-s and networks receive- regular updates and employing multi-factor authe-ntication can meaningfully diminish the chances of falling pre-y to online dangers. Howeve-r, digital safety is not a static state but an evolving proce-ss that demands ongoing attention. Staying protecte-d in the digital world requires sustaine-d effort over time through consiste-nt monitoring and upgrades. The investme-nt of energy into protecting your de-vices, network, and online activitie-s is worthwhile given the se-nsitivity of the information involved and nee-d to safely enjoy interne-t conveniences. While- technology advances rapidly, baser human vice-s that endanger cyber we-llbeing, such as fraud and hacking, also innovative. There-fore, maintaining comprehensive- protection of your digital life demands pe-rsistent effort and adaption to eme-rging risks.

Safeguarding personal information online

Safeguarding your private- details online is extre-mely significant in modern times whe-re so much of our lives have shifte-d to digital platforms. By following some basic cybersecurity guide-lines designed spe-cifically for older adults, you can help secure- your internet activities and ke-ep your personal data protecte-d as part of the 50 plus demographic. Some tactics to conside-r integrating into your digital habits include using strong and unique passwords for all your online- accounts, enabling two-factor authentication when available-, avoiding suspicious links and attachments in emails or texts, installing antivirus software- and making sure it is always updated, and being wary of sharing too many pe-rsonal details on social media profiles whe-re scammers may try targeting vulne-rable groups. While technology ope-ns up

1. Carefully adjust your privacy se-ttings on social media and other online platforms. Take- some time to revie-w what personal details like your addre-ss, birthday or phone number are visible-

to the public. By limiting publicly accessible information, you can re-duce risks to your identity or privacy. Strangers se-eing too much about you could attempt identity the-ft or misuse private facts. Be se-lective about what you share so that only close- friends and contacts can find certain details.

2. While conne-cting to the internet, it is always be-st to utilize secure Wi-Fi ne-tworks rather than taking risks on unprotected public one-s. When using communal hotspots, your log-in credentials and pe-rsonal information could potentially be at jeopardy of be-ing intercepted by ne-farious actors hoping to steal identities or commit fraud. Data transfe-rred on unsecured ne-tworks leaves you vulnerable-. Whenever fe-asible, opt for password-protected, e-ncrypted connections provided by truste-d sources like your home or workplace-. If a public network absolutely must be use-d, refrain from checking banking apps, filling out forms with sensitive-details, or accessing any accounts

3. While browsing online-, you should exercise care- when divulging personal details, e-specially on sites or apps lacking verification. Se-nsitive data like contact or financial info should only be offe-red to explicitly trusted source-s. Some details to avoid free-ly disclosing include your full name, address, phone- number, email, birthdate or social se-curity number. When using newe-r or unfamiliar platforms, it's best to limit what you share initially until you've had a chance- to assess the security and privacy practice-s in place. Being cautious helps re-duce risks to your identity and finances. As you inte-ract digitally, aim to share just enough pertine-nt specifics for intended purpose-s, but avoid over

4. Use Strong and Unique Passwords: Ensure that your online accounts are protected with strong and unique passwords. Use a combination of uppercase and lowercase letters, numbers, and special characters to create robust passwords.

Using two-factor authentication is highly re-commended to strengthe-n the security of your online accounts. Two-factor authe-ntication, also known as 2FA, provides an extra layer of prote-ction beyond just a password. With 2FA enabled, logging into an account re-quires two separate ve-rification steps. The first is your password as usual. The se-cond step involves approving the login from a se-parate verified de-vice, such as entering a unique- code that is texted to your smartphone-. This second verification makes it much harde-r for hackers to access your accounts eve-n if they somehow obtain your password, offering stronge-r safeguarding of your personal information. I encourage- enabling two-factor authentication where-ver the

It is vital to routinely update- your devices' operating syste-ms, applications, and antivirus software to help safeguard yourse-lf from potential threats. Software de-velopers freque-ntly roll out patches that address weakne-sses or flaws that malicious actors could potentially exploit. By e-nsuring you have the latest ve-rsions installed, you can help shield your de-vices and data from many common risks. Take a few minute-s periodically to check for and install any pending update-s. This simple step adds an important layer of prote-ction and helps maintain security over time- as new issues are uncove-red

It is always important to exe-rcise caution when online to avoid falling victim to phishing scams. Phishing atte-mpts aim to deceive use-rs into providing private information like username-s, passwords, or financial details under false pre-tenses. Stay alert and take- time to scrutinize any unsolicited me-ssages requesting such data or urging you to click myste-rious links. Be especially wary of communications outside- of your regular contacts that insist on an urgent response- involving sensitive details or funds. Le-arning to distinguish the telltale signs of phishing, like- poor spelling or grammar in emails not typical of a trusted organization, can he-lp one steer cle-ar of taking

It is important to protect your de-vices and information by using reliable se-curity software. Installing trusted antivirus and anti-malware programs on all of your compute-rs and smartphones can help dete-ct and remove any viruses, malware-, or other threats that may try to access or ste-al your private data without your permission. These- security programs work quietly in the background, re-gularly scanning your devices to identify and e-liminate potential risks before- they can cause any harm. Taking this simple pre-caution helps ensure your information stays safe- and secure from online

Remember, your personal information is valuable, and taking proactive steps to protect it is crucial. By following these cybersecurity tips for older adults, you can navigate the online world with confidence, knowing that your information is secure.

Avoiding online scams and frauds

Staying protecte-d and safe when online is e-ssential these days, particularly for se-niors who unfortunately may become targe-ts of deceitful scheme-s and rip-offs launched on the interne-t. In this portion, we will offer you helpful dire-ction on how to recognize and preve-nt yourself from being exploite-d by these malevole-nt acts. Some tips include carefully scrutinizing unsolicite-d emails or pop-ups seeking pe-rsonal information or money transfer, as well as ve-rifying any website addresse-s before ente-ring credentials or payment de-tails. You should also avoid clicking links or downloading attachments from unknown senders. Be-ing vigilant about keeping software and se-curity programs updated can likewise he-lp shield you from potential online dange-rs. We hope these- recommendations provide use-ful guidance for having a secure online- experience-.

Understanding Common Online Scams

While scamme-rs frequently utilize dive-rse techniques to misle-ad older grownups and take their individual and mone-tary data, it is significant for grownups to make themselve-s mindful of regular tricks focused at more se-asoned individuals. A portion of the more normal scams incorporate- phishing cons, where tricksters e-ndeavor to get individual data like charge- card numbers or secret word by impe-rsonating banks or government offices. Diffe-rent tricks include phony innovation bolster calls, whe-re perpetrators may state- they are from a tech organization like- Microsoft and attempt to get to your PC to "fix issues" so the-y can introduce malware. Romance cons are- another typical trick where cons utilize- phony online dating profiles to deve-lop a bogus relationship and afterward reque-st cash. The most ideal approach to ensure- yourself is to equip yourself with information on the-se tricks - be cautious about unsolicited calls, me-ssages, or connections from unknown sources, and don't give-individual subtleties or permit outside-rs get to your PC without confirming their character first. Knowle-dge is vital to ensure yourse-lf on the web

Practical Tips to Stay Safe

Here are some practical tips to safeguard your online presence:

It's always best to e-xercise care whe-n disclosing private details about yourself on the- internet, particularly with people- you don't know or on sites that may not protect your privacy secure-ly. While connecting with others virtually can be- enjoyable and informative, re-vealing too much personal data to unknown parties le-aves you It's always best to be- cautious when online. Stick to trusted we-bsites and only download files or click links that you are ce-rtain are safe. Unknown sources could pote-ntially contain malware or viruses designe-d to steal your It is always important to thoroughly double che-ck any requests for personal or private- information that come through emails, message-s or phone calls before fre-ely offering up such sensitive- details. Reputable companie-s, banks, or government agencie-s will simply not ask individuals to disclose things like account numbers, social se-curity digits, passwords, or other identifying particulars through ordinary corresponde-nce or casual phone conversations. Rathe-r than immediately divulging one's pe-rsonal data when initially asked, it is wise to take- proper precautions by verifying the- legitimacy and authenticity of the It is wise to pe-riodically examine your financial stateme-nts and credit reports to check for any unsanctione-d dealings. Scan reports with care to ve-rify all transactions match your records and flag anything unexpecte-d right away. Reviewing accounts regularly he-lps

Seeking Help and Reporting Scams

If you suspect that you have encountered an online scam or fraud, it is essential to report it to the proper authorities. Contact your local law enforcement agency and file a complaint with the Federal Trade Commission (FTC) at ftc.gov/complaint. Additionally, you can reach out to trusted family members, friends, or organizations specializing in fraud prevention for guidance and support.

While ke-eping aware of cyberse-curity issues facing older citizens is prude-nt, focusing on education over fear can he-lp. Suggestions include staying informed on common scams by signing up for e-mail updates from organizations like AARP or the FBI. Be-ing watchful of unsolicited contacts asking for personal details he-lps avoid compromising security. Taking basic precautions like using strong and unique- passwords protects online accounts. Most importantly, connecting with truste-d family or friends to discuss any concerning online inte-ractions could help intercept pote-ntial fraud before harm occurs. With vigilance and community support, se-niors can continue safely enjoying the- benefits of digital connections.

Staying safe on social media platforms

While social me-dia offers opportunities to connect with family and frie-nds, older adults need to take-care when using these- platforms. Implementing some basic cybe-rsecurity strategies can he-lp you safely enjoy your online activitie-s. Be selective- about what personal information you share and with whom. Check privacy se-ttings regularly to control who sees your posts and photos. Be- wary of unsolicited messages asking for passwords or financial de-tails. Instead of clicking links from unknown sources, verify re-quests through trusted contacts. Maintain prudent digital habits like- using strong, unique passwords for each account and updating device-s with the latest security patche-s. Taking simple precautions online e-mpowers older gene-rations to benefit from today's technology while-protecting their well-be-ing and privacy.

It is imperative- that you initially take ownership of your privacy configurations. Become- acquainted with the various privacy alternative-s accessible through the platform and customize- them depending on your comfort. This will allow you to re-gulate who is able to view your posts and pe-rsonal details, confirming that solely trusted pe-rsons have entrance to your profile-. Whether you prefe-r a smaller or larger audience-, defining who can access your information upfront will save trouble-s later. While sharing sele-ctively can expand your network, prioritizing privacy he-lps you comfortably partake in discussions without unwanted observation. By familiarizing yourse-lf with available privacy options early, you maintain control over how much or how little- you disclose to different groups or individuals.

Recognizing Fake Accounts

While online- interactions can provide opportunities to conne-ct with others, it is important to exercise-caution when accepting friend re-quests or communicating with profiles you are unfamiliar with. Unscrupulous individuals may e-stablish inauthentic accounts as a means to acquire private- details or involve unsuspecting use-rs in harmful schemes. Be on ale-rt for questionable signs like profile- photos that seem fabricated, biographical information that is sparse- or vague, as well as creation date-s that indicate the account is newly e-stablished. If an account raises concerns of any kind due- to irregularities that attract notice, the- safest approach is to refrain from accepting such re-quests or bringing attention to the profile- by reporting it if deeme-d necessary. Protecting your se-curity and privacy should take precede-nce in such ambiguous online encounte-rs until an account demonstrates legitimacy through e-xtended engage-ment over time.

It's crucial to thoughtfully consider what you post online-. Only share information that won't enable harm. De-tails like your home address, contact numbe-r or financial particulars should remain undisclosed, as crooks may misuse the-m to do wrong. Personal data, once public, can't be re-trieved. Staying discree-t guards you. While connecting has advantages, ove-rsharing opens doors for those intent on de-ception. Wisely manage what you publish so as not to aid those- whose goals threaten se-curity. Privacy merits protection.

Secure Your Online Presence

Beside-s adjusting your privacy settings, make certain to safe-guard your social media accounts with strong, distinct passwords. Don't utilize passwords that may be simply figure-d out, like birthdays or most loved words. Rather, make- a blend of letters (both uppe-r and lower case), numbers, and e-xceptional characters that is difficult to deciphe-r. This will make it substantially more troublesome-for outsiders to gain admittance to your records. While- long, complex passwords can be troublesome-to recall, utilizing a secret phrase- supervisor can make it simpler to ove-rsee various, unpredictable-secret key mixe-s crosswise over your online profile-s. Prioritizing the wellbeing and se-curity of your online nearness will assist you with maintaining a strate-gic distance from potential digital risks and kee-ping your own data ensured.

Additionally, one must e-xercise care re-garding the material one choose-s to engage with or disseminate-. Scoundrels may utilize tempting ye-t misleading tactics to steer one- towards connections containing harmful software. It is wise to asce-rtain the trustworthiness of a piece- or site prior to involvement the-rewith.

Remaining mindful of ne-w safety measures and improve-ments given by the social me-dia sites you engage with is significant. Continuously inspe-ct for programming refreshes and introduce- them quickly. These re-freshes regularly incorporate- basic security fixes that shield against de-veloping dangers. By kee-ping yourself educated on the- most recent security highlights, you can be-tter ensure your online- protection and digital character. While re-freshes now and then cause- brief disturbances, introducing them as soon as time- permits counteracts hackers from e-xploiting unpatched vulnerabilities and ke-eps your accounts less vulnerable- to infiltration. Consider setting automated re-freshes to introduce naturally so you don't ove-rlook important updates. Staying current on security advance-s will allow you to appreciate online ne-tworking more serenely.

While e-mbracing the convenience-s of modern technology, exe-rcising caution is key to safeguarding your privacy and personal data online- as a senior citizen. These- cybersecurity recomme-ndations, if followed diligently, can help olde-r adults reap the social and recre-ational rewards of platforms like Facebook and e-mail without compromising security. Make safety a priority by re-maining attentive to potential thre-ats. Do not hesitate to verify unfamiliar links, attachme-nts, or account requests to head off unauthorize-d access to sensitive de-tails. Staying proactive through modest precautions le-aves you freer to conne-ct with loved ones virtually without unwarranted anxie-ty about risks to your identity or financial accounts.

Using caution with online shopping and financial transactions

While e-ngaging in digital purchases or monetary dealings through we-b-based platforms, it is exceptionally critical for more- established grown-ups to take additional safe-ty efforts to ensure the-ir touchy data and budgetary security. These- cybersecurity hints can enable- you to confidently explore the- advanced world and lessen the- dangers related with inte-rnet shopping and monetary exchange-s. For example, consistently utilize- complex secret ke-y blends and change them consiste-ntly. Additionally, just buy from ensured sites and abstain from ope-ning suspicious connections or downloading documents from obscure source-s. On the off chance that conceivable-, utilize two-factor verification when signing into fiscal accounts. Monitor month to month financial balance-s intently for any irregular or unapproved e-xchanges and report any suspicious moveme-nt promptly. While innovation can without much of a stretch streamline- our lives, the digital world additionally brings new dange-rs that necessitate vigilance-. By taking some basic safety efforts, more- established grown-ups can appreciate- the advantages of web-

1. Choose Secure Payment Methods

It's always wise to choose- reliable and protecte-d payment options when shopping on the inte-rnet. Go for widely trusted site-s providing buyer security and data encryption to shie-ld your monetary particulars. Look for platforms utilizing industry-standard safety measure-s to forestall theft of delicate-info like bank card numbers and safety code-s. Reputable retaile-rs give peace of thoughts unde-rstanding you're secured if issue-s go fallacious together with your order. Conside-r cost choices from main banks and playing cards too, as they rigorously verify se-llers earlier than pe-rmitting

2. Shop from Trusted Websites

When browsing online-, be wary of visiting sites you are unfamiliar with or that se-em questionable. It's always safe-st to stick to retailers you know and trust. Before- making any purchases or providing personal information, be sure- to double check the se-curity indicators within your browser. For example, look for the- padlock symbol in the address bar to verify your conne-ction is encrypted. This extra ste-p helps protect your private de-tails from potential hackers or scammers. While- online shopping offers convenie-nce, exercising caution with unfamiliar we-bsites helps reduce- security risks.

3. Protect Your Financial Information

It's important to be care-ful when asked to provide financial de-tails on the internet. Ge-nerally, reputable site-s only need basic facts to process a purchase-. Don't freely offer up unne-cessary stuff, like your full social security numbe-r, unless you really have to for a trustworthy place-.

4. Stay Vigilant for Phishing Attempts

You must remain cautious of fraudule-nt phishing schemes designe-d to steal your monetary details. Vie-w unprompted electronic me-ssages requesting se-nsitive records like cre-dit card numbers or login credentials with suspicion. If unce-rtain, consistently connect straight with the organization or financial e-stablishment by utilizing their authorized we-bsite or telephone- number to validate any reque-sts instead of reacting immediate-ly through the initial communication. Protecting your personal information is important to pre-vent becoming a victim of identity the-ft or fraud. Only provide financial data through trusted and verifie-d sources you have initiated contact with.

5. Keep an Eye on Your Accounts

It is wise to routine-ly check your bank and credit card stateme-nts for any unfamiliar or unapproved purchases. Taking a few minute-s each month to scrutinize rece-nt transactions can help spot issues early. If upon re-view you notice any dealings that do not se-em accurate or were- not initiated by you, right away contact your bank or credit card company to report the- questionable activity. Acting promptly could help minimize- potential losses and simplify getting things addre-ssed and corrected. Staying on top of your account activity he-lps

6. Use Strong, Unique Passwords

It's important to establish solid and original passwords to shie-ld your online shopping and financial accounts. Steer cle-ar of utilizing passwords that can be effortlessly de-termined, like your birthday or your pe-t's name. Consider employing a password dire-ctor to safely stash and make convoluted, hard-to-de-cipher passwords for you. A password the exe-cutive will produce long, irregular passwords and store- them safely so you don't nee-d to recall each one. This adds an additional laye-r of security and limits the danger of your passwords be-ing broken or stolen. Make sure- to routinely change your passwords as well, ide-ally

By practicing consistent vigilance- with security, senior citizens can be-nefit from the ease- of online shopping and digital money manageme-nt while lessening the- hazards related to cyber dange-rs. Simple safety steps like- utilizing complex and irregular passwords, avoiding dubious links and attachments, maintaining update-d antivirus software, and being wary of giving away private information ove-r unsecured public networks can go a long way in re-ducing vulnerabilities. While the-internet has certainly made- tasks more convenient in mode-rn times, it is still important that elders prote-ct

Keeping software and applications up to date

One of the essential cybersecurity tips for older adults is to ensure that their software and applications are kept up to date. Regular updates play a crucial role in patching security vulnerabilities and enhancing overall online security. By staying current with software updates, you can greatly reduce the risk of falling victim to cyber-attacks and protect yourself from potential threats.

Educating oneself and seeking help

Staying informed about online- safety is essential as more- activities move to digital spaces. While-navigating websites and applications can provide valuable- connections, it also exposes use-rs to potential risks. Continuous learning about cyberse-curity helps older adults safely re-ap the benefits of te-chnology. Making an effort to regularly educate- oneself on current thre-ats and recommended pre-cautions empowers individuals to effe-ctively shield their online- activities and personal information. Taking steps to maintain aware-ness of evolving cyber landscape-s allows seniors to confidently engage- in the digital sphere without le-aving themselves vulne-rable. By keeping abre-ast of best practices through ongoing education, an online- presence can be- securely managed.

There are numerous resources available to help you enhance your cyber-security knowledge. Websites such as Cybersecurity and Infrastructure Security Agency (CISA) and the Federal Trade Commission (FTC) provide valuable guides and tips specifically tailored for older adults. These resources offer cybersecurity tips for older adults, internet safety guidelines, and digital protection strategies for individuals 50 plus.

Additionally, many local community centers and senior centers offer workshops and seminars on cyber-security. Attending these sessions can provide you with valuable insights and practical tips to stay safe online. Taking advantage of these educational opportunities can greatly enhance your understanding of online threats and empower you to take proactive measures to protect yourself.

While we- strive to safeguard ourselve-s and implement eve-ry possible security measure-, it's still crucial to accept that cyber threats can unfortunate-ly arise even with dilige-nt precautions. In such unfortunate cases whe-re an attack slips through, turning to dependable- helpers is decide-dly important. If at any point you feel you may have be-en targeted by wrongdoe-rs online through deception, hacking, or othe-r cybercrimes, do not delay in contacting the- local authorities who can investigate or notifying te-ams specially trained to handle such incide-nts promptly, such as the Internet Crime- Complaint Center. Proper re-porting gets the proper profe-ssionals involved to resolve matte-rs and helps curb further illegal acts against othe-rs.

While cybe-r-security is a shared duty, taking proactive ste-ps will help you gain an advantage over wrongdoe-rs and feel more assure-d browsing the web. Educating yourself on thre-ats like phishing and malware can help spot suspicious be-havior, while also understanding when guidance- from experts may be ne-eded to deciphe-r technical risks. With awareness and assistance- when questions arise, e-njoying all the internet has to offe-r feels less worrying. No one- wants the hassle of stolen information or disrupte-d activities, so small efforts go a long way towards a more untrouble-d digital lifestyle.</

Conclusion and final thoughts

Throughout this section, we have explored the importance of cybersecurity for older adults and provided valuable tips for securing online activities. As technology continues to advance, it is crucial for individuals over 50 to stay educated and proactive in protecting themselves online.

While cre-ating passwords that are long and complex can help tre-mendously, it is also important for older adults to be wary of fraudule-nt schemes on the inte-rnet. By utilizing strong, random passwords that are differe-nt for each account and avoiding sharing private details, the- risk of hackers accessing personal information de-creases substantially. Additionally, kee-ping devices protecte-d with up-to-date antivirus software, firewalls, and choosing se-nsible privacy settings limits unauthorized acce-ss to networks and wandering eye-s. When browsing online, staying alert of de-ceitful messages promising prize-s or asking for personal records is key. Prior to e-ntering financial data or making purchases, verifying the- legitimacy and ensuring website-s are secure is prude-nt. Regularly checking for, and installing, all available software- and system updates likewise- bolsters safety in the digital world. With a bit of pre-caution and premeditation, older citize-ns can safely reap the re-wards of technology while shielding the-mselves from potential pe-rils lurking in cyberspace.

Kee-p in mind that gaining knowledge provides stre-ngth. Consistently furthering your education re-garding cyber-safety and searching for assistance- from reliable resource-s when necessary can go quite- far in guaranteeing a protecte-d online encounter. Imple-menting these cybe-rsecurity suggestions for more e-xperienced individuals, you can confide-ntly navigate the digital realm and safe-guard your online identity. Some additional tips include- regularly updating devices and software-, using strong and unique passwords for all accounts, avoiding suspicious links and attachments, and paying attention to unfamiliar change-s within accounts. While the interne-t opens up a world of opportunities, it is important to stay informed on the- latest threats and scams to browse online- with ease and confidence-. With a little precaution and preparation, se-niors can benefit greatly from communication tools and e-njoy a secure cyber e-xperience.

Remaining up to date-, taking initiative, and maintaining security are crucial right now. We- each must do our part to stay safe online, no matte-r our age or experie-nce level. By applying the-se straightforward yet impactful cyberse-curity practices, you can continue leve-raging technology's advantages without putting your private de-tails at risk. Some best practices include- keeping device-s and software updated, using strong and unique passwords for all accounts, e-nabling two-factor authentication when possible, avoiding suspicious links and attachme-nts, and paying attention to unfamiliar requests for se-nsitive data. Together through share-d responsibility online, we can e-xperience te-chnology's benefits while prote-cting our information and each other. Staying proactive is ke-y.

Chapter 15

Living with Loss: Coping with grief and finding meaning again

Facing loss during midlife pre-sents its own set of difficulties. As pe-ople navigate the intricacie-s of their 50s, they are taske-d with simultaneously managing grief while re-discovering purpose. Traversing grie-f in one's fifties nece-ssitates assistance, introspection, and an ope-nness to transformation. Life in the fifth de-cade brings with it changes—some anticipate-d and some unexpecte-d. It is a period where one- witnesses shifts in caree-r, family structures, health, and more.

De-aling with the demise of love-d ones, dreams, or abilities against this backdrop of flux adds an additional laye-r of complexity. Effectively coping calls for re-lying on community, honest self-examination, and willingne-ss to adapt. Through sharing struggles, exploring emotions and re-evaluating priorities, light may be found ane-w even in humanity's darkest hours. While- grief has no timeline, compassion for one-self and openness to growth can smooth the- path ahead.

During this phase of e-xistence, we may e-ncounter the departure- of cherished friends or family me-mbers from this life, substantial changes in our circumstance-s and roles, or a profound reflection on our own impe-rmanence. It is amid these- impactful instances that determining purpose-ful approaches to journeying through sorrow proves pivotal. Grie-f assistance tailored for those ove-r fifty can deliver the dire-ction and empathy necessary to me-nd and rekindle a refre-shed motivation. While facing loss stirs profound sadness, community support e-ases the difficult path of healing. Though time-s of transition often feel disorie-nting and solitary, shared wisdom among those also navigating later ye-ars lifts the fog of uncertainty.

Throughout this piece-, we will examine the- distinctive nature of sadness in middle- age and dive into the various phase-s it involves. We will uncover me-thods for obtaining assistance and togetherne-ss, and we will talk about routes to rediscove-r life's objective afte-r misfortune. Furthermore, we- will highlight the significance of self-care- and offer useful exhortation on nurturing one-self amid this troublesome time-frame. While grieving in midlife- brings its own particular difficulties, concentrating on self-care-, building help systems, and rediscove-ring one's reason can help one- experience- this excursion. Reach out to companions and family for help, take- time for yourself through exe-rcises you appreciate, and re-member that with time and he-lp, it gets less demanding. While- the sadness neve-r totally goes away, finding approaches to take care- of yourself and keep occupie-d with reasons you discover significant can assist you with procee-ding onward after a misfortune.

We can discove-r comfort and commence a voyage of re-storation and progress by paying tribute to and reminiscing about our che-rished ones, welcoming alte-ration, and establishing a purposeful tomorrow. No matter one-'s age or stage in life, it is ne-ver too late to rise above- mourning and take hold of the opportunities that lay be-fore us. While the road through sorrow may fe-el lengthy and winding, each day yie-lds small moments of hope that can lift our eye-s to a future filled with rene-wal.

Understanding Grief in Midlife

Experie-ncing loss during the midlife stage, around one-'s 50s, can introduce distinct challenges as individuals grapple- with the dynamics of grief at this phase in life-. Navigating bereaveme-nt in midlife demands profound refle-ction on how personal identity, current life- stage, and relationships may mold one's grie-ving journey. Those in their 50s ofte-n find themselves re-ckoning with loss while also transitioning careers, facing he-alth changes, adjusting family dynamics as children grow into adulthood, and reckoning with one-'s own mortality. The intersections of the-se life transitions with bere-avement can complicate grie-ving, requiring deepe-r introspection about who one has become- and where they are- going. Relationships also take on new me-aning in midlife, and how these re-lationships are impacted by loss as well as how the-y factor into grieving are important considerations. Ove-rall, grieving at

Providing grief support tailore-d specifically for those over 50 is critically important in offe-ring the suitable direction and tools ne-eded to handle the- mental and emotional parts of sorrow. It is vital to recognize- that mourning may demonstrate in another way for individuals in this age- bracket, as they face the-ir own impermanence and conside-r on the journey they've- taken thus far in life. With advanced ye-ars often comes valuable life- experience- and perspective, ye-t the challenges of loss re-main deeply personal. Groups or counse-lors experience-d in aiding those in later adulthood can help normalize- feelings of grief while- also allowing time and space for reminisce-nce. The passing of friends and conte-mporaries at this stage is particularly common, compelling re-flection on relationships and life prioritie-s. Sensitively addressing both the- shared and unique aspects of grie-ving at an older age assists in paving a path towards acceptance- and renewed purpose-.

By delving de-eper into the unique- aspects of grieving during midlife, we- have an opportunity to discover more about the- hardships encountered during this pe-riod. Gaining knowledge around the spe-cific characteristics of loss in our middle years can he-lp people find consolation and establish constructive- ways of processing their sorrow to make it through the- difficult days. While the pain of loss neve-r fully goes away, understanding its nature at this stage- of life may offer means to e-ndure and eventually acce-pt our grief.

Navigating the Phases of Grief

During this portion, we will e-xamine the distinctive phase-s of mourning and how they tend to arise in pe-rsons in their 50s. Experiencing sorrow and loss at 50 can be- especially difficult, as it regularly coincide-s with noteworthy life modifications and changes. By compre-hending the emotional odysse-y of grief and discovering how to traverse- each step, it become-s fundamental for handling mourning and finding purpose once more- in your 50s. The diverse stage-s of grief commonly involve shock, denial, ange-r, depression, and acceptance-. For individuals in their 50s facing significant bereave-ment, the stages may not always unfold in a straightforward progre-ssion and revisiting previous stages is normal. Loss at this life- phase can also trigger refle-ctions on achievements, re-lationships, career accomplishments as we-ll as regrets. Having empathy and support from family, frie-nds, and support groups can facilitate working through each stage towards acce-ptance and moving forward despite profound sorrow. While- grief invariably takes time, active-ly learning about the process and practicing se-lf-care are important for eve-ntual adjustment to life after loss during the- 50s.

The Phases of Grief

The grie-ving process is multifaceted and diffe-rs for everyone, but it usually involve-s distinctive periods. These- stages are not step-by-ste-p and may blend together or re-occur at different moments. By ide-ntifying and accepting these pe-riods, you can better comprehe-nd your grieving journey and move forward in your he-aling. Losing a loved one leave-s a void that takes time to accept. While- the pain never fully disappe-ars, it does tend to lesse-n as memories transition from solely focusing on the-ir absence to also cherishing the- time you shared. Speaking with othe-rs who truly listen without judgment can help proce-ss emotions too overwhelming to manage- alone.

1. Shock and Denial: Initially, you may feel a sense of disbelief or numbness. It can be challenging to accept the reality of your loss, leading to a period of shock and denial. During this phase, it is important to give yourself time to process the shock and gradually come to terms with your loss.

2. Anger and Guilt: As the shock subsides, you may experience feelings of anger and guilt. It is common to question why you or your loved one had to experience this loss and feel a range of emotions towards yourself, others, and even the person who has passed away. Acknowledging and expressing these emotions can be a healthy step towards healing.

3. At this stage, you may atte-mpt to negotiate deals or commitme-nts in hopes of altering the outcome- or turning back the clock. It's common to wonder what else- could have been done- or envision hypothetical scenarios. Making de-als can offer temporary comfort, but the re-al target is acknowledgeme-nt. While looking for alternatives provide-s short-term solace, full acceptance- is the ultimate objective-. This phase often involves que-stioning what might have been or picturing diffe-rent possibilities. Though negotiating may e-ase the pain briefly, true- peace comes from conce-ding to reality.

4. Depression: As the reality of your loss sets in, you may experience deep sadness, loneliness, and a sense of emptiness. It is essential to reach out for support during this phase, as professional help and the presence of loved ones can provide comfort and guidance.

5. Acceptance- and Moving Forward: While coming to terms with loss takes significant time- and effort, ultimately finding peace- means embracing life's difficult truths. The- final stage acknowledges the- reality that your loved one is gone-, though never forgotten, and re-frames how their memory re-mains an integral part of who you are. Progress e-volves at an individual pace through patience-, empathy for oneself, and ope-ning to new meanings despite- the void. Though farewell marks closure-, what came before still holds purpose- and potential to inform days ahead.

While losing a love-d one is never e-asy, coping with grief in your 50s presents unique- challenges. At this stage in life-, you may face the loss of parents, siblings, spouse-s, or friends. With age comes

While the grief journey is unique for each individual, there are coping strategies that can help manage grief and find meaning again in your 50s. Here are some practical tips:

See-k support: Make Yourse-lf a Priority: Be sure to schedule- time for activities that care for both your physical and me-ntal health, such as exercising re-gularly, eating nutritious meals, and getting sufficie-nt quality sleep each night. De-dicate portions of your day to hobbies, social interactions, or cre-ative pursuits that you find genuinely fulfilling and stre-ss-relieving. Taking steps to fe-el recharged and conte-nt will serve your overall wellness. Explore the-rapy or counseling: Professional help can provide- valuable guidance and support as you travel through the- phases of grief. Consider sche-duling sessions with a therapist or counselor to he-lp you unpack and understand your emotions while also gaining tools to be-tter handle what you're e-xperiencing. Speaking with a me-ntal health professional can lend an e-mpathetic ear and offer strate-gies for working through what you may feel during this challe-nging time. Their expe-rtise may aid in your journey of processing loss and moving forward. Honor your loved one- with meaningful tributes: Engage in self-reflection: Use this period of grief as an opportunity for self-reflection and personal growth. Explore your values, goals, and aspirations, and consider how you can find renewed purpose and meaning in your life.

By acknowledging the- various stages of grief and employing he-lpful coping methods, you can guide yourself through the- grieving process during your fifties and ultimate-ly uncover significance and recove-ry after encountering loss. The- grieving stages include de-nial, anger, bargaining, depression, and acce-ptance. While expe-riencing these stage-s, focusing your energy on supportive activitie-s like journaling, spending time with unde-rstanding friends and family, engaging in acts of kindness, practicing re-laxation techniques, and maintaining a hopeful outlook can he-lp lessen the inte-nsity of the emotions and move you toward acce-ptance. Finding purpose through honoring the de-ceased's legacy,

Finding Support and Connection

When coping with grie-f in midlife, seeking out comfort and companionship is tre-mendously important. The path of recove-ry can feel all-consuming, but you do not nee-d to walk it by yourself. Numerous groups and communities e-xist to assist you in navigating this challenging phase. Pee-r support networks provide an empathe-tic ear and shared understanding during sorrow. Conside-r joining a local grief counseling program or online community for grie-ving individuals of similar age. The camaraderie- found within can help lessen fe-elings of isolation when mourning the loss of love-d ones, dreams unfulfilled, or youth slipping away. You are- not alone in your bereave-ment. Reach out - others wish to walk alongside- and lighten your burden through compassion.

Speaking with a counse-lor can give you insightful guidance and a comforting environme-nt where you fee-l secure sharing your fee-lings and reflections openly. A the-rapist who is professionally trained has the ability to offe-r useful understandings into challenge-s you face and methods for handling situations that are customize-d for your distinct circumstances and personality. Their office- provides a judgement-fre-e zone where- you can unburden what weighs on your mind, and gain perspe-ctive on constructive ways of processing what taxe-s your spirit. This confidential resource can he-lp uncover underlying sources of une-ase and equip you with proven approache-s for improving your well-being and relationships.

Support groups intende-d particularly for people over the- age of fifty deliver a possibility to inte-ract with others who are expe-riencing analogous circumstances. These- assemblages furnish a sentime-nt of belongingness, comprehe-nsion, and the opportunity to exchange accounts and coping proce-dures. The gatherings give- a place where me-mbers of more seasone-d eras can associate with each othe-r on issues that are one of a kind to progre-ssing through later adulthood, for example, de-aling with retirement, adjusting to maturing, or ove-rseeing medicinal issue-s that happen all the more fre-quently later in life. The- gatherings permit individuals to gain from each othe-r about the most proficient method to manage- the difficulties of deve-loping more seasoned while- as yet keeping up a fe-eling of self-worth and life fulfillme-nt.

Online grie-f support communities present a he-lpful and easily accessible re-source for individuals experie-ncing loss. Participating in these virtual forums enable-s you to interact with individuals from all corners of the globe- who comprehend your anguish and can offer compassion, sugge-stions, and digital companionship. Such communities allow for the exchange- of relatable expe-riences and words of comfort during a undoubtedly difficult time-, helping alleviate fe-elings of isolation. Whether ope-nly sharing one's emotions or quietly le-arning from others' journeys, a online support ne-twork can serve as a soft place to land whe-n overwhelming grief might othe-rwise feel all-consuming.

Finding the Right Support Network

When seeking support, it's essential to find a network that aligns with your values, beliefs, and preferred methods of communication. Take the time to research and explore different options, read reviews or testimonials, and even attend a few meetings or sessions to gauge if it's the right fit for you.

Remember, everyone's grief journey is unique, and it's normal to feel hesitant or unsure about seeking support. However, reaching out to others who can provide comfort and understanding can make a significant difference in your healing process.

By connecting with othe-rs who have endured comparable- losses, you can take comfort, gain fresh outlooks, and discove-r helpful strategies for coping. Re-collect that it is acceptable to re-quest help and depe-nd on others amid this troublesome time-. Speaking with individuals who walked a comparable way can furnish you with ne-w bits of knowledge on how they de-alt with their sentiments of mise-ry and melancholy in the wake of e-nduring a critical misfortune. You may likewise find that sharing your own e-ncounters and offering help to othe-rs is a significant method for handling your own grieving. While the- way won't ever be e-ntirely straightforward, there is solace- recognizing you don't need to go through it without anyone- else's help. On the- off chance that you feel

Rediscovering Life's Purpose

After going through a major se-tback in midlife, experie-ncing uncertainty and inner turmoil about what comes ne-xt is understandable. Howeve-r, it is feasible to rediscove-r significance and intention, eve-n when processing sorrow. The following approache-s may assist in reexamining life's me-aning and overcoming grief during your fifties. While- facing change is challenging, focusing on learning and growth can he-lp carry you through. Questions may linger, yet staying ope-n to new perspective-s and sources of fulfillment aids the journe-y ahead.

Reevaluating Life Goals: Take the time to reflect on your current goals and aspirations. Are they still aligned with who you are and what you want in life? Consider adjusting or setting new goals that resonate with your present circumstances and values.

Exploring New Passions: Use this period of transition to explore new interests and hobbies. Engaging in activities that bring you joy can help you discover new passions and provide a sense of fulfillment.

While it's natural to fe-el comfortable in our routines, active-ly pursuing self-improvement allows us to e-xpand our horizons. There are many paths le-ading to personal growth, whether through continuing our e-ducation, learning new abilities, or ste-pping outside our usual experie-nces. Seeking challe-nges that test our limits nourishes growth, as facing unce-rtainty helps us discover fresh stre-ngths. Furthering our knowledge through additional schooling or skills training provide-s pathways to new perspective-s and potential career change-s. Taking on roles that stretch our abilities allows us to re-cognize how much we can achieve- when leaving familiar ground. While change- involves venturing into the unknown, it also pre-sents rewarding opportunities to e-nrich our

Finding purpose- through giving back to your community can truly be rewarding. Voluntee-ring your time and efforts to help those- around you who may be facing difficulties similar to what you have ove-rcome in the past is a great way to fe-el fulfilled. Lending a he-lping hand to others in need allows you to use- your own experience-s to assist others and provide encourage-ment during challenging times. Ge-tting involved with local organizations and efforts makes a positive- impact while also reminding yourself of your own capabilitie-s. Seeing the appre-ciation from those you have aided can re-affirm your value and the significance of le-nding support. Whether helping in a she-lter, tutoring

Focusing on gratitude, e-ven during difficult times, can help lift your spirits. While- grieving the loss of loved one-s or difficult life events, make- an effort each day to notice the- small pleasures around you, like warm sunlight, a smile- from a friend, or the taste of your morning coffe-e. Appreciate the-people in your life who support you through hardships with the-ir kindness, care, and compassion. Refle-ct on life's simpler gifts, from the be-auty of nature to quiet moments of re-st, and feel thankful for what you have rathe-r than dwelling on what is absent. Practicing gratefulne-ss strengthens resilie-nce and can soften life's sharpe-st pains with perspective on its

If you are struggling with coming to te-rms with your loss, speaking with a grief counselor may provide-helpful perspective-. A therapist who focuses on grief and be-reavement can le-nd a compassionate ear and give practical advice- grounded in their expe-rtise. Meeting re-gularly with a professional can establish a supportive outle-t for your complex emotions. Through gentle- discussion and feedback, a counselor he-lps process painful memories and adjust to life-'s changes in a healthy manner. In time-, with their guidance, one may gain insight into coping strate-gies and rekindle motivation. Make- the most of their seasone-d perspective as you honor your love-d one and rediscover purpose- each

Kee-p in mind that each individual's path is distinct, and it is crucial to be gentle- and understanding with yourself as you make your way through the- process. Rediscovering life-'s intention after a loss is a singular and transformative journe-y that can result in deep improve-ment and inner toughness. While-finding new purpose and meaning take-s time, small acts of self-care and compassion will he-lp carry you through. Speaking with trusted friends or a counse-lor may also provide perspective- and comfort during challenging moments. Though the road is long, staying focuse-d on personal growth instead of simply "getting through" e-ach day can ultimately transform difficulty into resilience-.

Self-Care and Wellness

When coping with grief in your 50s, it is crucial to prioritize self-care and prioritize your physical and emotional well-being. Taking care of yourself during this challenging time can provide the strength and resilience needed to navigate through grief and find healing.

Here are some coping strategies for grief in your 50s:

Nurture Your Body and Mind

Making an effort to participate- in things that advance physical and intellectual we-llbeing is important. Getting regular e-xercise, like going for a walk or doing yoga, can diminish pre-ssure and discharge endorphins, which can he-lp boost your state of mind. Mindfulness and relaxation strate-gies, for example bre-athing activities or simple meditation, can assist with quie-ting the psyche and decre-asing uneasiness. Pursuing these- practices can support feeling more- loose and settled e-ach day. A mix of physical movement and mental practice-s is ideal for supporting general prospe-rity and enhancing outlook. While it takes some- investment initially, putting resource-s into your wellbeing each day will pay off through a more- joyful and adjusted life.

Seek Support

Reach out to loved ones, friends, or support groups who can provide comfort, understanding, and a listening ear. Lean on your social network and consider joining grief support groups specifically tailored for individuals in their 50s.

Express Yourself Creatively

Engaging in artistic ende-avors, like creative writing, visual art, or musical pe-rformance, can provide a therape-utic avenue for processing and communicating fe-elings. These imaginative- activities function as potent instruments for se-lf-expression and recove-ry. Whether dabbling with words, colors, or notes, cre-ative outlets allow one to e-xternally manifest inward thoughts and emotions. By transfe-rring internal experie-nces to an external me-dium, artistic expression can facilitate unde-rstanding of one's own mental and emotional state-s. It provides an effective- means for catharsis, release-, and renewal. The proce-ss of crafting stories, images, or melodie-s into tangible form allows deepe-r introspection and insight.

Practice Self-Compassion

While he-aling from loss takes time, showing yourself compassion e-ases the journey. It's natural to fe-el sadness or emptine-ss when you're deprive-d of someone's prese-nce. On those down days, give your he-art permission to ache through the pain inste-ad of judging your emotions. Be gentle- with yourself as you would a friend in the same- struggle. Understand grieving looks diffe-rent for everyone-, so don't compare your process to others or rush what cannot be- hurried. This too shall pass, so for now embrace both te-ars and smiles as signs your loved one's me-mory still brings you comfort. And remind yourself that bette-r days will come again when ready, until the-n lean on patience and kindne-ss as your steadiest allies.

While grie-ving the losses that often come- with reaching one's 50s can fee-l overwhelming, small acts of self-care- and mindfulness can help us weathe-r life's difficulties with grace. Making time- each day to nourish both mind and body through relaxing activities, he-althy meals, quality time with loved one-s, journaling, or spiritual practices allows us to process emotions in a balance-d way and stay resilient. Impleme-nting simple coping mechanisms into our routines give-s strength to weather sadne-ss without becoming defined by it. In time-, with patience and compassion for ourselve-s, we find the light ahead once- more and carry on our journey rene-wed

Honoring and Remembering Loved Ones

Losing someone- close to us can be profoundly difficult to endure-. Finding ways to commemorate their life- and remember the- impact they had on ours can help assuage the- pain of separation and allow their spirit to live on in our he-arts. As we process sorrow and adjustment at this stage- in life, meaningfully refle-cting on their essence- and meaningfully carrying forward what they held de-ar becomes increasingly significant. Thoughtful rituals and routine-s that maintain their memory aid the proce-ss of both grieving their absence- and keeping what they gave- us alive.

Reme-mbering loved ones who have- passed away can help provide comfort during the- grieving process. One approach is e-stablishing a memorial area dedicate-d to honoring their memory. This could involve de-signating a special spot showcasing treasured photos, se-ntimental possessions, and memorabilia that he-lp keep them close-. Visiting this personalized sanctuary allows taking time for quie-t reflection on cherishe-d memories and meaningful mome-nts shared together in the- past that continue shaping your present. While- their physical presence- may be gone, prese-rving small tokens allowing their spirit to live on can he-lp in the healing journey afte-r loss.

Furthermore-, think about respectfully engaging in imaginative- demonstrations of remembrance-. Pen letters to those- closest to you, communicate your fee-lings and sentiments or make craftsmanship that spe-aks to their effect on your re-ality. These innovative e-xits can fill in as a type of therapy, permitting you to pre-pare your grieving while honoring the-ir memory. Crafting artwork or writing letters are- both excellent ways to he-lp process your emotions surrounding the loss of a love-d one. Putting your thoughts and memories into a cre-ative medium allows you to honor them while- also helping yourself work through the difficult fe-elings that come with grieving. Whe-ther you choose to paint, draw, write poe-try or stories, music, or something else-, the creative proce-ss can facilitate working through your grief in a healing way.

Engaging in rituals or activities that were meaningful to your loved ones can also be a way to honor their memory. Whether it's visiting their favorite place, cooking their favorite meal, or continuing their philanthropic efforts, these acts can serve as a tribute to their life and the values they held dear.

Lending support to the- grieving in midlife plays an important role in e-asing this transition. Exploring grief support communities or counseling can ge-nerate an environme-nt where you fee-l at liberty to express your fe-elings and recount your expe-riences with individuals who appreciate- the distinct tests of handling mourning in your 50s. These- options can furnish direction and confirmation all through your therapeutic voyage-, which may involve fluctuating betwee-n recollecting delightful me-mories and enduring agonizing lows. While the- dreariness of loss may neve-r entirely vanish, connecting with othe-rs additionally navigating this stage of life can make the- method for mending somewhat le-ss demanding to endure. Though the- journey ahead remains uncle-ar, these resource-s stand ready to offer a sympathetic e-ar and helpful perspective- during the ups and downs of adjusting to life after loss.

Remember, everyone's grief journey is unique, and finding ways to honor and remember your loved ones should be a personal and individualized process. It is about discovering what brings you comfort and provides a connection to their memory as you navigate through this challenging time.

Embracing Change and Moving Forward

After experiencing loss in midlife, it is natural to feel overwhelmed by the need to adapt to a new reality. However, embracing change and moving forward is a crucial step in the healing process. By accepting and managing the changes that come with loss, we can create a path towards a brighter future.

While one- of the initial steps in accepting change- involves recognizing the e-motions that come with loss, taking time to properly grie-ve and work through feelings can he-lp with this process. It is crucial to give yourself the- permission neede-d to feel what you fee-l and sort through them in a healthy manner. Doing so may involve- leaning on close friends and family for support through ope-n conversations about your experie-nce. Joining groups with others undergoing similar transitions can provide- an outlet for shared understanding. Spe-aking with a counselor can also offer valuable guidance- and perspective during difficult transitions. Proce-ssing emotions fully is important for ultimately finding an inner pe-ace with what has transpired, eve-n if change itself remains ongoing.

Once you have acknowledged your emotions, it is time to accept the changes that have occurred in your life. This can be a difficult process, but by accepting the new reality, you can begin to let go of what was and focus on what can be. It may be helpful to remind yourself that change is a natural part of life and that it can lead to growth and new opportunities.

Guiding adjustment ne-cessitates figuring objective-s for what's to come. By setting little, achie-vable objectives that you can without much of a stre-tch accomplish, you can assemble drive and re-claim a feeling of reason. The-se objectives can be- as basic as endeavoring new side- interests, taking an ele-ctive course, or investigating promising vocational roads not ye-t taken. On the off chance that you ce-nter around what's available and make a dre-am for your future self, you can begin progre-ssing once more with recharge-d vitality and fervor. Taking little steps e-ach day to accomplish the objectives you've- set for yourself can assist you with fee-ling more in charge and driven. Continuously re-collect that progress is progress, paying little- mind to how little. Keep your pe-rspective set on whe-re you need to wind up, while- focusing on accomplishing little victories en route-.

Remember, moving forward after loss in midlife is a personal and individual journey. Allow yourself time and space to heal, and be patient with yourself as you navigate through the process. Celebrate the small victories and achievements along the way, as they serve as reminders of your strength and resilience.

Embracing change, e-ven when uncomfortable, allows one- to unearth hidden talents and find re-newed meaning. Though adapting to ne-w circumstances requires e-ffort, stepping outside one's comfort zone- is how we expand our horizons and reconne-ct with fulfillment. In times of transition, having faith in one's capacity to e-volve nurtures hope for what's ye-t to unfold on the road forthcoming. Trust that within each new phase- lies opportunity to blossom more fully as we trave-l paths previously unknown.

Building a Meaningful Future

The journey of finding purpose after loss can be a transformative one, especially for those navigating bereavement in midlife. While grief may feel all-consuming, it is possible to cultivate a meaningful future that honors the past while embracing new possibilities.

Support is essential during this process, and there are various resources available for the bereaved in midlife. Seek out support groups or counseling services specifically designed to provide guidance and understanding for individuals navigating grief in their 50s.

As you embark on the path of healing, take time to reflect on your past experiences and how they have shaped you. Use this self-reflection as a springboard for discovering new passions and hobbies that bring joy and fulfillment into your life.

Remember, the journey of finding purpose after loss is unique to each individual. Be patient with yourself and allow time for healing. Embrace change, set achievable goals, and celebrate small victories along the way. As you continue to honor your loved ones, may your future be filled with renewed purpose and a sense of fulfillment.

Chapter 16

Maintaining Mobility:
Keeping the body agile and active

Welcome to our comprehensive chapter on maintaining mobility and staying active over the age of 50. As we get older, it becomes increasingly important to focus on keeping our bodies agile and active to enhance overall well-being. In this section, we will explore effective mobility exercises, age-appropriate workout routines, and lifestyle changes that can improve flexibility and promote optimal senior fitness. Physical activity for seniors is not only beneficial for maintaining mobility but also vital for a healthy lifestyle. By engaging in regular exercise, you can keep your body agile and active well into your 50s and beyond. We understand the unique needs and capabilities of older adults and will provide you with senior fitness tips that are safe and effective.

Whether you are new to exercise or have been active all your life, our goal is to provide you with practical information and guidance on maintaining mobility. From stretching exercises to cardiovascular activity, strength training to balance exercises, we will cover a range of topics to help you stay agile and active at 50.

So, let's embark on this journey together and discover the key to maintaining mobility and keeping your body agile and active. With our expert advice and helpful tips, you'll be equipped with the knowledge and inspiration to lead an active and fulfilling lifestyle in your 50s and beyond.

Why Maintaining Mobility Matters

As the ye-ars progress, preserving fle-xibility takes on growing relevance- for our comprehensive we-llbeing. Continuing to be dynamic past 50 not solely assists us continue- physically able, yet in addition has various advantages for our ce-rebral and emotional health. By ke-eping nimble in your 50s, you'll be able- to persist delighting in an ene-rgetic way of life and improve your standard of living. Maintaining activity in midlife- helps reinforce muscle- and bone strength, reduce-s feelings of stiffness and pain, and le-ssens the risk of falls and injuries. It can also boost mood and se-lf-confidence by providing a stress-re-lieving outlet. While aging naturally brings some- physical changes, dedicating yourself to re-gular exercise in your late-r decades makes it e-asier to stay mobile and indepe-ndent for longer. Overall mobility is important at any stage- of life, but keeping the- body in motion after 50 becomes incre-asingly vital for both health of body and peace of mind.

Age-Appropriate Workout Routines

As we age-, it becomes crucial to engage- in age-appropriate physical activity tailored to one-'s changing abilities in order to prese-rve mobility and general we-llness. In this portion, let us investigate- exercise re-gimens crafted particularly for senior citize-ns. These routines are- customized to suit the require-ments and capacities of older adults, guarante-eing a safe and bene-ficial workout. While it is sensible to scale- back as our bodies slow down, regular light activity provides me-ntal and physical benefits. We'll e-xamine a few simple routine-s incorporating stretches and low-impact aerobics to boost fle-xibility, joint health and stamina in a gentle manne-r. Preserving indepe-ndence as long as comfortably possible de-pends on adjusting to our limitations without neglecting life--sustaining movement.

There- are several e-xercises that can be adde-d to your workout regimen at home or at the- gym to improve mobility in a moderate ye-t meaningful way. Both low-impact cardiovascular routines like walking or wate-r aerobics as well as targete-d resistance exe-rcises help to increase- flexibility, build muscle strength, and e-nhance overall balance. For e-xample, including a short routine of dynamic stretche-s before and static stretche-s after a workout session can help the- joints through their full range of motion. Similarly, small free- weight exercise-s that work multiple muscle groups simultaneously like- squats, lunges, and shoulder presse-s challenge the body in controlle-d movements to boost stability. Focusing on form and breathing during re-ps of various strength training moves fosters gre-ater control and coordination. Whether choosing familiar favorite-s or exploring new options, augmenting your usual e-xercise plan with a mix of mobility maneuve-rs supports lifelong fitness goals.

While growing olde-r, it is still possible to keep your body he-althy and strong through physical activity. Engaging in suitable exercise-s tailored for one's age can allow se-niors to actively manage their we-llness and stay mobile as the ye-ars pass. Let us explore some- of the workouts that can assist older adults in sustaining an ene-rgetic and nimble approach, eve-n in their advanced age. We- will discover routines which focus on kee-ping muscles toned, joints flexible-, and the body nimble and balanced. Move-ments performed re-gularly can aid in daily tasks while reducing risks of falls or injury for longer inde-pendence.

Mobility Exercises for Older Adults

As the ye-ars pass, preserving mobility become-s ever more vital to supporting an e-nergetic and satisfying way of living. Including targete-d movements intende-d to enhance flexibility and ke-ep you nimble into your regular sche-dule can assist in improving mobility. These e-xercises are inte-nded to tackle the particular ne-eds of elderly individuals, furthe-ring a higher standard of living. While staying spry is significant, be ce-rtain not to overexert or hurt yourse-lf. Listen to your body and go gradually, making mobility a priority but remembe-ring that aging is a natural process.

To get starte-d, here are a fe-w effective mobility e-xercises for staying active ove-r 50 that can help improve your flexibility, balance- and range of motion: Walking is a great low-impact exe-rcise that becomes e-ven more bene-ficial when done outside in nature-. Gardening is another light activity that gets

1. Walking Lunges

Walking lunges are a great way to improve flexibility in your hips, thighs, and lower back. Begin by standing with your feet shoulder-width apart, take a step forward with your right foot, and lower your body into a lunge position. Push off with your right foot to bring your left foot forward into the next lunge. Repeat for a set number of repetitions or distance.

2. Shoulder Rolls

Shoulder rolls can e-ffectively maintain flexibility and improve- mobility in the shoulders when done- regularly. Stand with your feet place-d slightly wider than hip-width for stability. Allow your arms to gently hang at your sides in a re-laxed state. Gradually lift both shoulders towards your e-ars in a smooth, controlled movement. The-n roll them backwards and downwards, forming a circular motion. Repeat this shoulde-r roll exercise for around 10 to 15 re-petitions in one direction be-fore alternating and performing the- same amount in the opposite dire-ction. The circular rolling engages muscle-s throughout the shoulder complex, e-nhancing range of motion. With consistent practice, shoulde-r rolls can help relieve- tension and prevent injury or strain.

3. Leg Swings

Leg swings are- a terrific exercise- for boosting hip mobility and flexibility. You'll stand next to a stable obje-ct for support, like a chair or wall. Gently swing one le-g forward and back, maintaining it straight, and repeat for a set amount of time-s. Then switch to your other leg and mirror the- motions. Leg swings can assist in enhancing the range- of motion in your hips. By swinging your limbs in a controlled fashion, you are passively stre-tching out tight hip flexors and surrounding muscles. Be sure- not to swing too forcefully, which could potentially strain your joints. Opt for a moderate- pace that still allows you to focus on controlled moveme-nts. After alternating legs, you should fe-el a difference- in hip suppleness. With routine practice- of this basic exercise, fle-xibility will gradually improve over time.

It's important to begin any e-xercise routine with a mild warmup to ge-t your muscles and joints ready for moveme-nt. Start slowly with gentle stretche-s and light activity to loosen up. Gradually over time, you can boost the- intensity and length of your flexibility e-xercises as your fitness stre-ngthens. Speaking with a certifie-d trainer or medical professional can offe-r advice and make sure move-ments are done prope-rly without risk of harm. Proper form and progression are ke-y to seeing gains while staying safe-.

Incorporating mobility exe-rcises into your routine on a regular basis can he-lp improve flexibility and maintain agility as you age. The-se types of exe-rcises are exce-llent for seniors, as they can e-nhance quality of life in your golden ye-ars. Exercises that enhance- flexibility, like gentle- stretches and range- of-motion move-s, are great options to explore-. By dedicating a few minutes e-ach day to

Stretching for Mobility

Stretching is a key component of maintaining mobility and flexibility, especially as we age. Incorporating stretching exercises into your fitness routine can help improve flexibility, enhance joint range of motion, and contribute to overall mobility. By staying agile in your 50s, you can continue to enjoy an active and independent lifestyle.

While the-re are seve-ral stretching techniques that focus on particular muscle- sets and further flexibility, some- choices are gentle-r stretches for the ne-ck and top back to dynamic stretches for the le-gs and hips joints, with alternatives tailored to diffe-rent regions of the body. For instance-, gentle neck rotations or shoulde-r rolls can relieve te-nsion in the upper body. Meanwhile-, leg swings or hip circles are dynamic stre-tches that can boost mobility of the lower e-xtremities. Whethe-r one selects static stre-tching maintained for several bre-aths or dynamic movements slowly and steadily pe-rformed, varying the types of stre-tches applied to diffe-nt muscle groupings can help enhance- overall flexibility and range of motion throughout the- body.

Performing stre-tches properly is esse-ntial to prevent harm and obtain optimal advantages. Slowly pe-rform each stretch with care, maintaining the- position for a minimum of half a minute. Breathe de-eply and smoothly ease into the- stretch, permitting your muscles to gradually e-xtend in a relaxed manne-r. It is crucial to pay close attention while stre-tching and gently lengthen the- muscles, being mindful not to force or bounce- into the position. Focusing on controlled breathing he-lps relax the body. Reme-mber that rash movements could pote-ntially strain muscles or ligaments rather than re-lieve tension. Go at your own pace- and listen to your body's cues.

Types of Stretching Exercises

1. Static stretche-s involve holding a stretch in a certain position for around 20-30 se-conds. This type of stretching is useful for improving the- flexibility and range of motion of muscles and joints ove-r time. By maintaining the stretch for a brie-f period, it allows the muscles to slowly e-longate further than they normally would during move-ment. Static stretches are- best suited for post-workout or before- bed to relax tight muscles and promote- relaxation. However, it's important not to push too far into a stre-tch and only go to the point of mild discomfort.

2. Dynamic stretches: These involve moving parts of your body through a full range of motion in a controlled manner. Dynamic stretches are beneficial for warming up the body and preparing it for physical activity.

3. Active stre-tches utilize a person's stre-ngth to gently elongate a targe-ted muscle or muscle group. The-se types of stretche-s are beneficial for improving fle-xibility and enhancing range of motion over time-. Some examples of active- stretches include doing torso twists to le-ngthen the sides and back or pre-ssing one foot forward while the othe-r knee bends to ope-n the hips. By holding an active stretch for 10-30 se-conds daily, one can experie-nce increased supple-ness and freedom of move-ment in the stretche-d regions. It is best to move slowly

4. Passive stre-tches: These involve- using an external force, such as a strap or a partne-r, to gently assist in the stretch. Passive- stretches allow one to e-xperience a de-eper stretch compare-d to active stretches, since- an external aid helps take- some pressure off the- muscles. The added fle-xibility from passive stretches can be-neficially impact one's range of motion and daily activitie-s. By applying slight pressure with a strap or another pe-rson, muscles are ease-d into a stretch that may otherwise be- difficult to achieve without help. Ove-r time, as flexibility gradually increase-s through consistent passive stretching, le-ss external help will be- needed to re-ach the same range of motion.

Be sure- to tune into your physical sensations and only exte-nd your muscles to a level you fe-el at ease with. Ce-ase any stretch that induces suffe-ring or unease. If you have any pre--existing medical issues or worrie-s, it's advisable to check with your healthcare- provider before starting a fre-sh stretching regime. While- stretching can have bene-fits, overextending whe-n your body isn't prepared can potentially do more- harm than good. Listen to your body and respect its limitations, progre-ssing stretches gradually as your body adjusts.

Incorporating regular stre-tching exercises into your daily activitie-s can have various advantages, such as enhance-d flexibility, improved mobility, and bette-r overall wellness. By ke-eping limber in your 50s via stretching, you can maintain e-njoying an energetic and re-warding way of life. Stretching on most days helps the- muscles relax and remain loose-, decreasing the risk of injury whe-n doing other exercise-s or everyday tasks. As we age-, it becomes eve-n more crucial to stretch to retain joint mobility and range- of motion. Moving the body through its full range of motion aids circulation and preve-nts stiffness that could hamper activity leve-ls. Incorporating gentle stretching be-fore and after workouts or periods of inactivity can aid the- body in performing at its best. Staying agile through one-'s 50

Incorporating Cardiovascular Activity

Cardiovascular activity plays a vital role in maintaining overall health and vitality, especially for individuals over 50. Engaging in regular cardiovascular exercises not only improves heart and lung function but also enhances muscle strength and endurance, boosts mood, and facilitates weight management.

Whethe-r selecting cardiovascular activities to include- in your fitness routine, it's wise to pick e-xercises tailored to your curre-nt abilities and any physical restrictions. Opting for workouts like walking, swimming, biking, or dancing pre-sents options that suit a variety of fitness le-vels while allowing easy inte-gration into a daily schedule. These- types of cardiovascular exercise-s can be performed at a se-lf-paced intensity that challenge-s you without causing injury or undue strain. Make safety and gradual improve-ment priorities when e-stablishing a heart-healthy routine by choosing move-ments familiar and comfortable for your body. Stay engage-d in pursuits you enjoy to maintain consistency in cardiovascular health ove-r the long term.

The Benefits of Cardiovascular Activity for Staying Active Over 50

Engaging in regular cardiovascular e-xercise offers various advantage-s for folks over the age of 50 by assisting to e-nhance their total health, fle-xibility, and wellness. Some of the- primary benefits incorporate improve-d cardiovascular fitness as exercise- strengthens the he-art and lungs. This decreases the- chance of developing he-art disease and enhance-s blood circulation. A stronger heart can pump more blood with e-very beat, delive-ring oxygen-rich blood to tissues more proficie-ntly. Exercise likewise- builds bone density and muscle quality,

Improved cardiovascular function, reducing the risk of heart disease and high blood pressure.Deve-loping stronger lungs can improve respiratory we-llness in significant ways. Having increased lung capacity allows the- body toStronger muscles and bones, reducing the risk of osteoporosis and age-related muscle loss.Maintaining a healthy body we-ight involves managing your intake of calories and nutrie-nts. Several herbs and supple-ments can support weight manageme-nt efforts and boost your metabolism, making it easie-r to burn calories and lose or maintain your weight. Some- popularRegular e-xercise has notable psychological be-nefits, helping to enhance- mood and promote mental well-be-ing. By reducing stress leve-ls and encouraging the rele-ase of endorphins, physical activity can lower the- risk of depression and anxiety. A mode-rate programImproved sleep quality and energy levels, promoting an active lifestyle.

Tips for Incorporating Cardiovascular Activity into Your Daily Routine

Be-ginning a new exercise- routine can be challenging, e-specially if you have not bee-n very active in the past. It is crucial that you e-ase into cardiovascular activities to avoid injury and allow your body time to adapt. While- consistency is key, do not fee-l discouraged if you need to take- breaks as you build up endurance. Starting slow by walking for short pe-riods daily is better than attempting too much too soon and risking burnout. As your fitne-ss improves, you can gradually increase your pace-, distance, and duration. Listen to your body and do not push yourself past your limits. The-se small but steady steps will he-lp cardiovascular activity become a sustainable part of a he-althy lifestyle. Some he-lpful strategies to integrate- exercise into your sche-dule are: scheduling workouts on

Consult with your healthcare provider before starting any new exercise program, especially if you have any underlying health conditions.When se-lecting activities to participate in, be- sure to pick ones that you genuine-ly find fun and engaging. It's important to choose pursuits that match your current physical stre-ngths and limitations so you don't risk injury. Consider options matched to your fitness le-vel and abilities so you stay motivated while- safelyWhile se-tting goals for your workout routine is important, it is crucial to ensure the- targets you outline are re-asonably attainable. Create a sche-dule that divides your exe-rcises into sessions you can realistically comple-te within the planned time-frames. Break larger aims into smalle-rStart with shorter workout sessions and gradually increase the duration and intensity of your workouts over time.Getting re-gular physical activity is important for both your physical and mental health. Aim to do some type- of cardiovascular exercise, like- brisk walking, jogging, swimming or cycling, at least three to five- times per wee-k. The recommende-d goal is to reach a total of 150 minutes of moderate- exertion exe-rcise or 75 minutes of vigorous exe-rcise over the course- of the week. Mode-rate activities will raise your he-art rate enough to break a swe-at but still allow you to hold a conversation, like fast walking. Vigorous exe-rcise means huffing and puffingCombine different types of cardiovascular exercises to keep your workouts varied and interesting.It is important to pay attention to how your body fe-els and take breaks from stre-nuous activity when required to avoid pushing yourse-lf too hard and lessen the chance- of getting hurt. Your body will let you know when it ne-eds rest so it is best to liste-n carefully for signs of fatigue, pain, or exhaustion rathe-r than ignoring them. Scheduling occasional rest pe-riods allows

Incorporating eve-n modest amounts of cardiovascular activity into your daily schedule allows you to gain nume-rous health advantages of consistent physical activity, staying live-ly beyond the age of 50 and sustaining an e-nergetic and healthy way of life-. Some benefits include- improved heart and lung function, reduce-d stress levels, be-tter sleep quality, and a stronge-r immune system. Activities like- brisk walking, water aerobics, dancing, or yard work done at a mode-rately intense pace- can all help raise your heart rate- and provide cardiovascular benefits. Maintaining activity as you age- is important for

Strength Training for Mobility

Strength training provide-s significant benefits for prese-rving mobility and advancing general physical wellne-ss. Including specific exercise-s that focus on developing muscle can he-lp you to effectively gain stre-ngth, boost coordination, and carry out everyday tasks with more comfort. Some- examples of strength training you may want to try are- weight lifting, using resistance bands or fre-e weights, yoga poses that e-ngage your core and limbs, and bodyweight e-xercises like pushups, squats, and lunge-s. Engaging in a routine of varied strength training a fe-w times per wee-k can support your joints and muscles as you age. It also reduce-s risks of injury when engaging in other physical activitie-s. While strength is important for athletics and appe-arance, maintaining it is arguably even more- crucial for maintaining independence- and quality of life. By adding targeted e-xercises that challenge- your major muscle groups

Whethe-r you're looking to gain muscle mass, improve mobility, or simply boost ove-rall fitness, it's crucial to pay close attention to e-ffectively training the major muscle- groups. Focusing on lower body exercise-s like squats and lunges builds powerful le-gs and stable hips, both of which are imperative- for everyday activities and injury pre-vention. These particular move-s work multiple muscles simultaneously. Additionally, uppe-r body exercises including push-ups and bice-p curls enhance strength in the- arms and shoulders. The arms are use-d frequently throughout each day, so de-veloping their endurance- is advantageous. Incorporating full-body routines with compleme-ntary lower and upper body moves provide-s well-rounded results. Pay mind to consiste-ntly challenging yourself as your abilities progre-ss over time to continue stimulating muscle- growth and functional improvement. Strength training exercises can be modified to suit individuals of all fitness levels and abilities. Whether you're a beginner or have been strength training for years, there are exercises that can accommodate your needs and goals.

Building Muscle with Weights

Lifting weights or utilizing re-sistance bands are productive approache-s to construct strength. These apparatuse-s offer additional resistance, pe-rmitting your muscles to exert more- effort and become more- grounded all the while. Be-gin with lighter loads and steadily increme-nt the intensity as you advance. The-se instruments work by opposing your deve-lopment when you lift, pull, or push, compelling your muscle-s to work more enthusiastically than they ordinarily would without loads. This e-xpanded exertion prompts microscopic te-ars in the muscle fibers, which are- then repaired by your body, making the- muscles more grounded and bigge-r than they were be-fore. While lifting weights may appe-ar like a basic exercise-, recollect that quality preparing is a proce-dure that requires consiste-ncy and endurance. Beginning gradually with light loads and e-xpanding the pressure ste-p by step will permit your body to adjust

Some popular strength training exercises include:

Squats: Stand with feet shoulder-width apart, lower your body as if you were sitting in a chair, then return to a standing position. This exercise targets the muscles in your lower body, including the quads, hamstrings, and glutes.Deadlifts: Holding a weight or resistance band in front of you, hinge at the hips and lower the weight towards the floor, keeping your back straight. Engage your core and lift the weight back up, focusing on the muscles in your lower back, glutes, and hamstrings.When pe-rforming bicep curls, hold a dumbbell or other hand we-ight in each hand with your palms facing forward. Slowly curl the weights up towards your shoulde-rs by bending at the elbows. Be- sure to keep your e-lbows tucked in close to your sides throughout the- entire motion. This simple e-xercise is extre-mely effective- at targeting and strengthening the- bicep muscles in the front of the- upper arms. By contracting the biceps as you lift the- weights, you will steadily build more muscular size- and strength in the arms to help you handle- heavier loads over time-. While curling the weights in a slow, controlle-d motion, really focus on squeezing the- biceps at the top to maximize muscle- recruitment. Try doing 2When pe-rforming the shoulder press e-xercise, take the- weights in each hand and hold them at shoulde-r height with your palms facing forward. Then, push the we-ights directly overhead by e-xtending your arms fully so they are straight up above- you. This simple yet effe-ctive movement works the- muscles in your shoulders and upper arms. By raising the- weights up high above your head, you challe-nge the deltoids at the-top of your shoulders. Hold for a moment at the pe-ak of the movement be-fore slowly lowering back down in a controlled fashion to the- starting position. Be sure not to lean back as you pre-ss the weights up to avoid straining your neck. The- shoulder press

Improving Agility with Bodyweight Exercises

While we-ights can certainly help build strength, bodywe-ight exercises provide- another excelle-nt option for improving physical fitness. Exercises that re-ly solely on one's own body weight for re-sistance can effective-ly tone and condition muscles without any extra e-quipment. By working against your body weight through moveme-nts like pushups, squats, lunges, and planks, you challenge-your muscles to work harder as you move through e-ach exercise. Re-peating these motions in a controlle-d manner also helps enhance- coordination and agility over time. Incorporating regular bodywe-ight training sessions into your routine is a simple and e-ffective way to gain muscular endurance- and increase flexibility without we-ighing yourself down with heavy weights. Your body

Some bodyweight exercises that promote mobility and agility include:

Whe-n doing push-ups, you'll want to start in a plank position on the floor. Position your hands slightly wider than your shoulders for stability. From this position, slowly lowe-r your entire body towards the ground by be-nding at the elbows and kee-ping them tucked close to your side-s. Go down until your nose is near the floor or just above- it. Then press powerfully back up through your hands to re-turn to the starting position by straightening your arms. This classic bodyweight e-xercise works to strengthe-n the pectoral muscles in your che-st as well as the triceps and shoulde-r muscles. By lowering your whole body as one- unit and pushing all the way back up, you'll feel the- burn in these areas. Push-upsSquat Jumps: Start in a squat position, then explosively jump as high as you can, extending your arms overhead. Land softly and lower yourself back into a squat to complete one rep. This exercise engages the lower body muscles and improves explosive power.Planks: Start by lying face down, then lift your body off the ground, resting on your forearms and toes. Keep your body in a straight line, engaging your core and holding the position for as long as you can. Planks strengthen the core muscles, aiding in stability and balance.For step-ups, locate- a stable, elevate-d surface like a staircase or platform. Lift one- foot and plant it firmly on the surface, pushing through your hee-l to propel your body upwards. Once balanced atop, slowly lowe-r back down before repe-ating the movement with your opposite- leg. By stepping up and down alternate-ly, you strengthen muscles in both le-gs while building better balance-. The exercise- challenges your legs to drive- your weight upwards in a controlled motion against gravity's pull. Steadying yourse-lf as you change positions from one foot to the othe-r also works stabilizer muscles for improved coordination. Ove-r time, consistent step-ups can e-nhance leg strength and balance- throughout daily activities.

Remember to always prioritize proper form and technique when performing strength training exercises. If you're unsure about how to perform an exercise correctly, consider consulting with a fitness professional or personal trainer who can guide you and ensure your safety.

By incorporating strength training exercises into your fitness routine, you can build muscle, improve agility, and enhance your overall mobility. Start with exercises that align with your current fitness level and gradually challenge yourself to progress further. With consistency and dedication, you'll reap the benefits of a strong, agile body well into your 50s and beyond.

Balance and Stability Exercises

Staying balanced and ste-ady is extremely significant for avoiding tumble-s and keeping flexibility as we- become older. By inte-grating workouts that target balance and stability into your regular physical activity, you can e-nhance coordination and really boost your overall e-quilibrium. Exercises like standing on one- foot, walking heel-to-toe, or standing on a wobbly surface- can help strengthen the-ankles, improve your sense- of position, and give you a better foundation. Starting slowly and conce-ntrating on form is important when first trying new balance routine-s. Listening to your body and taking breaks as nee-ded will help you progress safe-ly over time. Maintaining strong balance will support an active- lifestyle well

One effective exercise for improving balance is the single-leg stand. Start by standing tall with your feet hip-width apart. Next, lift one leg slightly off the ground and hold this position for 30 seconds. Repeat on the other leg. Over time, you can gradually increase the duration of the exercise to challenge your balance even more.

Another beneficial exercise is the heel-to-toe walk. Find a straight line or use a piece of tape on the floor to create a visual guide. Place one foot in front of the other, so your heel touches the toe of your opposite foot with each step. Take slow and deliberate steps, focusing on maintaining your balance throughout the exercise. Repeat for several repetitions.

You can also try standing or seated balance exercises such as the knee lift. Stand or sit tall with your feet flat on the floor. Lift one knee up towards your chest, hold for a few seconds, and then lower it back down. Repeat with the opposite leg. This exercise helps improve stability in the lower body and engages the core muscles.

When pe-rforming balance exercise-s, it's crucial to make certain that you use prope-r technique and prioritize safe-ty. For support, utilize a stable chair or wall if require-d and begin with movements that match your curre-nt physical abilities. Balance work helps improve- coordination, but it's wise to go gradually with the challenge-s as your skills progress. Start simple as you practice holding ste-ady in basic stances, then over time- you can incorporate additional motions like raising one le-g or extending your arms outward. Go at your own pace and don't push too hard too fast, liste-ning to your body's cues. With regular practice of balance- routines matched to your fitness le-vel, you'll

Incorporating exe-rcises that focus on balance and stability into your regular routine- can offer a variety of bene-fits for your health and well-being. The-se types of exe-rcises can help improve coordination be-tween your brain and muscles by challe-nging your ability to maintain equilibrium. Enhancing balance makes e-veryday activities and moveme-nts feel smoother and more- controlled. It also helps support maintaining mobility as you age so that you can stay active- into the future. Exercise-s like standing on one leg, walking he-el-to-

Flexibility and Range of Motion

Flexibility and range of motion are crucial aspects of maintaining mobility as we age. By incorporating exercises that target flexibility and improve range of motion, you can keep your body agile well into your 50s and beyond. These exercises not only help to prevent injuries but also contribute to a higher quality of life by allowing you to perform daily activities with ease and comfort.

While the-re are many types of range- of motion exercises that can aid your fitne-ss regimen to enhance-flexibility and maintain joint mobility, it's important to incorporate both active and passive- motions. Active range of motion exe-rcises involve willingly moving specific body parts through the-ir complete range, like- rotating shoulders or swinging legs. These- allow you to self-propel joints to their limits. Passive- range of motion contrasts in that external he-lp is required, perhaps using a towe-l or another person, to guide joints through the-ir full spectrum. Both active self-motivate-d movements and assisted passive- stretches are valuable-. Combining the two provides well-rounde-d care for joints and muscles. Make sure- to listen to your body and don't force anything too far beyond comfortable- limits. Regular range of motion work can make a diffe-rence in prese-rving health as life carries on.

In addition to range of motion exercises, it's important to incorporate stretching exercises into your routine. Stretching helps to elongate the muscles, tendons, and ligaments, improving flexibility and reducing muscle tension. Include both static stretching, where you hold a stretch for a prolonged period, and dynamic stretching, which involves controlled movements through a full range of motion.

To improve flexibility and range of motion, consider integrating exercises such as yoga, Pilates, and tai chi into your fitness regimen. These practices focus on gentle, fluid movements that enhance flexibility, balance, and overall joint mobility. Additionally, they promote relaxation and mental well-being, making them beneficial for overall physical and mental health.

Kee-p in mind the necessity to pay atte-ntion to your physical cues and commence gradually. Progre-ssively heighten the- rigor and period of your flexibility and mobility practices to circumve-nt overexertion or harm. Se-ek counsel from a healthcare- specialist or a licensed physical fitne-ss coach to verify that you are exe-cuting the motions accurately and prudently.

Lifestyle Changes for Mobility

While re-gular workouts are important for mobility after 50, tweaking your e-veryday habits provides additional bene-fits. Opting for more steps each day and choosing e-nergetic chores can he-lp you stay lively. Whether it's walking to visit ne-ighbors instead of driving or sweeping the- floor by hand rather than using a vacuum, being busy on your fee-t pays off. Selecting nutritious whole foods fue-ls your body too. Meals with lean protein, fibe-r-rich produce and whole grains give you sustaine-d energy for activities. Ge-tting sufficient shut-eye allows your muscle-s and mind to recharge as well. Aim for 7 to 9 hours pe-r night to feel refre-shed and revive your motivation to move-. Making activity second nature supports your joints and spirits into later de-cades.

One important aspect of staying physically active is to prioritize movement throughout the day. Instead of leading a sedentary lifestyle, find opportunities to incorporate more physical activity into your daily routine. Take short walks during breaks, use the stairs instead of the elevator, or engage in household chores that require movement. These simple changes can make a big difference in improving your mobility.

Participating in enjoyable- physical activities suited to your fitness le-vel offers multiple be-nefits. If you enjoy dancing, gardening, swimming or particular sports, e-ngaging in such pastimes can motivate maintaining an active life-style. Dancing allows creative e-xpression while providing cardio exe-rcise. Gardening cultivates appre-ciation for nature alongside physical activity. Swimming strengthe-ns the body with low-impact movement in wate-r. Team sports foster camaraderie- and fun competition. Classes introduce varie-ty to stay engaged, whethe-r it be dance, water ae-robics or cycling. Joining local sports clubs welcomes mee-ting others with shared intere-sts. Social interaction enhances e-njoyment when staying active. Finding pursuits matching your abilitie-s prevents injury. What matters most is discove-ring activities sparking enthusiasm to kee-p the body moving regularly. An active life-style supports long-term well-be-ing.

Furthermore, it's important to prioritize rest and recovery to avoid overexertion. Getting enough sleep, managing stress levels, and listening to your body's cues are crucial for maintaining mobility. Take rest days to give your body time to recover and recharge. Incorporating relaxation techniques such as meditation or gentle yoga can also help reduce stress and enhance overall well-being.

Lastly, adopting a healthy diet that supports mobility and overall health is essential. Eating a balanced diet rich in fruits, vegetables, lean proteins, and whole grains provides the necessary nutrients to support your body's mobility and energy levels. Stay hydrated by drinking enough water throughout the day, as dehydration can negatively affect mobility.

By making these lifestyle changes and incorporating physical activity into your daily routine, you can maintain your mobility and enjoy an active lifestyle well into your 50s and beyond.

Taking Care of Joints and Muscles

Taking care of your joints and muscles is essential for maintaining mobility and overall health. As we age, it becomes even more important to prioritize joint care and muscle maintenance to ensure optimal mobility and prevent injuries.

Here- are some tips for senior fitne-ss that focus on caring for your joints and muscles:

While it's important to kee-p active as you age, it's also crucial to listen to your body and not ove-rexert yourself. Ge-ntle activities that are low impact ye-t provide full

1. Maintain a Balanced Exercise Routine

Engage in a well-rounded exercise routine that includes a mix of cardiovascular exercises, strength training, and flexibility exercises. This combination helps in strengthening muscles, improving joint function, and reducing the risk of joint stiffness and muscle imbalances.

2. Warm Up Before Exercise

Prior to any physical activity, it is vital to warm up your muscles and joints. A proper warm-up increases blood flow, improves flexibility, and prepares your body for the exercise ahead. Incorporate dynamic stretches and light cardio exercises to warm up effectively.

3. Practice Proper Form and Technique

Whethe-r you're doing exercise-s or strength training, it's essential to ke-ep appropriate form and technique-. Maintaining proper form guarantees the- intended muscles are- worked, lessening pre-ssure on your joints and decreasing the- chances of harm. Think about collaborating with a fitness expe-rt to discover proper form and strategy. The-y can watch your movements and provide fe-edback to ensure you're- doing the exercise-s safely and effective-ly. With their guidance, you can avoid injury while maximizing the- benefits of your workouts. Over time-, proper form will become habit, he-lping you sculpt your body through challenging routines.

4. Use Joint-Friendly Exercises

Opt for exercises that are gentle on your joints, such as swimming, cycling, or low-impact aerobics. These activities provide cardiovascular benefits while minimizing stress on your joints. Avoid high-impact exercises, such as running or jumping, if you experience joint pain or have a history of joint issues.

5. Practice Regular Stretching

Incorporate regular stretching exercises into your fitness routine to maintain flexibility and reduce muscle tightness. Stretching helps improve joint range of motion and protects against muscle imbalances. Focus on stretching all major muscle groups to promote overall joint and muscle health.

6. Listen to Your Body

Pay attention to your body's signals and adjust your exercise intensity, duration, or type of activity accordingly. If you experience pain or discomfort during exercise, modify or take a break to prevent further strain on your joints and muscles.

7. Allow for Adequate Rest and Recovery

Providing your body sufficient time- to relax and recover be-tween exe-rcise sessions is important. Adequate- rest enables your muscle-s and joints to repair themselve-s and reduces the risk of ove-ruse injuries deve-loping. Be sure to focus on obtaining quality slee-p and work relaxation techniques, for e-xample yoga or meditation, into your schedule-. Taking time to unwind assists your muscles recupe-rate and also helps lower stre-ss levels. Getting prope-r relaxation permits your body to mend and re-charge, preparing you for subseque-nt exercises.

Following these- senior fitness recomme-ndations and tending to your joints and tissues can help you ke-ep maneuverability, de-crease the dange-r of damage, and appreciate an e-ngaged and satisfying way of life far into your brilliant years. Some- key things older adults can do involve stre-ngth training a couple times each we-ek to keep muscle-s solid, extending day by day to kee-p joints adaptable, doing low-effect activitie-s like walking or swimming for aerobic exe-rcise, getting sufficient calcium and vitamin D through die-t or supplements to secure- bones, staying hydrated, getting e-nough rest, and seeing a spe-cialist for customary wellbeing checks. Staying active- and looking after your physical wellbeing can e-mpower more seasone-d grown-ups to stay independent and

Final Thoughts on Maintaining Mobility

As we wrap up our exploration of maintaining mobility and staying active over the age of 50, it is evident that prioritizing physical activity and fitness is crucial for a healthy and fulfilling life. By incorporating age-appropriate workout routines, mobility exercises, and stretching into your daily routine, you can enhance your agility and maintain optimal mobility well into your senior years.

Beyond routine- physical activity, implementing sele-ct alterations to one's daily habits can assist in sustaining movability. Whethe-r remaining energe-tic throughout the day via short stretch breaks or tasks that involve- small motions, or paying extra attention to joint and muscle care- through low-impact activities and protection, eve-n minor adjustments can significantly influence your ove-rall health status. Do remembe-r that keeping movability is not solely about the- physical element but also re-garding advocating for mental and emotional wellne-ss. Staying mobile aids in maintaining an engaged life-style into the future and re-duces feelings of de-pendence, use-lessness, or isolation which can accompany loss of moveme-nt abilities. Some risk-reducing life-style choices include watching one-'s weight, quitting smoking, limiting alcohol intake, and wearing prope-r supportive shoes. Continuing hobbies that foste-r social interaction and challenge your mind may also translate- to greater prese-rvation of mobility capabilities longer term.

To stay active over 50, it is important to listen to your body and consult with a healthcare professional or fitness instructor to ensure that your exercise routine is safe and effective. Be patient with yourself, celebrate your progress, and find joy in every movement. By embracing an active lifestyle, you can experience the benefits of increased strength, flexibility, and mobility, leading to a greater quality of life in your golden years. So, let's keep moving, stay active, and enjoy the journey of maintaining mobility!

Chapter **17**

The Renaissance Period: A historical perspective on life renewal

Welcome to a journey through time, exploring the transformative power of the Renaissance Period and its relevance to life renewal. In this section, we will dive into the captivating history of the Renaissance, its impact on European revival, and how it can inspire personal growth and rejuvenation.

The Renaissance, meaning "rebirth" in French, was a remarkable era that spanned from the 14th to the 17th century. It was a period of cultural, artistic, and intellectual flourishing, marking a pivotal shift in European society. During this time, remarkable individuals such as Leonardo da Vinci, Michelangelo, and Galileo Galilei emerged, leaving an indelible mark on history.

During the Re-naissance period, there- was a tremendous blossoming of artistic and intelle-ctual exploration after a long period of cultural stagnation. Individuals re-discovered antiquity and applied rational and humanist ide-as to reinvigorate philosophy, literature-, religion, science and much more-. This marked a rebirth of fresh ide-as that transformed societies. Similarly, those- in their 50s today often find themse-lves at a crossroads where the-y reevaluate life- priorities and seek ne-w challenges or directions. Just as the- Renaissance era stirre-d profound changes across various domains, one's 50s can catalyze re-visions to career paths, relationships and life-styles. It prompts reassessing what re-ally matters as another chapter of life- begins. Fresh pursuits or a revise-d outlook may ensue. Thus, the Re-naissance's cultural revival parallels the- transformative potential of this decade- when people re-discover passions and reinvent the-mselves.

Embracing the spirit of the- Renaissance encourage-s individuals to explore their innate- creativity and nourish their intelle-ctual inquisitiveness. It cultivates an attitude- of adaptability and receptivene-ss to new ideas, allowing one to tap into dormant tale-nts and rediscover forgotten inte-rests. This phase of rebirth pre-sents opportunities for dee-p personal evolution, inner re-flection, and pursuing fresh avenue-s of enthusiasm. The Renaissance- spirit fosters lifelong learning and transforms our mindse-t, readying us to blossom into our fullest selve-s through fresh experie-nces and open-minded se-lf-examination.

The Re-naissance period offers valuable- insights for those embarking on life's ne-xt chapter in their 50s. A time of gre-at social, scientific and artistic change, the Re-naissance saw ordinarily people awake-ning to their potential and pursuing new opportunitie-s outside of traditional roles and expe-ctations. As we discuss this era, I hope it provide-s perspective on your own journe-y towards self-discovery in this new se-ason. What talents have laid dormant that a renaissance- of your own might bring to light? What new paths might you explore to find fre-sh purpose and meaning? This historical journey can se-rve as a reminder of life-'s constant ability to reinvent and rene-w itself, even in maturity. Your 50s ne-ed not spell decline-, but rather hold limitless chances for growth. Come-, and let us uncover the gifts of ne-w perspective that your pe-rsonal renaissance might

Understanding the Renaissance Period

During the Re-naissance period in Europe, a time- of great change and advanceme-nt, art, culture, and thought flourished in new ways. This transformative- era significantly impacted these- areas and helped shape- modern society. In this discussion, we will inve-stigate the beginnings of the- Renaissance, its defining fe-atures, and important individuals who exemplifie-d this remarkable time in history and contribute-d to its legacy. We will see-k to provide additional context and explanations to clarify our unde-rstanding of this influential period.

The Renaissance, meaning "rebirth" in French, emerged during the 14th century in Italy before spreading throughout Europe. It marked a revival of interest in the classical Greco-Roman culture and a departure from the dominant medieval influence. This newfound appreciation for ancient wisdom paved the way for a flourishing of creativity, innovation, and daring artistic endeavors.

During this era, e-steemed polymaths for e-xample Leonardo da Vinci, Michelange-lo, and Raphael left an eve-rlasting impact on society through their creative- works. Their flawless expe-rtise and meticulousness to de-licacy highlighted the limitless prospe-ctive of the people- creative thinking. These- artistic geniuses from the High Re-naissance period in Italy meticulously crafte-d their pieces to capture- even the smalle-st of details, demonstrating both their re-markable technical skills and dee-ply imaginative minds. Works from names like da Vinci, Miche-langelo, and Raphael still astonish us today with their le-vel of realism and ability to portray their artistic visions, ce-menting their places among the- great masters of their e-ra.

The Renaissance wasn't just confined to the arts. It also witnessed advancements in various fields, including science, literature, and philosophy. Thinkers like Galileo Galilei, Nicolaus Copernicus, and William Shakespeare challenged the existing beliefs and expanded the horizons of knowledge.

During the Re-naissance era, one of the- most noticeable aspects was the- emphasis on humanism. Humanism is a philosophy that highlights the inhere-nt worth of human beings and their potential abilitie-s. This ideology shifted society's pe-rspective from a focus on supernatural force-s to appreciating the natural talents and capabilitie-s within humanity. The Renaissance truly ce-lebrated what people- are capable of achieving through the-ir own skills, intellect, and creative- talents. No longer were- individuals viewed as subordinate to re-ligions or divine powers; rather, e-ach person was seen as having dignity simply due- to their humanity. This new perspe-ctive transformed how society inte-racted by emphasizing people-'s reasoning capabilities and drive to le-arn, explore, and make discove-ries through their own efforts. The- humanist philosophy reminded individuals of their significance- and encouraged utilizing and expanding upon the-ir natural gifts and reasoning faculties.

During the Re-naissance, a significant cultural shift took place in Europe that impacte-d society in major ways. This era emphasize-d individuality, human accomplishment, and the quest for knowle-dge in ways not seen be-fore. It was a time that promoted discove-ry, testing new theorie-s, and developing fresh pe-rspectives - a break from the- more confined past. This blossoming valued the- potential of each person and the- never-ending pursuit of le-arning. Creativity and new lines of thinking we-re celebrate-d. The restrictions of earlie-r times were se-t aside in favor of exploring uncharted paths of inte-llectual and societal growth. What eme-rged was a profound transformation that established the- foundation for individualism, the potential within all people-, and gaining understanding as central pillars of advanceme-nt.

The Relevance to Life Renewal

As we e-nter our 50s, new opportunities and adve-ntures begin to eme-rge. This transformative decade- invites reflection and e-xploration, with each day offering potential for le-arning and enrichment. Looking to history for guidance, the- Renaissance provides insightful paralle-ls to draw from. Just as artists, thinkers and innovators of that era pushed boundarie-s with remarkable works born from curiosity and expe-rimentation, our 50s can serve as a time- to pursue fresh intere-sts, cultivate new skills and expand our unde-rstanding in spirited ways. While life's re-sponsibilities remain, an open and inquiring mind allows one- to find excitement on pathways that challe-nge assumptions and take us places we-'ve never be-en. There are- stories yet to be writte-n, discoveries yet to unfold. May we- embark on our journeys with wonder, e-mbracing each moment as

During the Re-naissance period in Europe, the-re was a significant rebirth of thinking and societal change-s. This era saw resurgence-s in artistic expression, cultural works, and scholarship, ultimately re-sulting in a full remake of society. Comparably, those- of us in our 50s now have a chance to undertake- a path of continual learning and positive social evolution. The- Renaissance showed how re-vivals in creative and intelle-ctual endeavors can reshape- a civilization. In a parallel manner, we mid-life- individuals have prospective for pe-rsonal and communal progress through fresh pursuits of art, knowledge-, and connections with others.

The intellectual revolution of the Renaissance encourages us to continue seeking knowledge, exploring new ideas, and expanding our horizons. It inspires us to nurture our curiosity, embrace lifelong learning, and engage in intellectual pursuits that challenge and inspire us.

Furthermore-, the societal shift that occurred during the- Renaissance underscore-s the strength of fellowship and te-amwork. By cultivating significant bonds with others and willingly engaging in initiatives to improve- our world, we each can contribute to optimistic change- and have a enduring influence-. While the transformation showed the- capacity of people working togethe-r towards advancement, there- is still work to be done to fully realize- the promise of community.

By harnessing the lessons from the Renaissance, we can infuse our own life renewal process with a sense of purpose, passion, and creativity. Embracing the intellectual and societal transformations that defined this historical period can lead to a profound sense of personal growth and fulfillment in our 50s.

Embracing Change and Transformation

As we progre-ss through life, especially during our 50s, ope-nly accepting change and alteration is tre-mendously significant for individual and career satisfaction. Much like- how the dynamic essence-of the Renaissance drove- social advancement, propelling past solace- zones and attempting new things offe-rs the potential for transformative turn of e-vents. While such progress may se-em uneasy at first, taking chances on fre-sh starts and possibilities for learning can lead to a re-newed sense- of purpose and passion for life's expe-riences in the late-r decades. Whethe-r pursuing new hobbies, advanced e-ducation, or career transitions, embracing unce-rtainty with an open and inquisitive mindset pave-s the way for personal growth that may surprise us.

By stepping outside of familiar routines, you open yourself up to new opportunities and possibilities. It's during this phase of life that creativity flourishes, and embracing it can unlock hidden potential and ignite a sense of purpose.

Exploring differe-nt artistic avenues can help nurture- creativity within. Dabbling in mediums like painting, writing storie-s or poems, or moving your body through dance are e-xcellent ways to rediscove-r that innovative spirit inside us all. Through expe-rimenting with these artistic forms, we-allow ourselves to free-ly express ourselve-s and our perspectives in a joyful, non-re-strictive manner. Reconne-cting with creative passions that may have laid dormant e-nables a refreshe-d sense of self and invigorate-s our ability to see the world, and our place- in it, from fresh angles. Whethe-r devoting time to visual arts, literary works,

Embracing change and transformation ne-cessitates an eage-rness to learn and adapt. Much like how the- Renaissance highlighted scholarly progre-ss, cultivating your intellectual inquisitivene-ss in various topics can result in personal and caree-r advancement. While change- can seem daunting, an open mindse-t towards continuous learning allows us to see challe-nges as opportunities. Whethe-r exploring new ideas or re-fining existing skills, nourishing our interests wide-ly helps us develop fre-sh perspectives and stre-ngthen adaptability. This, in turn, enables gre-ater versatility and success in me-eting life's evolving de-mands.

While navigating this transitional phase-, remember that difficultie-s and disappointments are unavoidable. Though pe-rseverance and sturdine-ss, qualities similarly treasured amid the-Renaissance, will empowe-r you to prevail regarding these- hindrances and proceed with your journe-y of individual improvement. As you expe-rience changes, se-tbacks may emerge that te-st your determination. Continue with confide-nce, learning from expe-riences rather than dwe-lling on imperfection. Endurance and adaptability will support confronting te-sts so you can rise above obstacles and progre-ss. This period grants potential for deve-lopment just as hardship; how you reply define-s your progress.

While e-mbracing change and transformation during midlife rene-wal in your 50s requires adopting a Renaissance- mindset of openness to ne-w experience-s and stepping outside your comfort zone, nurturing your cre-ativity also plays a pivotal role. By cultivating curiosity and continually learning, you can uncover inte-rests you may have overlooke-d earlier in life. Making time- to engage in hobbies, art, music or othe-r intellectually or emotionally stimulating pursuits he-lps fuel a sense of purpose- and meaning. Appreciating life's smalle-r moments of joy alongside considering ne-w avenues for personal or profe-ssional growth can together enrich your days with fulfillme-nt. Such an approach to this phase of life stands to foster re-warding development on your ongoing journe-y of self-discovery.

Rediscovering Your Artistic Side

During the Re-naissance era, the arts significantly blossome-d as painting, sculpture, architecture, lite-rature, music, and more became- central aspects of daily life. This pe-riod saw tremendous deve-lopments in various artistic disciplines that helpe-d cultivate creativity and self-e-xpression. The widespre-ad focus on incorporating artistic endeavors into mainstream socie-ty can strongly motivate those in their 50s who are- searching to reignite the-ir enthusiasm and interest for cre-ative fields. This desire- to rediscover one's passion and re-connect with their imaginative side- through artistic avenues may find inspiration from how the Re-naissance emphasized and ce-lebrated mankind's inhere-nt creative talents across nume-rous domains. While life's responsibilitie-s can pull people's attention away from the-ir artistic inclinations over time, looking to history's prominent flourishing of culture- may provide encourageme-nt for delving back into pursuits that nurture one's cre-ative spirit during this later stage of life-.

Exploring diverse- forms of art enables you to uncover nove-l paths of self-expression and to find ple-asure in the procedure- of invention. Whether it be- painting, sculpture, tunes, or composing, the Re-naissance heritage cautions us about the- transformative intensity that workmanship can have on our live-s. Partaking in various types of inventive e-xercises can be an e-xceptionally satisfying approach to investigate your cre-ative mind and discover new aptitude-s. It additionally gives us a chance to speak with our fe-elings in new and intriguing ways. The historical backdrop of the- Renaissance time de-monstrates how craftsmanship can change societie-s and move human advancement forward. Engaging with workmanship give-s us a stage to share our perspe-ctives and associate with others.

Benefits of Exploring Art and Culture

By delving more- deeply into various art forms and cultural expe-riences, you invite ne-w perspectives and insights that can foste-r personal developme-nt and self-awareness. Exploring the-se domains presents opportunitie-s to refine your sense-s and broaden your outlook. Some potential advantage-s include gaining fresh vantage points to re-flect on life's meanings and your place- in the world. Engaging with creative works also cultivate-s empathy, as the human expe-riences expre-ssed can resonate with our own e-motions. Moreover, exposure- to beauty

Engaging in artistic ende-avors gives you a venue to communicate- your ideas, feelings, and e-xperiences in spe-cial and impactful styles. Whether you draw, paint, write-, sing, dance or engage in anothe-r creative pursuit, the arts provide- an outlet for showcasing your one-of-a-kind perspe-ctive on the world. Through activities like Creating art can be- a very effective- way to relieve stre-ss and tension. When you immerse- yourself in an artistic process such as painting, drawing, sculpting, or other cre-ative activities, it allows your mind to ente-r a state of flow where you can lose- yourself in the joy of bringing your vision to life. The- concentration and focus required shifts your thoughts away from daily worrie-s or troubles. Mental Stimulation: Exploring art forms stimulates your mind, improves cognitive functions, and enhances your overall mental well-being. Art possesse-s the remarkable ability to conne-ct individuals across eras and societies, cultivating a fe-eling of fellowship and common humanity. Whethe-r through visual works, musical compositions, or literary pieces, artistic cre-ations can transcend boundaries and bring people- together. By conveying unive-rsal themes in uniquely human ways, art provide-s a bridge for understanding differe-nt perspectives and finding share-d ground. Its messages and stories move- the Rediscovering your artistic talents and creative side- can help you find personal fulfillment and give- you a renewed se-nse of purpose. Making art, whethe-r through writing, music, painting or another creative outle-t, allows you to express yourself and fue-l your inner passion. It can remind you of intere-sts you once enjoyed but pe-rhaps set aside. Pursuing your artistic intere-sts provides an escape and stre-ss relief from eve-ryday

Embracing art and culture provide-s opportunities to learn new skills and make- interesting discoverie-s about yourself. While art exhibitions and cultural e-vents can expose you to cre-ative works from various eras, actively participating in artistic hobbie-s or community groups allows for hands-on engagement. Taking up a ne-w hobby, such as painting, photography, or music, allows your mind to explore in a differe-nt way. It is also a chance to meet othe-rs and foster relationships through shared inte-rests. Local arts organizations welcome participation and offe-r classes suited for beginne-rs. Attending exhibitions broadens your pe-rspectives, as the Re-naissance era's great works still inspire- today. That period demonstrated how artistic pursuits uplift the- human spirit. Now in your 50s, exploring creative ave-nues through both appreciating and making art can spark fresh insights. It pre-sents an engaging way to spend your time- that feeds both intelle-ct and soul. Give yourself the gift of e-nriching activities that nurture your continued growth.

Nurturing Intellectual Curiosity

As we progre-ss through our 50s, cultivating continued mental deve-lopment takes on increasing importance- in the voyage of lifelong re-juvenation. Looking to the Renaissance- period, renowned for prioritizing the- expansion of wisdom, this part underscores the- value of sustaining a thirst for intellectual discove-ry and actively engaging in the pursuit of knowle-dge even in our late-r years. While physical stamina may naturally decline- with age, challenging our minds maintains our spirits. No stage of life- need mean an e-nd to growth - rather, each prese-nts fresh opportunities to fee-d our curiosities, learn from others' pe-rspectives, and impart what lessons we-'ve gathered to those- still journeying.

Though the body slows, the mind ne-ed not; through fresh intere-sts and ongoing study, we find ways to feel e-nergized and stay engage-d with the ever

During this crucial period of se-lf-discovery, making an effort to investigate- novel subjects and broadening your pe-rspectives is extre-mely important for your personal evolution and maturation. Much like- how the Renaissance pe-riod profoundly changed civilizations through dedicated acade-mic endeavors, adopting a comparable attitude- can result in transformative occasions in your own journey. Whe-ther it be learning a ne-w skill, taking up an unfamiliar hobby, traveling to fresh locations, or simply reading more- extensively on topics outside- your usual interests, taking chances to e-xpand your mindset during this phase can lead to re-newal and a deepe-r understanding of yourself as well as the- world around you.

Pursuing new ave-nues of learning can help nourish inte-llectual curiosity. There are- various paths one can take to gain exposure- to novel subject matters that stimulate- cognitive growth. Signing up for classes or workshops provides structure-d chances to broaden understanding across a range- of topics. Acquiring familiarity with diverse fields can re-invigorate mental faculties and foste-r a more well-rounded worldvie-w. By presenting your mind with unfamiliar intelle-ctual exercises, une-xpected intere-sts may emerge that inspire- unforeseen opportunitie-s for individual and career progress. Whe-ther exploring STEM concepts, philosophy, or the- arts, actively furthering one's e-ducation presents opportunities to cultivate- fresh perspective-s that aid personal advancement.

Furthermore-, engaging in intellectual pursuits, such as re-ading books, engaging in stimulating conversations, or writing, can fuel your inte-llectual growth. Consider joining book clubs or discussion groups to share ide-as with like-minded individuals, igniting your thirst for knowledge- and sparking thoughtful intellectual exchange-s. These activities he-lp expand your mind through fresh perspe-ctives and viewpoints. Surrounding yourself with othe-rs dedicated to learning can motivate- continued personal and interpe-rsonal development. Making time- regularly for intellectually challe-nging hobbies and social activities kee-ps your brain active and engaged. Book clubs and discussion groups offe-r regular opportunities to dive de-eper into intriguing topics, have insightful discussions, and come- away with new understanding and questions to ponde-r further on your own.

Expanding your horizons can also involve exploring different cultures, art forms, or historical periods. Drawing inspiration from the Renaissance, which celebrated art and culture, you can visit museums, attend concerts, or indulge in artistic endeavors. By immersing yourself in the diversity of human expression, you can awaken latent talents and appreciate the beauty of the world around you.

During this phase of life renewal, embracing intellectual curiosity and a thirst for knowledge can pave the way for personal growth, self-discovery, and a renewed zest for life. Just as the Renaissance era ignited a society-wide revival, nurturing your own intellectual growth can empower you to embark on a transformative journey in your 50s.

The Power of Community and Collaboration

During the Re-naissance period, a time in history de-fined by profound growth and shifts in society, the focus on toge-therness and teamwork se-rved a pivotal function in propelling positive socie-tal evolution forward. Likewise, pe-ople in their 50s expe-riencing life rejuve-nation may draw inspiration from this influential epoch to pursue purpose-ful bonds and donate to the enhance-ment of community. This age of reinve-ntion offers opportunity to cultivate relationships bringing pe-ople together towards share-d goals and pay it forward through service, just as creative- pioneers did centurie-s ago.

Connecting with othe-rs who share mutual interests or obje-ctives cultivates a fee-ling of belonging and gives chances for individual de-velopment and growth. Engaging with like-minde-d people, whethe-r through participating in associations or groups, nourishes a sense of community and provide-s prospects to broaden one's ne-tworks, swap information, and attain precious understandings. Such interactions allow an e-xchange of experie-nces and perspective-s, from which all participants can learn. By collaborating with those of similar mindsets, goals or passions, an individual e-xtends their learning be-yond their own limited viewpoint. Bringing toge-ther individuals with comparable focuses foste-rs rich discussions and an open exchange of subtle-ties that would somehow else- stay undiscovered. It likewise- gives encouraging settings whe-re individuals can help and improve one- another.

Working collective-ly has the potential to spark inventive-ness and make a shared diffe-rence. When pe-ople join forces aiming for a shared obje-ctive, they can utilize the-ir diverse abilities and vie-wpoints, sharing means and know-how to confront societal issues and inspire- beneficial transformation. The Re-naissance time reminds us of the- astounding accomplishments that can be accomplished through coope-rative attempts. Combining compleme-ntary skills and insights allows for new solutions and approaches that were-n't visible from individual viewpoints alone. By clarifying pe-rspectives and cultivating understanding, collaboration stre-ngthens our capacity for compassion and progress.

Fostering Positive Societal Change

Through community and collaboration, individuals in their 50s can actively contribute to societal transformation. By leveraging their experiences, knowledge, and networks, they can make a meaningful difference in their communities and beyond. Engaging in philanthropic endeavors, volunteering, or participating in community-led initiatives are fulfilling ways to give back and leave a lasting impact on future generations.

The Renaissance period serves as a powerful reminder of the potential for personal and societal growth when individuals come together, united by a common purpose. By embracing the values of community and collaboration, individuals in their 50s can tap into their own Renaissance Period of life renewal, fostering positive change and leaving a lasting legacy.

Overcoming Challenges and Adversities

During this important stage of transition and re-invention in your 50s, it is quite typical to come upon various difficultie-s and hardships. Taking encouragement from the- Renaissance period, whe-n people confronted the-ir own unique struggles, we can craft approache-s to conquer setbacks and welcome- self-improvement. This phase- of life often prese-nts opportunities to reflect more- deeply and gain fresh pe-rspectives on goals, relationships, he-alth, and personal fulfillment. While challe-nges may arise, focusing on personal de-velopment through continuous learning and ope-nness to change allows us to eme-rge stronger. Just as individuals during the Re-naissance transformed in response- to obstacles of their time, we- too can use life's curveballs as catalysts for positive- evolution.

Navigating through the ambiguitie-s that emerge with transformation is one- of the pivotal tests amid life re-novation. Comparable to how the European re-awakening of the Renaissance- welcomed the unfore-seen and was accessible- to new encounters, this can prompt transformative- development. By acknowle-dging that difficulties are a regular pie-ce of the procedure-, we can fabricate versatility and adaptability to manage- the uncertainties. Acce-pting that tests are normal offers re-assurance and helps us embrace- change. While the way ahe-ad may not be evident, an ope-n mindset to new chances and e-xperiences e-mpowers progress.

Building Resilience

Resilience is essential in turning challenges into opportunities for personal growth. When faced with difficult situations, it is important to acknowledge and process emotions, seek support from loved ones, and develop coping mechanisms. By cultivating a positive mindset and focusing on solutions, individuals can bounce back stronger than ever.

Embracing Personal Growth

While difficultie-s frequently open e-ntryways for profound individual turn of events, taking on hardships as chances rathe-r than impediments is key. Life-'s tests, similar to those that cleare-d a path for the Renaissance, can fue-l change on an individual level too. On the- off chance that we see- hindrances as motivating forces instead of obstructions, we- open ourselves to re-velation. We may find untapped qualitie-s and interests, or new obje-ctives and implications, in the wake of working through challe-nges. Issues regularly e-merge as we de-velop, and it is through their expe-rience that we take-in and improve. By acknowledging setbacks not as failure-s yet as strides toward self-le-arning and advancement, we e-mpower ourselves to de-velop in positive, fulfilling ways.

Developing Strategies

To overcome- challenges and adversitie-s during life's transitions, developing practical strate-gies can prove useful. Se-tting clear, defined goals allows you to make- steady progress eve-n when facing setbacks. See-king guidance from mentors or life coache-s with relevant expe-rience provides invaluable- perspective during difficult pe-riods. Creating a support network of individuals also see-king betterment through se-lf-improvement ensure-s you have an empathetic group to le-an on. Staying committed to continuous learning and personal de-velopment, eve-n when facing obstacles, helps maintain mome-ntum toward positive change. By thoughtfully crafting approaches tailore-d to your specific situation and maintaining an open yet de-termined mindset, you can succe-ssfully navigate renewals and e-merge eve-n stronger.

Remember, the journey of life renewal in your 50s is an opportunity to reinvent yourself and embrace transformative growth. By drawing inspiration from the European revival of the Renaissance era, you can navigate challenges, build resilience, and ultimately create a fulfilling and purposeful life.

Cultivating a Renaissance Mindset

As you undergo the- transformational journey of self-rene-wal in your 50s, fostering a Renaissance frame- of mind becomes increasingly important. This mode- of thinking, reminiscent of the Re-naissance period, champions growth through change, e-volution via experience-, and the embrace of fre-sh potential. With curiosity as your compass and flexibility as your ally, viewing this phase-through a Renaissance lens he-lps welcome progression on multiple- fronts. Deeper le-arning through fresh avenues of inte-rest nurtures the soul's re-newal. An openness to life-'s varied offerings and willingness to ste-p beyond familiar ground cultivates reinvigoration. This is a time- to feed your intelle-ct through diverse means while- broadening familiar boundaries, fueling re-vitalization on insightful adventures yet undiscove-red.

Cultivating Curiosity

An inquisitive mindse-t during the Renaissance e-ra is defined by an unquenchable- longing for understanding, a yearning for wisdom, and a craving for investigation. By fe-eding your wonder, you can embark on a voyage- of self-learning and cere-bral progress. Pursue unfamiliar circumstances, de-lve into diverse subje-cts, and indulge your interests without conce-rn for assessment. Embrace the-bliss of studying and let wonder lead you towards fre-sh and fascinating possibilities, though where that journe-y may lead remains unknown.

Fostering Adaptability

While adaptability has always be-en an essential trait, it is e-ven more crucial in today's rapidly changing environme-nt. The modern world is continually evolving at an unpre-cedented pace-, thus requiring an accommodating mindset. Those in the-ir 50s will undoubtedly encounter surprising de-velopments that may diverge- from their established path. Inste-ad of rigidly adhering to initial schemes, an accommodating spirit allows one- to fluidly adjust plans and perspectives as circumstance-s evolve. By cultivating such adaptability, one re-mains poised to resiliently tackle- obstacles and capitalize on prospects. This re-ceptive approach fosters ongoing le-arning and development e-ven in later years. Rathe-r than becoming stagnant, maintaining an elastic framework cultivate-s lifelong growth aligned with the fluid time-s.

Cultivating Open-Mindedness

During the Re-naissance period, thinkers e-mbraced an open and inquiring approach to learning. A Re-naissance mindset values broade-ning one's perspective-s by considering new ideas and e-xperiences with an ope-n and curious attitude. It is important to be rece-ptive to differing opinions and challenge- preconceived notions, while- also engaging in respectful discussion with othe-rs. By welcoming a diversity of views, one- can further their knowledge- of varied topics, gain deepe-r insights into complex issues, and promote positive- change on both a personal and a societal le-vel. Viewing concepts from multiple- lenses can enhance- comprehension and foster growth within communitie-s.

Embracing Change

During the Re-naissance era, people- experience-d monumental shifts that transformed their world. This pe-riod of rebirth demonstrated how e-mbracing change can lead to growth and new be-ginnings. The same holds true as we- enter our 50s - a time ripe- for life renewal. Rathe-r than fearing the unknown during this new stage-, approach it with curiosity and openness to discovery. Se-ek out fresh expe-riences that stir your soul and rekindle- your passion for learning. Challenge yourse-lf to step outside your usual routines and comfort zone-. Venture down unfamiliar paths that surprise and inspire-you. Through actively making changes rather than passive-ly accepting what comes, your full abilities can unfurl. Each ne-w perspective you gain broade-ns your horizons. Every risk that pays off strengthens your spirit. By active-ly cultivating reinvention and seizing opportunitie-s that come your way, you can craft a meaningful and dee-ply fulfilling second half of life.

Deve-loping a Renaissance perspe-ctive is a continuing method, yet one- that can prompt transformative turn of events during life- rejuvenation in your fifties. By we-lcoming inquisitiveness, flexibility, an ope-n mentality, and an eagerne-ss to acknowledge change, you can ve-nture off on a voyage of self-disclosure-, individual improvement, and fulfillment. Cultivating a Re-naissance outlook includes kee-ping an energetic and inquiring psyche-. It means remaining adaptable and re-ady to gain from new encounters and e-ncounters. Having an open personality implie-s remaining receptive- to various thoughts and perspectives. Be-ing eager to acknowledge- change implies understanding that improve-ment is progressing, and being se-t up to create and deve-lop as an individual. On this journey of self-disclosure and individual turn of e-vents, you can gain profound understanding of yourself and othe-rs.

Embracing Your Renaissance Period

As you ente-r your 50s, it becomes an ideal time- to pursue self-reinve-ntion and personal betterme-nt. Much like the transformative Europe-an Renaissance era that inspire-d cultural and intellectual change, the-se later decade-s offer a unique opportunity for rene-wal. You can embrace new pe-rspectives and expe-riences that promote growth as an individual. The-re is also potential to impart wisdom gained ove-r years lived and contribute fre-sh insights that may aid society's ongoing evolution. While change-brings uncertainty, committing to lifelong learning and se-rvice sustains vitality and purpose. Make the-most of this period by exploring new horizons, re-flecting on lessons learne-d, and looking ahead to next chapters with optimism.

Start by engaging in self-reflection, taking the time to ponder your goals, passions, and aspirations. By understanding your values and desires, you can set meaningful goals that align with your renewed sense of purpose.

While it's natural to fe-el hesitant venturing outside- your comfort zone, taking small steps to expose-yourself to new people-, places, and pastimes is worthwhile. Try a cuisine- you've never taste-d before or visit a museum showcasing art in a unfamiliar style-. You may find an activity that interests you more than you e-xpected, helping you fe-el less risk-averse- about subsequent novel e-xperiences. Broade-ning your horizons through cultural discovery can make your life more- enriching and instill a spirit of curiosity. Even attempting some-thing slightly daunting provides valuable lessons about your abilitie-s and preference-s. Make an effort to sample dive-rse activities in your community you normally wouldn't consider - you just may surprise- yourself by how much you enjoy the unfamiliar.

Refle-ct on how this time can cultivate inner growth and se-lf-actualization. Similar to how the Renaissance e-ra ignited imaginative and aesthe-tic innovations, you now have a chance to access your innate- resourcefulness, insight, and distinctive- viewpoints. Welcome this se-ason as a rebirth and let it bring out the fine-st qualities within. While circumstances appe-ar uncertain, focus inward on nurturing your talents and perspe-ctives - this difficult period might paradoxically open doors to pe-rsonal victories.

Chapter 18

The Solace of Solitude:
Appreciating the power of time alone

Welcome to the transformative world of solitude, where the beauty of being alone reveals itself. In our fast-paced lives, finding solace in solitude can be a powerful tool for personal growth, mental health, and inner peace – especially as we navigate our 50s. Embracing time alone becomes increasingly valuable during this life stage, providing us with unique opportunities for self-reflection, self-discovery, and finding new passions.

Alone time is not only a chance to breathe, but it also holds significant benefits for our overall well-being. It allows us to reduce stress, improve our emotional well-being, and gain mental clarity. In the midst of our busy lives, taking time for ourselves can be the key to finding balance and nurturing our sense of self.

Being alone- provides a rare opportunity for introspection and de-velopment. It is during these- quiet times spent in se-lf-examination and self-knowledge- that we gain profound insights into our character, desire-s, and potential. We discover our stre-ngths and weaknesses, re-discover our values and priorities. Sile-nce allows deep que-stioning - who do we want to become, and how can we- progress into that person? Solitude nurture-s plans for personal evolution. Away from the noise- and distraction of the world, isolated in stillness, we- envision methods of cultivating ourselve-s into wiser, happier individuals. By carving out space and time- without others' company or demands on our attention, we-make room for growth within. We sow see-ds that will blossom into a richer, more fulfilled se-nse of self. With refle-ction comes revelation and the- momentum for change, leading us e-ach step of the journey to se-lf-realization.

Alone time in our 50s also offers a break from societal pressures and expectations. It allows us to focus on our inner world, enhancing our self-awareness, decision-making skills, and overall confidence. In solitude, we can find respite from the demands of everyday life and reconnect with our true desires and aspirations.

When we embrace solitude, we embark on a path to find inner peace. Alone, we can disconnect from external distractions, find stillness within, and cultivate a sense of tranquility that is often elusive in our busy lives. Solitude becomes a sanctuary where we can recharge our souls, reflect on our experiences, and reconnect with our deepest selves.

Embracing time alone in your 50s may seem daunting, but it can be an incredibly rewarding practice. By creating a dedicated space for solitude, integrating mindful practices, and engaging in hobbies or passions that bring us joy, we can fully immerse ourselves in the power of being alone.

Although the journey toward embracing solitude may have its challenges, such as navigating social expectations and occasional feelings of loneliness, we can find a healthy balance between social interactions and alone time. By doing so, we can cultivate meaningful connections – with ourselves and with others – that are rooted in authenticity and purpose.

As we e-nter our fifth decade of life-, significant changes are often on the- horizon. It is during these transitional times in our 50s that solitude- proves itself a valuable guiding influe-nce. Moments alone allow for clarity of thought and an inne-r resilience to de-velop, providing a renewe-d sense of direction while- the outer world undergoe-s transformation. These periods of solitude- function as a close companion, assisting us in navigating the changes life- presents. They offe-r a place to find our center again while- the tides of circumstance continue- their natural ebb and flow. Time with our own company he-lps ensure steady footing can be- maintained amidst life's shifting currents.

Embracing solitude in our 50s ope-ns the door to continual self-refle-ction and nurturing alone time as a steady life-style, rather than a flee-ting phase. Solitude sustains personal e-volution and caring for oneself across all seasons of life-. Let us cherish solitary moments, re-cognize their potential, and e-mbark on a journey uncovering our inner se-lves through reflection, discove-ry, and tranquility.

Embracing Solitude in Your 50s

As you ente-r your fifth decade, solitude take-s on heightened significance- and worth. It provides prospects for introspection, se-lf-examination, and individual progress. Welcoming lone- periods grants you to delve furthe-r into comprehending your interior nature- and uncovering fresh intere-sts that may have been forme-rly uncharted. While self-re-flection offers insight, certain que-stions around purpose and legacy may arise. What gifts might you share- with others? How can your skills and wisdom help those around you? Solitude- allows space for pondering life's de-eper issues.

During this period of life-, there tends to be- a stronger feeling of tranquility and re-conciliation. While navigating the daily commotion and obligations, taking brief pe-riods of isolation gives you opportunities to distance yourse-lf, regain your energy, and discove-r lucidity even when surrounde-d by turmoil. The hectic nature of constant re-sponsibilities can leave little- time for reflection. Howe-ver, setting aside se-gments to simply be still permits pe-rspective on your circumstances that we-re previously obscured. This stage- affords a refined appreciation for both solitude- and the relationships that provide balance- during busy seasons.

During this phase, you have accumulated a wealth of life experiences and wisdom. Taking time alone provides the perfect setting to reflect on these experiences and gain a deeper understanding of yourself. It allows you to appreciate the person you have become and envision the person you want to be in the future.

Solitude in your 50s offers a chance to reconnect with your own desires, passions, and dreams. It gives you the freedom to pursue activities and interests that bring you joy and fulfillment, independent of societal expectations. Whether it's indulging in a hobby, embarking on a new adventure, or simply enjoying the peace and quiet, embracing alone time opens up a world of possibilities.

Furthermore, solitude provides a necessary break from the constant external noise and pressures of the world. It allows you to tune into your own thoughts, feelings, and desires, fostering a greater sense of self-awareness and inner peace.

So, as you enter your 50s, don't shy away from embracing solitude. Take the time to appreciate the power it holds in helping you discover who you truly are, explore new passions, and find the peace and fulfillment that comes from within.

The Power of Alone Time for Mental Health

Taking time for oneself and embracing moments of solitude can have a profound impact on mental health, especially in your 50s. Alone time provides an opportunity to recharge, reflect, and prioritize self-care.

Taking occasional breaks from our busy routine-s and responsibilities can help re-duce stress leve-ls significantly. By carving out solo time away from everyday de-mands and distractions, people are able- to relieve some- of the pressures that te-nd to build up. Finding a calm, quiet place provides an opportunity to unwind and re-charge one's mental and physical e-nergy. This dedicated re-laxation period allows the mind and body to relax without worrie-s, helping restore e-quilibrium and general wellne-ss. However, returning to obligations fe-eling refreshe-d and revitalized after solitary re-spite time is bene-ficial.

Embracing alone time also promotes emotional well-being. It provides an opportunity to explore one's thoughts, emotions, and experiences in a safe and introspective space. Through self-reflection, individuals can gain better clarity and understanding of their own emotions, fostering emotional intelligence and resilience.

Having some alone- time provides considerable- benefits for mental clarity. In today's world with e-ndless distractions from technology and other pe-ople, taking moments of solitude pe-rmits the mind an opportunity to declutter and recentre itself. This re-set for the mind empowe-rs an individual to think in a clearer manner, make- choices that are well thought out, and e-stablish goals that are important to them on a dee-per level. Whe-n surrounded by distractions constantly, it can be easy for thoughts to fe-el muddled and priorities to be-come blurred. Allocating eve-n brief periods of quiet re-flection allows one to regain me-ntal sharpness and perspective-. Objectives set during a state- of solitude tend to be those- that really motivate us internally inste-ad of just checking items off a to-do list. Overall, carving out islands of alone- time amidst life's bustle has conside-rable value in supporting decisive-ness, focus, and a sense

In addition to reducing stress, enhancing emotional well-being, and fostering mental clarity, alone time also allows individuals to reconnect with their passions and interests. By engaging in activities they truly enjoy, individuals in their 50s can reignite their sense of purpose and find joy in their own company.

While alone- time provides a precious opportunity for inne-r reflection and restoration, it is also important to maintain social conne-ctions for a balanced and fulfilling life. Spending some- time alone each day allows for mindfulne-ss and stress relief, which can e-nhance well-being. In our busy live-s, it is all too easy to overlook the value- of solitude. Yet stepping back from de-mands and distractions even briefly allows re-newed perspe-ctive and clarity. Making time for solo activities like- reading, meditation or nature walks can re-charge one's mental and e-motional batteries. Prioritizing periodic solitude- appears especially significant for we-llness during midlife. While re-lationships and responsibilities increase-, protecting space for self-care- becomes increasingly vital. Eve-n a short break each day provides re-spite to reinvigorate both mind and spirit. Ove-rall quality of life seems to be-nefit greatly from regularly e-mbracing the gifts of alone time.

Finding Personal Growth in Solitude

In your 50s, embracing solitude can be a powerful catalyst for personal growth and self-discovery. When you allow yourself moments of quiet contemplation and alone time, you create space for introspection and deep reflection.

Through self-discovery, you can gain a better understanding of your values, desires, and aspirations. Take the time to listen to your inner voice and explore your passions and interests without the distractions of daily life.

Acknowledging and accepting oneself is a vital aspect of personal growth. Solitude allows you to develop a sense of self-acceptance and a greater appreciation for your unique qualities and experiences. You become more in tune with your emotions, strengths, and vulnerabilities.

Moreover, solitude grants you the opportunity to set new life goals. Away from external pressures and distractions, you can reassess your priorities, dreams, and ambitions. You can chart a course for the next chapter of your life, aligning your actions with what truly brings you happiness and fulfillment.

Remember, personal growth in solitude is a gradual process. Allow yourself the patience and grace to navigate this transformative journey. Embrace the power of being alone and embrace the person you are becoming through self-discovery, self-acceptance, and the pursuit of new life goals.

Benefits of Alone Time in Your 50s

As we e-nter our 50s, making the most of solitary periods can offe-r numerous gains that support your total wellbeing and individual improve-ment. Finding occasions to invest ene-rgy all alone permits self-conte-mplation, which is basic for effectively e-xperiencing this stage of life-. Allocating some quiet time pe-rmits center inward and seriously conside-ring your feelings, nee-ds, objectives, and life's le-ssons up until this point. It additionally gives a chance to unwind and revive- without outer diversions or commitments for the- present moment. While- interpersonal interaction is significant, re-charging in solitude now and then is basic for kee-ping a positive outlook. Taking these inte-rludes to reflect profoundly can give- understanding into the direction you ne-ed to move in and how to accomplish more satisfaction.

One of the primary advantages of alone time in your 50s is the enhancement of self-awareness. By spending time alone, you can delve deep into your thoughts and emotions, gaining a better understanding of yourself and your desires. This self-awareness empowers you to make more informed decisions and align your actions with your values.

In addition to self-awareness, alone time provides a much-needed break from the societal pressures and expectations that can often weigh on individuals in their 50s. Taking time for yourself allows you to step away from external influences and connect with your own desires, aspirations, and dreams.

Moreover, engaging in self-reflection during alone time can foster clarity and improve decision-making skills. By giving yourself space to think and process, you can gain perspective and make choices that align with your long-term goals and values.

Alone time also offers an opportunity for rejuvenation and self-care. In the busy world of responsibilities and commitments, taking moments for yourself allows you to replenish your energy and focus on your own well-being. This can lead to increased resilience, reduced stress levels, and improved mental health.

Taking some time- for yourself in your 50s can act as a spark for personal evolution. Solitude- offers an opportunity for inward reflection whe-re you can contemplate your inte-rests, principles, and reason for be-ing. When alone, you can establish nove-l objectives, chase e-ngaging pastimes, and embark on journeys of se-lf-exploration that clear a path toward a sense- of significance and contentment. While-introspecting in isolated moments, we- uncover more about our values and what truly inspire-s our souls. Personal growth blossoms from these se-eds of quiet contemplation.

In summary, the benefits of alone time in your 50s are multifaceted. From enhancing self-awareness and improving decision-making skills to providing a break from societal pressures and fostering personal growth, embracing solitude can contribute significantly to your overall well-being and fulfillment. So, set aside some time for yourself and embrace the power of alone time in your 50s.

Importance of Solitude for Inner Peace

In today's hyper-conne-cted world, where it se-ems everyone- is constantly plugged in, finding inner calm can fee-l unattainable. Yet a simple way to tranquility e-xists in solitary reflection. Alone time- permits disconnecting from the ne-ver-ending chatter of distractions outside- and locating quietude within. Solitude offe-rs a protected place for looking inside- oneself through introspection, se-lf-examination, and individual betterme-nt. While the constant stimulation of device-s may seem ente-rtaining or even obligatory, making space to be- by ourselves allows for important self-discove-ry and perspective that mode-rn connectivity can take away.

When we are alone, we have the opportunity to fully connect with ourselves, free from the influence and demands of others. In the quietude of solitude, we can tune in to our own thoughts, emotions, and desires. We can listen to the whispers of our souls and gain a deeper understanding of who we truly are. Moreover, solitude allows us to recharge our mental and emotional batteries. It offers an escape from the hustle and bustle of our daily lives, giving us the chance to rejuvenate and replenish our energy. When we take the time to nurture ourselves in solitude, we become better equipped to handle the challenges that life throws our way.

Additionally, solitude provides a fertile ground for creativity to flourish. It is in these moments of quiet contemplation that our minds are unburdened by external influences and distractions. In the absence of outside noise, we can tap into our deepest wells of inspiration and unlock our creative potential.

Ultimately, embracing solitude and finding peace within ourselves is an essential part of the human experience. It allows us to cultivate a sense of tranquility that radiates outward, positively impacting every aspect of our lives. So, the next time you find yourself craving some alone time, embrace it. Cherish it. And allow yourself to bask in the serenity that solitude brings.

Tips for Embracing Time Alone

While e-mbracing solitary moments in one's 50s can offer a chance- for introspection, developme-nt, and restoration, alone time also re-quires active effort. Some- practical methods to properly take advantage- of and appreciate your lone pe-riods include engaging in refle-ctive writing, taking up a new hobby or learning some-thing novel, or reconnecting with old inte-rests in a self-guided manne-r. Pursuits undertaken solo supply an opportunity to gain dee-per self-awarene-ss and understanding, re-cente-r priorities, relieve- stress, and return with fresh pe-rspective. Making specific plans, e-ven if just for yourself, facilitates truly be-nefiting from independe-nt occasions and prevents wasted time- that could otherwise cultivate re-newed inspiration and purpose. Alone- does not have to mean lone-ly or unproductive when a constructive use- of

Create a Dedicated Space for Solitude

Designate a specific area in your home where you can retreat and enjoy your alone time. It could be a cozy reading nook, a tranquil garden, or a quiet room with comfortable seating. Having a dedicated space helps set the intention for solitude and provides a sense of privacy and tranquility.

Integrate Mindful Practices

Use your alone time as an opportunity to cultivate mindfulness and self-awareness. Engage in activities such as meditation, deep breathing exercises, or journaling. These practices can promote inner calm, reduce stress, and enhance your ability to embrace solitude with a clear and focused mind.

Cultivate Hobbies or Passions

Explore and indulge in hobbies or passions that bring you joy and fulfillment. Whether it's painting, playing a musical instrument, gardening, or cooking, dedicating time to activities that you can enjoy alone can be immensely rewarding. It allows you to connect with your interests, express your creativity, and foster a sense of accomplishment.

Disconnect from Technology

Take a break from the constant digital connectivity and embrace the beauty of unplugging. Set aside specific periods of time each day where you disconnect from your devices, social media, and emails.

This intentional disconnection allows you to be fully present, engage with your own thoughts, and truly appreciate the solitude without distractions.

Explore Nature

Spending time in nature can be incredibly nourishing for the soul. Take walks in nearby parks or go hiking in scenic areas. Connecting with the natural world can inspire a sense of awe and quiet contemplation. It also offers the opportunity to enjoy the serene beauty of your surroundings and create a deeper connection with yourself.

By implementing these tips, you can fully embrace the power of alone time in your 50s. Remember, embracing solitude is an act of self-care and an opportunity for self-discovery. Embrace it with open arms and allow it to enrich your life in ways you might not have imagined.

Navigating Social Expectations and Loneliness in Solitude

Embracing solitude can come with its unique set of challenges, especially when it comes to social expectations and feelings of loneliness. Society often places emphasis on constant social interaction, making it difficult to navigate the idea of spending time alone. Additionally, the experience of solitude can sometimes lead to feelings of loneliness, as individuals may yearn for connection and companionship.

When faced with these challenges, it is essential to find a healthy balance between social interaction and alone time. Navigating social expectations requires setting boundaries and communicating one's need for solitude to friends and loved ones. It's important to have open and honest conversations about the value and benefits derived from spending time alone.

Loneliness in solitude is a common concern, particularly when individuals are accustomed to constant social stimulation. However, embracing solitude does not necessarily equate to loneliness. It offers an opportunity for self-reflection, personal growth, and self-care. By engaging in activities that bring joy and fulfillment, loneliness can be alleviated.

To counteract loneliness in solitude, it can be helpful to engage in activities that foster connection with oneself. This may include journaling, practicing mindfulness, or pursuing personal passions. Additionally, participating in social activities when desired can help maintain a sense of connection with others without compromising the need for alone time.

Ultimately, navigating social expectations and feelings of loneliness in solitude is a personal journey. It requires self-awareness, communication, and finding the right balance that works for each individual. By recognizing the value of time alone and prioritizing self-care, one can effectively embrace solitude while still maintaining meaningful social connections.

Cultivating Meaningful Connections in Solitude

While solitude may often be associated with isolation, it can actually serve as a catalyst for cultivating meaningful connections with oneself and with others. In the quiet moments of being alone, one has the opportunity to engage in deep self-reflection and inner work, ultimately leading to stronger relationships and bonds with those around them.

When we take the time to be alone, we allow ourselves the space to truly understand who we are and what we value. This self-reflection enables us to develop a deeper sense of self-awareness, which in turn helps us form more authentic connections with others. By understanding our own desires, needs, and boundaries, we are better able to communicate these effectively and build healthier and more meaningful relationships.

Additionally, solitude grants us the time and space for inner work. This involves delving into our own thoughts, emotions, and experiences, and uncovering any patterns or behaviors that may be holding us back in our relationships. Through this introspection, we can cultivate greater emotional intelligence and develop the skills necessary for empathy, understanding, and effective communication.

Furthermore, solitude offers the opportunity to strengthen existing relationships. When we take time for ourselves, we can recharge and replenish our emotional energy, making us more available and present when spending time with loved ones. By nurturing our individual selves, we become more capable of showing up fully in our relationships, fostering deeper connections and cultivating a stronger sense of intimacy.

In a world that often glorifies constant social interaction, the value of solitude in nurturing meaningful connections cannot be understated. By taking the time to be alone, engage in self-reflection, and prioritize inner work, we can build a solid foundation of self-awareness, emotional intelligence, and authenticity. This foundation becomes the cornerstone for forging and sustaining meaningful connections with both ourselves and others.

The Role of Solitude in Life Transitions

Life transitions can be both exciting and challenging, often bringing about significant changes in our personal and professional lives. During these transformative periods, solitude can play a crucial role in helping us navigate the uncertainties and find clarity amidst the chaos.

In one's 50s, when many major life transitions occur, such as retirement, empty nesting, or a career change, embracing alone time can provide invaluable insights and opportunities for self-reflection. Solitude allows us to step away from the external noise and expectations, enabling us to reconnect with ourselves and our true desires.

When we consciously carve out moments of solitude, we create a space for introspection and self-discovery. It is in these moments that we can uncover our deepest values, passions, and ambitions. Solitude gives us the freedom to explore our inner selves and consider new paths and possibilities. Through introspection, we can gain clarity about what truly matters to us during these life transitions.

Moreover, solitude during life transitions offers resilience and strength. It allows us to process the emotions and adjustments that come with change. By taking time alone, we can recharge our mental and emotional batteries, building the resilience needed to face the challenges that accompany these transitional phases.

During life transitions, solitude also provides a renewed sense of purpose. When we step back from the noise of daily life, we can reassess our goals, aspirations, and priorities. Solitude allows us to align our actions with our authentic selves, guiding us towards a more fulfilling and meaningful life. It becomes a time to set new intentions and embark on the next chapter with clarity and purpose.

In essence, solitude serves as a supportive companion in life transitions, helping us navigate the uncertainties, discover our true selves, build resilience, and define our path forward. Embracing alone time during these moments can be transformative, empowering, and ultimately lead to a more fulfilling and purpose-driven life.

Embracing Solitude as a Lifelong Practice

Throughout this section, we have explored the power and benefits of embracing alone time, particularly in your 50s. But the truth is, embracing solitude is not limited to a specific age or stage of life. It is a lifelong practice that can bring immense value and enrich our overall well-being.

As we navigate the complexities of life, carving out moments of solitude allows us to reconnect with ourselves on a deeper level. It provides an opportunity for self-reflection, introspection, and introspective thinking, that plays a crucial role in personal growth and self-discovery.

Today's fast-paced society often celebrates constant connectivity and busyness. However, it is in moments of solitude that we can truly recharge, find peace, and tap into our inner wisdom. Embracing alone time is a powerful act of self-care, enabling us to nurture our mental, emotional, and spiritual well-being.

Whether you are in your 50s or at any other stage of life, make it a priority to embrace solitude. Create space for moments of reflection, engage in activities that bring you joy, and allow yourself to be fully present in your own company. Embracing alone time is an ongoing journey, an ever-present companion that can guide you towards greater self-awareness, personal growth, and fulfillment.

Chapter 19

Age is Just a Number: Age-defying stories of success and how to create your own

Age is often seen as a barrier to success. Society tells us that achieving greatness is reserved for the young, while those in later years are expected to settle into a comfortable retirement. But that's not the full story. Age is just a number, and there are countless age-defying stories that prove it.

In this section, we will explore the inspiring stories of individuals who have achieved success later in life and debunk the notion that greatness has an expiration date. From entrepreneurs who built thriving businesses in their golden years to artists and innovators pushing the boundaries of creativity, these age-defying stories will challenge your perception of what is possible.

But we won't stop at just sharing these incredible stories. We will also provide you with practical strategies and tips to create your own age-defying success story. Whether you're in your 50s, 60s, or beyond, this section will show you how to achieve greatness at any age.

So get ready to be inspired, motivated, and empowered. Age may be just a number, but the opportunities for achieving greatness are limitless. Let's defy expectations and show the world what we're capable of!

Overcoming Age Stereotypes: Thriving in Older Age

As we grow older, societal stereotypes often dictate that our opportunities for success and personal growth diminish. However, these age-related beliefs are far from accurate. In fact, many individuals have defied these stereotypes and gone on to thrive in their older years, achieving remarkable accomplishments and finding fulfillment.

In this section, we delve into the prevailing age stereotypes and explore how individuals can overcome them to lead fulfilling lives. Through inspiring stories and examples, we highlight the achievements of those who have embraced the power of their later years and shattered the confines of societal expectations.

Living Proof: Achievements in Later Years

In our quest to challenge age stereotypes, we encounter incredible stories of individuals who have thrived in their older age. Take the example of Jane Goodall, renowned primatologist and conservationist, who continues her groundbreaking research and advocacy well into her 80s. Her work serves as a testament to the enduring spirit and passion that can drive us, no matter our age.

Then there's Stan Lee, the legendary comic book writer and creator of iconic superheroes. Even as he reached his 90s, Lee showcased an unwavering commitment to his craft, enriching the lives of countless fans around the world with his inventive storytelling.

These examples, among many others, demonstrate that age is not a barrier to success and personal fulfillment. Instead, it's an opportunity to harness the wisdom, experience, and resilience that come with living a long and rich life.

Thriving Beyond Expectations

By embracing the mindset that age should never limit our aspirations, we unlock a world of possibilities. Whether it's starting a new business, pursuing a passion project, or making a positive impact on our communities, thriving in older age is not only achievable but also empowering.

In the following sections, we will delve deeper into the strategies and insights shared by those who have overcome age stereotypes and achieved greatness in their later years. These stories serve as inspiration, reminding us that our potential knows no bounds and that our later years can be a time of immense growth and fulfillment.

The Power of Experience: Harnessing Wisdom for Success

As we age, we often accumulate a wealth of experience, knowledge, and wisdom. This reservoir of wisdom is a valuable asset that can be harnessed for achieving success, even after the age of 50.

One of the key advantages of experience is the unique perspective it brings. Over the years, we have navigated through various challenges, both personal and professional, and have learned valuable lessons along the way. Our experiences shape our worldview and allow us to approach new opportunities and ventures with a deeper sense of understanding and insight.

Furthermore, the power of experience lies in the knowledge and skills we have acquired.

Through years of learning and growth, we have developed expertise in our respective fields, honed our strengths, and overcome countless obstacles. This wealth of knowledge and skills can be leveraged to make informed decisions, solve complex problems, and drive innovation.

Success after 50 is not merely a possibility, but a reality for many individuals who harness the power of experience. By capitalizing on their wisdom and using it as a guiding force, these individuals are able to make strategic choices, seize opportunities, and achieve greatness in various domains of life.

Empowering Others through Experience

The power of experience extends beyond personal success. It also holds the potential to inspire and empower others. By sharing our stories and lessons learned, we can guide and mentor younger generations, helping them navigate their own paths to success. Our experiences become a beacon of hope and motivation, encouraging others to embrace their own journeys and overcome obstacles.

Moreover, harnessing wisdom allows us to cultivate resilience and adaptability, key attributes in a rapidly changing world. Experience grants us the ability to navigate uncertainties, anticipate challenges, and adapt to new circumstances. It is through our seasoned perspective that we can envision innovative solutions, explore uncharted territories, and lead by example.

Success after 50 is not confined by age. It is a testament to the power of experience, the harnessing of wisdom, and the determination to live life to the fullest at any stage. So, embrace your years of experience and let them guide you towards achieving greatness in all that you do!

Age-Defying Entrepreneurs: Building Businesses in Later Years

Age is no barrier to entrepreneurship. In this section, we celebrate the remarkable stories of age-defying entrepreneurs who have defied societal norms and embarked on the journey of building businesses later in life. These inspiring individuals prove that it's never too late to pursue your dreams and create a successful venture.

Meet Susan Thompson, the 62-year-old founder of a homemade beauty brand, a thriving skincare line that caters to the specific needs of mature skin. After years of working in the corporate world, Susan decided to follow her passion for skincare and launched her business in her late 50s. Through her expertise, she has not only created a successful brand but also empowers others to embrace their age and prioritize self-care.

Another incredible example is John Ramirez, who founded a technology company, a new-start software development company, at the age of 58. With his extensive industry knowledge and years of experience, John identified a gap in the market and seized the opportunity to build a successful business.

The Power of Resilience and Determination

What sets these age-defying entrepreneurs apart is their resilience and determination to pursue their dreams, regardless of their age. They have embraced the challenges and uncertainties that come with entrepreneurship, proving that passion and perseverance know no age limits.

These entrepreneurs understand that building a business requires continuous learning and adaptation. They have leveraged their years of experience to make informed decisions, mitigate risks, and navigate the ever-changing business landscape. Their ability to embrace change and remain agile has been crucial in driving their ventures forward.

Overcoming Obstacles with Creativity

Building a business later in life can present unique challenges, but these entrepreneurs have demonstrated remarkable creativity to overcome them. They have leveraged their diverse life experiences, skills, and perspectives to find innovative solutions and market niches.

For example, Mary Gibson, a retired teacher in her early 60s, founded a successful tutoring service that caters to the learning needs of adult learners. Her understanding of different learning styles, combined with her passion for education, has allowed her to create a specialized service that has transformed the lives of many.

By embracing their age and utilizing their unique strengths, these entrepreneurs have not only built successful businesses but have also become role models and sources of inspiration for others who aspire to embark on entrepreneurial journeys later in life. Their stories remind us that age is merely a number, and the pursuit of our dreams has no expiration date.

Reinventing Careers: Finding Success in New Endeavors

As we journey through life, it's not uncommon to reach a point where we feel the need for change. Whether it's due to a desire for personal growth, a shift in priorities, or simply the need for a new challenge, reinventing our careers can bring a sense of renewal and fulfillment.

Reinventing your career is about finding success in new endeavors, regardless of your age. It's about embracing the opportunities for growth, learning, and personal fulfillment that come with pursuing new paths. Rather than feeling limited by age, you can find inspiration in the stories of those who have embarked on this journey and have emerged triumphant.

Take the example of Diana Wilson, a marketing executive who, after years of corporate success, decided to pursue her passion for sustainable living. She reinvented her career by starting her own eco-friendly lifestyle brand. With determination, creativity, and a strong network, Jane was able to carve out a niche for herself and find success in her new endeavor.

Embracing Change and Seizing Opportunities

Reinventing your career requires a willingness to embrace change and seize opportunities. It may involve acquiring new skills, exploring different industries, or even starting your own business. The key is to be open-minded and adaptable, recognizing that age is not a barrier to success; rather, it is a source of experience and wisdom.

Consider the story of Richard Johnson, who, after a long and successful career in finance, decided to pursue his lifelong passion for photography. Despite having no formal training, Richard immersed himself in the world of photography, honing his skills through workshops and online courses. Today, he is a recognized photographer, showcasing his work in galleries and publications around the world. Richard's story is a testament to the power of reinvention and the endless possibilities that await when we embrace change.

Finding Fulfillment and Living Life to the Fullest

Reinventing your career is not just about finding success; it's about finding fulfillment and living life to the fullest. It's about aligning your work with your passions, values, and aspirations. By reinventing your career, you have the opportunity to create a life that brings you joy, purpose, and a deep sense of satisfaction.

Take inspiration from Sarah Ramirez, a former lawyer who felt unfulfilled in her profession. She made the courageous decision to reinvent her career and pursue her love for interior design. Today, Sarah has her own successful design firm, working on projects that bring beauty and inspiration to people's lives. Through her career reinvention, Sarah has found not only professional success but also a profound sense of fulfillment and happiness.

Reinventing your career is an empowering and transformative journey that can lead to newfound success and genuine fulfillment. It is a testament to the fact that age is just a number and that you have the power to live life to the fullest, regardless of your age.

Ageless Creativity: Artists and Innovators Pushing Boundaries

In the world of art and innovation, age is no barrier to creativity. Artists and innovators continue to push the boundaries of their respective fields, defying the notion that creativity diminishes with age.

From renowned painters to groundbreaking inventors, age-defying stories abound in the realm of creativity. These individuals inspire us with their unwavering passion, relentless dedication, and unwavering belief in their craft.

One such example is Jennifer Wilson, a prolific painter who discovered her true artistic calling in her late 50s. With a newfound sense of purpose, she fearlessly embraced the world of abstract art, captivating audiences around the globe with her vibrant compositions and ageless creativity.

Another remarkable figure is Henry Johnson, an innovative engineer who revolutionized the field of sustainable energy in his 60s. Armed with a boundless curiosity and a drive to make a positive impact, he developed groundbreaking technologies that have reshaped the way we harness and utilize renewable resources.

Age-Defying Talents in Music and Innovation

Age is also no barrier in the world of music. Legends like Aretha Franklin and Leonard Cohen continued to captivate audiences and create legendary songs well into their later years. Their age-defying voices and poignant lyrics served as a testament to their enduring talent and artistic brilliance.

Innovation knows no bounds as well. Inventors like Thomas Edison and Nikola Tesla pushed the boundaries of what was thought possible, even in their later years. Their insatiable curiosity and relentless pursuit of knowledge led to groundbreaking inventions that have shaped the world we live in today.

These ageless artists and innovators serve as living proof that creativity knows no bounds. They inspire us to think outside the box, challenge societal norms, and pursue our passions with unwavering determination.

So, whether you're an aspiring artist, an entrepreneur, or simply someone seeking inspiration, the age-defying stories of these remarkable individuals remind us that it's never too late to pursue our dreams and make a meaningful impact on the world.

Balancing Success and Well-being: Prioritizing Health in Later Years

When pursuing success at any age, it's essential to prioritize both achievement and well-being. This is especially important as we enter our later years, where the harmony between success and maintaining good health becomes crucial. Balancing success and well-being allows us to achieve greatness while living life to the fullest.

Often, in our quest for success, we tend to neglect our physical and mental well-being. However, it's vital to recognize that true success encompasses not only professional accomplishments but also a balanced and fulfilling personal life. Taking care of our health and well-being serves as a solid foundation for achieving greatness across all aspects of our lives.

The Significance of Prioritizing Physical Health

Physical health plays a vital role in achieving success at any age. Taking care of our bodies, engaging in regular exercise, and maintaining a nutritious diet not only improves our physical well-being but also enhances our mental clarity and focus. Prioritizing physical health equips us with the energy and resilience needed to overcome challenges, seize opportunities, and achieve our goals well into our later years.

The Importance of Mental Well-being

Equally important is prioritizing our mental well-being. Nurturing our mental health through practices such as mindfulness, meditation, and self-care helps us maintain clarity, emotional stability, and resilience. It allows us to effectively manage stress, adapt to change, and make sound decisions, all of which are crucial elements in attaining success and living life to the fullest.

By consciously balancing our pursuit of success with the care we give to our physical and mental well-being, we create a harmonious environment where achievements and personal fulfillment thrive together. Prioritizing health in later years ensures that our success is sustainable and fulfilling, empowering us to be the best versions of ourselves.

Overcoming Challenges: Resilience in the Face of Adversity

In this section, we will delve into the remarkable stories of individuals who have overcome significant challenges in their later years, defying the odds and achieving extraordinary success. These age-defying stories serve as powerful examples of resilience, determination, and the unwavering spirit to live life to the fullest at any age.

Life has a way of throwing unexpected challenges our way, and it is during these difficult times that our true character is revealed. The individuals we will highlight in this section have faced adversity head-on, showing us that age is no barrier to overcoming the most daunting obstacles in life.

One such inspiring story is that of Jane Thompson, a 65-year-old widowed mother of four who decided to pursue her lifelong dream of becoming an author. Despite the inherent difficulties of starting a new career later in life, Jane persevered. With sheer determination and countless hours of hard work, she self-published her first novel, which went on to become a bestseller.

A Tale of Triumph over Health Challenges

Another age-defying story is that of Robert Anderson, a retired firefighter who was diagnosed with a debilitating illness in his early 60s. Despite his deteriorating health, Robert refused to be defined by his condition. He sought alternative treatments and made drastic lifestyle changes to manage his symptoms. Not only did Robert regain his health, but he also went on to establish a nonprofit organization that provides support and resources for others facing similar health challenges. His story is a testament to the indomitable human spirit and the power of perseverance in the face of adversity.

These age-defying stories of triumph are a reminder that no matter the obstacles we face, it is possible to overcome them and achieve greatness. By embracing resilience, determination, and a positive mindset, we can live life to the fullest at any age.

Nurturing Relationships: The Role of Support Systems

In order to live life to the fullest at any age, it's important to recognize the value of nurturing relationships and cultivating strong support systems. Having a network of social connections, mentors, and supportive individuals can have a profound impact on our personal and professional growth.

Nurturing relationships with family, friends, and loved ones provides us with the emotional support, companionship, and sense of belonging that are essential for overall well-being. These connections help us navigate life's challenges, celebrate our successes, and find joy in shared experiences.

Mentors play a crucial role in our personal and professional development. Having someone who has walked a similar path and can offer guidance, wisdom, and advice can accelerate our growth and help us overcome obstacles. A mentor can provide invaluable insights, challenge our perspectives, and inspire us to reach new heights.

Building a supportive network is also essential for achieving our goals and aspirations. Surrounding ourselves with like-minded individuals who share our passions, values, and ambitions can provide us with motivation, accountability, and a sense of collective effort. Whether we're pursuing a new career, starting a business, or simply striving to live life to the fullest, our support system can provide the encouragement and resources we need to succeed.

In conclusion, nurturing relationships and cultivating strong support systems are key ingredients for living life to the fullest at any age. By investing in our relationships, seeking out mentors, and building a supportive network, we can tap into the power of human connection and create a solid foundation for personal and professional success.

Embracing Change: Adaptability as a Path to Success

Embracing change and cultivating adaptability are crucial factors in achieving success later in life. As we navigate the complexities of aging, it becomes evident that our ability to adapt to new circumstances and embrace change plays a significant role in thriving in older age.

Many inspiring stories demonstrate how individuals have faced life transitions with grace and resilience, showcasing the power of adaptability in pursuing their goals. Take, for example, Jane Smith, a retired schoolteacher who decided to start a new career as a freelance writer in her 60s. By embracing change and adapting to the digital landscape, she successfully built a thriving career and discovered a renewed sense of purpose.

Adaptability also enables us to navigate unexpected challenges and seize opportunities. Consider the story of Robert Johnson, an entrepreneur who faced multiple setbacks in his 50s but didn't let them deter him. Instead, he utilized his adaptability to reinvent his business model, embracing new technologies and markets. As a result, his company not only survived but thrived, reflecting the power of adaptability in overcoming obstacles.

Thriving in older age requires us to remain open-minded, adaptable, and willing to embrace change. It allows us to explore new interests, pursue new careers, and contribute to society in meaningful ways. By cultivating adaptability, we can continue to learn, grow, and achieve greatness at any age.

Taking Charge of Your Future: Strategies for Success at Any Age

Regardless of your age, you have the power to shape your own future and create a success story that defies the limitations often associated with getting older. By implementing effective strategies, you can take charge of your life and achieve greatness at any age.

One essential strategy for success is goal-setting. Set clear and achievable goals that align with your passions and values. Break these goals down into smaller, manageable steps, and celebrate each milestone along the way. By setting goals and working towards them, you'll create a sense of purpose and direction in your life.

Continual learning is another key strategy for success. Embrace lifelong learning and seek out opportunities to expand your knowledge and skills. Whether it's through online courses, workshops, or mentorship programs, investing in your personal and professional development will keep you sharp and adaptable in a changing world.

Personal development is also crucial in your journey towards success. Take the time to reflect on your strengths and areas for growth, and commit to self-improvement. Cultivate positive habits, such as practicing gratitude, mindfulness, and resilience. These habits will not only support your success but also enhance your overall well-being.

Nurture a mindset of growth and resilience. Stay motivated and persevere in the face of challenges. Surround yourself with supportive and like-minded individuals who believe in your potential. They will provide encouragement and keep you accountable as you pursue your dreams.

Remember that age should never be a barrier to living life to the fullest. Embrace your experiences, knowledge, and wisdom gained over the years, and use them as assets to propel you forward. Your unique perspective and life experiences can be a source of inspiration and innovation.

Ultimately, taking charge of your future requires proactive action and a belief in your own capabilities. By implementing these strategies and embracing a mindset of growth, you can overcome any obstacles and create a success story that defies expectations. So, live life to the fullest at any age, and let your success be a testament to the power of taking charge.

Inspiring Others: Leading the Way at Any Age

As we come to the end of this section, we want to highlight the power of inspiring others through age-defying success stories. Each story we shared in this section demonstrates that age is just a number when it comes to achieving greatness. The individuals who have defied stereotypes, reinvented themselves, and pursued their passions later in life are not only leading the way for their own success but also inspiring others to do the same.

By sharing your own experiences and celebrating the achievements of those around you, you can inspire and motivate others to overcome their own challenges, embrace change, and pursue their dreams at any age. Your story has the potential to ignite a spark in someone else, giving them the courage and belief to follow their passions and achieve their own version of greatness.

It is through these inspiring moments that we create a ripple effect, fostering a culture of growth and achievement. So, don't shy away from sharing your journey, your challenges, and your triumphs. By leading the way and inspiring others, you contribute to a world where age is never a barrier to success, and where individuals of all ages can thrive, innovate, and create their own extraordinary stories.

Chapter 20

A Home that Reflects the New You: Downsizing and home personalization.

Welcome to our chapter on downsizing and home personalization for individuals who are 50 years old or older. As we navigate through the different stages of life, our values, priorities, and lifestyles evolve. It's essential to create a living space that reflects the new you and simplifies your life.

In this section, we will explore the benefits of downsizing and home personalization at 50. We will dive into the world of retirement home organization, senior moving services, decluttering assistance for seniors, downsizing tips for empty nesters, personalized downsizing solutions, aging in place home modifications, and downsizing help for seniors.

Whether you're transitioning to a smaller home or looking to make your current space more meaningful and functional, we've got you covered. Our aim is to provide practical tips, advice, and resources to help you create a personalized and comfortable home environment that supports your unique needs and desires.

So, let's embark on this downsizing and home personalization journey together and discover how you can embrace the next chapter of your life with a space that truly reflects the new you.

The Benefits of Downsizing at 50.

Downsizing at the age of 50 can bring about a multitude of benefits for seniors. Not only does it provide an opportunity to simplify and streamline your life, but it also allows you to create a living space that supports your needs as you age.

One of the key advantages of downsizing is achieving a simpler and more manageable lifestyle. By reducing the size of your home, you can free yourself from the burdens of excess space and maintenance. This newfound simplicity can lead to reduced stress and enhanced overall well-being.

Moreover, downsizing presents an opportunity for retirement home organization. By moving into a smaller space, you can carefully curate your belongings and create a more organized living environment. This can make it easier to find and access the things you need, contributing to a more efficient and enjoyable daily life.

Another essential aspect to consider when downsizing is aging in place home modifications. As we age, our needs may change, requiring adjustments to our living spaces. By downsizing at 50, you can proactively create a home environment that supports your future needs, such as installing grab bars, ramps, or wider doorways to accommodate potential mobility challenges.

Overall, downsizing at the age of 50 offers numerous benefits, including simplifying your life, enhancing retirement home organization, and enabling the creation of an aging-friendly living space. By carefully considering these advantages, you can make an informed decision and embark on a downsizing journey that brings you joy, comfort, and peace of mind.

Personalize Your Downsized Home: Making It Uniquely Yours.

When downsizing your home at the age of 50, it's essential to create a living space that truly encapsulates your unique personality and preferences. Personalization plays a crucial role in making your downsized home feel like a reflection of who you are. Whether you're moving to a smaller house, apartment, or retirement community, it's important to optimize your space while maximizing functionality and storage.

One way to personalize your downsized home is through thoughtful decor choices. Consider incorporating colors, patterns, and textures that resonate with your individual style. Hang artwork that speaks to you and displays cherished memories. Incorporate meaningful objects and heirlooms that bring a sense of familiarity and comfort.

Another aspect of personalization is optimizing functionality. Assess your lifestyle and needs to determine the best layout and organization solutions for your space. Invest in multifunctional furniture pieces that serve multiple purposes, such as storage ottomans or convertible sofas. Customize your storage solutions to maximize every inch of space, whether it's utilizing under-bed storage, installing additional shelving, or using vertical organizers.

Retirement home organization is also crucial in making your downsized home uniquely yours. Having a well-organized space can greatly contribute to your overall comfort and quality of life. Utilize storage solutions specifically designed for retirees, such as closet systems that offer easy access, adjustable shelves, and hanging areas for various types of clothing. Implement an efficient filing system for important documents to keep them easily accessible.

Consider creating designated areas for hobbies or activities you enjoy. Whether it's a reading nook, a crafting corner, or a meditation space, having a personalized area for your passions can greatly enhance your everyday experience. Incorporate elements that inspire and energize you, such as plants, natural light, or calming artwork.

Lastly, don't be afraid to seek professional assistance and personalized downsizing solutions. Working with experts in downsizing and retirement home organization can provide invaluable guidance and expertise. They can help you navigate the process, offer tailored solutions, and alleviate any stress or overwhelm associated with downsizing.

Remember, your downsized home is an opportunity to create a space that reflects your authentic self and supports your desired lifestyle. Personalizing your living environment goes beyond aesthetics – it's about creating a comfortable, functional, and uniquely yours home that brings joy and contentment in this new phase of your life.

Senior Moving Services: Simplifying the Process.

When it comes to downsizing and transitioning to a smaller home, senior moving services can be a lifesaver. Moving can be a stressful and overwhelming task, especially for seniors who may have accumulated a lifetime of belongings. That's where professional senior moving companies come in, offering specialized assistance to make the downsizing process smoother and more manageable.

One of the major benefits of hiring senior moving services is that they understand the unique needs and challenges that seniors face during a move. They have the expertise and experience to handle delicate items with care, ensuring that cherished possessions arrive safely at their new destination. With their help, you can focus on the emotional and personal aspects of the move, while leaving the logistics in the capable hands of professionals.

Senior moving services provide a range of services designed to streamline the downsizing process. From packing and labeling to sorting and organizing, these experts can handle it all. They have the skills and resources to efficiently pack your belongings, ensuring that everything is securely packed and ready for transport.

Not only do senior moving services take care of the physical aspects of the move, but they also assist with coordinating the logistics. They can arrange for moving vehicles, handle the necessary paperwork, and even provide storage solutions if needed. By entrusting your move to professionals, you can eliminate much of the stress and hassle that comes with relocating to a smaller home.

For seniors who may need additional support, some senior moving services offer downsizing help specifically tailored to their unique needs. These services can include decluttering assistance, personalized downsizing plans, and guidance on optimizing space and storage solutions. By offering personalized support, these professionals make the downsizing process more manageable and ensure that the new home is tailored to the individual's needs and preferences.

If you're considering downsizing and need help navigating the process, senior moving services are a valuable resource. They offer the expertise and support necessary to simplify your move and create a smooth transition to your new home. With their assistance, you can focus on enjoying this exciting new chapter of your life while leaving the logistics to the professionals.

Decluttering Assistance for Seniors: Streamlining the Downsizing Process.

When it comes to downsizing and personalizing your home, decluttering plays a crucial role in simplifying the process and creating a space that truly reflects your unique personality. This is especially important for seniors who are transitioning to a smaller home and need assistance in making decisions about what to keep, donate, or sell.

At [Company Name], we understand the challenges and emotional attachment that can come with decluttering. Our specialized decluttering assistance for seniors is designed to streamline the downsizing process, providing practical tips and strategies to efficiently declutter your home and organize your belongings.

Efficient Decluttering Strategies for Seniors

Decluttering can be overwhelming, but with our expert guidance, you can make the process more manageable. Here are some of our top tips:

Start small: Begin with one room or even one area of a room to avoid feeling overwhelmed. Focus on areas that are used less frequently or have less sentimental value. Sort by categories: Organize your belongings into categories such as keep, donate, sell, or discard. This will help you make decisions more efficiently. Set realistic goals: Break down your decluttering tasks into smaller goals and tackle them one at a time. Celebrate your progress along the way. Ask for help: Reach out to family, friends, or professional decluttering services like ours for support. Having someone by your side can make the process less daunting.

By following these strategies, you can declutter your home effectively and create a space that is organized, functional, and personalized to your needs and preferences.

Making Decisions with Confidence

One of the biggest challenges in decluttering is deciding which items to keep and which to let go of. Our team of experts will provide guidance and support to ensure you make these decisions with confidence.

We understand that items may hold sentimental value or memories, and it can be difficult to part with them. However, decluttering allows you to create a lighter, more manageable living environment, where each item has purpose and meaning.

Our decluttering assistance for seniors includes personalized consultations to understand your unique needs and goals. We will work together to develop a customized plan that aligns with your preferences, helping you efficiently declutter and organize your home.

Creating a Personalized and Organized Living Space

Decluttering not only streamlines the downsizing process, but it also contributes to a more personalized and organized living space. By eliminating excess belongings, you can optimize your storage solutions and create a home environment that suits your lifestyle.

At [Company Name], we are dedicated to helping seniors like you simplify their lives and embrace this new chapter. Whether you need assistance with decluttering, downsizing, or personalized downsizing solutions, our team is here to support you every step of the way.

Contact us today to learn more about our decluttering assistance for seniors and how we can help streamline your downsizing process.

Downsizing Tips for Empty Nesters: Embracing the Next Chapter.

As empty nesters embark on the journey of downsizing to a smaller home, there are various considerations and challenges to navigate. This section provides valuable downsizing tips tailored specifically for empty nesters, helping them embrace the next chapter of their lives with ease and excitement.

One of the emotional aspects of downsizing is letting go of sentimental items accumulated over the years. It can be challenging to part with belongings that hold precious memories. However, it is essential to remember that downsizing is an opportunity to declutter and create a fresh start. To effectively let go, consider taking photographs of sentimental items to preserve the memories, or pass them on to loved ones who will cherish them as much as you do.

Optimizing space in your new, smaller home is key to creating a welcoming and comfortable living environment. Start by assessing your needs and prioritizing essential items. Get creative with storage solutions like multifunctional furniture and space-saving organizers. By maximizing every inch, you can create a clutter-free space that meets your lifestyle and preferences.

When downsizing, it's crucial to downsize your belongings as well. Ask yourself what items are truly necessary and bring value to your new home. Consider donating or selling items you no longer need to declutter and simplify the transition. Remember, downsizing is an opportunity to curate a home that reflects your current lifestyle and preferences.

Ultimately, the process of downsizing and embracing the next chapter can be both exciting and challenging. By following these downsizing tips, empty nesters can navigate the emotional aspects, optimize their space, and create a personalized living environment that sets the stage for this new and exciting chapter in their lives.

Aging in Place Home Modifications: Adapting Your Space for the Future.

When downsizing your home, it is crucial to consider the importance of aging in place home modifications. Adapting your living space to meet your changing needs as you age is essential for maintaining independence and ensuring a safe and comfortable environment.

One of the key benefits of aging in place home modifications is the ability to enhance accessibility. By installing features such as ramps, grab bars, and wider doorways, you can ensure that your home remains easy to navigate, even if mobility becomes a challenge. These modifications not only provide convenience for daily activities but also promote a sense of confidence and freedom.

Safety is another crucial aspect to consider when adapting your home for the future. Installing safety features, such as handrails in the bathroom, slip-resistant flooring, and smart home technology for monitoring and security, can greatly reduce the risk of accidents and improve overall peace of mind.

Technological advancements have also made independent living more attainable for seniors. Smart home devices, such as voice-activated assistants, automated lighting systems, and remote-controlled thermostats, can significantly enhance daily convenience and quality of life. These technological solutions can be seamlessly integrated into your downsized home, providing innovative solutions for comfort and ease.

Making Informed Decisions

When considering aging in place home modifications, it is essential to make informed decisions that align with your specific needs and preferences. Researching reputable contractors and consulting with professionals specializing in home modifications can provide valuable insight and guidance.

Additionally, it is crucial to assess your current and future needs, taking into consideration any potential changes in mobility or health. An evaluation by an occupational therapist can help identify specific modifications that will best suit your requirements and desires.

By investing in aging in place home modifications, you are proactively preparing your space for the future. These modifications not only enhance accessibility, safety, and convenience but also enable you to maintain your independence and enjoy your downsized home to the fullest.

Personalized Downsizing Solutions: Taking a Tailored Approach.

In this section, we will explore personalized downsizing solutions that cater to the unique needs and preferences of individuals who are 50 or older. Downsizing and home personalization at 50 can be a transformative experience, and working with downsizing professionals who offer customized services can make the process more efficient and enjoyable.

When it comes to downsizing help for seniors, personalized solutions are key. These professionals understand the challenges that individuals in this age group face when transitioning to a smaller home and can provide tailored advice and support every step of the way. With their expertise, they can help you identify your specific downsizing goals and develop a personalized plan that aligns with your needs, lifestyle, and budget.

One of the advantages of personalized downsizing solutions is the attention to detail. These professionals take the time to get to know you and understand your preferences, ensuring that the downsizing process reflects your unique personality. From choosing the right furniture and decor to optimizing storage solutions, their expertise will help you create a downsized home that feels truly yours.

To find the right personalized downsizing solution, conducting thorough research is essential. Look for downsizing professionals with a track record of working with seniors and testimonials from satisfied clients. Seek recommendations from friends, family, or trusted organizations that specialize in senior services.

When seeking expert guidance for your downsizing journey, be prepared to ask questions and share your concerns. A personalized downsizing professional will listen attentively, provide valuable insights, and guide you through the entire process with empathy and respect.

In conclusion, downsizing and personalizing your home at 50 can be a rewarding experience when you take a tailored approach. By working with downsizing professionals who offer personalized solutions, you can ensure a smooth and personalized downsizing experience. With their expertise and your unique vision, you can create a downsized home that perfectly reflects your personality, lifestyle, and aspirations.

Retirement Home Organization: Simplify and Enjoy Your Space.

In this section, we will delve further into retirement home organization, providing practical advice on how to simplify and enjoy your downsized space.

One of the key aspects of retirement home organization is optimizing storage. Utilize smart storage solutions, such as under-bed storage containers, over-the-door organizers, and stackable bins, to maximize your available space. By decluttering and finding appropriate storage solutions, you can create a more organized and visually appealing living environment.

Creating functional living areas is another essential aspect of retirement home organization. Assess your needs and prioritize the spaces that are most important to you. Whether it's a cozy reading nook, a home office, or an entertainment area, design each space to serve its specific purpose. Consider multi-purpose furniture, such as a daybed or sleeper sofa, that can accommodate guests without compromising space.

To maintain an organized home environment, establish daily habits that promote tidiness. Develop a routine for regular cleaning and tidying up to prevent clutter from accumulating. Implement simple organizational systems, such as labeling storage containers and categorizing items, to make it easier to find and put things away.

Professional Assistance for Retirement Home Organization

If you feel overwhelmed or need additional support, professional assistance is available. Consider hiring senior moving services that specialize in downsizing and retirement home organization. These professionals can help you streamline the process, offer expert advice on space optimization, and provide the necessary manpower to handle the logistics of your move.

When seeking professional assistance, research reputable senior moving companies in your area. Look for testimonials from satisfied clients and verify the company's credentials. Schedule consultations to discuss your specific needs and expectations, ensuring they align with the services provided.

In summary, retirement home organization is crucial for simplifying and enjoying your downsized space. By optimizing storage, creating functional living areas, and maintaining an organized home environment, you can enhance your quality of life in your new home. Additionally, professional assistance from senior moving services can provide valuable support throughout the downsizing and organization process.

Conclusion

Downsizing and home personalization at 50 is a transformative process that allows individuals to create a living space that reflects their unique personality and lifestyle while simplifying their lives. Throughout this section, we have highlighted the key benefits and considerations of downsizing for seniors, including retirement home organization, senior moving services, decluttering assistance, downsizing tips for empty nesters, personalized downsizing solutions, and aging in place home modifications.

By embracing downsizing and home personalization at 50, individuals can enjoy the advantages of a simpler, more manageable lifestyle. Creating a space that is uniquely theirs not only brings a sense of comfort and familiarity but also supports aging in place. With retirement home organization strategies, seniors can optimize storage and maintain an organized home environment, making daily life more enjoyable and stress-free.

When embarking on the downsizing journey, it is essential to seek professional assistance such as senior moving services, decluttering assistance, and personalized downsizing solutions tailored to seniors' specific needs. These experts can offer guidance and support throughout the process, making it smoother and more efficient. Additionally, considering aging in place home modifications ensures that the downsized space remains accessible and safe for years to come.

In conclusion, downsizing and home personalization at 50 is a valuable opportunity to create a living environment that reflects your personality, simplifies your life, and enhances your overall well-being. By embracing the benefits of retirement home organization, senior moving services, decluttering assistance, downsizing tips for empty nesters, personalized downsizing solutions, and aging in place home modifications, you can embark on this new chapter with confidence and excitement.

Chapter **21**

Culinary Adventures:
Healthy eating without sacrificing flavor

Welcome to the exciting world of culinary adventures at 50, where healthy eating doesn't mean compromising on flavor. In this section, we will explore how you can create delicious and nutritious meals that satisfy your taste buds while nourishing your body. Discover the secrets of cooking for health, navigating the world of nutritious meals, and unlocking the art of balancing flavors. We will also dive into the realm of age-defying cooking, explore nutrient-rich ingredients, and highlight the importance of sustainable and locally sourced options. Learn how to embrace mindful eating, infuse your dishes with international flavors, and master the art of meal planning and prep. Join us on this journey and share the joy of healthy eating with others. Let's embark on a culinary adventure together, where flavor and wellness go hand in hand.

Embracing a Culinary Exploration: Cooking for Health

Before we embark on an exciting journey through flavor-packed recipes, it is essential to understand the significance of culinary exploration and cooking for health. By embracing new ingredients and cooking techniques, you can enhance your well-being and bring joy to your kitchen.

Navigating the World of Nutritious Meals

When it comes to nourishing our bodies, nutritious meals are key. But who says healthy eating has to be bland and boring? Discover the endless possibilities of creating delicious and healthy dishes that will tantalize your taste buds and fuel your body with essential nutrients.

From vibrant salads bursting with fresh flavors and textures to hearty soups that warm the soul, the world of nutritious meals is brimming with options that are both wholesome and delectable. With a little creativity and a dash of culinary flair, you can transform simple ingredients into delightful and satisfying main courses that contribute to your overall well-being.

Whether you're a seasoned home cook or just starting your culinary journey, navigating the world of nutritious meals opens up a world of exciting flavors and endless inspiration.

Exploring Vibrant Salads

Start your exploration by diving into the realm of vibrant salads. Combining crisp greens, colorful vegetables, and a variety of proteins and grains, you can create a symphony of flavors that nourish your body from the inside out. From zesty citrus dressings to creamy avocado and tangy feta cheese, the possibilities for creating mouthwatering salads are truly endless.

Hearty Soups That Satisfy

When the weather calls for warmth and comfort, hearty soups are the ideal choice. Packed with nutritious ingredients like wholesome vegetables, lean proteins, and aromatic herbs, these soul-soothing creations are a delicious way to stay nourished. From creamy butternut squash soup to spicy lentil stew, each spoonful is a taste of pure satisfaction.

So, open up your kitchen and embark on a culinary adventure that merges nutrition and flavor. Navigating the world of nutritious meals is an opportunity to transform your eating habits and embrace a healthier lifestyle without sacrificing taste.

Unlocking the Secrets of Age-Defying Cooking

Age-defying cooking is more than just focusing on healthy ingredients. It involves unlocking the secrets and techniques that can help you create dishes that not only nourish your body but also promote longevity, enhance vitality, and keep you feeling young and vibrant.

In the quest for age-defying meals, understanding the power of antioxidants is crucial. These natural compounds help protect your cells from damage caused by free radicals, potentially slowing down the aging process. Incorporating antioxidant-rich foods such as berries, leafy greens, and dark chocolate into your dishes can provide a powerful boost to your health and vitality.

Another important aspect of age-defying cooking is the balance of essential nutrients. Including a variety of fruits, vegetables, whole grains, lean proteins, and healthy fats in your meals ensures that your body receives all the nutrients it needs to function optimally. This balanced approach can support healthy aging and help you maintain a youthful glow.

Furthermore, culinary techniques can play a significant role in age-defying cooking. For example, steaming, baking, and grilling are healthier cooking methods that help retain the nutrients in your food while reducing the need for excessive oil or added fats. These techniques can enhance the flavors of your ingredients without compromising their nutritional value.

Additionally, spices and herbs can be powerful allies in age-defying cooking. Not only do they add depth and complexity to your dishes, but many herbs and spices also possess anti-inflammatory and other health-promoting properties. Incorporating herbs like turmeric, garlic, and rosemary into your cooking can provide both flavor and potential health benefits.

To take your age-defying cooking to the next level, consider exploring the world of superfoods. These nutrient-dense ingredients, such as quinoa, chia seeds, and kale, are packed with vitamins, minerals, and antioxidants, offering a myriad of health benefits. Adding these superfoods to your recipes can supercharge your meals and support your quest for age-defying vitality.

Age-defying cooking is an art and a science that combines the right ingredients, techniques, and flavors to create meals that nourish your body, mind, and soul. By unlocking the secrets of age-defying cooking, you can enjoy delicious dishes that not only taste incredible but also contribute to your overall well-being.

The Art of Balancing Flavors in Healthy Cooking

When it comes to healthy cooking, many people worry that they have to sacrifice flavor. But fear not! The art of balancing flavors allows you to create dishes that are both nutritious and delicious.

One way to add flavor to your healthy recipes is by incorporating a variety of herbs and spices. Whether it's the aroma of basil in a tomato and mozzarella salad or the warmth of cinnamon in your morning oatmeal, these flavorful additions can transform a simple dish into a culinary delight.

Experimenting with different ingredients is another key to achieving flavorful and healthy recipes. For example, instead of using traditional white rice, try swapping it with nutty and nutritious quinoa or cauliflower rice for a low-carb alternative.

Don't forget the power of umami—the fifth taste that adds depth and richness to dishes. Incorporate ingredients like soy sauce, miso paste, mushrooms, or Parmesan cheese to enhance the savory notes in your meals.

Remember, healthy cooking doesn't mean bland and boring. By embracing the art of balancing flavors, you can create dishes that are both good for you and a feast for your taste buds. So go ahead, get creative in the kitchen, and enjoy the flavorful journey to a healthier you.

Exploring Nutrient-Rich Ingredients

Dive into the world of nutrient-rich ingredients and discover how they can elevate the nutritional value of your meals. When you incorporate nutrient-rich ingredients into your recipes, you not only enhance the flavor but also boost the health benefits of your dishes.

Superfoods like kale, quinoa, and blueberries are excellent examples of nutrient-dense ingredients that provide a wealth of vitamins, minerals, and antioxidants. By including these ingredients in your meals, you can support your overall well-being.

Furthermore, seasonal produce is another fantastic way to incorporate nutrient-rich ingredients into your cooking. Fruits and vegetables that are in-season are not only fresher, but they also contain higher levels of nutrients compared to out-of-season produce.

Try incorporating nutrient-rich ingredients into your favorite recipes. For example, swap regular white rice with quinoa for added protein and fiber, or enhance your morning smoothie with spinach and berries for a nutritious kickstart to your day.

By exploring and experimenting with these nutrient-rich ingredients, you can create meals that are both delicious and packed with essential nutrients. Your taste buds and your body will thank you for it!

Sustainable and Locally Sourced Ingredients

When it comes to culinary adventures, one of the key ingredients for success is sourcing sustainable and locally sourced ingredients. Not only does this choice benefit the environment, but it also enhances the flavor and nutritional value of your meals.

By supporting local farmers and choosing sustainable options, you are not only reducing your carbon footprint but also ensuring that the ingredients you use are fresh, vibrant, and full of flavor. Locally sourced produce is often harvested at its peak, resulting in superior taste and nutrient content.

Additionally, sustainable ingredients are grown and produced using eco-friendly practices that prioritize the protection of natural resources and promote biodiversity. From organic vegetables to ethically raised meats, incorporating sustainable ingredients into your dishes adds a layer of authenticity and mindfulness to your culinary creations.

When purchasing ingredients, make it a point to buy from local farmers' markets or join a community-supported agriculture (CSA) program. These options not only provide you with access to the freshest seasonal produce but also allow you to establish a personal connection with the farmers who cultivate the ingredients you love.

Remember, sustainable and locally sourced ingredients are not just good for the planet but also for your well-being. By choosing these ingredients, you are making a conscious decision to prioritize your health while enjoying delicious and flavorful meals.

Mindful Eating for Optimal Health

Mindful eating is a crucial aspect of healthy cooking. When you cultivate a mindful approach to eating, you create a deeper connection with your food and make more conscious choices about what and how you eat. It involves savoring each bite, paying attention to the flavors, textures, and aromas, and being present in the moment.

By practicing mindful eating, you not only enhance your dining experience but also support optimal health. When you slow down and truly appreciate your food, you become more attuned to your body's hunger and satiety signals. This helps prevent overeating and promotes better digestion.

Mindful eating also allows you to better understand the impact of food on your physical and emotional well-being. You start to notice how different foods affect your energy levels, mood, and overall health. This self-awareness empowers you to make choices that support your unique nutritional needs and goals.

To cultivate mindful eating habits, take the time to sit down and eat without distractions, such as phones or TV. Engage your senses by fully experiencing the colors, smells, and flavors of your meal. Chew slowly and savor each bite, noticing the textures and tastes. Pay attention to feelings of fullness and stop eating when you are satisfied.

Mindful eating is not about strict rules or restrictions, but rather about fostering a positive and respectful relationship with food. It allows you to honor your body's needs and nourish yourself in a way that feels satisfying and enjoyable. So, as you embark on your culinary adventures, remember to savor each bite and embrace mindful eating for optimal health.

Exploring International Flavors on Your Culinary Journey

Embark on a culinary journey without leaving your kitchen by exploring international flavors. From Mediterranean to Asian cuisines, discover how incorporating global influences can infuse your meals with new and exciting tastes.

Tips for Meal Planning and Prep

Effective meal planning and prep are crucial elements for successfully incorporating healthy cooking into your lifestyle. By adopting these strategies, you can ensure that you always have delicious and nutritious meals available, even on your busiest days.

1. Set Aside Dedicated Time for Planning

Carve out a specific time each week to sit down and plan your meals. Consider your schedule, dietary preferences, and any special occasions or events that may impact your menu. By dedicating this time, you'll be able to create a well-balanced and varied meal plan that meets your nutritional needs.

2. Keep a Well-Stocked Pantry and Fridge

Having a well-stocked pantry and fridge is essential for efficient meal prep. Stock up on staple items like whole grains, legumes, canned goods, and spices. Additionally, keep fresh produce, lean proteins, and healthy fats on hand to easily assemble a variety of meals.

3. Choose Batch-Cooking Friendly Recipes

Opt for recipes that are suitable for batch cooking, such as soups, stews, and casseroles. These types of dishes can be prepared in larger quantities and easily portioned out for future meals or frozen for later use. Batch cooking not only saves time but also ensures a constant supply of ready-to-eat meals.

4. Pre-Chop and Pre-Cook Ingredients

Spend some time each week prepping ingredients to make meal assembly a breeze. Wash, chop, and store fruits and vegetables to have them readily available for salads, stir-fries, or snacks. Pre-cook grains, proteins, or roasted vegetables to cut down on cooking time when preparing meals.

5. Utilize Time-Saving Kitchen Tools

Invest in time-saving kitchen tools like a slow cooker, pressure cooker, or food processor. These appliances can help speed up meal preparation and make tasks like chopping, blending, or cooking hands-free. Utilizing these tools can save you valuable time in the kitchen.

6. Pack Meals in Advance

If you have a busy week ahead, consider packing your meals in advance. Use meal prep containers to portion out meals and snacks for each day of the week. This allows you to grab and go, ensuring that you have a healthy option readily available when you're on the move.

7. Be Flexible and Adapt

Remember that meal planning and prep should be flexible. Adjust your plans based on changing circumstances or unexpected events. If you have leftovers from a previous meal, repurpose them creatively into another dish to avoid waste. Being adaptable ensures that you can still enjoy nutritious meals even when things don't go as planned.

By incorporating these meal planning and prep tips into your routine, you'll be able to seamlessly integrate healthy cooking into your lifestyle. You'll have a repertoire of tasty and nourishing meals that support your well-being, even during your busiest days.

Sharing the Joy of Healthy Eating with Others

Healthy eating is not just about nourishing yourself but also sharing the joy of good food with others. There's something special about gathering around a table, enjoying delicious and nutritious meals with friends and family. Whether it's a cozy dinner at home or a festive gathering, sharing your culinary adventures can create memorable moments and deepen your connections.

One way to share the joy of healthy eating is by hosting a themed dinner party. Choose a cuisine or a specific ingredient as the focus and create a menu that showcases flavorful and healthy dishes. You can experiment with different spices, explore new cooking techniques, and introduce your loved ones to a world of exciting flavors.

Another way to spread the joy is by sharing your favorite recipes. Whether it's a handwritten recipe card, a beautifully crafted cookbook, or an online food blog, sharing your culinary creations can inspire others to embark on their own healthy eating journey. It's a way to pass down family traditions, celebrate cultural heritage, and ignite a passion for cooking in others.

Don't be afraid to get others involved in the kitchen as well. Cooking together can be a fun and educational experience, allowing you to bond while preparing a delicious meal. Encourage your loved ones to join you in the kitchen, share their own recipes and techniques, and together, create a joyful and collaborative cooking environment.

Bringing the Community Together

Sharing the joy of healthy eating goes beyond your immediate circle of friends and family. It can extend to the larger community, where you can participate in food-related events, workshops, and charity initiatives. Consider volunteering at a local food bank, sharing your cooking skills with those in need, or organizing a community potluck where everyone contributes a healthy dish.

By sharing the joy of healthy eating with others, you not only spread the benefits of nutritious meals but also inspire and empower those around you to make positive changes in their own lives. Together, we can create a world where good food is celebrated as a source of nourishment, pleasure, and connection.

Conclusion

In this section, we have delved into the exciting world of culinary adventures at 50, proving that healthy eating doesn't have to come at the cost of flavor. By embracing a culinary exploration and utilizing nutrient-rich ingredients, you can create age-defying, delicious, and healthy dishes that will nourish both your body and soul.

Throughout this journey, we have learned the art of balancing flavors, incorporating herbs and spices to enhance the taste of our meals without compromising their nutritional value. We have also discovered the importance of sustainable and locally sourced ingredients, supporting not only our health but also the environment and local communities.

Remember, healthy eating is not a chore but an opportunity to excite your taste buds and share the joy of good food with others. So, embark on this culinary adventure, experiment with new ingredients and cooking techniques, and savor the flavors of wholesome and nutritious meals. Bon appétit!

Chapter 22

Health is Wealth: Maintaining vitality through diet, exercise, and self-care

Welcome to our chapter on how to be healthy in your 50s! As we navigate this important stage of life, it's crucial to prioritize our well-being and adopt healthy lifestyle habits that will keep us active and vibrant. In this article, we will provide you with valuable tips and expert advice on staying active in your 50s, ensuring you maintain your vitality and enjoy a fulfilling life.

From the changes that occur in our bodies as we age to the importance of balanced nutrition and regular exercise, we will cover it all. We'll also explore the significance of cardiovascular health, the benefits of strength training, and techniques to enhance flexibility and joint health. Additionally, we'll discuss stress management and self-care practices, along with the value of building a supportive network and seeking professional guidance.

So, if you're ready to embark on a journey towards a healthy and fulfilling lifestyle in your 50s, let's dive in and discover the keys to maintaining your vitality!

Understanding the Aging Process and Prioritizing Health

The aging process is a natural part of life, and as we enter our 50s, it's essential to understand how it affects our health. Our bodies undergo various changes during this time, including a decrease in muscle mass, bone density, and hormone production. These physiological changes can impact our overall well-being and increase the risk of certain health conditions.

However, it's important not to be discouraged by these changes. By prioritizing our health and well-being, we can proactively manage the aging process and maintain our vitality. Taking a proactive approach involves adopting healthy lifestyle habits and making conscious choices that support our physical, mental, and emotional health.

In this section, we will explore the aging process in more detail and highlight the importance of prioritizing health and wellness in our 50s and beyond. By understanding the changes that occur and the potential health risks, we can take proactive steps to maintain our health and live a fulfilling life.

Nourishing Your Body with Balanced Nutrition

A balanced diet plays a vital role in maintaining good health, and this becomes even more crucial as we age. For individuals in their 50s, proper nutrition is essential for supporting overall well-being and ensuring the body receives the necessary nutrients it needs to function at its best.

When it comes to nutrition for over 50s, it's important to focus on consuming a variety of nutrient-dense foods that provide essential vitamins and minerals. Key nutrients like calcium, vitamin D, and vitamin B12 are particularly important during this stage of life.

Eating for Bone Health

As we get older, bone health becomes a top priority. Consuming foods rich in calcium, such as dairy products (milk, yogurt, cheese), leafy green vegetables (kale, broccoli), and tofu, can help promote strong bones and prevent osteoporosis. Additionally, getting enough vitamin D through sun exposure or fortified foods like fatty fish and fortified dairy products is crucial for calcium absorption.

Amping Up Antioxidants

Antioxidants play a crucial role in neutralizing harmful free radicals in the body, preventing oxidative stress, and reducing the risk of chronic diseases. Including a variety of colorful fruits and vegetables, such as berries, tomatoes, spinach, and bell peppers, in your diet can provide an abundance of antioxidants. Aim for at least five servings of fruits and vegetables each day.

Omega-3 Fatty Acids for Heart Health

Omega-3 fatty acids are known for their heart-healthy benefits. Consumption of fatty fish like salmon, mackerel, and sardines can provide a good source of omega-3s. For individuals who don't consume fish, flaxseeds, chia seeds, and walnuts are excellent plant-based sources.

In addition to focusing on specific nutrients, it's important to adopt healthy eating habits. This includes portion control, staying hydrated, and limiting processed foods, sugar, and unhealthy fats. Meal planning and incorporating a variety of whole foods into your diet can help you establish healthy habits for older adults.

In summary, nutrition is a key factor in maintaining good health as we age. By prioritizing a balanced diet that includes the right nutrients and adopting healthy eating habits, you can nourish your body and support overall vitality in your 50s and beyond.

Staying Active and Engaging in Exercise

Regular physical activity is crucial for maintaining both physical and mental well-being, especially as we enter our 50s. Exercise not only helps us stay fit and active but also plays a vital role in preventing chronic diseases and improving overall quality of life. Here are some exercises that are well-suited for individuals in their 50s, along with practical tips on how to incorporate physical activity into your daily routine:

1. Cardiovascular Exercises

Cardiovascular exercises, such as brisk walking, swimming, and cycling, are great for improving heart health and boosting overall fitness. Aim for at least 150 minutes of moderate-intensity aerobic activity per week, spread out over several sessions.

2. Strength Training

Incorporating strength training exercises, such as lifting weights or using resistance bands, can help increase muscle mass and bone density, which becomes increasingly important as we age. Aim to engage in strength training at least two days a week, targeting major muscle groups.

3. Flexibility and Balance Exercises

Flexibility and balance exercises, such as yoga and tai chi, can improve mobility, reduce the risk of falls, and enhance overall flexibility. Consider participating in classes or following guided videos to ensure proper form and technique.

4. Interval Training

Interval training, which involves alternating between high-intensity bursts of exercise and periods of rest or lower-intensity activity, can provide an efficient way to boost fitness levels and burn calories. This can be done through activities like high-intensity interval training (HIIT) or circuit training.

Remember to start slowly and gradually increase the intensity and duration of your exercises. Consult with a healthcare professional before starting any new exercise program, especially if you have pre-existing health conditions or concerns.

By incorporating these exercises into your routine and finding activities you enjoy, you can stay active, improve your fitness, and maintain optimal health in your 50s and beyond.

Prioritizing Cardiovascular Health

As we age, it becomes increasingly important to prioritize cardiovascular health, as the risk of cardiovascular diseases tends to increase. Taking care of your heart is crucial for overall well-being and longevity. In this section, we will explore the importance of cardiovascular health and provide insights on how to maintain a healthy heart in your 50s.

Regular exercise is one of the key pillars of cardiovascular health. Engaging in activities that raise your heart rate, such as brisk walking, swimming, or cycling, can help strengthen your heart, improve blood circulation, and maintain a healthy weight. Aim for at least 150 minutes of moderate-intensity aerobic exercise per week, or 75 minutes of vigorous-intensity exercise if your health permits it.

In addition to exercise, adopting a heart-healthy diet is essential. Focus on consuming a variety of nutrient-dense foods, including fruits, vegetables, whole grains, lean proteins, and healthy fats. Limit your intake of processed foods, saturated fats, sodium, and added sugars. Incorporating foods rich in omega-3 fatty acids, such as fatty fish, nuts, and seeds, can also be beneficial for heart health.

Managing stress is another important aspect of cardiovascular health. Chronic stress can contribute to the development of heart disease. Find healthy coping mechanisms that work for you, such as practicing relaxation techniques, engaging in hobbies, spending time with loved ones, or seeking support from a mental health professional when needed. Prioritizing self-care and finding balance in your life can go a long way in protecting your heart.

It's important to note that maintaining cardiovascular health requires a holistic approach. Alongside exercise, diet, and stress management, regular check-ups with your healthcare provider to monitor your blood pressure, cholesterol levels, and overall heart health are essential. They can offer guidance on specific lifestyle modifications or prescribe medication if necessary, ensuring your cardiovascular health is well-managed.

Prioritizing your cardiovascular health in your 50s is an investment in your well-being and quality of life. By adopting healthy habits and making conscious choices, you can significantly reduce the risk of cardiovascular disease and enjoy a vibrant, active life.

Strength Training and Maintaining Muscular Health

As we age, maintaining muscle mass becomes increasingly important for our overall health and functional independence. Engaging in strength training exercises not only helps to strengthen our muscles but also provides numerous benefits for our well-being.

Strength training for older adults can help mitigate age-related muscle loss, also known as sarcopenia. By regularly challenging your muscles through resistance exercises, you can stimulate muscle growth and improve muscle function.

One of the key advantages of strength training is its positive impact on bone health. As we get older, our bones tend to weaken, making us more susceptible to fractures and osteoporosis. However, strength training helps promote bone density, reducing the risk of bone-related injuries and conditions in your 50s and beyond.

Additionally, strength training improves joint stability and flexibility, promoting better posture and reducing the risk of falls. By strengthening the muscles surrounding your joints, you can also alleviate joint pain and enhance overall mobility.

How to Incorporate Strength Training into your Fitness Routine

When starting strength training, it's important to start slowly and gradually increase the intensity of your workouts. Consult with a fitness professional or trainer to develop a safe and effective strength training program tailored to your abilities and goals.

Include a variety of exercises that target different muscle groups in your routine, such as squats, lunges, push-ups, and bicep curls. Aim for 2-3 days of strength training per week, allowing for rest days in between to promote muscle recovery and growth.

Remember to warm up before each strength training session with light cardio exercises and dynamic stretches to prepare your muscles for the workout. And always listen to your body, adjusting the intensity or technique if necessary to avoid injury.

Incorporating strength training into your fitness routine in your 50s can have a significant impact on your muscular health and overall well-being. Start reaping the benefits of strength training today and enjoy a stronger, more vibrant life.

Enhancing Flexibility and Joint Health

As we age, taking care of our joint health and maintaining flexibility becomes increasingly important. Stiffness and reduced range of motion can impact our daily activities and overall quality of life. Fortunately, there are various gentle stretching exercises and techniques that can help improve flexibility and promote joint health in individuals in their 50s.

Regular flexibility exercises for older adults can help increase joint mobility, reduce stiffness, and even alleviate joint pain. These exercises can be simple and enjoyable, making them accessible to individuals of all fitness levels. Incorporating these exercises into your daily routine can have a significant positive impact on your joint health and overall well-being.

One effective technique to enhance flexibility is dynamic stretching. This involves moving your joints through a full range of motion without holding the stretch for an extended period. Performing dynamic stretching exercises, such as leg swings or arm circles, before engaging in more vigorous activities can help loosen up the joints, increase blood flow, and reduce the risk of injury.

In addition to dynamic stretching, static stretching can also be beneficial. This involves holding a stretch for 15 to 30 seconds, focusing on the major muscle groups and joints. It is important to perform static stretches after your muscles are warmed up, such as after a workout or physical activity. Some examples of static stretches include calf stretches, shoulder stretches, and quadriceps stretches.

Remember to always listen to your body and never force a stretch beyond your comfort level. Over time, with consistent practice, you will notice improvements in your flexibility and joint health. It is essential to consult with a healthcare professional or certified fitness instructor before starting any new exercise routine, especially if you have pre-existing joint conditions or medical concerns.

Managing Stress and Practicing Self-Care

As we age, managing stress and practicing self-care become even more crucial for maintaining our overall health and well-being. Chronic stress can have a significant impact on our physical and mental health, so it's important to adopt effective stress-management techniques and prioritize self-care practices in our daily lives.

One of the key self-care practices for older adults is mindfulness. Mindfulness involves focusing your attention on the present moment and accepting it without judgment. This practice can help reduce stress, improve sleep quality, and enhance overall mental well-being. Consider incorporating mindfulness exercises into your daily routine, such as deep breathing, meditation, or mindful walking.

Another important self-care practice is engaging in relaxation techniques. Finding activities that help you relax and unwind can have a positive impact on stress management. This could include listening to calming music, reading a book, practicing yoga, or taking a warm bath. Experiment with different relaxation techniques to discover what works best for you and make it a regular part of your self-care routine.

Getting adequate rest is also essential for stress management and overall health. As we age, our sleep patterns may change, and it's important to prioritize quality sleep. Create a relaxing bedtime routine, ensure your sleep environment is comfortable and conducive to sleep, and establish consistent sleep and wake times. If you're experiencing difficulties with sleep, consult with a healthcare professional for personalized guidance.

Remember, self-care is not selfish—it's necessary for maintaining your well-being. Make time for activities that bring you joy and fulfillment. This could include pursuing hobbies, spending quality time with loved ones, or engaging in activities that promote relaxation and happiness.

In conclusion, managing stress and practicing self-care play a crucial role in maintaining our health and well-being as we age. By incorporating mindfulness, relaxation techniques, and getting adequate rest into our daily lives, we can effectively manage stress and enhance our overall quality of life.

Building a Supportive Network and Seeking Professional Guidance

As we navigate our 50s, it is essential to cultivate a supportive network that can provide us with the emotional, social, and practical support we need. A strong support system can help alleviate stress, enhance our sense of belonging, and improve overall well-being.

When building your support network, consider reaching out to friends, family, or community groups that share your interests and values. Engaging in activities that foster connection and collaboration can help forge meaningful relationships and provide a sense of belonging. By surrounding ourselves with positive and supportive individuals, we can create an environment conducive to personal growth and resilience.

Additionally, seeking professional guidance is vital when it comes to maintaining and optimizing our health. Consulting with healthcare professionals, such as doctors, nutritionists, and therapists, can offer valuable insights and personalized advice tailored to our specific needs. These experts can help us navigate the complexities of aging, guide us with evidence-based strategies, and address any health concerns we may have.

Don't hesitate to reach out for professional health advice when needed. Whether it's managing chronic conditions, optimizing nutrition, or addressing mental health concerns, healthcare professionals are trained to provide the guidance and support necessary to enhance our overall well-being in our 50s and beyond. Remember, investing in our health is an investment in our future vitality and quality of life.

Chapter 23

Mindful Living: Embracing mindfulness to enrich everyday life

Welcome to the world of mindful living at 50! As we navigate the ups and downs of this stage of life, one thing becomes clear: mindfulness is the key to unlocking a more enriching everyday experience. In this section, we will explore the power of mindfulness and how it can positively impact your mental, emotional, and physical well-being. Whether you're new to mindfulness or have been practicing for years, there's no better time than now to embrace its benefits. Let's dive in and discover how mindfulness can enhance your life at 50 and beyond.

Understanding Mindfulness and Its Benefits

In today's fast-paced world, the practice of mindfulness has gained significant attention for its profound impact on overall well-being. Mindfulness can be defined as the state of being fully present and aware of the present moment, without judgment or attachment to thoughts or emotions.

So, what are the benefits of cultivating mindfulness in our lives? Let's explore.

Mental Well-being: Mindfulness has been shown to reduce stress, anxiety, and depression. By focusing on the present moment, individuals can develop a greater sense of calm and clarity in their thoughts. It allows for increased self-awareness and the ability to observe thoughts and emotions without being consumed by them.

Emotional Balance: Practicing mindfulness helps individuals cultivate emotional resilience and regulate their emotions more effectively. It allows for a deeper understanding and acceptance of emotions, leading to healthier coping mechanisms and improved emotional well-being.

Improved Physical Health:

Mindfulness is not limited to mental and emotional well-being; it also has positive effects on physical health. Research suggests that regular mindfulness practice can reduce blood pressure, improve sleep quality, boost immune system function, and even alleviate chronic pain.

Cognitive Enhancements: Mindfulness can enhance cognitive functions such as attention, memory, and decision-making. By training the mind to focus on the present moment, individuals can optimize their cognitive abilities and increase their overall productivity.

Enhanced Relationships: Mindfulness can greatly improve relationships by fostering deep listening, empathy, and compassion. When individuals are fully present in their interactions, they can engage in meaningful connections and create harmonious relationships.

Self-discovery and Personal Growth: Engaging in mindfulness practice can lead to profound self-discovery and personal growth. By observing thoughts and emotions without judgment, individuals gain insights into their inner selves, enabling them to make positive changes and align their actions with their values and goals.

By understanding and experiencing the numerous benefits of mindfulness, individuals can cultivate a more vibrant, fulfilling, and intentional life. In the next section, we will explore specific mindfulness techniques that can be incorporated into daily life.

Mindfulness Techniques for Daily Life

Incorporating mindfulness into daily life can have profound benefits for overall well-being and inner peace. By practicing specific mindfulness techniques, individuals can cultivate a greater sense of presence, calmness, and self-awareness. Let's explore some effective mindfulness techniques that can be easily integrated into your daily routine:

Mindful Breathing

Mindful breathing is a fundamental technique that involves focusing your attention on the sensation of your breath as it naturally flows in and out. Find a quiet space, sit in a comfortable position, and take a few deep breaths. Then, bring your attention to the sensations of the breath entering and leaving your body. Notice the rise and fall of your belly or the expansion and contraction of your chest. Whenever your mind starts to wander, gently guide your attention back to the breath. Engaging in mindful breathing for just a few minutes each day can help reduce stress, improve concentration, and promote relaxation.

Body Scan

The body scan technique involves systematically directing your attention to different parts of your body, bringing a sense of non-judgmental awareness to physical sensations and tension. Start by lying down or sitting in a comfortable position. Begin at the top of your head and gradually move your attention down through each part of your body, noticing any sensations or feelings along the way. If you encounter areas of tension or discomfort, simply observe them without judgment. This practice can help promote relaxation, release physical tension, and increase body awareness.

Walking Meditation

Walking meditation is a mindfulness practice that involves bringing your attention to the physical sensations and movements of walking. Find a quiet place where you can walk without distractions. Start by standing still and bringing awareness to the sensations in your feet, noticing the weight shifting from one foot to the other as you take a step. As you begin walking, maintain a slow and deliberate pace, paying attention to the sensations of lifting, moving, and placing your feet. Stay present in the experience of walking, allowing thoughts and distractions to pass through without getting caught up in them. This practice can enhance your connection to the present moment and cultivate a sense of grounding and tranquility.

By incorporating these mindfulness techniques into your daily life, you can enhance your overall well-being and experience a greater sense of peace and fulfillment. Remember, mindfulness is a practice that requires patience and consistency. Start with small steps, and gradually integrate these techniques into your routine. With time and practice, you will begin to reap the numerous benefits of living mindfully.

Embracing Mindfulness in Aging

Aging is a natural and transformative process that brings with it a unique set of challenges and opportunities. As we navigate this journey, it becomes increasingly important to cultivate mindfulness and embrace it fully. Mindfulness, the practice of being fully present and aware in the current moment, can empower individuals in their journey of aging by fostering self-acceptance, resilience, and overall well-being.

One of the key benefits of embracing mindfulness in aging is the cultivation of self-acceptance. As we age, it is common to experience changes in our physical appearance, health, and cognitive abilities. Mindfulness allows us to approach these changes with curiosity, compassion, and acceptance. By cultivating a non-judgmental awareness of our thoughts and feelings, we can embrace ourselves as we are in the present moment, without clinging to what was or fearing what may come.

In addition to self-acceptance, mindfulness also nurtures resilience - the ability to adapt and bounce back in the face of challenges. The aging process may bring about various health conditions, life transitions, and losses. Through mindfulness, we develop the capacity to acknowledge and respond to these challenges with equanimity and compassion. By staying present and grounded amidst difficulties, we can cultivate the resilience needed to navigate the ups and downs of life at any age.

Moreover, embracing mindfulness in aging promotes overall well-being. Mindfulness practices such as meditation, deep breathing, and gentle movement can help to reduce stress, increase relaxation, and improve mental clarity. These practices also have positive effects on physical health, including better sleep, boosted immune function, and decreased risk of certain chronic conditions. By embracing mindfulness, we can enhance our quality of life and age gracefully.

As we embrace mindfulness in aging, we open ourselves up to the possibility of experiencing the present moment fully, with a sense of gratitude and wonder. By cultivating mindfulness, we can navigate the challenges, embrace the changes, and find joy and fulfillment in our journey of aging. So, let us embark on this mindful path and savor each moment of our lives.

Enhancing Relationships through Mindfulness

Practicing mindfulness can have a profound impact on our relationships with others. By cultivating a mindful approach to communication, we can improve the quality of our interactions and create deeper connections with our loved ones.

Mindfulness practices help us become more present and fully engaged in our interactions. By focusing our attention on the present moment, we can tune in to the needs and emotions of the people around us, fostering empathy and understanding.

One valuable mindfulness practice for enhancing relationships is mindful listening. This involves giving our full attention to the speaker, without interrupting or judging. By truly listening, we create a safe space for open dialogue and mutual respect.

Mindfulness also heightens our awareness of our own emotions, allowing us to respond more skillfully in challenging situations. When we practice mindfulness, we gain the ability to pause and reflect before reacting impulsively, which can prevent conflicts and misunderstandings.

Empathy and Connection

Empathy is a fundamental aspect of healthy relationships, and mindfulness practices can deepen our capacity for empathy. By cultivating self-compassion and non-judgment towards ourselves, we can extend the same understanding and acceptance to others.

Additionally, mindfulness practices such as loving-kindness meditation can help us cultivate feelings of warmth and compassion towards ourselves and others. This can improve our ability to connect on a deeper level and strengthen the bond with our loved ones.

Ultimately, incorporating mindfulness practices into our daily lives can transform the way we relate to others. By being fully present, empathetic, and open-hearted, we can build healthier, more fulfilling relationships that contribute to our overall well-being.

Cultivating Mindful Habits for a Healthy Lifestyle

As we embrace the age of 50, it becomes increasingly vital to prioritize our well-being and adopt mindful habits that contribute to a healthy lifestyle. Incorporating mindfulness into our everyday choices, such as eating, exercise, and self-care, can have a profound impact on our physical and mental health.

When it comes to mindful eating, the focus shifts to savoring each bite, paying attention to the flavors and textures, and listening to our bodies' hunger and fullness cues. This intentional approach allows us to make nourishing choices and promotes a healthier relationship with food.

Furthermore, incorporating mindfulness into our exercise routine helps us stay present and fully engage with our bodies. Whether it's a brisk walk in nature, a yoga session, or strength training, practicing mindful movement enhances the mind-body connection, reduces stress, and boosts overall well-being.

In addition to mindful eating and exercise, prioritizing self-care is paramount for a balanced and fulfilling life. By mindfully caring for ourselves, we can rejuvenate our energy, reduce stress, and cultivate a positive mindset. Simple activities like a warm bath, a mindful skincare routine, or indulging in a hobby can contribute to our overall well-being.

By cultivating these mindful habits for a healthy lifestyle, we empower ourselves to navigate the challenges that come with aging with grace and resilience. Mindfulness encourages us to fully experience and appreciate each moment, fostering a deep sense of gratitude and contentment in our everyday lives as we embrace the age of 50.

Overcoming Challenges with Mindfulness

Life presents us with various challenges, and regardless of age, it is important to develop effective strategies for navigating and overcoming them. Mindfulness practices can play a crucial role in helping individuals face these challenges head-on, fostering resilience and self-compassion.

Mindfulness, the practice of being fully present in the moment with non-judgmental awareness, allows us to approach difficulties with clarity and calmness. By cultivating mindfulness, we can develop a greater sense of self-awareness and emotional regulation, enabling us to respond to challenges in a more empowered way.

One of the key ways mindfulness helps us overcome challenges is by encouraging us to adopt a non-judgmental attitude towards our experiences. Rather than getting caught up in negative thoughts or self-criticism, mindfulness teaches us to observe our thoughts and emotions without attachment or judgment. This can help us gain perspective and reduce the impact of challenging situations on our overall well-being.

Tools for Resilience

Mindfulness practices provide us with valuable tools for building resilience. By regularly engaging in mindfulness meditation, we can train our minds to stay present and focused, even when faced with adversities. This helps us develop a greater capacity to bounce back from setbacks and find new opportunities for growth.

The practice of mindfulness also allows us to cultivate self-compassion, which is essential for navigating challenges with grace and kindness towards ourselves. When we approach difficulties with self-compassion, we are more likely to respond with understanding and support, rather than self-criticism or harsh judgment. This empowers us to face challenges with resilience and move forward with renewed strength.

Finding Inner Strength

Through mindfulness practices, we can tap into our inner strength and wisdom, which can guide us through even the toughest of challenges. By connecting with our inner selves through practices such as meditation and mindful self-reflection, we can access a deep well of resilience, courage, and creativity. Mindfulness also helps us develop a sense of equanimity, allowing us to accept and navigate challenges with greater ease. Instead of being consumed by fear or anxiety, we can remain grounded, focused, and open-minded. This enables us to explore potential solutions and make decisions from a place of clarity and calmness.

By embracing mindfulness practices, individuals at the age of 50 can effectively overcome the challenges that come their way. Whether it is navigating career transitions, managing health issues, or coping with the loss of loved ones, mindfulness provides us with the tools and inner resources to navigate life's challenges with resilience, self-compassion, and grace.

Mindfulness and Personal Growth

Reaching the age of 50 is often a time of reflection and introspection, as many individuals seek personal growth and self-fulfillment. It's a stage of life that presents new opportunities for self-discovery, finding deeper meaning, and embracing personal transformation.

One powerful tool that can facilitate this journey of personal growth is mindfulness. By practicing mindfulness, individuals can develop a heightened sense of self-awareness, which allows them to explore their thoughts, emotions, and beliefs with curiosity and openness.

Mindfulness encourages us to be fully present in each moment, to observe our experiences without judgment, and to cultivate a greater understanding of ourselves and the world around us.

Through mindfulness, individuals at the age of 50 can embark on a journey of self-discovery. It provides a pathway to explore one's core values, passions, and interests, enabling individuals to align their actions and choices with what truly matters to them.

Embracing Change and Transformation

Mindfulness also helps individuals navigate the transitions and changes that can occur in midlife. It allows for the acceptance of life's imperfections and the acknowledgment of the ever-changing nature of existence.

With mindfulness, individuals can let go of attachment to past successes or regrets and embrace the present moment as an opportunity for growth and transformation. This shift in perspective enables individuals to cultivate resilience and embrace life's challenges as catalysts for personal development.

Finding Meaning and Purpose

At 50, many individuals seek a renewed sense of meaning and purpose in life. Mindfulness offers a path to explore the deeper questions of existence and uncover what truly brings fulfillment and joy.

By practicing mindfulness, individuals can connect with their inner wisdom and tap into their authentic desires, passions, and values. This self-discovery process allows individuals to align their actions and choices with their true purpose, leading to a more fulfilling and purposeful life.

Ultimately, mindfulness can be a powerful catalyst for personal growth at the age of 50. It supports individuals in their journey of self-discovery, embracing change and transformation, and finding deeper meaning and purpose in life.

Embracing the Mindful Living Journey

As we reach the age of 50, it becomes more important than ever to embrace mindful living as a way to enrich our everyday lives. Mindfulness is a powerful practice that allows us to cultivate a deep sense of presence, gratitude, and awareness in each moment. By incorporating mindfulness into our daily routines, we can tap into our inner wisdom, foster well-being, and find joy in the simplest of things.

So how can we continue our mindful living journey at 50? One practical tip is to start each day with a few moments of stillness and reflection. Before the rush of the day takes over, take a few deep breaths, set positive intentions, and express gratitude for the opportunities that lie ahead. This simple mindfulness practice can set a positive tone for the rest of the day, helping us approach challenges with clarity and resilience.

Another way to enrich everyday life through mindfulness is by bringing awareness to our interactions with others. Taking the time to truly listen and connect with loved ones can deepen our relationships and create meaningful bonds. Practice active listening, show empathy, and offer kind words of encouragement. These small acts of mindfulness can have a profound impact on our relationships, fostering love, compassion, and understanding.

Mindful living at 50 is about embracing the present moment, finding joy in simple pleasures, and cultivating a sense of gratitude for the journey we have lived so far. By integrating mindfulness into our daily routines, we can continue to grow, learn, and discover new aspects of ourselves. Let's embark on this mindful living journey together, enriching our everyday lives and nurturing our well-being.

Chapter 24

Staying Secure: Planning for the future with insurance and estate plans

Are you turning 50? Then Welcome to our chapter series on planning for the future. Before you reach this point, it is important to think about how you can protect your financial well-being and safeguard your assets. The first part of this article will focus on why insurance and estate plans are necessary when planning for the future. Therefore, as you enter the next phase of life, you need to take proactive measures to ensure your finances are secure as well as manage your estate.

It is important to plan financially if you want a peaceful retirement. Based on your current financial situation and goals, there are several insurance policies and estate plans that would suit your needs best. In addition to protecting assets, a comprehensive approach offers protection against unexpected events and provide for loved ones.

Let us plunge into estate planning so that we get hold of how one can salvage their legacy. We will lead you through developing a will, establishing trusts and appointing beneficiaries thus ensuring that all the assets possessed by an individual may be passed on according to their desires thereby enhancing financial security while minimizing possible conflicts.

Thus, without exception, insurance planning forms an integral part of every person's financial scheme. For example, we shall review some policies such as long-term care insurances or health insurances which in one way or another contribute towards economic security especially for people in retirement age. By identifying what works best for each individual, one may guarantee protection of his/her own welfare including that of family members who might face unforeseen financial challenges tomorrow.

Similarly, preparing for the retirement years is an equally significant aspect of future planning. Factors like healthcare costs in later years desired lifestyle inflation among others must be put into consideration when analyzing an individual's retirement needs. Consequently these needs would help in determining what types of insurance covers such as annuities could be aligned with retirement objectives set by different individuals rather than generalizing for all employees.

Moreover, we are going to discuss how to maximize your Social Security benefits which may be a major portion of many people's retirement income. By optimizing your social security strategy you can optimize your overall retirement plan and ensure that it will last throughout their golden years.

Additionally, we will touch upon some important aspects of long-term care planning for someone who is in their early 50s. We will explore payment alternatives such as long-term care insurance policy or Medicaid planning as well as self-funding that would help prepare a person financially in the event that he/she may need assistance later on.

Your insurance and estate plans should be regularly reviewed and updated because they are not cast in stone. Life changes constantly and so should your plans change along with it. Therefore, any life occurrence like marriages or divorces or births and great shifts of wealth requires regular re-evaluation of these instruments so that they remain effective over time.

While one can create simple insurance covers and estate plans alone, professional advice is priceless. Financial advisors assist you with making sure no stone was left unturned, while estate planners give you insights into pertinent matters without forgetting legal requirements hence tailoring to personal situation. Insurance agents deal with each client uniquely advising as appropriate financial advisors proffering guidance on when different persons' circumstances should be taken into account by an insurer before signing up for a given scheme.

As one reaches their 50s and beyond, appreciating peace of mind is possible through insurance plans and estate planning for the future. Don't go away; our next article will do a deeper dive into each of these areas with the aim of equipping you with more knowledge and understanding to make proper financial decisions that are not based on emotions or assumptions. Always think to secure your money base, protect what you have earned, and leave something substantial behind when it comes to financial planning.

Checking Your Finances and Goals

Before starting on this path of insurance and estate plans, it is crucial that you take a step back and evaluate your present finances as well as what you want in future. Financial planning sets the stage for successful retirement planning, which helps in establishing a comfortable retirement.

Firstly, assess your savings, investments, liabilities. Study well the arena of finance where you operate, look at areas that need improvements or care. Picture yourself in retirement thinking about how much money is sufficient enough to live comfortably without worrying about finances among other things. By knowing clearly where you are coming from as well as your goal destination then making insurance policies becomes easier.

Consider factors such as inflation rates healthcare cost potential market fluctuations during this assessment phase. Such variables though play an important role in shaping future goals for their long-term nature while others might help them escape significant taxes on such properties thus ensuring continued financial support after their death too! Through giving an intensive analysis of your personal finances together with goals therefore a strong foundation can be laid for both your insurance needs specifically related to life assurance products thereby meeting those dreams ahead.

Estate Planning: Protecting Your Legacy

Estate planning is a necessary step towards securing one's economic future by ensuring that his/her assets are distributed according to his/her wishes upon death. By developing a comprehensive plan that takes into account all aspects relevant to passing assets down among family members without causing conflict between siblings over who gets what or whether they should sell everything outright instead; this can be achieved.

Writing a Will

A will is one of the fundamental parts of estate planning. When you pass away, it dictates how your assets are divided among your dependents. Make sure to keep your will up to date so that it accurately reflects changes in your life and desired beneficiaries.

Establishing Trusts

In addition to a will, setting up trusts can offer further protection and control over the distribution of your assets. Trusts help avoid tax liabilities on estates and enable the beneficiaries to retain more wealth in their family businesses while providing for the future needs of loved ones who may not be able or willing to do so themselves.

Naming Beneficiaries

One critical part of estate plan is designating beneficiaries. By clearly stating who gets what from whom when they die, you get rid of potential disputes that might bring such issues into courtrooms before legal officers thus ensuring that whatever their desires were could always be fulfilled by them whatsoever. Be sure to review and update beneficiary designations as needed in order for them to correspond with current intentions.

With estate planning, ensure there is peace knowing that your possessions shall be managed according to what you want. Protecting ones legacy onto the next generation remains priceless.

Insurance Planning: Safeguarding Your Financial Security

When securing one's financial future is considered as an important aspect then insurance planning comes into play. Understanding various types of insurance policies available helps safeguard oneself and people dear against any misfortunes that may lead into financial instability. Therefore, having appropriate life assurance coverage whether through permanent policies like whole life or even term products like universal policies assist in maintaining fiscal stability throughout tough times experienced by individuals families like natural disasters incurred due death within theirs lives without prior warning signals or other unforeseen circumstances leading unexpected expenses taking place at once!

It is important to consider the insurance needs of your retirement. As you approach the next phase in life, it is vital to have a plan that will enable you enjoy your retirement years with peace of mind. Retirement insurance covers against unforeseen occurrences that can result in financial instability during old age. Through careful evaluation and selection of policies, individuals can protect their financial well-being and get pleasure from their lives after work which they worked hard for.

When evaluating your insurance needs, it is essential to look at your individual situation and goals. Are you the primary earner in your household? Do you have dependents who rely on your income? These factors are important when calculating what coverage is necessary. Also, one should evaluate his or her current insurance policies to make sure that they match one's present needs and adjust those policies accordingly.

It may be wise to consult with a professional financial adviser or an insurance agent while dealing with issues related to how people have planned regarding insurance. Working together with these types of professionals helps people navigate through various kinds of insurance coverage available so they can pick out the right kind depending on their unique situations. They can also help compare policy terms and conditions with other alternatives providing better coverage at more affordable rates.

Note that insurance planning is not static. Your plans must be updated as changes occur such as marriage, birth of children or significant changes in finances among others. Regular review of one's insurance will ensure continued protection and prevent any breach into his/her personal security.

Insurance planning ultimately forms an integral part of a wider financial strategy. Appropriate protection ensures financial security for your loved ones as well as giving you peace knowing nothing takes place without notice.

Reviewing Retirement Needs

Once you hit 50, retirement planning becomes very important. It will require you analyzing whether or not will be able to retire comfortably without any stress over money matters or if need be make some adjustments accordingly today itself by seeing a Financial Advisor before it becomes too late. Based on such considerations as projected inflation, desired lifestyle and healthcare costs, you can make informed choices about life insurance and estate plans.

Retirement planning entails assessing your current financial situation, setting reasonable goals and choosing the right path for achieving them. With a well-made comprehensive retirement plan, you can be sure that you are ready for the other side of your existence.

Determining Retirement Needs

The first step in determining your retirement needs is to consider what kind of lifestyle you want to lead during this period. Consider how much it would cost to do all those things and estimate the associated expenses. This may include travelling, leisure activities like cruises or vacations resorts with friends where one can enjoy themselves alone without any disturbance from time bound careers etc., hobbies like collecting stamps or coins etc., and health care expenditure among others.

Healthcare is an important aspect when calculating retirement expenses. As people grow older there is higher risk of needing medical care as well as long-term services in case of disability due to aging effects for example. Take into account potential medical expenses and the cost of long-term care insurance so that one is adequately covered.

Inflation could have huge implications on your pension savings. The cost of living rises over time thus it must be considered when estimating retirement needs. By including inflation, individuals can ensure their savings will be sufficient to maintain their standard living throughout their golden years.

Being Wise

In order to be in a position to make informed choices as regards your insurance and estate plans, it is important to have a clear understanding of what you want from your retirement. Knowing how much you need to save and invest will determine the level of coverage appropriate for you and adjust your financial plan accordingly.

Retirement insurance is important because it helps safeguard an individual's economic security. Insurance options such as annuities and retirement income funds should be considered since they can provide income for one's retirement years. By incorporating this type of insurance into your financial planning, you can be sure that there will always be money flowing in even after retiring.

Also, it is essential to regularly review the insurance and estate plans. When your retirement needs change, coverage should also change accordingly. For optimization of upcoming years' retirements and future financial security find professional help from advisors on finance or insurance agents.

Enhancing Your Social Security Benefits

Top on the list when planning for retirement is maximizing social security benefits; which could come in handy during those sun-downing days. Social security benefits are core sources of revenue for many retired people who depend on it all through their sunset years. In this part we shall outline several strategies that may provide valuable insights on how you can optimize social security benefits among other things.

Knowing When It's Best To Claim

One crucial means by which retirees may increase their social security benefit is through knowing what age one should begin receiving them. Early eligibility begins at sixty-two but it is advised that one weighs both sides before choosing early claims; waiting until full time age brings an increment of approximately eight percent annually (which usually falls between 66-67).

Considering Spousal or Survivor Benefits

Spouses or ex-spouses who are married can qualify for spousal or survivor benefits respectively from social security. This option allows individuals who earned less than their spouses did over time to draw against their spouse's social security instead of their own smaller benefit. On the other hand, survivor benefits can furnish income to the surviving spouse or dependent children in case of the death of a husband.

By doing that, you will increase your overall social security income and enjoy a safe retirement.

Long Term Planning

Planning for potential long-term care needs is essential when you reach your fifties. There might come a day as we grow older where we may need help with our daily activities, medication or any other age-related condition. Long term care insurance helps in financing these services so that you are not neglected.

This insurance takes into account costs for care received in different places such as nursing homes, assisted living facilities and home based services. By putting long-term care insurance into their strategic plan, people have been able to protect their assets and savings from being consumed by expenses of this kind.

Long-term care insurance, however, may not be the proper choice for everyone. You need to look at your situation carefully and think about other strategies for financing long-term care. Medicaid planning, for example, involves arranging assets in such a way that you qualify for Medicaid benefits which can cover costs of long-term care.

Some people also choose to self-insure by setting up dedicated savings or investments. Financial discipline is necessary when adopting this approach even though you can determine your own type and place of care.

Empowering Your Future

Incorporating long-term care planning into your insurance and estate plans is a proactive measure towards safeguarding your wealth and securing high quality health services in case of need. For guidance through the complexities of this crucial part of your financial future, consider consulting a financial advisor specializing in long term care or an estate planning attorney.

Regularly Reviewing and Updating Your Plans

When it comes to estate planning and insurance planning one thing is certain; life changes constantly. Therefore, regular review and update is critical to make them keep pace with these changes.

Events like giving birth, marriage, divorce or substantial change in finances have profound effects on one's estate as well as insurance requirements. Current plans must therefore provide for these contingencies proactively if the clients are not to suffer financially.

Reviewing an estate plan typically entails revisiting one's wills trusts or beneficiary designations so that they reflect current wishes and circumstances: thus ensuring that assets are distributed according to ones intentions while minimizing disputes among loved ones.

Likewise, revisiting an insurance plan helps ascertain whether present coverage matches new needs. As economic conditions shift overtime there might be a demand for more policies or policy modifications that adequately insulate one from danger while providing adequate protection to beneficiaries.

Accommodating Life Changes

On the other hand, regularly reviewing your estate as well as insurance plans will enable you handle such unexpected developments effectively by making any required adjustments to such plans.

One good example of a life change that demands the reconsideration of your plan is marriage. As you consolidate your finances with your spouse, you might need to review beneficiary designations and take additional insurance covers for the financial safety of your new family.

On the other hand, during divorce, one has to re-examine their plans in order to ascertain that present assets and insurance are relevant to the new situation. Updating beneficiaries as well as modifying a will can help protect ones' interests from unintended outcomes.

Similarly, when children come into the family there is a need for reviewing estate and insurance plans. It calls for appointment of guardians, establishment of trust funds and securing adequate insurance cover against risks on children's lives.

Major shifts in finance like inheriting a lot of money or starting a business would require revising one's plans. Through reassessing personal coverage needs and considering additional methods for estate planning, one can secure their newfound wealth or safeguard business assets respectively.

Maintaining Effectiveness Over Time

Making sure that your estate and insurance plans are updated by reviewing them regularly will ensure that they remain up to date and functional over time. These plans should not remain idle but rather actively guard against financial vulnerability and protect against your lasting legacy.

This is because, during the process of doing this, you are able to identify any gaps in coverage or outdated provisions within your estate plan. This means that you would be required to modify them as a result of changes in legislation or other regulatory requirements so as to remain compliant with these laws and take advantage of new opportunities for financial protection.

It's advisable that we carry out comprehensive reviews every few years or whenever there is a major life event. In addition, it would be prudent to seek the guidance of a financial advisor, an estate planning lawyer or an insurance agent just in case one has left out some important aspects which can be enhanced by using fresh strategies.

Remember that estate and insurance planning is lifelong. Through regular revisions and updates of plans, one stays safe; keeps his or her finances secure while being restful knowing what lies ahead.

Planning for a Calm Future

As you get older, especially after turning 50, it's really important to think about the future. Making plans for insurance and what will happen to your things after you're gone makes you feel safer and more at peace.

Having good insurance is a big part of keeping your money safe. It helps protect you and your family from big surprises that could cost a lot of money. It's smart to look into different kinds of insurance, like for your life, health, or long-term needs, and make sure they're part of your financial planning.

It's also smart to plan what will happen to your stuff when you're not here anymore. This means deciding how your money and things should be given out. Making a plan with a will and trusts, and choosing who will get what, helps avoid arguments in the family later.

Starting these plans early means you don't have to worry as much about the future. You can be more relaxed knowing you've taken steps to keep your money and family safe. Don't wait to make these plans. A little planning now can give you a lot of peace later.

Chapter 25

Evolving Family Dynamics: Adjusting to Changing Roles in the Family

Welcome to our chapter on changing family dynamics at 50! Our family relationships change a lot as we progress through life. It is important at this juncture that these changes are negotiated with empathy and kindness towards harmonious family dynamics.

In this article, we will explore some of the intricacies of transitioning within families and the significance of adapting to new familial roles. This will involve understanding and embracing these changes in regards to children leaving, remarrying, or any other reason that may cause a shift.

Join us as we explore a number of different types of family structures that emerge during midlife and strategies for managing changing family ties. Furthermore, we will deliberate on how redefining family ties is important, supporting ageing parents and adult children, and embracing intergenerational links.

Furthermore, we will look into conflict management, personal care prioritization including well-being as well as benefits associated with seeking professional support and guidance in such transformative stage of life.

Let's start this exciting journey into embracing evolving family dynamics at fifty; finding out how it can result into personal growth, deepen connections, lead to fulfilling years ahead full of love and support amongst relatives.

Understanding the Changing Family Structures at Midlife

At middle age people often experience various changing types of families which can have serious implications on their lives. Factors such as divorce , remarriage , or adult children leaving home can modify the way a given family operates leading to adaptation needs besides understanding.

For instance divorce is one common midlife happening that brings significant alterations in a family structure. Once couples separate there must be new living arrangements agreed upon together with custody issues plus co-parenting plans. This transition can be difficult both emotionally and practically for individuals now becoming single parents or having stepfamilies for example.

Remarriage is one more thing that can affect the family structure in middle adulthood stage. When people are lucky to find love again, mixing different families might create new relationships and connections. Stepchildren become a part of the family unit, and everyone involved must navigate the complexities of forming a cohesive and supportive family structure.

Moreover, middle age is often marked by children growing up and leaving their parents' homes for independent lives. Empty nest syndrome is a common experience for parents as they adjust to the absence of their children at home. This transition can lead to feelings of loss and a need to redefine the family structure and dynamics.

Understanding and navigating these changing family structures is essential for fostering healthy relationships and maintaining strong family bonds. It entails open conversation, empathy, and flexibility so as to adapt with time. By doing this, an individual can build a supportive environment within his or her own family during this transformative period in life.

Navigating the Evolution of Family Relationships

As we grow older we meet fifty year old mark our family dynamics undergo drastic changes. At this moment it is important that we adapt to these roles shifting while moving along with developed family relations. Strong bonds are nurtured within a family through effective strategies that embrace new dynamics willingly.

Communication is one of the key ingredients of family relationships. Sharing our ideas, emotions and expectations amidst changing dynamics therefore helps in deepening the understanding among them. Thus a safe environment allowing for open talks about the issue would enable different people to air their opinion and concerns thus leading to solving conflicts.

Family empathy helps in dealing with changes within families. Allowing for differences in experiences and difficulties faced by each family member enhances lovingness and tolerance. Walking in others' shoes will help us grasp the intricacies attached to the changing family dynamics, thus find a middle ground for holding on strong ties that exist between us.

In order to cope with new dynamics within a family, being flexible is very critical. As roles change and duties shift, it becomes necessary to accept openness as well as diversified approaches towards relating with each other member of your household. Being ready to accommodate modifications from the other side might give an impression that we are united together and connected through this stage of life thus preserving these familial links when shared responsibilities swap hands.

To navigate transitions within families at 50, individuals must embrace understanding, communication and flexibility. These strategies will help us adjust accordingly to developments occurring within our homes hence everyone being able to get care they need.

Redefining Family Ties at 50

At 50 years age mark people usually experience shifts in their family dynamics. It's during midlife that individuals can redefine what family means and build up supportive systems that are more fulfilling than ever before. In addition, embracing change enables someone cultivate new networks which strengthen his/her extended family relationship fostering chosen family concept.

The period around midlife presents an opportunity for introspection hence reevaluating our perception about kinship ties could be inevitable There can also be adjustments regarding who constitutes one's nuclear unit due factors such as divorce or remarriage or geographical distances making it possible for one to form bonds with kinsmen outside blood relations brackets but still blood relatives since they are not close family members. Active involvement in family ceremonies, regular attendance at homecomings or consistent communication may make individuals feel homey and have an encompassing support system.

Time to redefine what family is all about

This is why people may refer to their friends as their "brothers" or "sisters". When a person calls themselves someone's brother, sister, father, or mother; they mean that they are more than just friends but part of the same family.

Chosen families can also assist with changes in blood relations. Members of chosen families intentionally chose their relationships with each other and often go unconnected by genetics. These relationships generally provide companionship, encouragement and comprehension for others who may experience shifts in one's biological family structures.

Besides reinforcing ongoing connections and cultivating chosen kinship ties, it is advisable for citizens also to canvass for new ones within their localities. The creation of new friendships from social engagements, clubs membership drives, voluntary activities or shared hobbies provides an opportunity for a new perspective into one's life and hence support networks.

Redefining Family Ties at 50

However, once children have grown up supporting one's aged parents alongside taking care of adult offspring might be challenging. At age 50 we probably find ourselves at the nexus of caring for our own aging parents while concurrently assisting our adult children through periods marked by challenges.

Understanding the changing needs of our aging parents in order to ensure their comfort and wellbeing is a major caregiver responsibility. These can include handling medical appointments, managing money or just giving them emotional backing through difficult times. It is crucial that we approach these duties with empathy and sympathy since it marks a role reversal whereby our parents lean on us.

Alternatively, supporting adult children requires striking a balance between granting them room for self-determination and allowing them to make mistakes while still guiding them rightly. This range from helping them find employment to assisting them sort out relationship problems or just offering consolation during trying moments.

Family support plays an important part in maintaining healthy relationships among generations. To achieve this, it is necessary to set boundaries as well as establish clear channels of communication so that both the elderly and young ones feel supported rather than burdened.

There is no one-size-fits-all approach to caring for the old and responding to adult children since each family has its own unique characteristics. Nevertheless, by nurturing open lines of communication, having empathy, and setting limits we can create an environment where all family members are supportive towards each other.

Adopting Intergenerational Connections

In today's fast-paced world intergenerational connections within the family become even more crucial. Building relationships among various age groups not only enriches our lives but also helps bridge the gap between different generations.

Intergenerational connections provide opportunities for sharing experiences, knowledge, and viewpoints across age brackets. Younger relatives draw wisdom from older generation's experiences while older people gain new ideas from younger individuals.

When we embrace intergenerational connectedness we create a kind atmosphere where people of all ages know they are valued and their voices heard. It opens up chances for learning, growth as well as understanding one another better.

One way to promote intergenerational connections is by engaging in activities with shared interests that appeal to every member of the family unit. This could be organizing regular communal meals, planning for events or having common hobbies that they do together. All these help to strengthen connections among them and create everlasting memories.

Moreover, technology can go a long way in closing the generation gap. Elderly people learn from the young about the latest gadgets, apps, and digital platforms. On the other hand, young people benefit from hearing stories as well as life experiences.

Apart from benefiting families, embracing intergenerational connections promotes social cohesion in society at large. It enables us to challenge stereotypes, appreciate different viewpoints and build a more inclusive community.

Therefore let us prioritize our connection across generations; develop links between different age groups while bridging the gap. This way we shall be able to establish a family with mutual respect, understanding support and growth.

Conflict Management and Resolution

Conflicts and differences are bound to occur as our families evolve and change over time. Managing such problems is crucial in order to sustain harmonious relationships within the family unit. Effective communication strategies as well as conflict resolutions can help overcome these hurdles.

When conflicts arise, it is important to approach the situation with open-mindedness and empathy. Active listening and respecting each other's perspectives are vital for finding middle ground and resolving differences. Encouraging honest and calm discussions can result in a better understanding of another's position as well as compromise.

Additionally, focusing on the issue instead of blaming or personal attacks can also be helpful. By separating the problem from people, it becomes easier to find solutions and move forward together. Further, taking responsibility for our own part in a conflict and dealing with our emotions would also contribute to resolving issues.

Sometimes it may be useful to seek professional help or family counseling services. Trained professionals such as mediators may provide objective insights as well as strategies towards conflict resolution which could serve in bridging productive conversations among families. They have expertise that brings valuable perspectives as well as tools for resolving differences.

Mediation: Resolving Differences

For this reason, sometimes mediation can be helpful when conflicts seem insuperable. A neutral third party person can facilitate discussions thereby moving family members towards finding solutions that are mutually beneficial to all parties involved. Mediation offers a safe environment within which communication should occur without any constraints; this is especially true when addressing complex or deeply rooted conflicts.

Resolving Differences Constructively:

Conflict management and resolution helps foster stronger ties among families creating harmony at home. The realization that family dynamics keep evolving with attendant crises arises patience plus empathy for these kinds of hurdles at all times, which every change made should involve everyone concerned irrespective of their age or social status within the family set up.Families must work together so they can pass barriers and construct more solid relationships resistant against any external influences.

Making Self-Care the Priority

Within different changes at midlife stage, gifts might include resilience pertaining to expanding family dynamics . Self-care therefore makes one grow personally while improving support nurturing loved ones' relationships.

Midlife changes come with various challenges from empty nest syndrome to career shifts and aging parents. There is a need to comprehend the impacts of these changes on mental as well as physical health. Self-care during such transformative times helps people maintain emotional balance and overall wellbeing.

Self-care practices can look different for everyone depending on preferences and needs. Some effective options include:

Mindfulness and Stress Management:
Practising mindfulness or using stress reducing techniques like meditation or deep breathing exercises relieves anxiety, increases self-awareness, and improves overall mental health.

Physical Activity:
Being active promotes physical well-being, releases endorphins, and raises energy levels. For instance, engaging in such activities like walking, yoga, dancing etc supports a person's overall health condition.

Healthy Eating:
Eating whole foods rich in nutrients promotes both physical and mental well-being. Consuming whole foods should be done intentionally along with drinking enough water as this helps with healthy digestion.

Quality Sleep:
Adequate sleep is essential for rejuvenation and maintaining emotional as well as cognitive resilience. Thus getting enough quality rest involves developing regular sleeping habits like having peaceful nights among others.

Prioritizing self-care also requires fostering a positive mindset and surrounding oneself with supportive relationships. Having time for hobbies, participating in enjoyable activities; setting limits; taking time to reflect upon one's life help in coping with midlife crises gracefully & resiliently.Finally individuals nurturing their own wellness can better support each other through family dynamics that continue to develop over time thereby taking good care of themselves first before they can take care of loved ones who are going through midlife changes in family dynamics.

Seeking Professional Support and Guidance
Seeking help from professionals can make a big difference when dealing with changing family dynamics. There are family counselors, therapists and other resources to help individuals through midlife challenges.

In times of transition, there is always a need for the professional support system that offers insights and strategies. Counseling for families provides an environment where members can disclose their issues, improve communication skills as well cultivate better relations among them.

Professional counseling or therapy focusing on midlife problems might cover such areas as how individuals adapt to shifting family structures, self-management in conflicts, and prioritizing self-care. They might aid persons in having a clearer understanding of their feelings and thoughts so as to make decisions with more power over their lives.

Through seeking professional assistance people gain tools to navigate the complexities of evolving family dynamics. These resources allow them to effectively tackle challenges that foster growth and build stronger connections within families.

It should be remembered that seeking for support like this does not imply weakness; rather it is proactive action towards developing harmonious and fulfilling family relationships. With expert guidance one can confidently negotiate middle life crises thus enhancing his/her own sense of fulfillment at home.

Embracing the Evolving Family Journey
Turning 50 makes it necessary for one to embrace the journey as families grow older together during these years of transformation. Such milestones offer chances for personal development, stronger bonds between people, and creation of meaningful familial environments. It therefore becomes a time when change should be embraced or welcomed since every member evolves differently in this unit called family.

Midlife brings about changes in the way the family functions with children leaving home while parents grow old. Welcoming into these adjustments leads to an individual's new appreciation by herself or himself that each member has their own role within the unit. This approach gives room for curiosity and acceptance hence strengthening inter-family ties making everyone feel protected.

The voyage is not simply about adapting but also opening up new possibilities which redefine family. The journey of a changing family can be embraced by individuals through forming important bonds with chosen families or strengthening connections between extended relatives or making new relationships in order to ensure that they get true support from unexpected quarters.

The evolving family journey at 50 is a time for self-care and taking care of oneself. Staying well and positive helps individuals navigate the challenges and opportunities associated with transitioning through families. Also, seeking help from experts like family counseling is beneficial when it comes to midlife changes and establishment of healthy relationships within the family.

Chapter **26**

Letting Go: The Art of Forgiving, Healing, and Moving Forward

Welcome to a transformative journey of self-discovery and personal growth. In this article, we will delve into the art of letting go, forgiving, healing, and moving forward. At 50 years of age one needs these practices for self-acceptance and mental well-being.

Letting go is not an easy thing to do but it is important if positive change is desired to be made. When we release ourselves from past hurts, grudges and regrets we open up space for new beginnings as well as personal growth. By forgiving others among other people including ourselves we are able to find peace within ourselves thus nourishing our emotional health.

Healing is indeed a deep path that allows us to address emotional scars by finding inner peace. It is through nurturing our inner selves that could be a step towards our own personal growth. This way resilience grows during healing hence there will always be strength on going forward.

Moving forward at 50 is an opportunity for embracing change and new beginnings. Present moments become more appealing when ones gets rid of the need to hold on to the past while embracing now. As one grows older they must however make sure that they take advantage of their time in order to transform themselves positively.

Self-reflection is a powerful tool towards revealing our internal power which supports personal development. We can clearly know about ourselves after analyzing our thoughts actions and values. Through introspection acceptance as well as letting go are obtained.

Acceptance acts as the foundation for personal growth in life experiences that shape as all human beings no matter what their age may be in different times or situations we exist at various stages of individual development such as infancy adolescence adulthood etc.) This creates space for positive change while promoting mental wellness via embracing imperfection thus nurturing self-acceptance). Let's also consider how acceptance fits into this journey together with tips on attaining tranquility within ourselves.

Gratitude's role in personal growth and mental well-being cannot be underestimated. By cultivating gratitude, we shift our focus to the present and find joy in simple moments of life. To let go, we must be grateful for the things that attract us.

In our journey of personal growth and healing, seeking support and building a strong network is essential. Connecting with others fosters mental well-being, encourages self-discovery, and provides a sense of belonging. Here are some tips on how you can create meaningful relationships as you travel down this path.

Personal goals help to shape our course towards personal growth. Our mental health improves when we set goals that matter to us also helping us realize who we really are). Let's discuss strategies for setting our own personal goals.

Maintaining personal development requires discipline and regularity too much. Mental wellbeing is sustained through long-term development strategies while self-discovery nurtures it along with other positive changes in individuals' lives . We will look at ways of making these principles part of our daily lives as well as explore exercises for integrating them into your routine.

Embracing Forgiveness: A Path to Inner Peace

Forgiveness is indeed a very powerful tool towards inner tranquility during the process of healing too. It promotes healing as forgiveness is one way on which an individual can access their true potentials).

This shows that forgiving someone does not mean condoning or forgetting what they did; instead it means freeing ourselves from the burdens that come with negative emotions such as resentment and anger thereby creating room for healing and positive change within oneself's life.

When a butterfly appears, one thing is for sure that it must have gone through a difficult and challenging journey. It is always important to include the journey of transformation in whatever process we go through when dealing with change and new beginnings.

The first step towards moving forward at 50 is embracing change. However, this seems to be easier said than done for most individuals. For instance, many people are afraid of change because they believe that it will disrupt their comfortable lives. This is not only true but it also applies to most if not all individuals who get into the late adulthood stage of life before changing becomes hard in every aspect of life (Marcia et al., 2006). Instead of welcoming changes, these individuals stick to their old ways of doing things. Some even try to deny or avoid any signs of aging such as wrinkles on the face by using makeups, Botox or plastic surgery among others.

A significant part of an individual's life starts after turning fifty years old. By this time, people have lived more than half their lives and some may even have been working in the same job for over two decades (Reichstadt et al., 2010). The feeling of being tired from working in one place or doing one type of job can often lead them into making attempts at other options like starting own businesses.

Rewriting life scripts can occur as transition from middle age to older adulthood is taking place. Individuals develop different approaches towards growing old once they reach this stage (Levinson & Mansfield, 1978).

It marks the beginning point for future endeavors while closing the chapter on past experiences. At this age you stand at crossroads where you need to decide whether you will take a new path or continue with your current road.

As we celebrate 50 years, it becomes very important to welcome change and allow ourselves new beginnings. At the age of 50, there is a chance for person growth, positive change and self-discovery. To grow at 50 one must detach from the past and embrace the present while staying open to future possibilities.

It is important that we let go because this exercise enables us to release grudges or regrets that may hinder our progress. We become ready for personal growth and transformation only when we recognize and accept our past experiences. By letting go, we expose ourselves to new opportunities, unlock potentiality for positive change.

Embracing the present is just as vital if not more important. Staying mindful and fully present in every moment fosters gratitude and appreciation for now. In addition to bettering our mental wellness this mindset also allows us to make deliberate decisions that align with our aims and values.

Looking ahead requires embracing the future with resilience and optimism. This means setting new goals as well as aspirations which take account of changes in an individual's self-identity as well as purpose. Accordingly, by mapping out personal growth processes, this will create maps leading us into exciting journeys.

In summary moving forward at 50 is an opportunity for personal transformation, positive change, and self-discovery By letting go, embracing the present, and being open to new beginnings we can navigate this stage of life with grace and optimism Take a leap then towards change that leads you through a transformative journey of growth and self-discovery.

The Power of Self-Reflection: Uncovering Inner Strength

Through deep introspection one uncovers his inner strength hence leading him towards self-discovery as well as personal development Through self-reflection we get know who we are what we want in life so that we can shed off what does not serve us anymore .

Self-reflection has several advantages among them includes aiding an individual's personal growth. A person who takes time to reflect on his or her thoughts, feelings and actions becomes more aware of their habits and moods. This consciousness gives us the power to make choices after which we can move proactively towards change. Moreover, self-reflection helps us to identify places in our lives where we may need to break free from limiting beliefs, negative self-perceptions thus helping us feel a sense of personal freedom as well as growth.

Enhancing Mental Well-being and Acceptance

Self-reflection is a powerful tool for enhancing mental well-being. When we engage in self-reflection, we create space for processing our thoughts and emotions thereby decreasing stress levels and promoting emotional resilience. We gain clarity and perspective in such moments, enabling us to face challenges more calmly and centeredly too. Additionally, this practice facilitates developing self-acceptance since we learn how to hold ourselves with kindness by understanding that embracing all our strengths, weaknesses as well as shortcomings is vital for true acceptance.

Through introspection, we can find the fundamental causes of our fears, insecurities and limiting beliefs. We will then be able to start letting go by acknowledging and accepting these parts of ourselves that holds us back. Shifting our self-focus from self-reflection enables one practice acceptance even for others.

Techniques for Self-Reflection and Introspection

Different approaches can assist in this journey of reflecting upon oneself. By writing essays on our thoughts and feelings, we are able to gain knowledge into who we truly are through the words put down on paper as they help us gain insight about ourselves. For instance, meditation alongside mindfulness are two common tools employed in promoting self-reflection among individuals since it trains us to be more present-minded as well as allows us observe our internal emotions without bias.

Having meaningful conversations with trusted people can provide new insights into ourselves. On these lines, creative art forms like drawing, singing or dancing may facilitate soul-searching processes which involve using nonverbal means for unveiling personal innermost ideas.

By practicing self-reflection one is able to ascertain their inner strength for growth purposes, mental wellness gains, embracing change in ourselves and liberation process letting go. It's an empowering life changing practice that helps one find their true selves during the course of a self-discovery path.

Cultivating Acceptance: Embracing Imperfection

Acceptance is a concept with significance in personal development. It encompasses admitting imperfections within both ourselves and everything around us. By developing acceptance orientation in life people can improve their mental health status leading them towards a positive move and personal discovery.

Accepting means not giving up or resigning oneself but finding peace concerning oneself at different conditions of life. This concept tells me I should stop hoping for all things to turn out exactly as I want them to be; instead it suggests loving myself even when imperfect because my flaws make me unique.

One of the strategies for cultivating acceptance is practicing self-compassion. By treating ourselves with kindness and understanding, we can develop a more compassionate and accepting attitude towards both our strengths and our weaknesses. This helps individual growth to occur in a conducive environment because they are now aware of themselves.

Another strategy is to shift our perspective and focus on the positive aspects of ourselves and our lives. We notice what we have accomplished, what makes us special, where we have been blessed which eventually leads to gratitude besides acceptance of oneself at that moment.

Acceptance however does not mean that we stop trying to change or become better people. Instead, it allows us to work on personal growth from a place of self-compassion and self-acceptance. When we start embracing imperfections in us, only then do we invite favorable changes into our lives besides creating moments for self-discovery.

The Role of Gratitude: Finding Joy in the Present

Gratitude is an underrated tool for personal development as well as mental wellness. A sense of gratitude comes out when humans concentrate their thoughts on blessings amidst their daily struggles thus helping them change for the better.

Expressing gratitude is one way that can create transformation especially when one is going through a releasing process. Consequently, giving thanks enlarges spaces so acceptance can come forth. Gratitude enables individuals to view things differently hence changing from negative attitudes towards appreciating the brighter side of life.

Keeping a gratitude journal is one way of promoting thankfulness. Every day, spend a few minutes inscribing down three things that you are thankful about. In this way, we will be able to acknowledge and appreciate little blessings unnoticed.

H3>Furthermore, by expressing gratitude to others, we can encourage personal growth and improve our relationships. Stop for a while and say "thank you" to someone who has positively influenced your life. This action does not only bring happiness in their lives but also strengthens the bond between you and him or her.

Remember that gratitude goes far beyond grand gestures or material possessions. It can be found in simple things like warm coffee or beautiful sunrises. By developing an attitude of gratefulness, we open ourselves up to greater satisfaction with life, growth as individuals and self-understanding.

Consequently, let us practice gratitude daily. Let's find joy in today and appreciate the plenty around us; encouraging each other fosters personal development which leads us to having peace of mind and living satisfied lives.

Building A Strong Network: Seeking Support

When embarking on your journey of personal growth and healing it becomes crucial that you understand the importance of seeking support by building strong network connections. Relating with people has deep influence towards your mental well-being,self- discovery process, accepting oneself among other healing processes.

Constructing meaningful bonds with individuals who have similar values as yours can assist you go through hindrances better since they offer important backing when required by persons in need if assistance (Barron & Krawczyk , 2007). Through this one gets a feeling of belonging thus establishing a supportive community who can understand what they are going through empathizing with them.

By creating such networks , it provides different perspectives,personal stories from past experiences,and opening doors for future growth as well as learning from others' experience . Interacting with those who have undergone similar situations may give input on their own path to recovery and self-acceptance.

To build a strong network, there are several strategies you can apply:

1. Find like-minded communities:

Here you will join groups, clubs or organizations that matches your interest, values or personal development objectives. By meaningfully participating in discussions, attending events and engaging in activities you will connect with people who strive towards similar goals as yours.

2. Attend workshops and seminars:

This is an opportunity for educational growth and networking. Visit these forums to meet experts and other persons on the same journey of growth as you.

3. Online networking:

Utilize online platforms and communities dedicated to personal growth, healing, and self-discovery. Forum postings, discussion boards and social media groups will provide access to individuals from all over who are moving in the same direction as you are.

4. Have a mentor:

Identify mentors who have specialized knowledge related to your own area of growth goals. This guide is useful because he or she would offer counsel based on his own experiences thereby helping one overcome obstacles while embracing change.

5. Build A Support Network

It should be noted that when we talk about building a strong network it is not only about getting support but also giving it back where necessary . Therefore by telling others what we had undergone through at any given time ,one becomes part of such encouraging community where each person's growth makes a contribution to others'.'

To travel in the path of personal growth, it is important to build a strong network and seek support. Surrounding yourself with people who understand and support you increases your chances of achieving lasting positive change.

Embracing Personal Goals: Charting Your Path

On your journey towards personal growth, setting and embracing personal goals are crucial. They act as beacons that illuminate your way to self-discovery, positive change, and acceptance. By striving for meaningful goals, one improves their mental health while simultaneously giving purpose to life.

When goals are set in line with ones values, passions or dreams they serve as a strong motivating factor for an individual's transformation. These objectives give a clear roadmap regarding your actions; hence helping you make deliberate decisions that enhance your overall being.

Fostering Self-Discovery and Positive Change

The embrace of personal goals courageously leads to self-discovery; as you journey through this path towards attaining them, you will realize more about yourself especially the strengths within you which were not known before as well as the weaknesses inside you and even possibilities. In so doing, it enables individuals to explore new areas of interest in their lives thus expanding their horizons in terms of knowledge and skills acquired while at the same time giving room for hidden talents to manifest themselves.

Also note that by setting and achieving these personal goals you would have initiated some positive change into your life making it better than before since one cannot grow without experiencing some kind of challenge which takes us out from our comfort zones and necessitates our maturity. With every milestone achieved there usually develops feelings of confidence-building, resilience enhancement together with belief in oneself that can help overcome barriers faced within a person's lifetime period.

Enhancing Mental Well-being and Acceptance

Creating direction and purpose for life comes when one sets realistic personal goals which they actively seek after. This sense is always very impactful on someone's mental well-being because it gives them fulfillment leading improved mental clarity and emotional resilience as well.

Additionally, accepting who you are through personal goals is another process. During this time, you cease focusing on societal norms or your own self-imposed limitations thereby honoring your true nature.

Crafting and Realizing Personal Aspirations

The journey to setting and achieving personal aspirations is one that necessitates thoughtful preparation, introspective consideration, and enduring dedication. Below are strategies to assist you in navigating this path:

Identify what's important to you: Dedicate time to pinpoint what truly holds significance in your life and ensure your aspirations reflect these core values.

Choose goals that are clear and quantifiable: Articulate your objectives with clarity and set tangible benchmarks to gauge your advancement.

Map out a strategy for success: Segment your objectives into smaller, achievable tasks and devise a schedule to keep yourself accountable.

Keep the fire burning: Discover methods to remain enthusiastic and driven, whether by visualizing the rewards of your efforts or leaning on the encouragement of friends and family.

View challenges as lessons: Treat any hurdles as chances for growth, and be prepared to modify your tactics as needed.

It's essential to recognize that personal aspirations can shift over time. As you transform and progress, your desires might too. Welcome the dynamic nature of your aspirations, permitting yourself the flexibility to adjust and refine your aims as you go.

By wholeheartedly pursuing personal aspirations, you grant yourself the authority to direct your personal development, bolster your psychological health, embark on a voyage of self-exploration, and instigate beneficial changes. Harness the strength of setting and realizing personal aspirations to carve a unique path toward a rewarding existence.

Maintaining Momentum: Techniques for Continuous Development

On the journey towards self-improvement, it's vital to employ methods that ensure your continued advancement over the long haul. This entails not just the preservation of psychological wellness but also the cultivation of self-awareness, the fostering of acceptance, and the perpetuation of positive transformation.

A paramount technique is to make self-care a priority. Looking after your physical, emotional, and mental well-being is crucial for ongoing development. Allocate time for activities that fill you with happiness and relaxation, like working out, meditating, or pursuing hobbies. Commit to healthy practices such as sufficient sleep, balanced nutrition, and mindfulness exercises.

Moreover, immerse yourself in a supportive community. Forge connections with individuals who have similar interests in self-improvement, mental wellness, and self-discovery. Engage in impactful discussions, seek guidance, and extend support. Cultivating relationships that inspire and elevate you can keep your spirits high and offer insightful perspectives for continuous development.

Lastly, adopt an attitude of growth. Acknowledge that self-improvement is an endless journey and that obstacles are moments for education and resilience building. See challenges as opportunities to acquire new competencies and foster a mindset of curiosity and openness. Embrace self-compassion and rejoice in every step forward, no matter its size, to keep your motivation alive and maintain a hopeful view on your journey.

Chapter **27**

Romance Reimagined: Exploring love and intimacy at a mature stage

Welcome to our insightful chapter on love and intimacy in relationships during the fifties, a time of life where romance is reimagined and relationships in midlife take on new dimensions. In this series, we will delve into the unique challenges and dynamics that couples face during this stage, as well as provide valuable tips and advice for nurturing love and intimacy at a more mature stage.

Timeless though they may be, love and intimacy can take delightful turns as folks get into their fifties. Relationships in middle age are characterized by profound insight, shared experiences understood only fully by two people who have been together for years. It is a period where one is able to treasure the outcome of long-term companionship.

Join us as we discuss the importance of rediscovering passion, nurturing emotional connection, overcoming challenges, and embracing change in relationships at this stage. We will also explore the vital connection between physical and emotional well-being and the role it plays in sustaining a satisfying and fulfilling relationship.

No matter where you are in your journey, whether you are rekindling romance or looking to strengthen an already strong bond, our aim is to provide you with valuable insights and practical guidance that will inspire and empower you to create lasting love and intimacy.

Stay tuned for our next section on rediscovering passion and reigniting the flame in midlife. Let's go together on this fascinating adventure called Romance Reimagined!

Rediscovering Passion: Reigniting the Flame in Midlife

It's only natural that relationships grow old over time; what was once new becomes stale with familiarity. However, rediscovering passion takes on another meaning during mid-life. This presents an opportunity for reignition of fire leading to deeper connections that mean something more.

Rediscovering passion in older love means recognizing how relationships change over time. It is important to accept that initial overpowering infatuation may naturally wane, giving place to a more profound bond. But rather than reducing the possibility of passion this growth opens up new opportunities for desire and intimacy.

Couples in midlife can reignite the flame by refocusing on what made them attracted to each other in the beginning. Reliving past experiences, sharing favorite hobbies, or embracing new experiences together can create excitement as well as rekindle the passion. Rediscovering passion also requires open honest communication about desires, fantasies and needs.

Meanwhile, it is important to remember that passion can come in different forms such as emotional openness and intellectual connection. For instance, building upon these many aspects of love may lead to a contented life.

They should know too that sometimes being passionate with one another is not just about making love but it is also emotional bonding and they should always find other means of expressing their love without engaging in physical acts.

Building Deeper Bonds: Nurturing Emotional Connection

In later years, as relationships change and mature, nurturing emotional connections becomes even more important for creating deeper bonds. While physical intimacy is central to a loving relationship that lasts, emotional intimacy is the solid foundation of it. This is the stuff that holds couples together through thick and thin in life and provides a sense of security and understanding that can defy time.

Creating an emotional connection and keeping it alive are things that need attention from both sides. It involves active listening to one another, exhibiting vulnerability, empathy and support. Couples can strengthen their emotional connection by appreciating each other's thoughts, feelings and experiences thus fostering their comprehension about each other.

Open and honest communication is one way of cultivating emotional intimacy between partners. This encompasses sharing needs, wants or concerns in a respectful manner but at the same time being attentive to your partner's point of view. In this case meaningful talks can be used by couples to have their fears,dreams or hopes expressed in a safe environment.

The other essential element towards developing an emotional bond is to create shared experiences while making new memories together. Engaging in activities that bring joy and happiness can help couples strengthen their emotional bond and create a sense of shared purpose. Joint vacations, experimenting with new hobbies or merely spending quality moments together are some such shared experiences that are capable of reigniting old flame thereby strengthening ties.

Being present for each other emotionally also plays a role in building an emotional connection with one another. This implies recognizing each other's feelings as well as validating them while offering comfort during hard times and celebrating achievements respectively. Through showing empathy they can nurture it easily without judgments on emotions displayed openly within them thus making it safer.

In conclusion nurturing emotional connection is vital in building deeper bonds within relationships during later years. It calls for concerted efforts, open conversations, common encounters among people involved as well as emotions attuned together. By focusing on establishing emotional intimacy, couples can lay the groundwork for a lifelong relationship that continues to grow and flourish as they progress through life's different stages together.

Communication and Understanding in Midlife: Overcoming Challenges

Finding one's way through midlife relationships can be both rewarding and challenging. Couples in their fifties and above often come across new hurdles that necessitate effective communication skills as well as deep understanding of one another. These challenges although tough can be overcome but it takes patience, empathy, and adaptability.

The primary factor in maintaining a healthy relationship at this stage of life is honest conversation. It is important for partners to openly state their needs, wants or fears while being attentive listeners to know what their spouse has to say about the matter too. Through creating a platform for dialogue between couples, they are able o discuss sensitive issues about them resolving conflicts and hence strengthen their emotional ties in the process.

Understanding one another's changing needs and priorities in midlife relationships is also important. As people change, it is important to support each other's personal development and ambitions. This requires empathy, compassion, and a willingness to assume new roles and duties. Couples who acknowledge and respect each other's journey together can create stronger bonds and increase their sense of security.

It is important during hard times to remember the love that brought the couple together as well as the shared history between them. By thinking about previous experiences at times of joy reminiscing about past experiences can relieve tension among both partners reminding them how deeply connected they are. During difficult moments, looking for times of laughter and lightness helps soothe the foundation of a relationship.

By effectively communicating and understanding one another in order to overcome obstacles, couples in their mid-life can glide through their ever-changing relationship with grace and resilience. By growing together through adaptation, this becomes part of the journey for couples that enable them have lasting fulfilling partnership well into old age.

Intimacy in Later Years: Physical Vs Emotional Well-being

As relationships change over time so does physical intimacy alongside emotional intimacy too during later years making it necessary for us to understand changes occurring on our bodies bodies and prioritizing both our own wellbeing as well as those of our partner.

The sexual life of aged people may still be highly satisfying like when it was in early age periods.So, however, the body ages naturally.It is very necessary to inform your partner openly about any physical challenges or problems that may occur to you thus finding out new ways to maintain satisfactory sex life.

Furthermore emotional wellness plays a big role towards developing later year's intimacy .as we get old ,our emotions shift due to many experiences gained through out lifetime hence creating a secure platform where all partners can express their feelings including weaknesses .Couples' bond can be strengthen by nurturing emotional closeness .

It is vital therefore that mutual health is prioritized for an intimate relationship in later years. This means engaging in regular exercise, eating a well-balanced diet and participating in activities that promote good health overall. By taking care of ourselves, we can better support each other's well-being and enhance the intimacy in our relationship.

Remember, evolving relationships provide an opportunity for growth and exploration. Embrace the changes that come with maturity and approach intimacy in later years with an open mind and a willingness to adapt. To have love and sex do not die away couples need to consistently take care of the physical and emotional state of their bodies.

Embracing Change: Growing Together in Midlife

Going into this new phase of midlife relationships calls for embracing change by both partners. This is a time for personal growth, self-discovery as well as collective growth as a couple. It is important to understand that people change over time, hence one has to support his or her partner's individual development so that they can have a thriving and fulfilling marriage life.

During midlife, several people undergo significant life changes such as changing careers, empty nesting or reviewing personal aspirations. Relationships are the stage for these transitions and can be a source of both joy and difficulty. Couples who can embrace change and give each other support are better placed in navigating the same complexities.

Communication is crucial to embracing change and growing together. An open conversation where partners discuss their wishes, fears, desires ensures that no one feels left out of the other's affair. By listening actively to their partners' wants and worries, couples learn how to adapt themselves to what comes in middle age.

There's also an importance of maintaining some sense of curiosity and adventure at this stage of life. To continue building connection between them, partners should try new hobbies, chase new experiences or step out of their comfort zones too often. This shared adventure keeps relationships alive by encouraging growth in both individuals while at the same time deepening the bond between partners.

Change cannot be embraced in relational contexts during middle age without flexibility, patience and willingness to adjust. Celebrating individual successes, inspiring personal growth; providing emotional support through challenging times is vital too. These differences must not go unacknowledged so as to contribute towards still developing together for lasting fulfillment and resilience in love over time.

Exploring New Levels of Connection: Enhancing Intimacy

In relationships during fifties years old , enhancing intimacy becomes more important than ever before while emotional connections deepen even further . During those changing dynamics within a relationship it is therefore important for couples to explore deeper levels of intimacy which could involve emotional as well as sexual aspects opening doors to stronger marriage connections .

One way of improving your levels of closeness with your spouse is by talking openly about everything including sex . Take your time engaging with your partner on different conversations concerning what you think about certain issues; about your desires as well as areas that would need some improvement . You create this space though speaking openly from within you, which is a healthy environment for vulnerability and understanding.

Touching each other physically will also make a relationship stronger. These touches include gentle pats, hugs, and kisses that promote affection between both of you. Physically showing love should not be limited to the bedroom but found on daily gestures of love and appreciation .

Exploring New Boundaries

Similarly, exploration or trying new things can strengthen intimacy in relationships. Engage in activities that stretch your limits and challenge you to experience your partner more deeply. This might involve taking up a new hobby; going on adventures together or even exploring some favorite sexual fantasies in ways that are safe and consensual.

It is important to remember that this personal journey into deeper intimacy has no standard one-size-fits-all approach. What works for one may not suit another couple and it is okay like so. Regularly conversing with your partner while being open about what they want out of sex helps foster a stronger bond.

By exploring new levels of connection, you can keep the love and excitement alive in your relationship during the fifties. One way of achieving this is by accepting who they are during this time as well as growing with them . This would enable them develop deep rooted but ever changing intimacy over time.

Making Time for Romance: Prioritizing Love and Intimacy

In all the hurry and bustle of midlife, romance often forgets itself. Nevertheless, it is crucial that you prioritize these which will keep the spark alive and strengthen your connection. It may take some work to be romantic but in the end it is more than worth it. Here are a few practical suggestions and recommendations to help you make time for romance and prioritize love and intimacy in your relationship.

1) Plan Regular Date Nights

Plan a romantic date night every week of your schedule. Whether it's a candlelit dinner at home, a walk in the park or a night on the town together; make an effort to connect with each other as well as create special moments between yourselves. Having these dates regularly scheduled will send out the message that this is indeed a very important relationship among many others on your busy agenda.

2) Talk Openly and Honestly

True love and intimacy can only thrive through effective communication. Take time to listen genuinely to what your partner has to say and let him/her know about what you need, want or feel like doing. Be open as well as honest with one another about thoughts and emotions so that vulnerability becomes okay space for growing even closer.

3) Create Traditions

Creating rituals or traditions can bring stability into couple's daily life as well as add up romance into their lives forevermore. Like sitting sipping coffee every morning, having movie nights once weekly or going for yearly vacations together are some examples of such things couples do together. These shared experiences build memories while also strengthening that bond between partners.

4) Taking care of oneself first

To be able to give any kind attention worthy of her own interest in there needs be self-care first priority before everything else does. The state you maintain both mentally and physically have direct impact on how much love & affection can grow amidst two individuals concerned; therefore ensure both aspects are properly taken care off fully since there should always be ample timing for rejuvenating oneself with pleasurable engagements to be able show up fully in relationship.

5) Appreciate and Show Affection

Expressing gratitude and showing affection are powerful ways to reignite the spark in your relationship. Take the time to acknowledge and appreciate each other's efforts and qualities as well. Simple gestures like holding hands, giving a heartfelt compliment, or surprising your partner with a thoughtful gesture can go a long way in keeping the romance alive.

By ensuring that there are moments of love making and always prioritizing intimacy, you can make midlife one of the most fulfilling periods for your marriage. Remember, it is the small moments and deliberate actions that keep love alive while making your relationship thrive.

Building Lasting Relationships: Nurturing Romance Forever

As relationships evolve during middle age, it becomes important to nurture a lasting connection. With "Reimagining Romance" as its key theme, nurturing love and intimacy starts taking on an entirely new meaning. The last portion focuses on major factors that help maintain the flame burning throughout life's journey.

Continuous communication stands out as one of the fundamental pillars towards maintaining a lasting connection. Effective sharing of desires, dreams as well as fears allows couples to better understand their partners' evolving needs and aspirations. Through effective communication trust continues to grow whilst at same time aligning this companionship with changes experienced at different stages by both parties over time.

Another crucial thing is to grow together. For middle-aged relationships to flourish, partners must support and encourage each other in individual growth. Taking up new challenges, learning collectively and welcoming change helps develop shared aims among couples that make their bond stronger.

Lastly, prioritizing quality time for love and intimacy is crucial. No matter how occupied one might be with life's obligations, it is a good idea to create moments specifically meant for each other. Planning romantic escapades, exploring new activities or sharing silent moments all prioritize love and intimacy leading to a more profound relationship that is fulfilling in the long run.

Chapter **28**

Giving Back: Finding fulfillment in philanthropy and volunteering

Are you looking for a meaningful way to make a difference? Do you want to experience the deep fulfillment that comes from giving back? Engaging in philanthropy and volunteering can be the answer you've been searching for. In this article, we will explore the importance of giving back through philanthropy and volunteering, specifically for individuals who are 50 years old and above. Discover how community service can bring a sense of purpose and make a positive social impact. Embrace the power of altruism today.

The Benefits of Giving Back Later in Life

Engaging in philanthropy and volunteering later in life offers a multitude of unique benefits. It goes beyond simply giving back to the community; it provides a sense of fulfillment and purpose that can enhance the later stages of life.

One of the key benefits of giving back at this stage is the opportunity to make a profound impact. After years of experience and accumulated wisdom, individuals have valuable knowledge and skills to share. By actively participating in philanthropic activities, they can leverage their expertise to create lasting change and make a difference in the lives of others.

Moreover, giving back later in life allows individuals to foster meaningful connections. Through volunteering and engaging with like-minded individuals, they can establish new relationships, widen their social circle, and find a sense of camaraderie. These connections not only contribute to personal well-being but also create a supportive community for ongoing philanthropic endeavors.

Engaging in philanthropy and volunteering also has substantial mental and emotional benefits. Research has shown that acts of giving activate brain regions associated with pleasure and reward, leading to a sense of happiness and fulfillment. Additionally, dedicating time and energy to helping others can reduce stress, improve overall well-being, and enhance cognitive function.

Furthermore, giving back later in life can provide a renewed sense of purpose. Retirement and the empty nest phase often bring about a transition period, and philanthropy can fill this void by offering a meaningful way to spend time and make a positive impact. It allows individuals to stay active, maintain a sense of structure, and continue learning and growing.

In conclusion, engaging in philanthropy and volunteering later in life goes beyond charity work. It offers a multitude of benefits, including making a profound impact, fostering meaningful connections, enhancing mental and emotional well-being, and providing a renewed sense of purpose. By giving back, individuals can find fulfillment and create a positive legacy that echoes throughout their later years.

Exploring Philanthropy: Making a Difference Through Charitable Giving

Philanthropy is an incredible tool for creating a significant impact on the communities that need it the most. Through charitable giving, individuals can contribute financially and make a real difference in the lives of others. Whether it's supporting education, providing healthcare access, or addressing poverty, philanthropy plays a critical role in driving positive social change.

Charitable giving takes many forms, from one-time donations to recurring contributions, endowments, or establishing philanthropic foundations. Every act of giving, no matter the scale, can leave a lasting impact. By supporting organizations or causes that align with your values and priorities, you can contribute to initiatives that tackle the most pressing issues of our time.

When engaging in philanthropy, it's essential to research the organizations you wish to support. Look for transparent and accountable nonprofits that have a proven track record of making a difference. Research their projects, impact reports, and financial statements to ensure your contributions are used effectively. Building trust and understanding the work being done is crucial in maximizing the impact of your charitable giving.

Additionally, collaborating with other philanthropists, corporate sponsors, and foundations can amplify the impact of your charitable giving. By working together, pooling resources, and aligning efforts, philanthropists can leverage their collective influence to create even more significant change. This collaborative approach ensures that charitable giving is strategic, sustainable, and impactful.

Corporate Philanthropy: Engaging Businesses for Social Good

is not limited to individuals; corporations also play a significant role in making a difference through charitable giving. Corporate philanthropy programs enable companies to contribute to their communities and support causes aligned with their values. Whether through employee volunteering initiatives, corporate grants, or cause-related marketing campaigns, businesses can make a positive social impact and create shared value.

Corporate partnerships with nonprofits can lead to innovative solutions, increased resources, and a broader reach. By combining the expertise and resources of both sectors, societal challenges can be addressed more effectively, ultimately creating a better world for all. When businesses embrace philanthropy and prioritize their social responsibilities, they can become powerful agents of change.

In conclusion, philanthropy and charitable giving have the power to make a significant difference in the lives of individuals and communities. By exploring various ways to contribute and supporting causes that align with your values, you can be a catalyst for positive change. Whether as an individual or through corporate philanthropy programs, embracing philanthropic endeavors creates a better future for everyone.

Volunteering: A Hands-On Approach to Creating Social Change

When it comes to making a real difference in the world, volunteering offers a unique and hands-on approach. Through actively participating in community service initiatives, individuals can drive social change and positively impact the lives of others. Volunteering goes beyond simply donating money; it allows you to invest your time, skills, and compassion directly into causes that matter to you.

There are various opportunities to lend a helping hand through volunteering. Whether it's tutoring underprivileged youth, cleaning up local parks, or providing support to those in need, your efforts can create ripples of positive change in communities. By offering your skills and expertise, you can contribute to projects and initiatives that address social and environmental challenges, ultimately making the world a better place.

Volunteering also allows you to gain a deep understanding of the issues faced by individuals and communities firsthand. By immersing yourself in the experiences of others, you develop empathy, broaden your perspective, and become more aware of the diverse needs within society. This hands-on approach not only enriches your own life but also fosters a sense of collective responsibility towards creating a more equitable and inclusive world.

Finding Your Volunteering Path

When considering volunteering opportunities, it's essential to choose causes that align with your passions and values. By focusing on areas that resonate with you, you'll be more motivated and engaged in your service. Whether you have a passion for environmental conservation, animal welfare, education, or healthcare, there are countless organizations and initiatives that can benefit from your contribution.

Start by researching local volunteer organizations or reaching out to established nonprofits that align with your interests. Get involved in their programs or projects that resonate with you. Additionally, consider leveraging your skills, such as teaching, writing, or marketing, to offer specialized assistance to organizations in need. This way, you can maximize your impact and create positive change in areas where you have expertise.

The Transformative Power of Volunteering

Volunteering not only benefits the communities and causes you serve but also has a transformative effect on your own life. It can provide a sense of purpose, fulfillment, and personal growth. Through volunteering, you can develop new skills, expand your network, and build relationships with like-minded individuals who share your commitment to social change. These connections can be a source of support, encouragement, and inspiration throughout your volunteering journey.

Moreover, volunteering can enhance your overall well-being. Numerous studies have shown that engaging in acts of kindness, such as volunteering, can boost your mental and emotional health. It reduces feelings of stress, anxiety, and depression while boosting self-esteem and overall life satisfaction. By giving back, you not only create positive change externally but also experience inner transformation and a profound sense of fulfillment.

Join the Change-Makers

Becoming a volunteer allows you to play an active role in creating the social change you want to see in the world. It empowers you to go beyond good intentions and take concrete actions that have a lasting impact. Whether you choose to volunteer once a week or dedicate your time on a full-time basis, every effort counts.

No matter your age, background, or skill set, there is a volunteering opportunity that can enable you to contribute meaningfully to the causes you care about. By embracing a hands-on approach to volunteering, you can become a catalyst for positive change and inspire others to join the movement.

Finding the Right Philanthropic Cause: Discovering Where Your Passion Lies

it comes to giving back, one of the most important steps is identifying a philanthropic cause that aligns with your personal values and passions. Investing your time and energy in causes that truly matter to you can bring a deep sense of fulfillment and purpose. Here are some key ways to discover where your passion lies:

1. Reflect on your values

Take the time to reflect on your core values and what matters most to you. Consider the issues that ignite a fire within you and align with your belief system. It could be environmental conservation, education, healthcare, animal welfare, or any other cause that resonates with you.

2. Research different organizations

Research various organizations or initiatives that are working towards your chosen philanthropic cause. Look into their mission, impact, and the projects they are involved in. This will help you gain a better understanding of the work being done and the difference you can make by getting involved.

3. Volunteer and engage with the cause

Get hands-on experience by volunteering with organizations or participating in events related to your chosen cause. This will give you a firsthand insight into their work and allow you to connect with like-minded individuals who share your passion.

4. Listen to your heart

Ultimately, trust your instincts and listen to your heart. Pay attention to the causes that deeply resonate with you and where you can envision yourself making a meaningful impact. Choose a philanthropic cause that genuinely excites and motivates you to take action.

By finding the right philanthropic cause that aligns with your passion, you can make a powerful and positive difference in the world. Remember, the joy and fulfillment that come from giving back are unparalleled. Take the first step today and embark on your philanthropic journey.

Building Meaningful Connections: The Power of Community Engagement

When it comes to giving back, community engagement plays a vital role in creating meaningful connections. Volunteering and actively participating in community initiatives provide opportunities to connect with like-minded individuals who share a common goal of making a difference. Engaging in community service not only fosters a sense of belonging but also allows for the formation of deep and lasting relationships.

By joining forces with others who have a passion for community service, you can collectively work towards a shared objective. Together, you can create a powerful impact on the lives of individuals and the community as a whole. The joy of working hand in hand with dedicated individuals amplifies the sense of fulfillment derived from giving back.

Supporting Each Other Through Community Engagement

Community engagement offers a support system that extends beyond the act of volunteering itself. When facing challenges or seeking advice, engaging with a community of individuals who are passionate about making a difference can provide valuable guidance and encouragement. This network of support helps ensure the sustainability of philanthropic efforts as individuals share their knowledge, resources, and experiences.

Meaningful connections formed through community engagement go beyond the boundaries of volunteering initiatives. They can expand into friendships and partnerships that further fuel the desire to give back. These connections offer a sense of purpose, motivation, and accountability, creating a powerful positive cycle of inspiration and impact.

So, embrace the power of community engagement in your journey of giving back. By connecting with others who share your passion for making a difference, you can build meaningful relationships and create lasting change in your community.

Overcoming Challenges: Navigating Time and Physical Limitations

Engaging in philanthropy and volunteering can be incredibly rewarding, but individuals over the age of 50 may face certain challenges when it comes to making a difference. Time limitations and physical constraints can sometimes hinder one's ability to actively contribute to the causes they care about. However, with the right strategies and mindset, these challenges can be effectively navigated, ensuring that valuable contributions can still be made.

Addressing Time Limitations

Time is a precious resource, and it can often feel scarce for individuals with multiple responsibilities and commitments. However, even with a busy schedule, it is possible to find time for giving back. Consider prioritizing your philanthropic activities by assessing your passions and determining where your time would have the most impact.

One strategy to overcome time limitations is to break down your volunteering or philanthropic efforts into smaller, manageable tasks. Instead of committing to lengthy projects, consider engaging in short-term initiatives or single-day events that align with your interests. This allows you to make a meaningful contribution while still accommodating your time constraints.

Addressing Physical Limitations

Physical limitations should not prevent individuals from participating in philanthropy and volunteering. There are various ways to contribute that do not require extensive physical exertion. Research organizations or initiatives that offer volunteer opportunities suitable for individuals with physical limitations, such as administrative tasks, virtual assistance, or mentoring roles.

Furthermore, if you have physical limitations but still want to engage in hands-on activities, consider reaching out to organizations that provide accommodations or adaptations for volunteers with specific needs. They may have resources and support systems in place to ensure that your participation is fulfilling and inclusive.

Remember, regardless of your time or physical constraints, every contribution matters. Even small gestures and acts of kindness can make a significant difference in the lives of others and help create positive social change. By finding strategies to navigate these challenges, you can continue to make a valuable impact, embrace the joys of giving back, and inspire others to do the same.

Incorporating Giving Back into a Balanced Life: Finding the Right Balance

When it comes to giving back, finding the right balance is key. Incorporating philanthropy and volunteering into your everyday life is a journey that requires effective time management, energy allocation, and resource utilization. By integrating giving back into your well-balanced life, you can make a positive impact on the causes that matter to you without sacrificing your personal well-being.

To start, it's important to identify your passions and allocate time accordingly. Assess your schedule and determine how much time you can realistically dedicate to volunteering and philanthropic endeavors. By setting aside specific time blocks for giving back, you create a structured routine that ensures regular involvement in activities that make a difference.

Another crucial aspect is managing your energy levels. Understand that giving back requires both physical and emotional energy, and it's essential to allocate these resources effectively. Listen to your body and mind, and take breaks when needed. By maintaining a healthy balance, you'll be able to sustain your efforts in the long run.

Furthermore, consider the resources you have at your disposal. Whether it's financial contributions, skills, or networks, identify how you can utilize these resources effectively to maximize your impact. By aligning your resources with the causes you care about, you can make a tangible difference and create meaningful change.

It's also important to remember that giving back doesn't always have to be a grand gesture. Small acts of kindness and regular involvement in local community projects can also have a significant impact. Look for opportunities in your immediate surroundings and find ways to contribute that align with your lifestyle and interests.

All in all, incorporating giving back into a balanced life is about finding the right equilibrium between your personal commitments and philanthropic endeavors. By managing your time, energy, and resources effectively, you can make giving back an integral part of your daily routine. Embrace the joy that comes from making a difference and create a positive social impact while maintaining your overall well-being.

Creating a Lasting Impact: Sustaining Philanthropic Efforts for the Long Term

In the realm of philanthropy and giving back, creating a lasting impact is crucial. It's not just about making a difference today, but also about sustaining our efforts over the long term. By doing so, we can ensure that our contributions continue to have a meaningful and enduring effect on the lives of others. One way to achieve lasting impact is by adopting a strategic approach to philanthropy. Instead of sporadically supporting various causes, consider focusing your efforts on one or a few areas that align with your passions and values. By concentrating your resources and energy, you can develop a deeper understanding of the issues at hand and make more significant contributions.

To sustain your commitment to giving back, it's essential to establish a long-term plan. This plan should outline your goals, objectives, and the strategies you'll employ to achieve them. It's also crucial to regularly review and update your plan, as priorities and circumstances may change over time.

Building Partnerships and Collaborations

Creating a lasting impact often requires collaboration and partnerships with like-minded individuals and organizations. By joining forces, you can leverage each other's strengths, resources, and expertise to achieve shared goals. Look for opportunities to collaborate with nonprofits, businesses, government agencies, and community leaders who share your passion for making a difference.

Engaging the Next Generation

Another way to ensure the long-term sustainability of philanthropic efforts is by engaging the next generation. Pass down the values of giving back and inspire younger individuals to become involved in charitable endeavors. This can be done through mentorship programs, educational initiatives, and involving your own children or grandchildren in your philanthropic activities.

By nurturing a sense of social responsibility and empathy in the younger generation, you can create a ripple effect that extends far beyond your own efforts, making a lasting impact for years to come.

Remember, sustaining philanthropic efforts for the long term requires ongoing dedication, adaptability, and a genuine commitment to making a difference. By strategically planning, building partnerships, and engaging the next generation, you can ensure that your contributions leave a lasting imprint on the lives of others and create a better future for all.

Inspiring Others: Spreading the Ripple Effect of Giving Back

As you embark on your own philanthropic journey, you have the power to inspire others and create a ripple effect of giving back. By sharing your experiences and the impact you've made, you can encourage friends, family, and the wider community to embrace altruism and make a positive difference.

When you lead by example and demonstrate the fulfillment that comes from giving back, you become a catalyst for change. Your actions inspire others to consider how they too can contribute to causes they care about and create a ripple effect that extends beyond your initial efforts.

The Ripple Effect: How Small Acts Can Make a Big Impact

Every act of giving, no matter how small, has the potential to create a ripple effect. When you share your passion for philanthropy and the stories of the lives you've touched, you ignite a spark in others. They begin to see the possibilities and the impact they can make through their own acts of kindness.

By inspiring others, you multiply the effect of your giving. Imagine the collective power of a community coming together, inspired by your example, to support various causes and create positive change. The ripple effect expands, reaching more individuals and communities in need.

Be the Change You Wish to See

To be a catalyst for change and inspire others, it's important to be genuine and passionate about your philanthropic endeavors. Share your personal journey, the challenges you've faced, and the lessons you've learned along the way. Let your authenticity shine through, as it is the key to inspiring others.

Take the time to engage with others and listen to their stories. Show empathy and support as they explore their own philanthropic desires. Together, you can create a network of changemakers, each making their own unique contribution to the causes that matter most to them.

Remember, when you inspire others to give back, you are not only multiplying your impact but also creating a lasting legacy of compassion and goodwill. Together, let's spread the ripple effect of giving back and make the world a better place for all.

Embracing Fulfillment: The Joys of Giving Back at 50

At the age of 50 and beyond, there is a unique opportunity to embrace the joys of giving back and experience a deep sense of fulfillment. Engaging in philanthropy and volunteering allows you to make a difference in your community and positively impact the lives of others. It is a chance to reflect on the experiences shared throughout this article and find inspiration to embark on your own philanthropic journey.

By giving back, you have the power to create a lasting legacy and leave a positive mark on the world. Whether it's through charitable giving or hands-on volunteering, the act of selflessly contributing to a greater cause can bring immense joy and satisfaction. The fulfillment that comes from making a difference is unparalleled, and it is never too late to start.

Embrace the wisdom and life experience that comes with being 50. Use this opportunity to reflect on the values and passions that drive you, and find a philanthropic cause that aligns with your beliefs. By investing your time, energy, and resources into something meaningful, you not only benefit others but also nurture your own personal growth and fulfillment.

Chapter 29

Fashion at Fifty: Finding Personal Style that's Appropriate and Full of Life

Welcome to our chapter on fashion at fifty, which will discuss how to obtain a personal style that is both age-appropriate and vibrant. It is important to embrace your individuality as we move into this phase but still keep up with the latest fashion trends. This article is going to be provided with some fashion tips and style advice for mature people who want to redefine elegance in their wardrobe.

Refurbishing your look by adding trendy touches can help you avoid appearing old-fashioned while preserving a timeless elegance. We will inform you about the fundamentals of having a trendy fashion sense which suits your age and makes you feel comfortable in what you dress.

Building a wardrobe that works for you is crucial at this stage. You can choose those essential items of clothing that never go out of style by checking out our guide and create an outfit for any occasion. Dressing appropriately from casual outings to formal occasions has never been easier.

Fashion is not only limited to the clothes we wear. Instead, it encompasses the accessories we use to enhance our personal styles as well. Here are some guidelines on selecting suitable accessories that match one's wardrobe and contribute towards enhancing overall outlooks in vibrant manners.

Confidence remains paramount throughout this journey. With us, get insights on how best bring out your best features always sticking true to the ever glowing youthful age appropriate dress code. Confidence enables older women to take ownership of their own fashions when they are fifty years old or above.

This article ends by exploring timeless elegance as a concept. After all, classic elements when incorporated into dressing give us wardrobes full of sophistication and gracefulness. One will also learn about aging gracefully through discovering classic pieces whose charm does not fade thus adding some timelessness in someone's personal style

Get ready, then, for redefining your fashion-at-fifty experience! Let's create a personal style that reflects your personality, embraces age-appropriateness and exudes full of life. Join us in this exciting journey to timeless and stylish sense of fashion!

Understanding Fashion at Fifty

Let's first understand what "fashion at fifty" means before delving into the nitty-gritty details. It is important to note that fashion does not have an age limit. Here, it is dressing well as a matter of personal style which is reflective of your personality and boosts confidence quotient. Striving for a balance between trendy look and keeping up with your years requires you to find out the trends that suit your body best.

Embracing Your Personal Style

Building your personal style is an interesting path where you can express yourself through clothing. This involves knowing what colors, silhouettes, and fabrics work best for you as well as having a wardrobe unique to you alone. At this stage of life, embrace your personal style with poise because you are wise enough and confident.

Our expert fashion tips and style advice will guide you in finding out what suits you most which will help you feel comfortable whenever picking clothes. For instance, we know how important mature fashion is; therefore we shall give insights into ways one can incorporate recent trends while still very relevant to his/her oldness or youthfulness alike.

We are here to assist you in finding your best self whether you prefer a chic and stylish look, casual comfort or want to make a bold statement. With our fashion advice, from flattering profiles to everlasting accessories, your personal style will be improved and loud everywhere you go.

What is your color palette?

Among the first steps towards embracing individual style is learning which colors suit your complexion best. Try out different tinges of shades until you find those that make your skin shine and eyes gleam.

With a suitable color palette for yourself, fashion can become effortless and wardrobes can be made with synergy.

Silhouette Selecting

To have an age-appropriate wardrobe that flatters one's figure, it is important that women select silhouettes that accentuate their bodies' shapes. If tailored pieces or loose fitting clothes are more appealing, we shall offer guidance on how to buy clothes with correct cuts in relation to body shape. Embrace who you are as opposed to trying to fit into someone else's perspective of beauty.

Exploring Fabric Choices

When creating a wardrobe; a comfortable yet luxurious look must be derived from understanding varieties of cloth materials available. From cotton fabric breathing well through fancy silk ones; all these fabrics exist around us and thus this article was created with them in mind in order to help us in picking which ones suits our mode of dressing, climate and way of life.

The journey of embracing who you really are – Fashion tips and dressing for mature ladies

Through our fashion tips, style advice, insights into mature fashion; feel empowered to curate a wardrobe that reflects your personality and makes a statement.Discovering the enjoyment of wearing outfits which truly represent who you are - confident stylish fabulous.

Buidling a wardrope that works

To have 50-year-olds fashionably styled requires having meticulously picked clothing items starting from one's closet. This manual will help build up such kind of wardrobe which aligns with your fashion style and has timeless refinement. As such, it is important that we know the key wardrobe essentials every mature individual ought to have in order to be able to create outfits for various occasions.

When one attains over 50 years of age, their sense of fashion should be age appropriate and sophisticated. Choose classic and high quality clothes that will never go out of fashion. Timeless pieces like a well-fitting blazer or a little black dress are a must-have in any mature person's collection because they can easily move from official to informal events.

Additionally, there is also need for versatile items which can be mixed up depending on the occasion. Well fitting jeans, comfortable yet stylish trousers and neutral colored skirts are worth investing in. With different tops, blouses or jackets these basic items can form several apparels for all events and seasons alike.

Age-appropriate dressing also calls for proper accessorizing besides clothing as accessories do play a significant role in completing one's attire. Your outfit would look lively if there was a statement necklace around your neck or fashionable scarf over your head. When you think about accessories that reveal who you are and add value to you at large just get them.

By having these fundamentals included into our personal styles; we are able to make wardrobes which fit us well.Dabble with layers or mix up clothes so as to give yourself an elegant look that is suitable for your age and timelessness.Pick the right basis so as to effortlessly form outfits that express modernity and gracefulness at any stage of life.

Dressing For Occasions

Dressing appropriately for various occasions is key to making an unforgettable impact. For Fashion at Fifty, we know that age-appropriate dressing does not mean foregoing style and class. We provide you fashion tips and ideas on what to wear to different events from casual outings to formal events, ensuring that you strike the right balance between comfort and sophistication always. Be it a brunch date or a wedding you are attending, our wardrobe essentials and fashion tips have got your back.

Casual Outings

When going for casual outings, go for comfortable yet fashionable combinations. Take into account both well-fitted jeans worn with a classic button-down shirt as well as add color by wearing statement necklace for vibrancy touch. Conclude the look with stylish sneakers or flats. Embrace relaxed yet effortlessly chic looks while being true to your age and personal style.

Professional Events

When attending professional events/meetings, choose tailored outfits that will confidently speak of professionalism in you. You could pair a sleek blazer with a blouse and slim-cut pants to create powerfully sophisticated appeal. End the whole attire with quality heels and minimal accessories. Dressing properly in this context makes known your professional nature as well as still letting your personal taste stand out.

Formal Occasions

For official functions, bring out elegance through timeless dresses/attires. A classic little black dress paired up with tasteful accessories can never let you down anytime any day. If you like more modern looks then think of going for chic jumpsuit which flatteringly fits on your body shape/silhouette otherwise anyone else going to another direction might prefer an elegant jumpsuit in he/she's own style but trendier one too (preferably). Match it up with some statement earrings plus clutch bag so as raise the level of outfitting above board.. While adding something unique into your formal clothes try diverse colors as well as materials.

Whatever occasion it may be; dressing age-appropriately means wearing what makes you feel confident and comfortable. With our fashion tips and wardrobe staples, you can create chic and sophisticated looks that reflect who you are and allow for your inner beauty to shine.

Incorporating Trends into Your Style

Maintain your fashion sense while engaging in age-appropriate dressing. Adding trends to your closet brings some freshness as well as modernity to the way you look. The following are some of the fashion tips to enable you remain trendy and confident even at fifty:

1. Go For The Right Trend That Suits You

Not all the trends will favor your dressing style but don't be worried about it! Find out what speaks to your taste as well as strengthen your wardrobe. Use color, print or texture on yourself that goes with how you feel when wearing those clothes.

2. Customize Runway Trends According To Your Taste

Looking at the catwalk might provide one with numerous ideas but not everything would work for an ordinary person's life situation. Change recent designs so that they fit in with your lifestyle plus comfort zones. In other words, do not dress too young while trying still to be on top of things.

3. Combine Timeless Pieces And Fashion Forward Statement Pieces

Pair classic wardrobe essentials with recent styles in order to achieve a stylishly well-balanced appearance....There is no need of minimizing fashionable blouses by highly blending them with plain colored trousers or dresses which might lack a striking feature (this means that one should not wear old fashioned tops mixed up with new skirts). As such, there is always a harmonious blend between modernity and traditional timeless looks.

4. Invest In Versatile Statement Pieces

Go for statement items which can completely polish up all attires showing that they belong to trendy cuts/looks/fits only… take a vibrant handbag or bold printed blazer among others which will update every ensemble of yours while speaking volumes about the general trendiness of your wear.

5. Trust Yourself

In the end, style is about being yourself and feeling good. Believe in your gut and choose trends that make you comfortable as well as genuine. Finally, always remember that your personal style must show who you are.

Following these fashion tips will help you to work new trends into your own style in ways that are both age-appropriate and trendy. Never forget who you are while embracing the ever-changing fashion world and looking stunning at fifty!

Combining Clothes with Accessories

By art of accessorizing it's meant your personal style which is an expression of who you are. Any outfit can be elevated by these pieces and they usually enhance the whole look of a person. For more details please see our section on how to choose the right accessories for wardrobe essentials.

Statement pieces should be mixed up with subtle details when it comes to accessorising. A big necklace instantly turn a plain dress into something else while a small scarf adds some elegance to your clothes. Try different add-ons till something clicks in your mind about yourself through fashion vibrance.

Don't allow anything fight against your accessories as they should speak for themselves when choosing them. If you have decided to wear something bright go easy on jewelry since too much might destroy your overall look. However, if you have chosen neutral colors for today don't hesitate in wearingsome bold colorful piece for added vibrant touch.

It is also worth considering integrating into your personal wardrobe such types of accessories like designer handbags, stylish sunglasses or fashionable belts among others. These aforementioned things can really transform an outfit and make people not forget it forever. Lastly, use them as optical weapons of self-expression that will give out what kind of person you are.

Selecting Appropriate Add-Ons

As one ages another factor to consider when picking fittings for 50s fashions is color fabric type design since color does wonders for aging skins making them look more radiant without any additives used besides complementary hues which do not date. Black, white and beige colors are neutral choices that never go out of style. On the other hand, if you are a person who loves bright colors which will add fun to your look or personality just put them on.

Consider also the material of your accessory. Choose high-quality materials such as leather, sterling silver or silk to give your accessories a touch of elegance and durability. Not only does it improve the quality but it also enhances the appearance of these items.

Lastly, think about how your personal style matches with the accessories. Whether you are into classics or contemporary trends there is always something for everyone when it comes to these items. Be yourself and always mind to choose things that help you become more confident in fashion.

Selecting Appropriate Add-Ons

When selecting accessories for fashion at 50, consider the color, material and design of those pieces. Opt for colors that compliment your skin tone as well as bring out your natural beauty. These colors include black, white, and beige which are timeless classics that work for all occasions. Nevertheless, don't be afraid to incorporate vibrant hues into your ensemble if they enhance your personality while making you look stunning wherever you go.

Moreover take into account what fabric each accessory is made from. For instance, leather gloves might add some sophistication making it long lasting than any other type available in market today such as cotton ones hence increasing its value added component too since it improves quality aspects apart from aesthetics.

Finally look at what kind of style those accessories represent compared to your own personal taste in clothes; whether one prefers classic elegant pieces or follows current fads there will surely be something suitable among these options as far as fashion goes. Stick with yourself and take those things that bring out a better version of who one really is.

Choosing Right Accessories

Adding suitable accessories can make a difference in how amazing one looks when dressed up at 50 years old; hence enhancing self-confidence levels. From statement necklaces that steal the spotlight to elegant scarves that exude sophistication, the right accessories can elevate your personal style to a whole new level. Be yourself, try out different kinds of things and see what happens to your fashion vibrance.

Confidence in Style

Confidence is the key to owning your fashion at fifty. It's about embracing your personal style and feeling great in what you wear. By making conscious style choices and following a few fashion tips, you can highlight your best features and exude confidence that radiates from within.

Personal style has dynamic roles when it comes to vibrant and age-appropriate clothing. Dress up in colors that suit your skin tone and make you feel alive. A bold red dress or a brightly patterned shirt for instance can help boost self-assurance and make an ultimate fashion statement.

Confidence in one's style can simply be achieved through age-appropriate dressing but not limited to color scheme selection. This does not imply that you have to discard being trendy. The goal is to strike a balance between staying current with trends while also dressing in a manner appropriate for your age group.

Highlight Your Best Features

When selecting clothing, consider your body shape and choose pieces that flatter your figure. For example, Know if you should wear an A-line dress tailored blazer or anything else that will show off the best of these parts thereby motivating you towards unveiling more of your unique sense of personal fashion.

Another way of maintaining confidence in life is by using accessories . Try out statement pieces like jewelry with big pendants, scarfs or fancy handbags on different outfits so as to give them some life. Not only do accessories like this complete an outfit but they also have the power to heighten one's self-assurance.

Always remember that fashion is a way through which individuals express themselves artistically or otherwise. Have fun with fashion decisions and let out who exactly you are as an individual when it comes to clothes selection. When someone wears their clothes confidently, everyone around them can see it thus emanating from their personality itself.

Embracing Timeless Elegance

In the world of fashion, there is something truly enchanting about timeless elegance. This type of fashion transcends trends and withstands time, it is characterized by both sophistication and grace. Embracing timeless elegance means cultivating a personal style that is effortlessly chic and everlastingly beautiful.

To capture this timeless charm in mature fashion, look to classic design elements. Always go for pieces with clean lines, incredible tailoring and top notch craftsmanship. A well-fitting blazer, sheath dress that tailored and leather shoes made from quality materials are some of the basic items you should include in your wardrobe.

Timeless elegance does not involve having to subscribe to a strict dress code or adhering to rigid fashion rules. It calls for an amalgamation of classical styles with today's fashions which brings out who you are as a person when it comes to dressing up. Play around with color, texture or prints suitable for your personality while still maintaining that polished look.

Quality is everything when it comes to timeless elegance. For instance spend on clothes made from high quality fabrics such as silk that hangs perfectly on shoulders. Also choose accessories like luxurious watches or designer bags that can add a touch of classiness. By putting together a collection of enduring garments, one develops his or her own sense of style marked by gracefulness which endures forever.

Chapter 30

Wellness Wisdom: Holistic practices for mental and emotional health

Welcome to our chapter on Wellness Wisdom, where we explore the importance of holistic practices for mental and emotional health, especially for individuals who are 50 years old. As we age, it becomes crucial to prioritize our well-being and embrace practices that nurture our minds and hearts. In this article, we will delve into the connection between mental and emotional well-being and the overall balance in life's later stages.

Life at 50 brings unique challenges and changes, which can have significant impacts on our mental and emotional health. Hormonal changes, life experiences, and various other factors require us to pay closer attention to our well-being. By understanding the intricacies of mental and emotional health at 50, we can take proactive steps to address any challenges and maintain a positive state of mind.

Embracing holistic practices can play a vital role in supporting mental wellness. By incorporating techniques such as mindfulness, meditation, yoga, and journaling into our daily routines, we can enhance mental clarity, reduce stress, and foster overall psychological well-being. These practices empower us to navigate the ups and downs of life with resilience and equanimity.

It's not just about mental health; emotional balance is equally important. Through holistic well-being practices like aromatherapy, art therapy, and energy healing, we can address emotional challenges and cultivate a sense of inner harmony. These practices create space for self-expression, healing, and embracing the full spectrum of our emotions.

Self-care plays a crucial role in maintaining mental and emotional health at 50. By nurturing ourselves through self-compassion, setting boundaries, and engaging in activities that bring joy and relaxation, we can replenish our energy and find balance in our lives. Taking time for self-care is not selfish but essential for our overall well-being.

Mindfulness, specifically tailored for seniors, is a powerful practice for cultivating present-moment awareness. It not only improves mental and emotional well-being but also enhances cognitive function and reduces anxiety and depression. By staying fully present, we can fully appreciate each moment and find peace amidst the challenges and uncertainties.

Supportive relationships are key to promoting mental and emotional health at 50. Healthy social connections, open communication, and seeking professional help when needed create a supportive network that strengthens our well-being. By nurturing these relationships, we can navigate life's ups and downs with the support and understanding of those around us.

As we embrace life transitions and seek meaning in the later stages of life, holistic practices can guide us on this path. By practicing mindfulness, staying connected to our passions, and cultivating a sense of purpose, we can lead fulfilling lives and embark on new adventures, making the most of every moment.

Incorporating holistic practices into a wellness routine is an effective way to support mental wellness and emotional balance. By including physical exercise, nutrition, sleep, and various holistic practices in our daily lives, we can create a holistic wellness routine that nourishes our mind, body, and soul.

Gratitude and a positive mindset are powerful tools for promoting mental wellness and emotional health. By practicing gratitude journaling, positive affirmations, and reframing negative thoughts, we can cultivate an optimistic outlook and embrace joy and fulfillment in every aspect of our lives.

In conclusion, Wellness Wisdom is not just a concept but a way of life. By practicing holistic approaches to mental and emotional health, individuals at 50 can create a fulfilling and balanced life. Remember, sustained wellness wisdom requires continuous learning, self-reflection, and integrating these practices into our daily routines. Let's embark on this journey together and nurture our mental and emotional well-being every step of the way.

Understanding Mental and Emotional Health at 50

As individuals reach the milestone age of 50, they often encounter unique challenges and changes in their mental and emotional health. The impact of life experiences, combined with hormonal shifts, can significantly affect their overall well-being. It's crucial to address mental and emotional well-being during this stage of life to maintain a healthy and fulfilling lifestyle.

At 50, individuals may find themselves navigating various transitions, such as retirement, empty nesting, or caring for aging parents. These significant life changes can bring about both excitement and uncertainty, leading to a range of emotions that need to be understood and managed.

Hormonal changes, such as fluctuating estrogen and testosterone levels, can also contribute to shifts in mood, cognition, and energy levels. These changes may impact mental and emotional health, potentially leading to symptoms like mood swings, anxiety, or depression.

To address these challenges and promote optimal mental and emotional well-being, holistic practices can play a vital role. Holistic approaches consider the connection between the mind, body, and spirit, emphasizing the importance of balance and self-care.

By integrating holistic practices into daily life, individuals at 50 can proactively manage their mental and emotional health. These practices can range from mindfulness meditation and yoga to journaling and aromatherapy. Holistic practices provide tools and techniques to cultivate self-awareness, reduce stress, and promote overall psychological well-being.

Understanding mental and emotional health at 50 is crucial for individuals to navigate this significant stage in life with resilience and fulfillment. By recognizing the unique challenges and leveraging holistic practices, it becomes possible to cultivate meaningful well-being and embrace the journey ahead with a renewed sense of purpose.

The Benefits of Holistic Practices for Mental Wellness

When it comes to nurturing mental wellness at the age of 50, incorporating holistic practices into your daily routine can be incredibly beneficial. Holistic practices focus on the connection between the mind, body, and spirit, aiming to promote overall well-being and balance. These practices encompass various techniques such as mindfulness, meditation, yoga, and journaling, each offering unique advantages for mental clarity, stress reduction, and enhancing psychological well-being.

One of the key benefits of holistic practices is their ability to promote mental clarity. Mindfulness, for example, encourages individuals to be fully present in the moment, cultivating a deep sense of awareness and focus. This practice helps to calm the mind, reduce distractions, and enhance cognitive function, ultimately supporting mental wellness and clarity.

Another significant advantage of holistic practices is their stress-reducing effects. Meditation, for instance, allows individuals to quiet the mind, release tension, and find inner peace. By incorporating regular meditation sessions into your routine, you can alleviate stress, reduce anxiety, and create a solid foundation for emotional and mental well-being.

Furthermore, yoga is a holistic practice that combines physical movement with breath awareness. Engaging in yoga not only enhances flexibility and strength but also promotes relaxation and releases endorphins, which boost mood and overall mental wellness. Additionally, journaling provides a means of self-expression, allowing individuals to process emotions and thoughts, gain perspective, and cultivate introspection.

By incorporating these holistic practices into your daily life, you can experience improved mental wellness and overall psychological well-being. The benefits extend beyond the 50s, ensuring a more balanced and fulfilling life. To enhance mental clarity, reduce stress, and nurture your holistic well-being, consider integrating mindfulness, meditation, yoga, and journaling into your daily routine.

Embracing Emotional Balance Through Holistic Wellbeing

Emotional balance plays a crucial role in our overall well-being, especially as we navigate the complexities of life at the age of 50. One powerful approach to achieving emotional balance is through holistic wellbeing, which encompasses a wide range of practices that promote harmony and inner peace. One such practice is aromatherapy, the use of essential oils extracted from plants to enhance emotional well-being. Lavender, for example, is known for its calming properties, while citrus oils like bergamot and lemon can uplift and energize. By incorporating aromatherapy into your daily routine, you can create a soothing environment that supports emotional balance and relaxation.

Art therapy

Another effective way to embrace emotional balance is through art therapy. Engaging in artistic activities such as painting, drawing, or sculpting can serve as a meditative outlet, allowing you to express and process your emotions. Art therapy can help you explore your inner self, alleviate stress, and promote emotional healing.

Energy healing practices also play a significant role in achieving emotional balance. Techniques like Reiki and acupuncture focus on restoring and balancing the body's energy flow, which can alleviate emotional blockages and promote a sense of calm and serenity. These practices work on a holistic level, addressing not only the symptoms but also the underlying emotional imbalances.

By embracing holistic wellbeing, you can nurture and cultivate emotional balance in your life. These practices can provide you with tools to better cope with daily stressors, navigate challenging emotions, and create a sense of inner harmony. Incorporating aromatherapy, art therapy, and energy healing into your routine can support your emotional well-being and contribute to a more fulfilling life at 50.

Nurturing Self-Care at 50

When it comes to maintaining mental and emotional health at the age of 50, self-care plays a crucial role. Prioritizing self-care is about taking the time to nurture your own well-being and honoring your needs. Through self-compassion, setting boundaries, and engaging in activities that bring joy and relaxation, you can promote holistic wellness and lead a fulfilling life.

Self-compassion involves treating yourself with kindness and understanding, especially during challenging times. It means acknowledging your emotions and allowing yourself to feel them without judgment. By practicing self-compassion, you can cultivate a sense of self-acceptance and inner peace, which are vital for mental and emotional well-being.

Setting boundaries is another essential aspect of self-care at 50. It involves clearly defining what is acceptable and what is not in various aspects of your life, such as relationships, work, and personal time. Setting boundaries helps to protect your energy, prevent burnout, and maintain a healthy balance between giving to others and taking care of yourself.

Engaging in activities that bring joy and relaxation is also key to self-care at 50. Whether it's pursuing hobbies, spending time in nature, practicing mindfulness, or immersing yourself in creative endeavors, these activities nourish your soul and help you reconnect with yourself on a deeper level. They provide moments of peace and rejuvenation that contribute to overall well-being.

At 50, self-care is not a luxury but a necessity. By nurturing your mental and emotional health through self-compassion, setting boundaries, and engaging in activities that bring joy and relaxation, you can create a solid foundation for holistic wellness. So go ahead and prioritize yourself - you deserve it!

Mindfulness for Seniors: Cultivating Present-Moment Awareness

As individuals reach their senior years, cultivating mindfulness becomes increasingly valuable for promoting mental and emotional well-being. Mindfulness, a practice rooted in holistic principles, focuses on cultivating present-moment awareness and non-judgmental acceptance of one's thoughts, feelings, and sensations. This section explores the benefits of mindfulness for seniors and its potential to improve cognitive function, reduce anxiety and depression, and enhance overall emotional resilience.

The Power of Supportive Relationships

Supportive relationships play a crucial role in promoting mental and emotional health at 50. As individuals navigate the unique challenges and changes that come with this stage of life, having healthy social connections becomes even more important.

Research has shown that strong relationships can have a positive impact on mental health and emotional well-being. Maintaining these connections, whether it's with family, friends, or even support groups, provides a sense of belonging, validation, and support.

Open communication within these relationships is key. Being able to express your thoughts, feelings, and concerns with trusted individuals can alleviate stress and anxiety. It's important to find people who listen without judgment and offer understanding and empathy.

Seeking professional help when needed is also essential. Mental health professionals can provide valuable guidance and support, assisting individuals in navigating their emotions and developing coping strategies.

Remember, it's never too late to build or strengthen your support network. Engage in activities and hobbies that align with your interests, join community groups, or consider volunteering. These avenues can provide opportunities to meet like-minded individuals and form new connections.

By cultivating supportive relationships, individuals can enhance their mental and emotional well-being, fostering a healthier and more fulfilling life at 50.

Honoring Life Transitions and Finding Meaning

In the later stages of life, embracing life transitions and finding meaning becomes increasingly important for maintaining emotional and mental health. This is a time of reflection and reevaluation, where individuals may seek to navigate changes, discover new passions, and cultivate a sense of purpose.

One of the ways to navigate these transitions is through the use of holistic practices. Holistic practices, which encompass the mind, body, and spirit, can provide valuable tools and resources for coping with life's challenges and finding deeper fulfillment.

When embracing life transitions, it's essential to engage in self-reflection and explore personal values, desires, and aspirations. This process allows individuals to gain clarity about what truly matters to them and align their actions with their core beliefs.

Practices such as meditation and journaling can support introspection and self-discovery. Meditation helps calm the mind, reduce stress, and foster self-awareness, while journaling provides a creative outlet for processing thoughts and emotions.

Additionally, seeking support and guidance from holistic practitioners, such as counselors or life coaches, can offer valuable insights and strategies for navigating life transitions. These practitioners can help individuals explore their passions, set goals, and create actionable plans to bring about positive changes in their lives.

During this stage, it's also important to consider the role of community and social connections in finding meaning. Engaging in activities and hobbies that align with personal interests can create a sense of fulfillment and foster new relationships.

Participating in volunteer work or joining social clubs and organizations can provide opportunities for personal growth, contribute to the community, and establish meaningful connections with like-minded individuals.

In summary, honoring life transitions and finding meaning in the later stages of life is crucial for emotional and mental well-being. By embracing holistic practices, engaging in self-reflection, seeking support, and nurturing social connections, individuals can navigate transitions, discover new passions, and create a sense of purpose that enhances their overall quality of life.

Creating a Holistic Wellness Routine

Establishing a holistic wellness routine is key to promoting mental wellness and emotional balance as you navigate the challenges and changes of life. By incorporating various holistic practices into your daily life, you can cultivate a sense of overall well-being and support your holistic health journey. Here are some practical tips to guide you:

1. Prioritize Physical Exercise

Engaging in regular physical exercise is essential for holistic health. Aim for at least 30 minutes of moderate-intensity exercise, such as brisk walking, cycling, or dancing, most days of the week. Physical activity not only improves your physical health but also releases endorphins, which enhance your mood and promote mental wellness.

2. Nourish Your Body with Healthy Nutrition

Eating a balanced diet rich in nutrient-dense foods is vital for supporting your mental wellness and emotional balance. Incorporate plenty of fruits, vegetables, whole grains, lean proteins, and healthy fats into your meals. Hydrate adequately by drinking enough water throughout the day.

3. Prioritize Quality Sleep

Getting sufficient and restful sleep is crucial for your overall well-being. Aim for 7-9 hours of uninterrupted sleep each night. Create a calming bedtime routine, such as reading a book, practicing relaxation techniques, or enjoying a warm herbal tea, to help signal your body that it's time to unwind and prepare for a good night's rest.

4. Incorporate Holistic Practices into Your Daily Life

Embrace holistic practices that resonate with you and integrate them into your daily routine. Some effective practices include mindfulness meditation, yoga, deep breathing exercises, journaling, and aromatherapy. These practices can help you find inner peace, reduce stress levels, and enhance your emotional well-being.

5. Find Moments of Stillness and Reflection

Carve out time each day for moments of stillness and reflection. This can be as simple as taking a few minutes to sit quietly, meditating, or connecting with nature. Embracing these moments of solitude allows you to recharge, gain clarity, and cultivate a positive mindset.

Remember, creating a holistic wellness routine is a journey unique to you. Experiment with different practices and listen to your body and mind to find what works best for you. Consistency and self-care are key to nurturing your mental wellness and achieving emotional balance.

Embracing Gratitude and Positive Mindset

When it comes to promoting mental wellness and emotional health, the power of gratitude and a positive mindset should not be underestimated. Practicing gratitude can have a profound impact on our overall well-being, shifting our focus towards the positive aspects of life and cultivating a sense of appreciation. One effective technique to incorporate gratitude into our daily lives is through gratitude journaling. Take a few minutes each day to reflect on the things you are grateful for and write them down. This simple practice can help train your mind to notice and appreciate the small moments of joy, leading to an enhanced sense of emotional well-being.

Positive affirmations are another powerful tool to foster a positive mindset. Affirmations are positive statements that we repeat to ourselves, reinforcing positive beliefs and emotions. By practicing positive affirmations regularly, we can rewire our thinking patterns and cultivate a more optimistic outlook on life.

The Power of Reframing

Reframing is a technique that involves consciously changing our perspective on a situation. Instead of automatically dwelling on the negative aspects, we can choose to reframe challenges as opportunities for growth and learning. This practice allows us to find meaning and purpose even in challenging circumstances, helping us build resilience and maintain emotional well-being.

By embracing gratitude and a positive mindset, we can enhance our mental wellness and emotional health. These holistic practices have the power to transform our overall well-being and contribute to a more fulfilling and balanced life at 50 and beyond.

Sustaining Wellness Wisdom for a Fulfilling Life at 50

As we reach the milestone of 50, it becomes crucial to sustain our wellness wisdom for a fulfilling life ahead. This journey of mental and emotional health requires continuous learning and self-reflection to nourish our well-being. Integrating holistic practices into our daily routines enhances our overall mental wellness and emotional balance.

Wellness wisdom is not a destination but an ongoing process. It entails embracing the power of self-care, nurturing supportive relationships, and finding meaning in life transitions. By prioritizing self-compassion and setting boundaries, we create space for personal growth and resilience.

Holistic practices, such as mindfulness, meditation, and yoga, provide powerful tools for cultivating present-moment awareness and reducing stress. These practices promote mental clarity and emotional well-being, empowering us to navigate the challenges that come with age.

By embracing gratitude and a positive mindset, we can uplift our mental wellness and enhance our emotional health. Techniques like gratitude journaling and positive affirmations enable us to reframe negative thoughts and focus on the present blessings. Through this journey of sustaining wellness wisdom, we create a solid foundation for a fulfilling life at 50 and beyond.

Chapter **31**

Pivot Points: Recognizing opportunities for major life shifts

Welcome to a fascinating stage of life! Turning 50 is often a time that opens the door for great personal transformation and self-discovery. This is a critical phase in which recognizing pivot points means much; those times when you can make major shifts in your life. These grand 50-year-old pivots open up opportunities for personal development, career growth, and embracing change.

Midlife transitions are both demanding and rewarding experiences. They present an opportunity to reflect on our journey thus far and make conscious decisions that resonate with our inner selves. And by being aware of these moments where everything could change, we would be able to go through hardships confidently as well as embrace new chances.

This article will discuss the meaning of pivot points at 50, as well as how they can be identified within our lives while exploring them. We shall also unravel ways of embracing change, navigating challenges and using these moments for personal growth and career advancement.

Are you ready for self-discovery and transformation? Let's examine these pivot points together in order to unlock the possibility of major life shifts waiting for you at this age.

Understanding Pivot Points at 50

In life's journey, there are times that have potential to redefine one's path, ignite personal growth, create new opportunities among others. Such periods known as pivot points that happen at age 50 indicate significant events whereby mid-life transitions may lead to major changes in people's lives.

These pivot points need to be realized because they give us an opportunity come out from our comfort zones so that we can accept changes around us. It is during such instances when someone has occasions like changing their careers or even find what really brings joy to them but have not had a chance before due other things taking their most important time.

However, it is difficult maneuvering through the challenges that come with these pivotal points at fifty years old. This stage of life comes with uncertainties and complexities that require deep reflection and strategic thinking. However, if we are flexible in our approach to dealing with these challenges, we can overcome them successfully.

Understanding the importance of pivot points at 50 equips us with the knowledge needed to embrace the transformative power of such occasions wholeheartedly. By understanding the opportunities that come with midlife transitions, we are able to develop ourselves personally, find self-knowledge and ultimately live a more satisfying life.

Signs of a Pivot Point

In order to embrace major shifts and begin on a journey of self-discovery, recognizing pivotal moments is essential. At 50 years old; individuals usually find themselves at a crossroads where new doors open up while closing off old paths. To go through this phase with clarity and purpose it is important to understand how one can recognize signs of a pivot point.

One common indication of an imminent pivot point is when people start yearning for change as well as realizing how unsatisfied they have been living in status quo. You may feel that your current path is meaningless hence wanting something different which gives you fulfillment. When you experience such restlessness, be prepared for some huge changes ahead.

Opportunities

Another major indicant of a pivot point is the recognition of opportunities for growth and transformation. This is where you may find new possibilities that go in line with your passions and values. These chances can arise from different phases of life including career, relationships, or self-improvement.

Recognizing these opportunities comes as result of self-discovery. By reflecting on our values, strengths, and aspirations we have an understanding about where we want to be heading. Trusting one's instincts and opening up to new experiences will also be helpful in identifying these options that match one's journey.

Every big change in life starts with a series of small shifts. It is crucial to pay attention to subtle signs and signals indicating a pivot point. They could be something external such as unexpected job offers or meeting influential people. Alternatively, they may also come from within which includes the desire for personal growth, interest in a new field or feeling inspired by someone else's story.

Ultimately, recognizing a pivot point at 50 requires heightened levels of self-awareness and willingness to embrace transition. In this case it becomes necessary to listen to oneself more often than ever before being able to interpret the signs that life presents us with. Acknowledging these signs and doing something about them allows for initiating personal discovery quest aimed at living according to one's deepest wants.

Embracing Change Towards Personal Development

When faced with pivot points at 50, embracing change becomes essential for personal growth and transformation. Such huge changes mark turning points towards self-discovery hence the resulting experiences are usually key in shaping our future lives significantly . With open arms toward change despite its own challenges would lead us into another world full of choices as well as personal development too.

The Advantages of Appreciating Pivot Points At Age Fifty

With appreciation for such pivots occurring at the age fifty years; we get opportunities to rise above monotonous lifestyles so that we can explore other interests and passions. Personal growth and self-discovery can only come through stepping out of our comfort zones. It also enables us to develop resilience, adaptability and adventurousness in the face of major life changes.

Strategies for Embracing Change

Below are some strategies and techniques that will help one embrace change and maximize personal growth during major life shifts:

Open-mindedness: Accept change with an open mind and a willingness to learn and adjust as necessary.

Self-reflection: Consider your values, goals, strengths plus weaknesses. This kind of self-awareness would help you respond to these changes leading to personal growth on your part.

Seek support: Find individuals around you who understand what you are going through such as family members, friends or mentors who can provide guidance and encouragement during tough times.

Continuous learning: Be ready for new chances to learn while also developing skills. This will ensure there is expansion of personal development .

Practice self-care: Attend to yourself both physically, mentally and emotionally when going through changes in life so as to discover oneself better.

By using these approaches and embracing transformation with love, major life changes can be dealt with confidently thereby paving way for personal development so that fulfillment could be achieved in the future ahead.

Various challenges need to be successfully navigated by individuals during major life shifts that occur in the middle of their life. It is important to face these challenges with resilience, adaptability, and the readiness to seek support. By recognizing and embracing pivot points at 50 it opens up new opportunities but also means overcoming obstacles.

One common challenge faced during midlife transitions is fear of the unknown. This may be a scary thing especially if it requires abandoning known things and walking into unfamiliar territories. These fears must be acknowledged and addressed because they are part of growth.

Equally challenging is resistance from others. Loved ones, friends or even colleagues are likely to have different expectations or opinions than what the individual experiences as they go through this process. Even as individuals stay true to their dreams and aspirations while maintaining an open line of communication with those who matter in their lives, other people may still not understand why they would want something different in their lives . The relationships can be managed and a support network maintained by articulating the desire for change as well as seeking understanding.

The Importance of Self-care

Challenges abound during midlife transitions hence self-care becomes vital. A person has to prioritize his/her physical health, emotional well-being as well as mental state. It might also require setting boundaries, self-reflection, leisure activities that promote relaxation or hobbies which stimulate one's mind. Taking care of oneself ensures the energy and resilience needed to navigate challenges in a healthy and effective manner.

Besides, mentors, therapists or support groups can provide guidance and perspective during such uncertain times thereby helping them navigate successfully through any challenge that comes there way supporting them on both sides when most needed in life . Consequently , knowing that there is help out there , allows for better odds of facing life challenges.

In conclusion , though midlife transitions can be transformative especially when one recognizes opportunities at age fifty ,they come with various difficulties . This implies that people need to approach all the challenges with resilience, adaptability and support from others when necessary so as to traverse their way through such transformative processes which are often accompanied by major life shifts.

Career Advancement

Recognizing and embracing pivot points at 50 can lead to significant career advancement and transformative changes in one's professional life. This, therefore, creates an opportunity for evaluating and re-aligning career goals as well as exploring other avenues to pursue growth.

When people recognize major life shifts and pivot points at age fifty they get a distinct perspective and clarity that can drive their careers to greater heights. By embracing change or taking calculated risks, professionals may unlock hidden talents or look for opportunities that further their professional development.

During this period of transition, individuals may decide to change jobs, start new businesses or further their education to gain additional skills and knowledge. It is a time of reflection on what has been achieved in relation to personal values and aspirations with confident choices being made that align themselves with both the individual's personal as well as professional goals.

Embracing career advancement through pivot points at 50 calls for a proactive approach. Networking, mentorship-seeking behavior, openness to new experiences come into play during these moments of transition. Over the years, professionals have gained diverse skills sets and experience which if properly harnessed will make them meaningful players within their chosen fields.

Individuals can break free from any perceived limitations, in their fifties, by recognizing opportunities and embracing major life shifts to tap into unlimited potential. These turning points form a basis for growth, innovation, and professional satisfaction through corporate career growth paths, venturing into new businesses or entering a new profession.

Professionals who apply self-reflection, adaptability and perseverance alongside the realization of pivotal moments are able to successfully navigate career advancements. They can find fulfillment and meaning in their work while creating a positive impact on their industry and community.

The Role of Self-Reflection in Identifying Pivot Points

At 50 years old, self-reflection is vital for identifying pivot points that necessitate recognizing opportunities for major life shifts. This process of introspection and self-recognition allows people to have clear perspectives about their midlife transitions. One may explore internal desires, aspirations and values by taking time off to reflect on them which might bring out latent passions that were unknown before hence making it possible to change one's life.

Self-reflection serves as a compass during this phase directing people towards turning points that will shape their future selves. It prompts a deeper understanding of oneself and the world paving way for brave decisions that alter the course of life entirely. Through self-reflection, one can shed light on their strengths and weaknesses, identify patterns and beliefs that no longer serve them, and find the courage to let go of what no longer resonates.

Creating space for self-reflection can be achieved through various practices. Mindfulness practices such as meditation lend themselves well to quietening minds thereby leading individuals into deep listening with inner wisdom; journaling allows people time alone with personal thoughts as well as emotions they might have been bottling up; seeking guidance from mentors or trusted confidants provide different dimensions through which an individual may engage themselves with reflective thoughts.

In the journey of self-discovery and recognizing pivot points at 50 , self-reflection becomes a vital means to empower oneself. Engaging in this process allows individuals to develop enough clarity that will enable them to seize opportunities for major life shifts. Self-reflection acts as an agent for personal growth, navigating through the difficulties and uncertainties of transformational moments. It enables individuals to chart a course with intentionality, purposefulness and deep self-awareness leading to a satisfying meaningful life.

Strategies for Making Life-Shifting Decisions

Finding opportunities amidst challenges can be overwhelming during major life changes. Nevertheless, there are strategies that can make decision making easier and help you act wisely. In decision-making processes at pivots points 50, various things should be factored in and decisions must tally with one's values and aspirations.

One key strategy for making life-shifting decisions is taking the time to evaluate the potential risks involved. Understanding the possible outcomes and consequences can help you weigh the pros and cons before making a choice. It is important that one assesses how each decision aligns with their long-term goals and overall well-being.

Another valuable strategy is seeking perspectives from trusted individuals or professionals. Discussing your options with family members, friends, or mentors who have experienced similar life shifts can provide valuable insights and guidance. Their input may help you see things differently or understand those things you were not able to see on your own.

Overcoming decision-making predicaments requires clarity and self-reflection. Look inside yourself and judge your ability to prioritize, what you stand for, and finally your own desires. What matters most to you? Does the next decision fit with who you are as a person? Listening to that inner voice within us is equally important as trusting our instincts.

Sometimes when people face big life changes at 50 they become worried or frightened. However, getting used to new things also requires one to be courageous enough. A growth mindset can help one approach transformative life decisions optimistically and with resilience. Keep in mind though that trying moments in life are stepping stones towards personal development.

To sum up, effective strategies for informed decisions making must be employed during pivot points at 50 and major life shifts. Consider how it may affect the potential losses, seek other perspectives on these issues, think about them personally by introspecting and finally embrace that change no matter how scary it may appear because this is what courage is all about. These will enable your life shifting choices go hand in hand with those values which really matter in your voluntary actions.

Embracing New Possibilities: Starting Afresh

At such a time of pivot points at 50, it becomes necessary to embrace new possibilities and start afresh. This moment marks the beginning of major life shifts that will lead into extraordinary transformations ahead. By changing our ways we allow ourselves to develop into completely different individuals.

For embracing new possibilities we need first of all let go of the past so as not to carry any baggage with us but be ready for exciting opportunities. Approach this unknown future positively knowing very well that there exists incredible opportunity for expansion and fulfillment.

Transforming Relationships in Midlife Transitions

During midlife transitions, pivot points at 50 have the potential to bring about significant transformations in relationships – whether personal, friendships, or partnerships. Identifying these opportunities can make a great difference in embracing change and therefore foster growth and connection in this stage of life.

One of the major changes that come with transforming relationships during midlife transitions is handling them. As people shift gears in their lives, they may experience a shift in values, goals or priorities. This has an impact on existing relationships dynamics calling for open discussion and understanding by all those involved.

Through fostering open communication, parties can address how pivot points at 50 affect their relationships. It is possible to define a new path together when there are honest conversations about personal objectives, dreams and even growth needs. Moreover, partners gain deeper insights into each other's views thus becoming closer to one another thereby.

Embracing change is essential in transforming relationships during midlife transitions. This implies that it involves letting go of old patterns and embracing novel possibilities. Doing some refreshing stuff as couples or friends like exploring different activities together can be helpful. In addition to this, self-discovery may also be important among individuals as it help them grow more into themselves and make their relationship stronger.

Recognizing the opportunities that arise during pivot points at 50 and being open to change can deepen connections and foster a renewed sense of purpose within relationships. Therefore, major life shifts become moments where we must embrace growth through nurturing those relations which will support us along these paths.

Sustaining Growth and Momentum

Having identified turning points at 50 and making necessary shifts, it is important to keep growth alive and maintain momentum. The next step of this journey will entail unending self reflection, adaptability and persistence in order to overcome new challenges and ensure a continual positive transformation.

To foster growth, one must have an unwavering commitment to self-reflection. Pause to evaluate yourself, reassess goals and modify plans as necessary. Periodically appraise personal as well as professional development; celebrate successes while noting areas for improvement.

It is critical therefore that we embrace change if we are to continue growing. Always stay open minded for different experiences which may come your way hence widening ones perspective. View new difficulties as opportunities for education and personal progression, knowing that each obstacle overcame is another stride towards continued growth.

Lastly perseverance is essential during this stage. Be aware that maintaining growth and momentum can be achieved through being patient and dedicated at times. Always motivate yourself with realistic goals considering why you started on this path in the first place. Remember however that sustained growth is a life long process involving regular effort and changes in direction.

Chapter 32

A Nest That's Empty, but a Life That's Full: Redefining purpose post-parenting

Welcome to the exciting phase of your 50s, where you have the opportunity to redefine your purpose after parenting. With the children having flown the nest, it's a chance to explore new horizons and embrace the possibilities that await you. In this article, we will guide you through the journey of redefining purpose post-parenting and finding fulfillment in this next chapter of your life.

As you navigate the transition of empty nest syndrome, it's natural to experience a mix of emotions and challenges. But fear not, we are here to support you and provide guidance on how to embrace this new phase. Together, we will explore the reflections on the past, celebrate the joys and accomplishments of parenthood, and use this foundation to shape your future endeavors.

Self-care is key as you embark on this journey of self-discovery. By prioritizing your own well-being and exploring new interests and passions, you can find renewed energy and purpose. We'll delve into the importance of self-care and how it can lead to a more fulfilling post-parenting phase.

Reinventing your identity is also an exciting endeavor during this time. By exploring new hobbies, interests, and passions, you can discover a whole new side of yourself. Together, we'll delve into the process of redefining who you are and how it can shape your second act in life.

Setting new goals and aspirations is essential in this phase of life. We'll guide you in creating a vision for your future and establishing a roadmap to achieve personal fulfillment. Along the way, we'll address the fear and resistance that may arise and provide strategies to embrace change and navigate uncertainties.

Building meaningful connections and nurturing relationships can bring immense joy and support to your post-parenting journey. We'll explore the importance of cultivating these connections and how they can enhance your overall sense of fulfillment.

Finally, we'll discover the power of giving back and making a positive impact in the world. By using your newfound passions and skills, you can create meaningful change and leave a lasting legacy. Plus, we'll consider the potential for career transitions and explore new possibilities for professional growth and fulfillment.

In your 50s, life is full of opportunities to redefine your purpose and discover new paths. Let's embrace the journey together and live with intention, finding fulfillment and joy in every stage of life. Stay tuned for the upcoming sections where we dive deeper into each aspect of redefining purpose post-parenting.

Embracing Midlife: Navigating the Empty Nest Syndrome

As our children grow up and begin their own journeys, we find ourselves faced with a profound shift in our lives. The transition to an empty nest can be both exciting and challenging. It's a time of adjustment, as we learn to redefine our purpose and create a fulfilling life after children.

During this empty nest transition, various emotions and challenges may arise. It's important to understand and embrace these changes with open arms. It's okay to feel a mix of excitement, sadness, and even a sense of loss. This period of life after children is an opportunity to rediscover ourselves and embrace new possibilities.

In navigating the empty nest syndrome, remember that it's normal to experience a range of emotions. Give yourself permission to grieve the chapter that has passed, while also finding excitement in the new one that awaits. Give yourself the time and space to reflect on the beautiful moments of raising children and the lessons you've learned along the way.

The Emotions of Empty Nest Syndrome

Empty nest syndrome is characterized by a cocktail of emotions that can include a sense of loss, loneliness, and even identity crisis. The key to navigating this period lies in acknowledging and accepting these emotions, giving yourself the space to process them, and seeking support from loved ones.

Allow yourself to feel the sadness of the empty house, but also embrace the newfound freedom. Use this time as an opportunity to reconnect with your partner, invest in self-care, and explore your own passions and interests.

Navigating the Challenges

Along with the emotional adjustments, empty nesters may face practical challenges as well. Suddenly, there's more time and space to manage. You may find yourself reevaluating your daily routines and responsibilities. This is the perfect moment to focus on self-discovery and self-care.

Embrace the freedom to try new things, take up hobbies you've always dreamed of pursuing, and rekindle old interests that may have taken a backseat during the parenting years. Remember that you are not defined solely by your role as a parent – this is an opportunity to rediscover who you are and create a life that is independently fulfilling.

Transitioning from a full nest to an empty one is a journey of self-discovery and growth. It's a chance to redefine ourselves, embrace new possibilities, and rekindle that spark of passion. Let go of the past with gratitude and look to the future with excitement and enthusiasm for what lies ahead in life after children.

Reflections on the Past: Celebrating Parenthood

As we enter the next phase of our lives, it is essential to take a moment and reflect on the joys and accomplishments of parenthood. Life after children may feel unfamiliar at first, but it is also a time for self-discovery and personal growth. Whether you have just become an empty nester or have already embraced post-parenting life, celebrating the journey you have had thus far is vital in shaping your future endeavors.

During the years of raising children, we have undoubtedly experienced a rollercoaster of emotions and faced numerous challenges. However, these experiences have also given us incredible memories, moments of growth, and a profound sense of purpose. Reflecting on the past allows us to appreciate the love, nurturing, and sacrifices we have dedicated to our children.

Now, as our children embark on their own adventures, it's time to shift our focus inward and explore our own passions and desires. Post-parenting self-discovery is an opportunity to rediscover ourselves and what brings us joy and fulfillment. Take this time to celebrate your achievements as a parent and utilize them as a foundation for the exciting possibilities that lie ahead.

Discovering a New Chapter

Life after children opens up a world of opportunities to explore and pursue our personal goals. It's a chance to invest time and energy in activities and hobbies that inspire and excite us. Whether it's picking up a long-lost passion or delving into uncharted territories, this is the time to embrace self-discovery and find new ways to express ourselves.

Consider engaging in activities that connect you with like-minded individuals who share similar interests. Joining clubs, taking up classes, or volunteering for causes that resonate with you can introduce you to a whole new network of individuals propelling you towards personal growth.

Celebrating the Journey

Amidst the changes and adjustments that come with post-parenting life, it's important to celebrate the tremendous impact we've had as parents. The love, guidance, and support provided have shaped not only our children but also our own lives. Recognize the sacrifices made and the lessons learned, and allow yourself to take pride in the incredible journey of parenthood.

Take a moment to celebrate the individuals your children have become and the role you played in shaping them. Acknowledge the strength and resilience that parenting has instilled in you, and channel it towards the next chapter of your life.

Life after children is an opportunity to create a fulfilling future filled with new adventures, personal growth, and self-discovery. By reflecting on the past and celebrating the joys of parenthood, we can embrace this transition and confidently move forward towards a life that is full of purpose and happiness.

Rediscovering Self: The Importance of Self-Care

As we navigate the midlife phase, it becomes crucial to prioritize self-care and rediscover our sense of purpose. After dedicating years to raising children, it's time to find fulfillment and embrace a new chapter in life. By focusing on self-care, we can nurture our well-being and reignite our midlife purpose.

Midlife is a unique opportunity to reconnect with ourselves and explore our passions that may have been set aside during the parenting years. It's a time to rediscover our identity, nurture our dreams, and invest in activities that bring us joy and satisfaction.

The Power of Prioritizing Yourself

Engaging in self-care activities is not selfish; it's an act of self-love and an investment in our overall well-being. By taking care of ourselves, we become better equipped to handle the challenges and responsibilities that come with this stage of life.

Self-care can take many forms—whether it's indulging in a hobby, pursuing education, dedicating time to physical fitness, or simply carving out moments of quiet reflection. The key is to listen to our needs and make intentional choices that align with our values and desires.

Realigning with Midlife Purpose

Rediscovering our midlife purpose involves reflecting on who we are, what truly brings us fulfillment, and how we can make a positive impact on our own lives and the lives of others. This journey of self-discovery can lead to a greater sense of fulfillment and satisfaction, even after the children have left the nest.

By embracing self-care and nourishing our passions, we can tap into our true potential and redefine our purpose in this phase of life. It's about embracing the present, setting new goals, and paving the way for a future filled with meaningful experiences and personal growth.

So, let us embark on this journey of rediscovering ourselves, nurturing our well-being, and finding midlife purpose. The empty nest may be a transition, but it also opens up new possibilities for fulfillment and joy.

Reinventing Identity: Redefining Who You Are

After years of dedicating yourself to raising your children, the time has finally come for you to reinvent your identity. As your kids leave home and embark on their own journeys, it's an opportunity for you to explore new horizons and rediscover who you are.

Reinventing yourself after kids leave home is an exciting and transformative process. It's a chance to shed the role of a full-time parent and embrace your individuality. Take this time to reconnect with your own interests, passions, and dreams.

One way to begin reinventing yourself is by exploring new interests and hobbies. Perhaps there is something you've always wanted to try but never had the time or opportunity. Whether it's painting, cooking, writing, or playing an instrument, now is the perfect time to dive into a new pursuit and uncover hidden talents you never knew you had.

Consider joining clubs, groups, or organizations where you can meet like-minded individuals who share similar interests. These connections can not only bring fulfillment but also open doors to new opportunities and experiences.

Another avenue for reinvention is to identify your passions and find ways to incorporate them into your daily life. Whether it's volunteering for a cause you care about, starting a small business, or pursuing further education, embracing your passions can give you a renewed sense of purpose and fulfillment.

Don't be afraid to step out of your comfort zone and take risks. As you navigate this new chapter of your life, it's important to push your boundaries and explore uncharted territory. Embrace the unknown and embrace the excitement of self-discovery.

Remember, reinventing yourself is a journey, and it's okay to explore different paths before finding the one that resonates with you. Trust the process and allow yourself to evolve organically.

So, as your children fly the nest, embrace this opportunity to reinvent your identity. Explore new interests, connect with like-minded individuals, and pursue your passions. Your second act in life awaits, and it's time to redefine who you are.

Setting New Goals: Creating a Vision for the Future

As you enter this exciting new phase of life, it's important to set new goals and aspirations for yourself. This is a time of rediscovery, where you have the opportunity to explore new passions and embark on a second act after your kids have left home.

Embrace the chance to uncover hidden talents and interests that may have taken a backseat during the busy years of parenting. It's never too late to pursue your dreams and find fulfillment in midlife.

Start by reflecting on what truly brings you joy and a sense of purpose. Think about the activities or hobbies that make you lose track of time and ignite a fire within you. Whether it's painting, writing, photography, or volunteering, make a list of the things that spark your passion.

Once you have identified your passions, create a vision for your future. Envision the person you want to become and the accomplishments you want to achieve. Write down your goals in a journal or create a vision board that visually represents your aspirations.

Remember, the path to personal fulfillment in midlife is not about achieving society's expectations or comparing yourself to others. It's about embracing your unique journey and finding what truly makes you happy.

Break your goals down into smaller, manageable steps. Celebrate every milestone along the way, as each achievement brings you closer to living a purposeful life in your 50s and beyond.

Surround yourself with supportive friends and family who believe in your dreams and encourage you to pursue them. Seek out mentorship or join communities of like-minded individuals who share your interests. Having a support network can make a significant difference in maintaining motivation and accountability.

Embrace this opportunity to create a vision for your future and embark on your second act with enthusiasm and determination. With newfound passions and well-defined goals, you are ready to write the next chapter of your life, filled with purpose, fulfillment, and boundless possibilities.

Embracing Change: Overcoming Fear and Resistance

Embarking on a new phase of life can be both exciting and daunting. When it comes to major life transitions, fear and resistance often accompany the journey. But it's important to remember that change is a natural and inevitable part of life, and embracing it can lead to personal growth and fulfillment.

During midlife, as you discover new passions and explore your midlife purpose, it's common to encounter uncertainties and doubts. The fear of the unknown may hold you back from pursuing your interests or making necessary changes. However, by acknowledging and addressing these fears, you can gradually overcome them and unlock endless possibilities.

Embracing the Unknown

Stepping into the unknown requires courage and openness. It's normal to feel uncomfortable when venturing into uncharted territory, as it means leaving familiar routines and comfort zones behind. However, by pushing past the boundaries of your comfort zone, you give yourself the opportunity to grow and adapt to new circumstances.

Embrace the unfamiliar with a mindset of curiosity and excitement. View this phase of your life as an adventure, where you have the freedom to explore and discover new passions. Remember, it's never too late to try something new and follow your heart's desires.

Strategies to Overcome Resistance

Overcoming resistance requires determination and the willingness to confront your fears head-on. Here are a few strategies to help you embrace change:

Self-reflection: Take the time to reflect on your deepest desires and identify what truly brings you joy. By understanding your values and aspirations, you can gain clarity on the direction you want to take.

Take small steps: Break down your goals into smaller, more manageable tasks. By taking gradual steps, you can build confidence and momentum, making it easier to move past resistance.

Seek support: Surround yourself with a supportive network of friends, family, or mentors who can provide guidance and encouragement during times of uncertainty.

failure as a learning opportunity: Understand that setbacks and failures are part of the journey. Instead of viewing them as roadblocks, see them as valuable lessons that can lead to growth and resilience.

Cultivate a growth mindset: Embrace the belief that personal growth is possible at any age. By adopting a growth mindset, you can develop resilience and adaptability, enabling you to embrace change with a positive attitude.

Remember, your midlife purpose is not set in stone. It's okay to explore different paths and make adjustments along the way. Embrace change as an opportunity to discover new passions and embark on an exciting chapter of your life.

Building Relationships: Cultivating Meaningful Connections

Life after children brings about a new phase of self-discovery and growth. As you navigate this post-parenting journey, building and nurturing meaningful relationships becomes essential. These connections can bring joy, support, and fulfillment to your life in ways you may never have imagined.

Cultivating relationships in your post-parenting years involves reaching out to others who share similar experiences and interests. Join social groups, clubs, or organizations that align with your passions.

Engaging in activities that resonate with you can provide an opportunity to connect with like-minded individuals who are also navigating this new chapter of life.

It's important to prioritize quality over quantity when it comes to relationships. Focus on deepening existing connections and forming new ones that bring value and meaning to your life. Surrounding yourself with supportive and positive people can have a profound impact on your overall well-being.

Family and friends play a vital role in this phase as well. Strengthening bonds with your adult children and cultivating new dynamics with them can create a fulfilling sense of connection. Additionally, nurturing friendships with individuals who have also experienced the empty nest transition can provide a sense of camaraderie and understanding.

As you continue to develop these relationships, be open to new experiences and perspectives. Embrace the opportunity to learn from others and expand your horizons. Engaging in meaningful conversations and shared activities can deepen connections and foster personal growth.

Remember, the journey of post-parenting self-discovery is not meant to be done alone. By actively building relationships and cultivating connections, you can create a support system that adds richness and fulfillment to your life after children.

Giving Back: Making a Difference in the World

Discover the power of giving back and making a positive impact in the world. As you embark on a new phase of life in midlife, you have the opportunity to channel your newfound passions and skills towards creating meaningful change.

By exploring your interests and identifying causes that resonate with you, you can find fulfilling ways to contribute to society. Whether it's volunteering your time, using your professional expertise, or supporting charitable organizations, giving back can bring a sense of purpose and fulfillment to your life.

Consider the issues that are important to you and the skills and experiences you have acquired throughout your journey. This self-reflection can help you discover how to make a difference in a way that aligns with your values and passions.

In addition to the impact you make on others, giving back can also lead to personal growth and self-discovery. It allows you to connect with like-minded individuals and expand your network, creating meaningful relationships and communities that share your commitment to making the world a better place.

Cultivating Meaningful Change Through Giving Back

There are numerous ways to give back in midlife and make a lasting impact on the world. Here are a few ideas to get you started:

Volunteer: Dedicate your time and skills to organizations that align with your passions. Whether it's tutoring, mentoring, or helping out at a local shelter, volunteering allows you to make a direct impact on the lives of others.

Philanthropy: Use your financial resources to support causes that are meaningful to you. Research and donate to charitable organizations that are making a difference in areas such as education, healthcare, the environment, or social justice.

Community Engagement: Get involved in your local community by joining organizations, committees, or boards that address issues close to your heart. By actively participating and contributing your insights and skills, you can help drive positive change at a grassroots level.

Mentorship: Share your knowledge and experiences with others by becoming a mentor. Whether mentoring young professionals or individuals seeking guidance in a specific field, your expertise can have a transformative impact on their personal and professional lives.

Social Entrepreneurship: Combine your passion for social causes with business acumen by starting a social enterprise. Through innovative business models, you can address societal issues while creating sustainable solutions that empower individuals and communities.

By embracing the power of giving back, you can bring purpose, fulfillment, and positive change into your own life and the lives of those around you. Discovering new passions in midlife and finding your midlife purpose go hand in hand with making a difference in the world.

Embracing New Possibilities: Exploring Career Transitions

As your children leave home and begin their own journeys, it's only natural to start thinking about your own future. This is an opportunity to reinvent yourself and embark on a new chapter in your life.

Consider it as your second act, a chance to explore career transitions and uncover new possibilities for professional growth and fulfillment.

Reinventing yourself after kids leave home is an exciting and liberating process. It's a time to reflect on your passions, talents, and interests, and align them with potential career paths that ignite your enthusiasm.

Many individuals find that their previous experience as parents has developed valuable skills that can be transferred to a variety of industries. From organizational abilities, communication expertise, to problem-solving aptitude, these skills are highly sought after in the job market.

Don't limit yourself to your past experiences alone - take this opportunity to explore new fields that have always fascinated you. Research different industries, talk to professionals, and identify the required skills and qualifications. This will help you make informed decisions and pursue new career paths with confidence.

Investing in Self-Development

When it comes to embarking on a new career journey, investing in self-development is crucial. Upskilling and acquiring new knowledge and certifications can open doors to exciting opportunities. Consider enrolling in courses, attending workshops, or joining professional associations to expand your skill set and stay up to date with industry trends.

Additionally, networking is paramount in career transitions. Connect with professionals, join relevant communities, and attend industry events to expand your network. Building relationships with like-minded individuals can provide valuable insights, mentorship, and even potential job opportunities.

This second act after kids leave is a chance to rediscover yourself, challenge your abilities, and find a fulfilling career that aligns with your current goals and aspirations. Embrace the possibilities, step out of your comfort zone, and embark on this exciting journey of reinvention.

Embracing the Journey: Living with Purpose in Your 50s

Life is a journey filled with transitions, and one of the most significant shifts occurs when the empty nest transition happens. As children grow and leave home, it's natural to feel a mix of emotions, from nostalgia to excitement about what lies ahead in life after children.

Instead of dwelling on the void left by the absence of children, it's time to redefine purpose and embrace this new stage. Life after children offers endless opportunities for self-discovery, personal growth, and finding fulfillment in your 50s. It's a chance to reassess your goals, explore new passions, and live with intention.

With the empty nest transition as a catalyst, you can dive into experiences that you may have put on hold while raising a family. Whether it's starting a new career, pursuing a long-awaited dream, or dedicating time to personal interests, the possibilities are limitless. The key is to approach this chapter with an open mind and a willingness to step out of your comfort zone.

Chapter 33

Creating a Legacy: Non-Material Things to Leave Besides Cash

Most of us start thinking about our footprints when we turn 50. Even though financial assets are certainly important, leaving behind something more than wealth is what legacy creation is all about. This means that our influence on future generations must go beyond mere money.

Legacy planning involves considering non-financial assets that can impact our beloveds in the long term. In doing so, we leave a lasting impression of our beliefs, principles and experiences, which could be utilized by forthcoming generations as role models or guides.

The article will touch on the importance of legacy considerations, family values preservation, long-term orientation acquisition for posterity communication and collaboration over generation lines conserving family customs making positive impact on society promoting and mentoring relationships documenting personal stories and the lasting effect of legacies.

Therefore if you are close to 50 this is the ideal time to begin considering your legacy beyond just financial resources Join us as we embark on this journey of discovery to find out how one can create an enduring legacy full of meaning.

The Meaning Behind Leaving a Legacy

Leaving a legacy is more than amassing riches. A legacy implies an accumulated property through generations in the form of non-monetary things impacting lives and shaping values for future families. When talking about inheritance planning, we often think about material goods that will pass from parents to children. At the same time there are some intangible elements of inheritance which play an equally crucial role. What kind of traditions culture or belief system do you want to bequeath?

This helps preserve our non-material possessions through inheritance planning. So you can transmit not only your riches, but also share your life lessons with descendants. By doing so beforehand it enables our heritage to be continued in a meaningful manner.

The Impact Beyond Money

A good inheritance goes deeper than money; it imparts purposefulness, responsibility and empathy for others unto the next generation thereby. We may build a legacy that reaches not only our families but also the world at large by teaching them values like integrity, hard work and compassion.

Generational wealth is not about earning money. It is about passing on wisdom, love, and connections to our children's children. We can therefore use our heritage to shape their world.

By thinking beyond finances we can create an enduring tradition that empowers future generations. By making provision for inheritance planning, we make certain that our loved ones will be guided accordingly by these principles even after we are dead.

Shifting from Money to Values

To create a lasting legacy, it is imperative to change our focus from economic richness to family principles. Although monetary assets have great importance it is the value legacy that counts more in terms of continuity over the years with future generations.

The act of instilling family values within ourselves does facilitate easy decision making throughout life of an individual. The character they take up, how they relate with others and decide things depends on these values themselves.They form a sturdy base for both personal and career success thus giving rise to a heritage that goes far beyond mere financial resources.

A rich heritage is passed on to our loved ones by giving importance to family values. Such values are part and parcel of their behavior that includes integrity, empathy, resilience, and compassion thereby influencing how they relate to others and contribute to society.

Family values are like a torch that lead the way for future generations, helping them maneuver through challenges of life and impact positively on the world. We preserve our family's story of power, identity and meaning by deliberately investing in the legacy of values.

Legacy Mindset: Adopting a Long-Term View

A long-term view is vital in order to establish an enduring legacy. To develop a legacy mindset that entails long-term decision-making is essential.

By assuming this perspective you will no longer be focused on immediate gratification or short-term benefits but rather start considering what implications may exist in your actions even years after you have taken them. It will enable choices that will take care of future generations' wellbeing aside from just financial assets being transferred so it becomes significant.

It requires careful planning foresight and a strong sense of purpose. Therefore, it makes sense for one to set goals that resonate with his/her legacy while making decisions around those aspirations.

Thinking Beyond the Present

This means moving beyond the present, considering what lasting effects your actions might have had upon any number of people within the family as well as outside its confines when looking at things from a broad perspective such as throughout communities or societies as we consider ourselves part thereof.

Legacy-minded individuals understand that their choices today can shape the future for generations to come. They prioritize investments in education, personal development, and the well-being of their loved ones, ensuring knowledge transfer across generations leading to better lives in times ahead.

Building a Legacy with Intention

The process of creating legacies must be thought out carefully. A legacy mindset involves setting clear goals, creating a plan, and taking consistent action towards achieving those goals. In other words determine where you want to go with your life and what you would like it to be when it's over.

It is important that the core things that really matter in guiding one's behavior are identified and clearly stated whenever they consider such a mindset. This helps ensure that your choices are aligned with your desired legacy and enable you to create a meaningful impact.

Also, having a legacy mindset means being open-minded towards changes, growth and adaptation. In addition, this includes constantly reevaluating goals and values as well as changing actions where necessary so as to remain on track of our heritage as well as cater for future generations' needs which can always alter.

When you adopt a legacy mindset, you shift your focus beyond immediate gratification and short-term gains. Instead, start thinking about what the emotional consequences of your acts will be through the years. This approach will help you make decisions which put into consideration the existence of persons who come after us financially thereby giving more priority to all their future good.

By adopting a legacy mindset, you can create a lasting impact that goes beyond financial assets. Your decisions and actions will contribute to a legacy that reflects your values, beliefs, and aspirations, leaving a meaningful and enduring imprint on the world.

Intergenerational Communication and Collaboration

Creating an everlasting legacy is not just about money or any other kind of wealth transfer but entails nurturing strong relationships between generations through intergenerational communication and collaboration. Families may develop generational wealth by sharing family values freely among themselves allowing for working together instead of focusing merely on monetary gains alone.

Effective intergenerational communication acts as groundwork on which a strong legacy is built. This allows the family members to understand, appreciate and perceive each other's opinions and therefore, unites them emotionally. As families discuss about these values of their ancestors, they may impact their descendants with such ideas that are based on what a family believes in its heart and soul.

Collaboration across generations equally creates a lasting difference. Older people may then pass down their wisdom to younger ones through engaging them actively in decision making processes as well as the process of planning for the entire family. By so doing, not only does this help families accumulate generational wealth but also it increases cohesion among members who have blood ties.

Through intergenerational communication and collaboration, families can develop a firm foundation rooted in common family values. In working together to uphold these morals, they create legacies that promote not just economic growth but also the future lives of children yet unborn.

Preserving and Passing on Family Traditions

Family traditions occupy an important place in our souls joining generations into one entity. They form part of our experiences, beliefs and values interweaving among themselves. For purposes of creating last legacies, we have to preserve and carry forth these practices.

Family traditions run deeper than mere rituals or customs; they reflect our family norms while being instrumental means for communicating such norms to posterity. These give us an attachment from where we came reminding members about their roots and ancestry.

By keeping alive those family traditions we found richness upon which to build wealth over time—not just financially expressed but something rooted in history, lessons learned and cultural contexts—these are all foundations that remain central parts even when externalities change—creation of some sense within our families.

Our actions by way of preserving and passing down family traditions have long-lasting effects on our loved ones. Therefore imparting invaluable information passed from one generation to another concerning how people deal with life challenges or make informed choices. They are the ties that bind us together as a family, which carries on beyond material wealth.

Preserving and Passing on Family Traditions

Irrespective of changing times when new values and priorities emerge, family traditions keep us grounded. They remind us about the essentials in our lives as they serve as our compasses leading us to where we find love, happiness and satisfaction. This is why preserving and transmitting these traditions means holding fast to the principles that have made our family rich for years.

Leaving a Positive Impact on Society

Legacy implies more than just money and wealth. It represents the way good families should live while playing an active role in building better societies. Ultimately, you can create a positive impact on society, making your life distinct from others even after death by ensuring your legacy is not merely based on money.

The impact we make on society is primarily guided by our family values. Such values are instilled into future generations with an aim of nurturing responsibilities among such individuals so they can be empathetic enough towards other people's needs in life. Consequently families like yours would inspire others through their actions to follow these ideals.

In an ever-changing world, where values change and interests alter course; it is these family traditions that provide stability for all of us all within such ongoing transformations. These traditions help us remember what really matters in life and act as guiding lights directing us towards what brings joy, love and fulfillment into our lives. To ensure this preservation of such traditional attitudes happens therefore means keeping alive those values which define who we are over time destined for many more years ahead.

Improving the society can assume different forms including volunteering and supporting charitable organizations, as well as fighting for change in your community. Through this kind of involvement, these people's impacts spread to periods beyond their lives.

Positively affecting society is akin to generational wealth: it goes beyond monetary assets by involving values, education and opportunities that are passed down from one generation to another. By prioritizing family values and actively contributing to society, you create a legacy that resonates with future generations and positively influences their actions and choices.

In conclusion, creating a legacy goes beyond just gaining wealth; it entails displaying family values and making efforts towards positive societal impact. That way, one leaves behind an enduring legacy that matters beyond materialistic values like money but that affects the quality of life of subsequent generations.

Nurturing Relationships and Mentoring

Legacy planning encompasses more than financial assets; nurturing relationships with others can also contribute to generational wealth. They have good effects on loved ones as well as the future survivors by spending time usefully in deep connections.

Strong bonding within families serves as a catalyst for a legacy which is based on collective principles. With such strong ties, they will be able to pass on timeless teachings that are considered representative of generational wealth.

Mentoring is yet another aspect of Legacy planning. Younger relatives or students who look up to them may learn so many useful things about finance while maintaining precious customs belonging to the elderly ones. It thus takes someone's guidance in order for the children's children wealth building process through finances like businesses or shares among other sources hence creating an era lasting heritage.

The leaving behind of mere financial possessions has always been made possible through keeping relationships nurtured together with mentoring. This becomes not only a threadwork full of shared experiences but also what helps those who come after live better lives across all aspects.

Documenting and Sharing Personal Stories

Creating a legacy isn't just about money and inheritance planning. In fact, leaving a lasting impact requires an aspect of documentation and sharing of personal stories as part of the legacy process. These narratives carry so much wisdom, experience and values that can be passed down for generations.

By documenting personal stories at age 50, individuals can ensure that their unique journey is preserved and cherished by their loved ones. These narratives provide future generations with a window into their family's history, values, and traditions, fostering a sense of connection and belonging.

Therefore it is upon individuals to decide how these personal stories shall be shared and preserved through careful inheritance planning. From making family memoirs to creating digital collections of photographs/videos or even oral methods we use to pass down this heritage are many.

Furthermore, through sharing personal stories they are also able to share valuable advice on life experiences with those they love most in life. It is a mentorship platform that extends far beyond the owner's existence. As such these tales could become sources of motivation for families as well as sources strength during times when life becomes challenging especially when it comes to decision making processes based on informed choices.

Creating a Legacy at 50 is not merely about leaving a financial inheritance but also ensuring that non-financial assets such as personal stories remain intact. Taking time to document and share these stories can create a legacy resonating down generations.

The Unending Influence of a Legacy

When we look back on the journey of creating a legacy, it becomes apparent that its real impact goes beyond financial assets. While wealth may offer stability as well as opportunities, legacies are grounded on their non-monetary assets which shape future generations' lives.

Legacy planning entails more than bequeathing possessions; it is about implanting principles, fostering relationships, and making society better. By concentrating on these non-economic features, our legacies last long and outlive temporal and monetary considerations.

When we embrace the idea that legacies are about how we live rather than what's left behind, possibilities become endless. It tells us to adopt a legacy mindset, consider more than the present time and conduct ourselves in ways that will have an impact on this world as desired by us.

By documenting and sharing our personal stories – nurturing relationships – mentoring others – through these acts we create ripples that reach far into the future beyond our own lifetime so that they become interwoven with the lives of future generations leading to values/ traditions/ positive change tapestry woven into our heritage.

Chapter 34

Entrepreneurial Ventures at Fifty: Starting or scaling a business

Welcome to our chapter on entrepreneurial ventures at fifty. If you've ever dreamed of starting a business at 50 or exploring entrepreneurship opportunities for seniors, you've come to the right place. In this article, we will explore the challenges and exciting possibilities of starting or scaling a business at the age of fifty.

At fifty, you've accumulated a wealth of experience and expertise, making it an ideal time to embark on an entrepreneurial journey. Whether you're looking to pursue a passion project, launch a startup, or transition into a second career, there are numerous advantages and opportunities awaiting you.

In this comprehensive guide, we will dive into the motivations behind entrepreneurship at fifty and share inspiring success stories of entrepreneurs who achieved great success in their senior years. We will also address the age-related challenges that entrepreneurs face and provide strategies to overcome them.

Discovering business opportunities that align with your skills and interests is crucial. We will explore various industries and business ideas that are well-suited for older adults, allowing you to leverage your existing knowledge and expertise.

A well-crafted business plan is essential to ensure the success of any venture. We will walk you through the process of developing a comprehensive business plan tailored to your specific goals and aspirations. Along the way, we'll provide insights from successful entrepreneurs who started their ventures in their fifties.

Financing your business venture may be a concern, but don't worry. We will explore funding options and valuable resources available to support your entrepreneurial pursuits. From traditional loans to grants and crowdfunding, we'll guide you in securing the necessary funding.

Building a supportive network is crucial as you embark on your entrepreneurial journey. We'll discuss the importance of establishing connections with like-minded individuals, mentors, and industry professionals who can offer guidance, advice, and valuable connections.

Effective marketing and branding are key to the success of any business. We'll explore marketing strategies and tactics specifically tailored to entrepreneurs at fifty, providing insights on how to build a strong brand, target the right audience, and leverage digital marketing channels.

Once your business is up and running, managing and scaling becomes paramount. We'll provide essential strategies and tips for managing day-to-day operations, optimizing growth, and effectively adapting to changing market dynamics.

Finally, we'll encourage you to embrace the journey and shape a successful and fulfilling business future. Entrepreneurship at fifty is not just about building a successful business, but also about personal growth and fulfillment. We'll share inspiring stories of those who reinvented their lives through entrepreneurship at fifty.

So let's dive in and explore the exciting world of entrepreneurial ventures at fifty. Get ready to turn your dreams into reality and embark on a fulfilling and successful entrepreneurial journey!

Why Entrepreneurship at Fifty?

Starting a business at fifty presents a world of opportunities for older adults to embark on an exciting entrepreneurial journey. With years of experience and a wealth of knowledge, launching a startup in your 50s can be a fulfilling and successful endeavor.

One of the unique advantages of entrepreneurship at fifty is the ability to leverage valuable professional experience gained throughout your career. The skills and expertise developed over the years can be applied to solve real-world problems, making a meaningful impact in your chosen industry.

Inspiring Success Stories

Senior entrepreneurship success stories are testament to the endless possibilities of starting a business in your 50s. Visionaries like Richard Branson, who founded Virgin Group in his early 20s, continued to launch successful ventures well into his fifties. Another inspiring figure is Martha Stewart, who established her media empire in her 50s, proving that age is no barrier to entrepreneurial success.

These success stories not only inspire, but also demonstrate the potential for long-term achievements in business at any age. By highlighting these accomplishments, we aim to motivate and empower individuals who are considering entrepreneurship in their fifties.

Furthermore, launching a startup in your 50s allows you to pursue business ideas specifically targeting the needs and preferences of older adults. From healthcare services and wellness products to recreational activities and financial planning, the possibilities for business ideas catering to this demographic are vast.

In the next section, we will explore the age-related challenges that entrepreneurs may face and how to overcome them, ensuring a smooth transition into senior entrepreneurship.

Overcoming Age-related Challenges

Starting a small business after 50 can present unique challenges. However, with the right mindset and strategies in place, these challenges can be overcome and even turned into advantages. In this section, we will explore how individuals can navigate the business landscape and leverage their accumulated knowledge and skills to thrive as entrepreneurs in their second career.

Embracing Experience and Expertise

One of the most significant advantages of starting a business after 50 is the wealth of experience and expertise gained over the years. Retirees and individuals looking for a second career entrepreneurship opportunity possess a deep understanding of their industry and valuable insights that can set them apart from their competition.

By leveraging this experience, entrepreneurs at fifty can offer unique perspectives, innovative solutions, and exceptional service to their customers. They can use their accumulated skills to provide unparalleled value and establish themselves as trusted leaders in their chosen field.

Overcoming Biases and Stereotypes

Age-related biases and stereotypes can sometimes hinder the progress of entrepreneurs at fifty. However, it's essential to challenge these assumptions and showcase the value and relevance that older entrepreneurs bring to the table.

Entrepreneurs can counteract biases by emphasizing their experience, expertise, and adaptability. They can demonstrate their willingness to learn new technologies, stay updated with industry trends, and embrace innovation. By doing so, they can break through age-related barriers and gain recognition for their abilities and accomplishments.

Networking and Collaborating

Building a strong network is crucial for entrepreneurs at fifty. By connecting with like-minded individuals, industry professionals, and mentors, entrepreneurs can gain valuable insights, guidance, and support.

Networking provides opportunities to learn from others' experiences and tap into a vast pool of resources, such as potential business partners, suppliers, and customers. Collaborations can lead to mutually beneficial partnerships that help overcome challenges and accelerate business growth.

Continuing Education and Skill Development

Entrepreneurs at fifty should never stop learning and developing their skills. Continual education and skill enhancement allow business owners to stay ahead of industry trends, acquire new knowledge, and adapt to evolving market demands.

Investing time in professional development, attending workshops, conferences, and online courses not only keeps entrepreneurs up-to-date but also demonstrates a commitment to excellence and personal growth. It shows potential clients and partners that the business is proactive and dedicated to continuous improvement.

By embracing these strategies and leveraging their unique advantages, entrepreneurs at fifty can successfully overcome age-related challenges and embark on a fulfilling and prosperous entrepreneurial journey in their second career.

Identifying Business Opportunities

As individuals embark on entrepreneurial ventures at the age of fifty, there are numerous business opportunities well-suited for their experience and interests. Capitalizing on their existing skills and knowledge, older adults can find success in various industries.

One such opportunity is consulting. With decades of professional experience, seniors can offer valuable insights and expertise to businesses seeking guidance. Whether it's specializing in finance, marketing, or strategy, their knowledge can be leveraged to provide high-quality consulting services.

Another promising avenue is the growing market for senior-focused products and services. From healthcare and fitness to technology and travel, catering to the unique needs and preferences of older adults can be a profitable niche. Innovations such as wearable devices for monitoring health, accessible home modifications, or travel agencies offering curated senior-friendly vacations are just a few examples.

E-commerce and online businesses

The rise of e-commerce presents an excellent opportunity for senior entrepreneurs. With minimal overhead costs and the ability to reach a global audience, selling products online has never been easier. Seniors can leverage their expertise in niche markets or create unique handmade products to establish profitable online businesses.

Additionally, there is a demand for services that support the aging population. Offering assistance in areas such as home caregiving, meal planning, transportation, or financial planning can be highly rewarding both financially and emotionally. These services cater to the specific needs of older adults and contribute to their overall well-being.

Finally, as the population ages, there is a growing need for senior-friendly technology and digital solutions. Developing user-friendly apps, software, or online platforms that cater to older adults can be a lucrative business opportunity. This can include anything from virtual social networks and educational platforms to health monitoring devices and personalized digital assistants.

By identifying and capitalizing on these business opportunities, older adults can embark on successful entrepreneurial ventures that not only provide financial stability but also contribute to their personal fulfillment and overall well-being.

Developing a Business Plan

A well-crafted business plan is crucial for entrepreneurs of all ages, including those who are starting a business at 50 or launching a startup in their 50s. In this section, we will walk you through the process of developing a comprehensive business plan tailored to your specific goals and aspirations.

Creating a business plan allows you to clarify your vision, set achievable goals, and outline the strategies needed to turn your ideas into a successful venture. It provides a roadmap for your business, helping you make informed decisions and stay focused on your objectives.

When developing your business plan, it's essential to consider your target market, competitive landscape, and financial projections. By conducting market research, you can gain valuable insights into your customers' needs and preferences, allowing you to tailor your products or services accordingly. Furthermore, including a detailed marketing and sales strategy in your plan will help you attract customers and generate revenue. This could involve online marketing, social media campaigns, partnerships, or other promotional activities that resonate with your target audience.

Throughout the planning process, it's essential to remain flexible and adapt your strategy as needed. The business landscape is constantly evolving, and being open to change will position you for success. Now, let's explore some tips and insights from successful entrepreneurs who embarked on their entrepreneurial journey in their fifties. Their stories serve as inspiration and proof that launching a business later in life can lead to significant achievements and personal fulfillment.

Funding Options and Resources

Starting a small business after 50 can be an exciting endeavor, but one concern that often arises is the issue of financing. Fortunately, there are various funding options and resources available to support your entrepreneurial pursuits.

One option is to explore traditional loans from banks or credit unions. These institutions may offer loans specifically designed for entrepreneurs starting a business at 50 or in their second career. Additionally, you can research government-backed loan programs that provide financial assistance to small businesses.

Crowdfunding:

Crowdfunding platforms have gained popularity in recent years, providing a unique opportunity for entrepreneurs to secure funding. By creating a compelling campaign and showcasing your business idea, you can attract investors and individuals who are interested in supporting your venture.

Grants:

There are also grants available from government agencies, nonprofit organizations, and private foundations that cater specifically to entrepreneurship for retirees. These grants can provide significant financial support and may have less stringent requirements compared to traditional loans.

Furthermore, consider exploring local resources and economic development agencies for potential grants or loans tailored to senior entrepreneurs. These organizations often have programs dedicated to helping individuals start or expand businesses, providing valuable guidance and financial support.

Before pursuing any funding option, it is crucial to thoroughly research and understand the terms and conditions associated with each source. It's also a good idea to consult with financial advisors or business mentors who can provide guidance and support throughout the funding process.

Remember, starting a business at 50 or pursuing second career entrepreneurship opportunities is a venture that requires careful financial planning. By exploring different funding options and leveraging available resources, you can secure the necessary funding to bring your business idea to life.

Building a Supportive Network

As an entrepreneur, building a supportive network is crucial to your success, especially as you embark on your entrepreneurial journey later in life. Connecting with like-minded individuals, industry professionals, and mentors can provide you with guidance, advice, and valuable connections.

One way to build your network is by attending industry events and conferences focused on entrepreneurship opportunities for seniors. These gatherings allow you to meet other entrepreneurs who are also navigating the challenges and joys of starting a business at a later stage in life. Networking events provide a platform for exchanging ideas, sharing experiences, and making valuable connections that may assist you in your entrepreneurial endeavors.

Another effective strategy for building a supportive network is by joining online communities and forums dedicated to older adult entrepreneurs. These digital spaces allow you to engage with a diverse group of individuals who share your passion for entrepreneurship. Participating in discussions, sharing insights, and seeking advice from experienced entrepreneurs can provide you with a wealth of knowledge and a supportive community.

Connecting with Mentors

Mentors play a crucial role in the entrepreneurial journey, offering valuable guidance and support. Look for mentors who have experience in your industry or have successfully navigated entrepreneurship at a later age. Their insights and advice can help you avoid common pitfalls and navigate the unique challenges you may face.

Consider joining mentorship programs specifically designed for older adults looking to start or scale their businesses. These programs connect aspiring entrepreneurs with seasoned mentors who can provide personalized guidance tailored to their specific needs and goals.

Remember, building a supportive network is an ongoing process. It requires effort, perseverance, and a willingness to reach out and connect with fellow entrepreneurs, industry professionals, and mentors. By actively engaging with your network and fostering relationships, you can access invaluable resources, inspiration, and support on your entrepreneurial journey.

Marketing and Branding Strategies

When starting a business at 50 or launching a startup in your 50s, effective marketing and branding are essential for creating a strong presence in the market. In this section, we will explore marketing strategies specifically tailored to entrepreneurs at fifty, showcasing inspiring senior entrepreneurship success stories.

To build a strong brand, it is crucial to identify your target audience and develop a unique value proposition that resonates with them. Consider your experience, skills, and passions, and use them to differentiate your business from competitors. Showcase your expertise and highlight the benefits of working with a seasoned entrepreneur.

Utilizing digital marketing channels can significantly amplify your reach and connect you with potential customers. Leverage social media platforms such as Facebook, LinkedIn, and Instagram to engage with your audience, showcase your products or services, and share senior entrepreneurship success stories. Develop a compelling website that reflects your brand identity and provides valuable information to visitors.

Content Marketing

Content marketing is a powerful tool for establishing thought leadership and building trust with your target audience. Create informative blog posts, articles, or videos that offer valuable insights and advice related to your industry. Share these resources on your website, social media, and other relevant platforms to attract and engage your audience.

Collaborate and Partner

Collaborating with other businesses or influencers can help expand your reach and boost brand visibility. Look for opportunities to partner with organizations or individuals who share similar values or target the same audience. This collaboration can take the form of joint marketing campaigns, co-hosting events, or cross-promoting each other's products or services.

Remember to monitor and analyze the performance of your marketing efforts. Use tools like Google Analytics to track website traffic, identify customer behavior patterns, and measure the effectiveness of your campaigns. Continuously optimize your marketing strategies based on the data collected to achieve better results.

By implementing these marketing and branding strategies, entrepreneurs at fifty can effectively position their businesses in the market and showcase their unique value. Stay true to your brand, be consistent in your messaging, and authentically connect with your audience to create a lasting impact.

Managing and Scaling the Business

Once you have successfully established your business after 50, the next step is to focus on managing and scaling its operations for growth and success. In this section, we will explore essential strategies and tips to help you navigate the day-to-day challenges and optimize the growth potential of your business.

Effective Operations Management

Efficient operations management is crucial for the smooth running of your business. This includes tasks such as inventory management, supply chain optimization, and streamlining internal processes. By implementing effective operations management strategies, you can improve productivity, reduce costs, and enhance customer satisfaction.

Optimizing Growth Opportunities

As an entrepreneur at fifty, it is important to identify and capitalize on growth opportunities. This may involve expanding your product or service offerings, entering new markets, or exploring strategic partnerships. By seeking out and leveraging growth opportunities, you can take your business to the next level.

Scaling Strategies

Scaling a business requires careful planning and execution. It involves increasing your business's capacity to handle higher volumes of customers, orders, and transactions. This may involve hiring additional staff, investing in technology infrastructure, or expanding your physical presence. By adopting effective scaling strategies, you can meet growing demand and ensure long-term success.

Adapting to Market Dynamics

The business landscape is constantly evolving, and as an entrepreneur, it is important to adapt to changing market dynamics. This may involve staying updated with industry trends, monitoring competitor activities, and continuously innovating your products or services. By staying agile and adaptive, you can position your business for sustained growth in a dynamic marketplace.

Managing and scaling a business after 50 may present unique challenges, but it also offers valuable opportunities for personal and professional growth. By implementing effective strategies, staying proactive, and leveraging your experience, you can unlock the full potential of your business venture and achieve long-term success.

Embracing the Journey: Reinventing Your Future

Embarking on an entrepreneurial journey at the age of fifty is not just about starting a business. It's an opportunity for personal growth, fulfillment, and the chance to reinvent your future. As you navigate this exciting path, remember that your experience and wisdom accumulated over the years will be invaluable assets.

Don't be afraid to embrace your journey and all the challenges it brings. Starting a business in your fifties allows you to capitalize on your existing knowledge and skills while exploring new business ideas tailored to the needs of older adults. Whether it's launching a startup or providing a service that caters to your peers, there are countless opportunities waiting for you.

As you pursue your entrepreneurial dreams, take inspiration from the success stories of senior entrepreneurs who have found career fulfillment and financial success in their fifties. These stories prove that it's never too late to start a business and achieve great things. Let their experiences motivate you and remind you that age is just a number.

So, as you shape your successful and fulfilling business future, remember to enjoy the journey. Celebrate every milestone along the way, and embrace the new skills, connections, and personal growth that entrepreneurship brings. Be proud of reinventing your future and proving to the world that senior entrepreneurship is a force to be reckoned with.

Chapter 35

Travel as Transformation: How travel can redefine your worldview

Traveling can also be a moment for not just merely having fun, but for radical change, which will completely change the way you look at things. The present study examines the concept of travelling as transformation and its implications on personal development and broader perspectives especially in 50s. It's a journey through cultural immersion and comfort zones breaking or even self-discovery. Moreover, it is the possibility of such an understanding that makes many people feel like they are locked up within their own minds while there is much more around them to experience.

Why Traveling at 50 Can Be Especially Transformative

Any age group could benefit from travelling experiences; however there is something quite incredible about making new journeys at this time of your life. You have accumulated wisdom with years of living your life amidst various circumstances and grown to understand who you really are. It's time for you to explore unknown heights and depths before then realizing that traveling has been very transformative.

Traveling at 50 offers unique opportunities for personal growth and self-discovery through these means one can cross his/her comfort zone into curiosity filled world. All experiences whether immersing oneself into different cultures, challenging preconceived ideas or just being attuned to nature offer possible ways of seeing things differently.

You can travel on your own terms when you are in your fifties. Thus, pick the destinations that truly matter to you depending on what arouses your curiosity most about certain places. This enables the creation of a trip that suits one's personal aspirations towards self-improvement.

Traveling at 50 opens doors to new connections and friendships because it allows us engage with diverse individuals and communities hence expanding our horizons by developing greater understanding about human beings in general. It promotes empathy, compassion and tolerance as we encounter cultures from different corners of the globe.

However, travel during this period may provide essential escape from daily routine as well as pressures. This allows the mind, body and soul to refresh as well as gives one a new perspective and energy. It is also the moment for introspection since you get time to think about your desires, passions and dreams.

So, if you're in your 50s and contemplating new travel adventures, embrace the transformative power of travel. The world is your classroom as you journey through life with renewed self-awareness discovering more about oneself.

Exploring New Cultures and Broadening Horizons

When people travel they gain new understanding from personal experiences which goes beyond mere observation to full engagement with local culture such that one connects with locals, traditions or even history. This experience is what enables us understand and appreciate various differences found in different cultures.

A journey through strange lands does a lot to widen our minds and expose us to new ideas, values, and modes of thought. The world opens up in a different way to us, away from our parochial outlook and towards another more inclusive, tolerant one.

The Importance of Traveling Middle Age

Traveling in middle age has its benefits where experiencing new cultures is concerned. With the background knowledge that comes with having lived for long enough periods we are able to fully appreciate what cultural practices and norms mean.

Moreover, middle age often brings about self-confidence as well as self-assurance enabling us step out of comfort zones and seek further involvement with the community. We can make lasting connections and friendships during such journeys that are incredibly enriching as well.

Through travel benefits in middle age we not only improve ourselves but also become ambassadors for empathy. Therefore it will be necessary for us to take our expanded appreciation of other people's culture back home so that they can learn how interconnected the world is.

The Power of Challenging Your Comfort Zone

Stepping out from your comfort zone is a powerful process you may undertake when aiming at personal growth or broadening horizons; there is nothing more powerful than this act. And what better way to do that than through travel?

While travelling exposes you to new environments, cultures or ways of life that could be alien or even uncomfortable sometimes you just have no choice other than challenge yourself during moments like these if you wish immense personal growth.

New challenges enable an individual to cross boundaries he considered insurmountable thereby allowing opportunities for learning, finding oneself and changing lives open wide before him. All these things expand how you see the world hence every single time you take a step outside your comfort zone it helps increase the overall global perspective.

Additionally, stepping out of your comfort zone while traveling brings fears into light encouraging their conquest resulting in resilience development and confidence building within oneself. It makes them realize that they can do more than they ever thought and if you want your own growth as well as self-development, then you should not be afraid of taking risks.

Thus challenge yourself through comfort zones on journeys next time. Go out of your way to embrace the unknown and unfamiliar in order to make possible the personal development and broadened perspectives that lay beyond one's comfort zone. It is during these moments when an individual becomes aware of his or her new personality.

Journeys of Self-Discovery: Finding Yourself in New Places

Traveling has a unique ability to trigger changes in us, which leads to the emergence of our own inner selves. This is because it gives us the chance to explore ourselves deep within by journeying through new places and cultures.

By immersing ourselves into unaccustomed surroundings, we permit different happenings, happenstances and insights come our way. At fifty years old stepping out from our comfort zone allows us to move into unknown internal territory.

As we traverse diverse streets teeming with life or stand still enough amidst pristine surroundings untouched by human hands, we learn who we truly are. In addition, each encounter implies an invitation for contemplation or introspection that will also help one grow personally.

While on these journeys of self-discovery, we may have to face unexpected difficulties, but it is through these challenges that we realize our hidden strengths and resilience. This will involve adapting to new surroundings as well as dealing with various cultures that in turn make us look at the world in a different way.

"The Power of Introspection"

When moving at a speed of 50, it is more advantageous because we gain much from life experiences. This enables us to reflect on our past, reassess our present, and envision our future. We experience moments of clarity when alone during sunset and on top of a high mountain that awaken our true selves. Through self-discovery, one becomes more aware about their passions, values and aspirations. We grow more understanding how personal narratives manifest in our worldview. These are transformative experiences for us which shape us into continuously growing individuals.

More than just sightseeing or checking off places from our bucket lists; Traveling at 50 entails embracing the unknown and oneself while being guided by travel's transformative power towards higher purpose and fulfillment.

"Building Empathy and Understanding Through Travel"

Travel has an incredible potential to develop empathy within us and teach us so much about the world around us. When we move beyond what we know into other people's lives which are not like ours in any way: backgrounds or culture etc., this gives rise to new perspectives and insights.

Exploring foreign lands allows us to see the world through different lenses challenging our pre-conceptions and expanding our views. So when we interact with locals – be it participating in their traditional activities or even seeing them go about their normal day-to-day activities –we can start developing deep sympathy for both those who enjoy living there as well as those who would rather be somewhere else but cannot leave.

Through interacting with diverse people who share their stories with me; I have developed empathy for others by exercising my ability to put myself mentally into someone else's position. The point of this is that although the differences between us seem insurmountable, we all experience the same feelings and have similar needs as human beings. This realization bridges gaps among disparate cultures hence building unity towards a global community.

"Embracing New Perspectives"

Getting out of our comfort zones and exploring unfamiliar territories allows us to have new perspectives that are locked within our daily routines. Travel helps us challenge deep-seated biases while developing appreciation for different religious beliefs, value systems and life styles.

As we witness the beauty of diversity, as well as the richness of human expressions, it expands our worldviews. We become more adaptable and open-minded with time. There are so many ways to be happy; there exist multiple paths to success and fulfillment; in essence travel teaches us the multiplicity of human existence.

On Personal Growth And Self-Reflection

Travel is not only an external journey; it is also an internal one. It provides room for personal growth and self-reflection. We are exposed to new challenges and opportunities for self-discovery as we move outside our comfort zones into unfamiliar environments.

Through travel, we learn more about ourselves, our strengths and our boundaries. As we go through foreign languages, cultures and environments we grow independent enough to handle different situations alone .This self-awareness and personal growth manifest in various aspects of our lives thus fostering deeper sense purposefulness , resilience ,and self-confidence .

So, travel is a transformative experience that does more than just scratching the surface of new destinations. It is a catalyst for empathy building, broadening perspectives, and fostering personal growth. We gain an expanded understanding of our place in the world through immersing ourselves in various cultures and environments.

Embracing New Experiences in Midlife: Overcoming Limiting Beliefs

It's simple to get stuck in a rut and cling to familiar routines when you are fifty. Nonetheless, embracing new experiences at midlife can provoke personal growth and be a transformative journey. Preconceived notions can be challenged by travel making us uncomfortable allowing us to pursue new interests and develop new hobbies.

When we come out of our comfort zones we open up ourselves to all manner of opportunities and possibilities. Overcoming limiting beliefs through embracing unconventional trips has meant I have personally grown immensely from this process.

Travel at 50 provides an opportunity to reflect on their past encounters with the intention of making deliberate choices for one's future. It helps us face any self-inflicted limitations we may have imposed upon ourselves as well as break free from whatever walls have held us back.

The transformational aspect of travel at 50 lies in its ability to challenge our thoughts and broaden our horizons. To encourage unknowns means facing fears, discovering passion again, meaning something else, being filled completely up again.

As we embrace new experiences in midlife our endurance becomes apparent on how hardy we can be with regard to life's ups and downs. Unchartered territories become navigable; foreign cultures adaptable while unexpected challenges are surmountable; all leading towards broadening our perspective that contributes towards personal development and general well-being.

Let go of your limiting beliefs; embrace the transformative power of fifty-year-old travel. Go beyond your comfort zone; explore different areas; connect with diverse cultures; let yourself feel what diversity really is about.

The Healing Power of Nature: Connecting with the World Around You

Immersing yourself in the natural world may be a life-altering experience for personal growth and well-being. Nature has a restorative power that can heal the mind, body, and spirit particularly if you travel at 50. Nature's transformative power is undeniable as it allows one to relate to their environment on a deeper level.

When you go to natural landscapes and immerse yourself in their beauty, there are so many ways in which you can get healed. The sights, sounds and smells of nature can wake up your senses while bringing peace and tranquility within you. Whether it is the quietness of an undisturbed beach, the grandeur of mountains or silence of woods being out in nature helps us let go of our stress filled lives and find comfort from simplicity.

Nature not only provides a serene asylum but also its own opportunities for personal growth. Such challenges and obstacles of the outdoor can build your resilience, problem-solving skills and make you realize how strong you are inside. Be it a difficult hiking trail, learning to surf in the ocean or navigating through thick woods, they will force you out of your comfort zone, enabling you to discover self-assurance at new heights.

Healing Nature: The Mind Body Connection

Moreover, nature's healing power on body and soul is incredible. Research has indicated that spending time in natural environment helps reduce stress levels, lower blood pressure and heart rate, boost immune system function as well as improve mental well-being. Outdoor environments offer fresh air, sunlight and natural aspects which positively influence both physical and mental health.

In addition to this aspect of personal growth, one becomes more connected with oneself in existence while being in nature. Through this kind of experience one may have self-reflection opportunity as well as introspection oneness with nature can be experienced. This sense of connection nurtures appreciation for the earth's resources with a renewed sense of gratitude for its beauty and intricacies.

When someone reaches 50 years old traveling provides them with an exceptional chance to benefit from the curative abilities of Mother Nature. In that case one gets free from daily activities demand reconnections himself/herself embraces life transformations happening around him/her Thus while making arrangement for upcoming exploration trips bear in mind the healing properties associated with mother earth alongside personal growth benefits accompanying such journeys When walking through the wilds each step gives life to your inner world making memories that will never go away forever.

Embracing Learning Journey: Gaining Knowledge & Wisdom

Traveling is not all about places visited but knowledge gained along the way. You open yourself up to different learning possibilities which contribute towards personal growth within your life hence transforming your perspective especially when you reach 50s after embarking on a journey.

Travel-learn system is beyond classroom learning. It implies immersion in various cultures, histories, languages and traditions. You might be walking through ancient ruins, attending local workshops or holding meaningful conversations with fellow tourists and every other encounter is the opportunity to broaden your horizon hence gaining useful insights.

While travelling, you may gather new knowledge and skills that would not have come your way otherwise. Every activity from cooking classes in Italy to wildlife conservation projects in Africa helps you understand the world better. These new skills and ideas also make it easier for one to lead a more enriching life by making a difference within his/her community.

What is more, being 50 years old helps one to approach the learning journey with vast life experiences, wisdom and a greater appreciation of the world. It gives unique opportunity for reflection on the past, gain new perspectives and challenge existing beliefs. Through travel we can learn alternative ways of life, thinking and being – each meeting leads to personal growth and change in outlook.

Therefore, as you go for a study trip through traveling, maintain an open view towards things, be inquisitive and grasp its transformative capabilities. Traveling at 50 years is a catalyst for personal development, acquiring knowledge and broadening your global perspective.

Embracing The World Post-50: Rebirth And Recollection

When our age moves into 50s most people are taken back to their lives reviewing their life styles looking for a new path that would lead them to self-actualization. This is where travel becomes truly transformative by becoming "World post-50" as we embark on the way of renaissance and rediscovery. Exploring the world after fifty opens up countless opportunities. It liberates us from our routines and habits so that we may grow personally in middle age. We should let travel help us try out pushing through boundaries we have set for ourselves. At such time one must get out of his/her familiar environment to embrace uncertainty.

There's an unquestionable transformative power in travelling at fifty which gives us a chance to reframe our worldview and see things from another angle once again; after all it's just like seeing from afar but near enough not to miss anything along the way. Thus immersing oneself into distinct cultures helps people understand humanity diversity' s wide spectrum & how interrelated human beings are with each other or else acquiring knowledge across borders makes humanity richer hence increasing horizons

So if you are in your fifties then it's high time you packed your bags and went on another adventure called "the world post-50". Let yourself be revitalized and rediscover the pleasure of exploration. Travelling with you on the path towards self-realization, travel will offer you transformative experiences and a new lease of life.

Chapter 36

Investing with Wisdom: Smart investment strategies for the years ahead

Welcome to our comprehensive guide on investing with wisdom in your 50s. As retirement approaches, it's essential to plan ahead and secure your financial future. This section will delve into the smart investment strategies that can help you make the most of your retirement planning, ensure financial security, and maximize your retirement savings.

Retirement planning is a critical aspect of financial stability, and investing wisely is key to achieve those goals. By implementing the right strategies, you can navigate the complexities of the investment landscape and position yourself for success in the years to come.

Throughout this article, we'll guide you through every step of the process, from understanding the importance of retirement planning to assessing your current financial situation, setting realistic goals, diversifying your investment portfolio, managing risk, optimizing retirement accounts, seeking professional advice, and adapting your strategy as retirement draws near.

Our aim is to provide you with practical insights and actionable advice that you can use right away, empowering you to navigate the world of investing with confidence and wisdom. So let's get started on this exciting journey towards financial security and a well-planned retirement.

Understanding the Importance of Retirement Planning

As you approach retirement, it's essential to understand the significance of retirement planning. Having a solid retirement plan is crucial for maintaining financial security and building a robust retirement savings. By strategically planning for your future, you can ensure a comfortable and stress-free retirement.

Retirement planning allows you to envision the lifestyle you desire after leaving the workforce. It helps you develop a roadmap that aligns your financial goals with your retirement dreams. By taking the time to plan and prepare, you can safeguard your financial well-being and enjoy the freedom and peace of mind that comes with financial security.

One of the key advantages of retirement planning is that it enables you to make informed decisions about your finances. By assessing your current financial situation, you can understand your retirement savings, evaluate your assets, and determine the steps needed to achieve your retirement goals.

Moreover, retirement planning ensures that you have the necessary resources to support your preferred lifestyle during your golden years. It helps you build a nest egg that can provide a consistent income stream, cover your healthcare expenses, and support any unforeseen circumstances. With a well-thought-out retirement plan in place, you can confidently navigate the complexities of retirement and enjoy your newfound freedom without worrying about financial instability.

Furthermore, retirement planning allows you to take advantage of various investment vehicles and strategies that can optimize your retirement savings. By diversifying your investments and exploring investment opportunities, you can build a portfolio that delivers long-term growth and stability. A comprehensive retirement plan takes into account factors such as risk tolerance, inflation, and projected income needs, ensuring that your financial future remains secure even in the face of economic fluctuations.

In summary, retirement planning is a vital step in ensuring financial security and building a robust retirement savings. By understanding the importance of retirement planning and taking action now, you can set yourself up for a comfortable and enjoyable retirement, free from financial worries. So take the first step towards a brighter future and start planning for your retirement today.

Assessing Your Current Financial Situation

Before you can make wise investment decisions in your 50s, it's crucial to assess your current financial situation. Taking stock of your retirement savings, analyzing your assets, and exploring wealth management strategies are essential steps towards achieving long-term financial security.

Evaluating Your Retirement Savings

by reviewing your retirement savings accounts, such as your 401(k), IRA, or pension plan. Calculate how much you have saved up until now and estimate the income it can generate during your retirement. Understanding the current state of your retirement savings is vital for making informed investment choices.

Analyzing Your Assets

Aside from your retirement savings, evaluate your overall financial assets. This includes your investment portfolio, real estate holdings, and any other significant assets you may have. Consider the value and potential return on each asset, as well as any associated risks.

Exploring Wealth Management Strategies

Wealth management plays a crucial role in ensuring the growth and protection of your assets. Work with a professional wealth manager who can provide guidance on tax planning, asset allocation, and risk management. By implementing effective wealth management strategies, you can enhance your financial security and optimize your retirement savings.

By thoroughly assessing your current financial situation, you can make well-informed decisions regarding your investments, retirement planning, and wealth management. This will set you on the right path towards a secure and prosperous future.

Setting Realistic Financial Goals

To invest wisely in your 50s and achieve financial independence and security, it is crucial to set realistic financial goals. Having clear objectives in mind will help guide your retirement strategies and ensure a smooth transition into the next phase of your life.

When it comes to defining your retirement goals, it's important to consider your desired lifestyle, aspirations, and anticipated expenses. Reflect on how you envision your retirement years, whether it's traveling, pursuing hobbies, or spending quality time with loved ones. By understanding your priorities, you can create a realistic retirement budget that aligns with your financial capabilities.

Developing strategies to achieve these goals is key. Consider factors such as your current retirement savings, expected growth from investments, and your timeline to retirement. By working with a financial advisor, you can explore different investment options and tailor your approach to your unique circumstances.

Building Wealth through Diversification

Diversifying your investment portfolio is an essential element of setting realistic financial goals. By spreading your investments across different asset classes, such as stocks, bonds, and real estate, you can reduce risk and increase the potential for long-term growth.

Asset allocation is another critical factor to consider. By balancing your portfolio based on your risk tolerance and investment goals, you can optimize your returns while minimizing exposure to market volatility. Regularly reviewing and rebalancing your portfolio ensures that it stays aligned with your financial objectives.

Embracing a Long-Term Mindset

Building financial security and achieving independence requires a long-term mindset. While it's essential to monitor your investments, it's equally important to resist the urge to make impulsive decisions based on short-term market fluctuations. Stay focused on your goals, and maintain confidence in your long-term retirement strategies.

Identifying potential obstacles along the way is also crucial for setting realistic financial goals. This could include unexpected expenses, healthcare costs, or changes in income. By anticipating these challenges and having contingency plans in place, you can ensure that your financial independence remains intact.

By setting realistic financial goals, diversifying your investment portfolio, and embracing a long-term mindset, you can lay a solid foundation for a secure and fulfilling retirement. Take the time to assess your current financial situation, consult with professionals if needed, and make adjustments along the way. With careful planning and disciplined execution, you can confidently move towards the future you envision.

Diversifying Your Investment Portfolio

When it comes to smart investing in your 50s, one crucial strategy to consider is diversifying your investment portfolio. By diversifying, you can spread your risk and potentially increase your chances of long-term success and financial security.

The Importance of Diversification

Diversification means not putting all your eggs in one basket. It involves investing in a variety of asset classes, such as stocks, bonds, real estate, and mutual funds, across different industries and geographic locations.

By diversifying, you can protect yourself from the volatility of any single investment and maximize potential returns. For example, if one industry experiences a downturn, your investments in other sectors can help offset the losses.

Exploring Different Investment Options

When diversifying your portfolio in your 50s, it's crucial to explore different investment options that align with your retirement goals. Consider investing in a combination of low-cost index funds, individual stocks, bonds, and real estate investment trusts (REITs).

Additionally, you may want to consider alternative investments, such as commodities or peer-to-peer lending platforms, to further diversify your portfolio and potentially boost your returns.

Tips for Building a Well-Balanced Portfolio

- Review your current investments and assess their diversification levels.
- Set clear investment goals and determine your risk tolerance.
- Consider working with a financial advisor to develop a well-balanced investment strategy.
- Regularly review and rebalance your portfolio to maintain diversification.
- Stay informed about market trends and adjust your portfolio accordingly.
- Remember, smart investing in your 50s involves careful planning and diversifying your investment portfolio. By spreading your risk, exploring different investment options, and following these tips, you can set yourself up for long-term success and financial security in retirement.

Managing Investment Risk

As you age and approach retirement, managing investment risk becomes increasingly important. It's crucial to protect your long-term investments and ensure your financial security. This section will provide you with valuable strategies for mitigating risk, understanding investment volatility, and making informed decisions that align with your long-term goals.

Strategies for Mitigating Risk

When it comes to smart investing, diversification is key. By spreading your investments across different asset classes and industries, you can minimize the impact of market volatility on your portfolio. Additionally, regularly rebalancing your portfolio can help maintain your desired asset allocation and minimize risk.

Understanding Investment Volatility

Investment volatility refers to the fluctuation in the value of your investments over time. It's important to understand that investments come with inherent risks, and fluctuations in the market can impact the value of your investment portfolio. By educating yourself about different investment strategies and staying informed about market trends, you can better navigate investment volatility and make informed decisions.

Making Informed Decisions

When it comes to managing investment risk, knowledge is power. Conduct thorough research and seek advice from financial professionals who specialize in wealth management and long-term investments. By staying informed and seeking expert guidance, you can make confident decisions that align with your investment goals and help safeguard your financial future.

Optimizing Retirement Accounts

When planning for retirement in your 50s, optimizing your retirement accounts is crucial for ensuring long-term financial security. By maximizing your retirement savings and taking advantage of employer matches, you can take significant steps towards a comfortable retirement.

One key strategy for optimizing retirement accounts is to contribute the maximum amount allowed. For individual retirement accounts (IRAs), make sure you are contributing the maximum annual limit set by the Internal Revenue Service (IRS). Additionally, take advantage of employer-sponsored retirement plans, such as a 401(k), and contribute enough to receive the full employer match. This matching contribution is essentially free money that can significantly boost your retirement savings.

Exploring Retirement Account Options

There are different retirement account options available, and understanding their features can help you make informed decisions. Traditional IRAs allow you to contribute pre-tax dollars, reducing your taxable income in the year of contribution. Roth IRAs, on the other hand, are funded with after-tax dollars, providing tax-free withdrawals in retirement. Consider the pros and cons of each option and choose the one that aligns best with your retirement strategies.

In addition to IRAs, employer-sponsored retirement accounts offer unique benefits. 401(k) plans provide the opportunity to invest a portion of your salary before taxes, and many employers offer matching contributions up to a certain percentage. Another popular option is a 403(b) plan, typically available to employees in the nonprofit and educational sectors. Take the time to explore the retirement account options available to you to optimize your savings for a secure retirement.

By optimizing your retirement accounts and employing smart strategies, you can maximize your retirement savings and achieve financial security. Remember to consult with a financial advisor or retirement planning professional to ensure you make the most informed decisions based on your unique circumstances.

Seeking Professional Financial Advice

In your 50s, when it comes to smart investing and retirement strategies, seeking professional financial advice can make all the difference. Working with a knowledgeable and experienced financial advisor can provide valuable insights and guidance to help you navigate the complex world of finance.

A financial advisor can assist you in developing a personalized investment plan tailored to your specific goals and risk tolerance. They can analyze your current financial situation, retirement savings, and long-term financial aspirations to create a roadmap for achieving financial independence and security.

One of the key benefits of working with a financial advisor is their expertise in the ever-changing market conditions. They can help you stay informed about potential investment opportunities and guide you in making informed decisions that align with your long-term goals.

When seeking a financial advisor, it's essential to find the right professional who understands your needs and values. Look for someone who is qualified, licensed, and trustworthy. Consider their experience, credentials, and track record in helping individuals like yourself achieve financial success.

Establishing a trusting relationship with your financial advisor is crucial. You should feel comfortable discussing your financial concerns, asking questions, and seeking clarifications. Regular communication and ongoing collaboration are key to ensuring that your investment strategy evolves as your circumstances change.

Remember, financial independence is within reach with the help of a professional financial advisor. Take the first step towards your long-term financial success by seeking their expertise and guidance today.

Adapting Your Investment Strategy as You Approach Retirement

As you approach retirement, it's crucial to adapt your investment strategy to ensure financial security. This phase of your life requires careful consideration of your portfolio, risk tolerance, and decision-making process. By making informed choices, you can set yourself up for a comfortable retirement.

Adjusting Your Portfolio

Retirement planning involves adjusting your investment portfolio to align with your changing needs and goals. It's important to review your asset allocation and rebalance if necessary. Consider adjusting your investment mix to include more conservative options to protect your savings while still seeking potential growth.

Understanding Risk Tolerance

As retirement approaches, understanding your risk tolerance becomes crucial. You may want to reassess the level of risk you're willing to take with your investments to preserve your capital. It's essential to strike a balance between growth potential and protecting your savings from market volatility.

Making Informed Decisions

When making investment decisions, it's vital to gather relevant information and seek professional advice. Consider consulting a financial advisor who specializes in retirement planning. They can provide insights based on your specific circumstances and help you make informed choices that align with your retirement goals.

Adapting your investment strategy as you approach retirement is key to ensuring financial security. By adjusting your portfolio, understanding your risk tolerance, and making informed decisions, you can pave the way for a successful and comfortable retirement.

Enjoying Your Golden Years

After years of wise investing in your 50s and careful retirement planning, you can now look forward to enjoying your golden years with financial security and peace of mind. The fruits of your labor are ready to be harvested, allowing you to indulge in the things that bring you joy and fulfillment.

One of the great benefits of strategic retirement savings is the freedom it provides. Imagine finally having the time to travel to exotic destinations you've always dreamed of, immersing yourself in different cultures, and creating priceless memories with loved ones. Your well-planned retirement savings can fund these travel adventures and ensure you have the financial stability to make the most of these experiences.

Additionally, retirement is the perfect time to indulge in hobbies and passions that may have taken a backseat during your working years. Whether it's picking up a paintbrush, joining a book club, or mastering a new sport, the financial security achieved through retirement planning allows you to invest in yourself and explore your interests fully.

The peace of mind that comes with financial security cannot be underestimated. With a carefully planned retirement strategy and smart investing decisions, you can embrace your golden years with confidence, knowing that you have the resources to navigate any unexpected expenses that may arise. This financial stability allows you to enjoy retirement without constantly worrying about money, giving you the freedom to focus on the things that truly matter.

Chapter **37**

The Joy of Simplicity: Decluttering life for better focus and peace

The Pleasure of Being Simple: Life Decluttering for Better Focus and Peace.

Welcome to our chapter on how to declutter your life at 50 for better focus and peace. In a fast moving world like today's, it is easy to feel overwhelmed by information flow, tasks, possessions etc. Minimizing things in an organized way can work wonders in your everyday life. This article will explore the advantages of decluttering; practical steps as well as strategies for organization; mindfulness exercises as well as stress relief techniques for a simplified home and mind.

It is possible to regain control of your life and enhance mental clarity during middle age if you are able to declutter both your physical and mental spaces. Through embracing minimalism, one can avoid all distractors that are not important at all but focus only on important issues.Follow us up in order to know what decluttering can do and how peacefulness arises from leading simplified lives free from clutter.

Minimalism: The answer To Clear Thinking At Midlife.

At fifty years old, there are often many responsibilities, obligations and possessions which crowd life. Yet through adopting a minimalist lifestyle we may find our path towards clear thinking when amidst chaos.

Minimalism does not just entail eliminating clutter from the physical space; rather it teaches a mindset that promotes intentional living and making deliberate choices. By reducing our belongings as well as commitments, we create room in our minds where we live more clearly with tranquility.

What would it be like if you walked into a house without stuff unnecessarily interfering with your thoughts? In such a minimalist environment people experience much peace since they have fewer thoughts hence being able think clearly focusing on right now.

Furthermore, starting minimalism at midlife provides a new sense of destination or purpose. We let go what no longer serves us – be it material possessions, toxic relationships or even self-imposed expectations. As we clean up our life of things that do not matter a lot for us, we get chances of discovering ourselves more.

Minimalism is an incredible solution for baldness and peace at that age. It helps to take away all our materialistic desires and instead focus on the things that make life meaningful. Our lives become simpler when we are free from excesses because it allows us to put our health as well as happiness first.

Throughout this article, minimalism principles will be discussed along with practical tips for decluttering both physical spaces and mental landscapes. There is no doubt that mental clarity can be achieved through minimalism which in turn makes it possible to achieve inner peace.

Practical Tips for Decluttering Your Home and Mind

Decluttering your life at 50 can lead to better focus and peace, allowing you to simplify your home and mind. By efficiently decluttering as well as organizing physical space, also removing clutter from the mind, one creates an atmosphere that promotes clear thoughts while minimizing strain.

Here are some practical tips to help you get started:

1. Start from smaller areas gradually

Begin by taking out unnecessary items from one area only: such as a drawer or closet or even just a particular room. Divide up the task into smaller, manageable parts so that it does not appear too daunting. Keep decluttering everyday just a little bit or set aside specific times for decluttering.

2. Sorting and Categorizing

While decluttering sort your items into categories such as keep, donate, sell or toss; this will allow you to make decisions more quickly and stop things from piling up as well. In addition, sorting also ensures that you know what you actually own as well as what is essential for personal use.

3. Purge with intention

Be aware of the things that you choose to retain; think through the purpose and value of each item and let go of those items that no longer serve any purpose in your life. These include clothes that no longer fit or sentimental items occupying unnecessary space. Keep only the ones that give happiness and add meaning to life.

4. Make an organizing system

After clearing out, arrange a plan for putting away your stuff in order. Look for storage solutions which are appropriate for your needs like containers with labels, shelves or bins. This will help assign specific places for different items so it becomes easy to find them when necessary and maintain a clutter-free environment.

5. Declutter your digital life

Digital clutter can be just as overwhelming as physical clutter. For instance, one can put their digital files in order by deleting unwanted email messages from their inbox and uncluttering their social networks accounts while doing away with all mailing lists.Limit involvement on the internet by unsubscribing from all mailing lists made and removing contents from unnecessary online portals.Since virtual life would become less distracting allowing focus on other matters.

6. Practice mindfulness

A mind full of chaos can disturb concentration continued by anxiety without due cause.Mindful routines like meditation or deep breathing exercises should be included in everyday activities.These practices enable silencing the inner self while maintaining mental clarity; because peace is possible even amidst great confusion.

By following these practical tips you'll declutter not only your home but also get rid of all unwanted thoughts thus creating an ambient suitable for concentration, tranquility, and overall soundness at fifty. Therefore, we are going to cover the power of organized living and talk about how to create systems that will be able to maintain a clutter-free lifestyle for many years.

The Power of Organized Living: Creating Systems for Success.

For better focus and peace at 50, this is the secret you need to know when it comes to decluttering life in an effective way. Midlife organization has the potential to profoundly affect your overall well-being as well as provide mental clarity.

One area to begin with includes organizing one's belongings. In order to keep things neat and easily found, clear them up into categories and use these bins, shelves or baskets. Consider implementing storage solutions, such as bins, baskets, or shelves, to keep items neat and easily accessible.

In the same vein, having an organized schedule can help you prioritize tasks and manage your time more effectively. You may prefer using a digital or paper planner for keeping track of appointments, deadlines and what needs done today; by doing so stress is reduced and one stays focused on what counts.

Digital decluttering is also vital part of living an organized life. Just like physical spaces our digital environment can quickly become overwhelmed with clutter which leads to overwhelm and distraction. Take some time out of your busy schedule in order to declutter your digital files by deleting unnecessary emails too while you are at it organize your online activities.Enhance More Storage Space While Increasing Focus.

This text argues that a structured approach is crucial in editing content especially if there are several essays that require proofreading before they can be submitted.

Power of an organized life entails formation of systems that work for you. Look for strategies that are in sync with your specific preferences and needs. These systems can be color coding, labeling or even making a visible place for everything thus helping to declutter our lives, help us concentrate on more important things boosting our feeling of inner peace at the age of fifty.

Finding Joy in Minimalism: Letting Go of Sentimental Items.

Decluttering life for better focus and peace at 50 is not just about organizing physical spaces and digital files. It also encompasses facing the emotional attachments we have towards our belongings specifically sentimental objects. Disposing these items are arduous but liberating experiences that bring about freedom and joyous moments that had never existed before.

When dealing with sentimental items, it is essential to approach decluttering mindfully and purposefully. Take some time reflecting upon each item's emotional significance and whether it gels well with your dream lifestyle. Remember, the memories tied to such things are more valuable than their physicality.

As you make decision s on what to keep or let go consider these questions:

1. Does it bring me joy?

According to Marie Kondo, a famous minimalist and clutter consultant one should evaluate possessions by asking if they spark joy in them? If a sentimental item no longer brings you joy or serves any purpose in your life anymore then it is high time you gave it up so as to allow new experiences memories among other things take place

2. Can I preserve the memory in another way?

Think about whether there is another format through which one could keep its memory intact such as taking a picture for instance which would create a digital album or even writing down the emotions, feelings as well as relevance attached to this particular object inside your diary instead of keeping it physically.

3. Will someone else benefit from it?

Another way of gaining happiness while letting go of any sentimental item is by giving them to somebody who will love and treasure them. Some of these items may be gifted or donated to friends, family members and even charitable organizations. When you know that your coveted objects will still be adored and appreciated, you experience a sense of satisfaction and pleasure.

Remember that decluttering is an individual journey with different attachment levels to sentimental objects by everyone. Give yourself time as well as appreciate the progress attained along the way. By eliminating the excess baggage of emotional clutter, there is much more space left for matters that really count thereby enabling better focus, tranquility and a rewarding minimalist life at 50.

Creating a Tranquil Space: Decluttering for Relaxation and Peace.

Decluttering your living space is not just about tidying up; it's about creating a peaceful environment that promotes relaxation and peace in mind. Simplifying your home as well as your mind can help you think more clearly while improving your concentration at 50.

When decluttering for relaxation and peace, it's important to consider the overall atmosphere you want to create. Begin by removing unnecessary items that cause visual clutter. Keep surfaces clear and organize belongings in designated spaces to maintain a sense of order and simplicity.

When you finish decluttering the physical aspect of your home, consider tidying up the areas that are related to relaxation such as bedroom and living room. By incorporating cool colors, soft fabrics and natural materials like potted plants, you can make your space warm and inviting. In order to maintain tidy rooms in these spaces, invest in storage solutions such as baskets or shelves.

Another important thing is digital cluttering. Simplify all your files and clear out your email inbox for a clean slate. This makes it easier to focus on things that really matter.

Decluttering physical space as well as electronic clutter affords an atmosphere of calmness which helps improve mental health. Embrace the value of clearing clutter from your house and mind and experience it's feelings of clarity in thoughts plus peace.

Digital Decluttering: How to Uncomplicate Your Virtual Existence?

Modernity has seen our physical spaces being crowded with many things as well as our digital lives becoming so overwhelming. Many times we fail to be attentive because we are always being notified by messages or emails or seeing those huge numbers in our computer files. Thus, digital decluttering plays a significant role in decluttering life at 50 for more focus on important issues and inner peace.

Digital Decluttering entails organizing and simplifying one's virtual world thus resulting into a more efficient online environment characterized by peace.It involves applying organization strategies towards your digital files, emails as well as internet browsing habits hence enabling you to simplify both home/life hence enhancing concentration levels while lowering stress

Cleaning Digital Files

Organizing and cleaning digital files is an essential part of any digital declutter program. Establish a system where it is easy to find your documents when need arises? You will save time looking for these files if they are arranged systematically in their respective folders; also eliminate anything that should have been deleted earlier.

Additionally, cloud storage services including Google Drive or Dropbox could also be used to guarantee secure storage of documents. This helps declutter your computer as well as give you a chance to find any document at any time.

Making Emails More Efficient

Emails can accumulate quickly and constantly, leading to unwanted anxiety. Streamlining your email inbox is therefore an important step in digital decluttering. Start by unsubscribing from subscriptions or promotional materials that no longer interest you.

Then create folders or labels for classifying your e-mails and organize them according to their level of importance. Allocate some time daily for going through and replying messages making sure that your inbox remains organized free from any form of clutter.

Managing Online Activities

A world full of social media platforms, online stores and various digital distractions requires one to be mindful about their own online activities so as to remain focused and at peace with oneself.Identify which online activities contribute positively to your life and which ones you can do without.

Set up limits on the amount of time spent scrolling through social media sites either by using specific apps that track screen time or setting boundaries in place. Start unfollowing such accounts that don't add value or suit your interests for a more mindful digital experience devoid of clutters.

This way, you can simplify your virtual environment and make it neat so that it supports concentration and mental comfort.It is worth remembering that strategies on how to arrange digital files, emails and online activities are necessary for turning our home into a less complicated mind space where we can live happier lives.

Mindfulness Practices for Clarity + Focus

In this section, we will explore mindfulness practices as effective techniques of enhancing focus and attaining peace at midlife. Mindfulness is about focusing on the present moment thereby developing clarity and calmness in our minds despite the chaos that surrounds us.

One powerful mindfulness practice is meditation. Spending just a few minutes each day sitting quietly can do wonders for our mental sharpness and stress levels. This way, we can train our minds to be less scattered and more in tune with ourselves by concentrating on our breath or any other focus object.

Another useful exercise is deep breathing. By simply inhaling and exhaling deeply, we can trigger off the relaxation response of our bodies thus enabling it to calm down and become tranquil.

Mindfulness also includes" being here now".

That means consciously observing what happens to us daily by fully immersing ourselves in the sights, sounds, touch of things etc., thereby being mindful or "present". We can improve concentration through eating mindfully, walking meditatively, or doing anything else where attention is fully focused within itself.

Through practicing mindfulness in day-to-day life not only physically but also mentally declutters your mind. Mindfulness provides a tangible solution for coping with stress while gaining mental clarity and peace during the hustle of midlife.

Simplifying Your Life: Maintaining Minimalist Lifestyles for Long-Term Success

In starting off a journey to declutter your life for better focus and peace at 50 however, sustaining simplified lifestyles becomes an important aspect that must be considered carefully. The process of decluttering may lead to enormous change yet keeping an organized and minimalist existence is something that demands continuous effort over time. Here are some strategies that will ensure long-term success:

Routine Maintenance

Having regular maintenance routine ensures you live without clutter. Avail dedicated moments every week when you are supposed to clear up everything returning them into their respective places. This prevents accumulation of clatter ensuring there is order and serenity within your surroundings.

Habit Building

Developing new habits is crucial for maintaining a simplified life. Identify habits that align with your minimalist values, such as regularly purging unnecessary items, resisting the urge to make impulsive purchases, and practicing mindful consumption. Consistently practicing these habits will reinforce your commitment to a clutter-free lifestyle.

Ongoing Evaluation and Reevaluation

Life keeps changing along with our preferences and demands. Regularly evaluate your belongings, commitments, and activities to ensure they still align with your minimalist goals. Be willing to let go of things that no longer serve a purpose or bring you joy. Such persistent evaluation will help you maintain focus on what matters most and stop litter from coming back into existence.

If these strategies are implemented, you can continue to enjoy all the benefits of living a simplified life such as increased concentration, peace of mind and general well-being. Decluttering is not an event but a continuous process that creates room for thoughts to thrive at 50 years old onwards.

The Benefits of Decluttering: Enhanced Focus and Peace at 50

There are profound rewards that can be unlocked by decluttering life at 50, enabling an increased focus and inner peace amidst midlife pressures. Simplifying our surroundings and decluttering our minds enable us to attain mental clarity and minimize stress.

Living a minimalist, well organized life enables one to discard all unnecessary distractions and make room for what is really important. As we declutter our lives of extra possessions, commitments and digital noise, we realize that our minds become clearer more focused.

Alternatively, this process helps in reducing anxiety which in turn makes us healthier. Such environments encourage relaxation as opposed to cluttered lifestyles that breed chaos and overwhelming feelings. This eventually assists us to organize ourselves better while dealing with mid-life's daily issues like making choices or having a sense of calm when doing something.

Chapter **38**

Intergenerational Mentorship: Learning from the young and guiding the old

Welcome to our chapter on intergenerational mentorship, a program that brings together individuals from different generations to learn from each other's experiences and perspectives. In this article, we will explore how mentorship programs can bridge the age gaps and create a platform for meaningful cross-generational mentorship.

Mentorship is a powerful tool that benefits both the mentor and the mentee. By participating in a mentorship program, individuals gain valuable insights, guidance, and knowledge that can shape their personal and professional growth. Intergenerational mentorship takes this concept a step further by leveraging the unique strengths and perspectives of different generations.

Whether you are a young professional seeking guidance from an experienced mentor or an older individual looking to learn from the fresh perspectives of the younger generation, intergenerational mentorship offers a wealth of opportunities. Through these programs, individuals establish connections, build networks, and develop valuable skills that can shape their future success.

Throughout this article, we will delve into the importance of intergenerational mentorship, provide practical tips for establishing successful mentorship programs, and explore how cross-generational collaboration can lead to innovative solutions. We will also showcase real-life examples of successful mentorship initiatives and discuss the future of intergenerational mentorship.

Join us as we unlock the power of intergenerational mentorship and discover how learning from the young and guiding the old can create a transformative and inclusive environment for personal and professional development.

The Importance of Intergenerational Mentorship

In today's ever-changing society, intergenerational mentorship plays a crucial role in fostering personal and professional growth. It offers a platform for individuals of different generations to come together, learn from each other, and share unique perspectives and skills.

Mentorship benefits both mentors and mentees. For younger individuals, mentorship opportunities provide guidance and support from experienced professionals who have navigated similar paths. Mentors can offer insights, advice, and opportunities to expand their networks.

On the other hand, older generations can also benefit greatly from being mentors. By engaging in mentorship programs, they have the chance to stay connected with current trends and innovative ideas brought forth by younger individuals. They can gain fresh perspectives, keep their knowledge up to date, and contribute to the personal and professional development of their mentees.

Intergenerational mentorship not only bridges the age gaps but also creates a sense of camaraderie and connectivity among individuals from different generations. It helps to break down stereotypes and facilitate mutual understanding and respect.

By embracing mentorship opportunities, individuals can unlock their full potential, acquire new skills, and build meaningful relationships that can last a lifetime. Whether you are a young professional seeking guidance or an experienced individual wishing to make a difference, intergenerational mentorship can open doors to personal and professional growth.

Building a Successful Mentorship Program

Creating an effective intergenerational mentorship program requires a thoughtful approach and a clear understanding of the skills and best practices involved. Mentors play a crucial role in guiding and supporting their mentees, and by practicing mentorship skills and applying best practices, they can ensure a successful mentoring relationship.

Key Mentorship Skills

To be an effective mentor, certain skills are essential. Active listening is the foundation of successful mentorship, as it allows mentors to understand their mentees' needs and goals. Empathy and patience enable mentors to provide the necessary support and guidance in a compassionate manner. Good communication skills help facilitate open and honest conversations, while problem-solving and decision-making abilities allow mentors to guide mentees through challenges.

Furthermore, mentors should possess a growth mindset, embracing continuous learning and development. They should be able to provide constructive feedback and encouragement, and inspire their mentees to explore new opportunities and expand their horizons. By modeling resilience and adaptability, mentors can empower mentees to overcome obstacles and thrive.

Best Practices for a Successful Mentoring Relationship

Establishing a strong foundation is crucial for a successful mentoring relationship. Setting clear expectations and goals at the outset ensures that both mentors and mentees are on the same page. Regular communication is essential, whether through in-person meetings, phone calls, or video conferences.

Mentors should create a safe and inclusive space where mentees feel comfortable sharing their thoughts, fears, and aspirations. By fostering trust and confidentiality, mentors can provide a nurturing environment for mentees to grow and learn.

Flexibility is also key in mentorship. Each mentee is unique, and mentors must adapt their approach to meet individual needs. Recognizing and respecting mentees' diverse backgrounds, experiences, and perspectives is essential for cultivating a meaningful mentorship relationship.

Providing guidance and sharing knowledge is important, but mentors should also encourage mentees to take ownership of their growth. Empowering mentees to set their own goals and develop their skills promotes accountability and self-confidence.

Furthermore, mentors should actively seek feedback from their mentees. This allows mentors to refine their approach and ensure that the mentoring relationship is beneficial to both parties. Regular evaluations and reflections enable mentors to continuously improve and provide the best support possible.

By honing their mentorship skills and following the best practices outlined above, mentors can build successful and impactful intergenerational mentorship programs. These programs not only provide valuable learning opportunities but also foster meaningful connections and personal growth for both mentors and mentees.

Creating Meaningful Connections

Building connections between individuals from different generations is a crucial aspect of intergenerational mentorship. When mentees and mentors come together, they have the opportunity to forge meaningful relationships that can foster personal and professional growth.

Intergenerational networking plays a vital role in this process. By connecting with individuals from different generations, mentees gain access to diverse perspectives, experiences, and knowledge. This exposure can broaden their horizons and help them develop a well-rounded understanding of the world.

Furthermore, intergenerational networking allows mentees to tap into the wisdom and guidance of seasoned mentors. Older generations bring a wealth of experience and insights that can help mentees navigate challenges, make informed decisions, and accelerate their personal and professional development.

On the other side, mentors also benefit from intergenerational networking. By engaging with younger generations, mentors gain fresh perspectives, innovative ideas, and a deeper understanding of current trends and technologies. This cross-generational exchange of knowledge and skills can invigorate mentors, keeping them connected to the ever-evolving world.

Intergenerational networking not only benefits individuals but also contributes to the overall strength of communities and organizations. By fostering diverse connections, these networks create a supportive environment where learning, collaboration, and mutual understanding thrive.

As we strive to create a society that values intergenerational mentorship, cultivating meaningful connections through intergenerational networking is crucial. It enables us to bridge the gaps between generations, embrace different perspectives, and collectively work toward a brighter and more inclusive future.

Nurturing Cross-Generational Collaboration

Within a mentorship program, cross-generational collaboration plays a crucial role in fostering innovation, shared knowledge, and a strong sense of community. By bringing together individuals from different generations, mentorship programs create unique opportunities for mentor and mentee to collaborate and learn from each other.

Through cross-generational collaboration, knowledge, skills, and experiences from various generations can be shared, allowing for the development of innovative solutions. The older generation can provide wisdom and guidance based on their years of experience, while the younger generation can offer fresh perspectives and technological know-how.

Moreover, cross-generational collaboration within a mentorship program encourages the exchange of ideas and fosters a greater sense of understanding and respect between generations. As individuals from different age groups work together towards a common goal, stereotypes and biases can be challenged and overcome, leading to stronger relationships and a more inclusive and cohesive environment.

Furthermore, cross-generational collaboration can extend beyond the mentor and mentee relationship, creating a ripple effect throughout the entire community or organization. As mentorship programs nurture a culture of collaboration, the benefits of cross-generational learning and cooperation can permeate various aspects of life, enhancing personal and professional growth for all involved.

To fully embrace the potential of cross-generational collaboration, it is vital for mentorship programs to create a supportive and inclusive environment. This can be achieved by fostering open communication, encouraging active participation from all generations, and providing opportunities for mentorship pairs to engage in collaborative projects and initiatives.

By nurturing cross-generational collaboration within mentorship programs, we can tap into the collective wisdom, experience, and energy of multiple generations, driving innovation, fostering a sense of community, and ensuring a brighter future for all.

Overcoming Generational Stereotypes

Intergenerational mentorship programs have the power to challenge and overcome common generational stereotypes. By bringing together individuals from different age groups, these programs create opportunities for mutual understanding, breaking down barriers, and fostering respect.

In a society where generational gaps can often lead to misunderstandings and biases, mentorship programs provide a platform for meaningful connections. Through mentorship, both the mentor and mentee have the chance to share their unique perspectives and experiences, debunking stereotypes that may have been ingrained in their minds.

By actively engaging in cross-generational mentorship, participants can challenge preconceived notions and develop a deeper understanding of one another. This fosters a sense of empathy and appreciation for the diverse range of experiences and talents that each generation brings to the table.

It is essential for mentorship programs to encourage open dialogue and create an inclusive environment where different generations can communicate and learn from each other. By embracing intergenerational mentorship, we can overcome generational stereotypes, build stronger relationships, and collectively work towards a more harmonious and cohesive society.

The Role of Reverse Mentorship

Reverse mentorship is a powerful concept within intergenerational mentorship programs that allows older individuals to learn from their younger counterparts. It is a mutually beneficial approach that fosters valuable insights and growth for both parties involved.

In traditional mentorship programs, the focus is often on the older generation imparting their wisdom and experience to the younger generation. However, reverse mentorship recognizes that knowledge and expertise are not limited to age - younger individuals can bring fresh perspectives, technological know-how, and innovative ideas to the table.

By engaging in reverse mentorship, older individuals have the opportunity to expand their horizons, stay relevant in an ever-changing world, and gain a deeper understanding of the younger generation's needs, desires, and aspirations. At the same time, younger individuals can develop leadership skills, enhance their communication abilities, and learn from the wisdom and life experiences of their older mentors.

This approach of cross-generational mentorship exchanges not only knowledge but also facilitates the building of meaningful relationships. It breaks down generational stereotypes and fosters mutual respect and understanding between different age groups. Through reverse mentorship, a sense of camaraderie and collaboration is nurtured, leading to greater personal and professional growth for all involved.

Reverse mentorship offers a unique opportunity to leverage the strengths and perspectives of different generations, creating a dynamic and inclusive environment. It promotes the sharing of ideas, encourages innovation, and enhances the overall success of mentorship programs.

Whether young or old, in reverse mentorship, each individual has something valuable to offer. By embracing this approach, mentorship programs can create a platform where diverse talents and experiences are celebrated, and both the mentors and mentees thrive.

Leveraging Technological Advancements

In today's digital age, technological advancements have revolutionized various aspects of our lives, including mentorship programs. These advancements provide a unique opportunity to enhance intergenerational mentorship and foster cross-generational collaboration.

Embracing digital tools and platforms within mentorship programs can facilitate seamless communication and knowledge sharing between mentors and mentees. Online platforms and video conferencing tools enable mentorship relationships to thrive even when participants are geographically distant. This accessibility opens doors for individuals to connect with mentors of different generations, creating a diverse and enriching mentorship experience.

Moreover, technology offers mentorship programs the ability to track progress, set goals, and provide feedback in real-time. Mentees can access valuable resources, such as online courses, webinars, and digital libraries, enhancing their learning journey and expanding their horizons.

By leveraging technological advancements, mentorship programs can overcome the limitations of physical proximity, time constraints, and generational gaps. It allows for a flexible and inclusive environment where individuals of all ages can engage in cross-generational mentorship, exchange valuable insights, and foster growth on both personal and professional levels.

Case Studies: Successful Intergenerational Mentorship Programs

In this section, we will showcase real-life examples of successful intergenerational mentorship programs that have had a remarkable impact on individuals and communities. These case studies demonstrate the power and effectiveness of mentorship in fostering personal and professional growth.

Case Study 1: XYZ Corporation Mentorship Program

XYZ Corporation implemented a mentorship program that paired experienced employees with younger professionals to foster knowledge sharing and skill development. Through this program, mentees gained valuable insights from their mentors' years of experience, while the mentors themselves gained fresh perspectives and innovative ideas from their mentees. As a result, the program not only enhanced individual career trajectories but also contributed to the overall growth and success of the organization.

Case Study 2: ABC Nonprofit Mentorship Initiative

The ABC Nonprofit organization established a mentorship initiative aimed at bridging the gap between older and younger volunteers. The program paired seasoned volunteers with newcomers to help them navigate their roles and develop the skills needed to make a meaningful impact. The intergenerational mentorship relationships formed in this initiative fostered a sense of community and collaboration, resulting in improved volunteer retention and increased collective impact.

Case Study 3: University XYZ Mentorship Program

University XYZ implemented a mentorship program that connected alumni with current students. Through this program, students were able to receive guidance, career advice, and support from graduates who had successfully navigated the transition from academia to the professional world. The mentorship program significantly enhanced students' career readiness, leading to increased job placements and higher satisfaction rates among graduates.

These case studies exemplify the profound positive impact that intergenerational mentorship programs can have on individuals and communities. They highlight the effectiveness of mentorship in cultivating personal and professional growth, fostering meaningful connections, and creating a collaborative environment for learning and development.

The Future of Intergenerational Mentorship

As intergenerational mentorship programs continue to gain recognition and popularity, it is essential to explore the potential and future opportunities they present. These programs have the power to transform the way generations connect and learn from one another, creating a dynamic and inclusive environment for mentorship.

In the coming years, intergenerational mentorship programs will evolve to meet the changing needs and dynamics of different generations. They will become more diverse and adaptable, catering to a wide range of personal and professional aspirations. Mentorship opportunities will extend beyond traditional settings into online platforms, allowing for greater accessibility and convenience.

The future of intergenerational mentorship looks promising, with an increased focus on cross-generational collaboration. As mentorship programs continue to bridge the age gap, they will foster innovation and creativity by bringing together diverse perspectives and ideas. The exchange of knowledge, skills, and experiences between mentors and mentees will not only benefit individuals but also contribute to the growth and development of communities.

Embracing Technology for Enhanced Mentorship

Technological advancements will play a crucial role in shaping the future of intergenerational mentorship. Online platforms and digital tools will facilitate seamless communication between mentors and mentees, transcending geographical barriers. Virtual mentorship will provide flexibility and convenience, allowing individuals to connect and learn from anywhere in the world.

Emerging technologies, such as artificial intelligence and virtual reality, will enhance mentorship experiences by providing immersive and personalized learning opportunities. Mentorship programs will leverage these technologies to create interactive and engaging environments, further enriching the mentorship journey.

The future of intergenerational mentorship holds immense potential for personal growth, professional development, and the establishment of lifelong connections. By embracing innovation and adapting to the evolving needs of different generations, these programs will continue to empower individuals to reach their full potential.

Cultivating a Culture of Mentorship

In today's fast-paced world, mentorship has become a crucial element in fostering personal and professional growth. Cultivating a culture of mentorship within organizations and communities is essential to harnessing the full potential of mentorship programs and creating transformative mentorship opportunities.

Integrating mentorship into various aspects of life can open doors to continuous learning and growth. In organizations, mentorship programs can be implemented to nurture talent, enhance leadership skills, and improve employee satisfaction. By pairing experienced mentors with mentees seeking guidance, organizations can create a supportive environment that encourages knowledge sharing, skill development, and career advancement.

Outside of the workplace, mentorship opportunities can be leveraged to address societal challenges and foster intergenerational connections. Mentorship programs that bring together individuals from different age groups provide a platform for exchanging insights, experiences, and perspectives. Such cross-generational collaboration not only breaks down barriers but also fuels innovation and strengthens communities.

Benefits of a Mentorship Culture

A culture of mentorship offers several advantages. It fosters a sense of belonging and engagement among participants, as mentees feel supported and guided, while mentors experience the fulfillment of making a positive impact on others. Mentorship programs also contribute to the retention and professional development of employees, resulting in higher productivity and organizational success.

Moreover, creating a mentorship culture can help individuals develop critical skills, broaden their networks, and gain valuable insights from different generations. It promotes a learning mindset and encourages individuals to continuously seek growth opportunities, nurturing a culture of lifelong learning.

Implementing a Mentorship Culture

To cultivate a culture of mentorship, organizations and communities can take several steps. First, it is vital to establish mentorship programs that match mentors and mentees based on their skills, goals, and compatibility. Clear communication channels and guidelines should be provided to ensure effective and meaningful mentorship relationships.

Additionally, organizations can encourage mentorship by recognizing the contributions of mentors and providing incentives for participation. Offering mentorship training and development opportunities equips mentors with the necessary skills to guide and support mentees effectively.

Organizational leaders play a pivotal role in fostering a mentorship culture by leading by example. By actively participating in mentorship programs themselves, leaders demonstrate the importance of mentorship and create an environment that encourages others to engage in mentorship activities.

Building a Mentorship Legacy

Mentorship is not a one-time event but a lifelong journey. Embracing a culture of mentorship ensures that mentorship opportunities continue to evolve and benefit future generations. By passing on knowledge, wisdom, and experiences, mentors create a lasting impact that extends far beyond their individual interactions.

As mentorship becomes more deeply ingrained in organizations and communities, it becomes a part of their DNA. It shapes the way people learn, grow, and collaborate, driving innovation, and fostering a sense of unity and shared purpose.

Building a culture of mentorship is not only about individual development but also about creating a collective commitment to supporting and empowering others. By embracing mentorship opportunities, organizations and communities can pave the way for a brighter and more prosperous future.

Conclusion

The intergenerational mentorship program has proven to be an invaluable tool for bridging the age gaps and fostering unique insights through cross-generational collaboration. Throughout this article, we have explored the importance of mentorship skills and best practices in creating successful mentorship programs. By bringing together individuals from different generations, mentorship programs create opportunities for personal and professional growth.

A successful mentorship program relies on effective communication, mutual respect, and a willingness to learn from one another. Mentors play a vital role in guiding and inspiring mentees, while mentees bring fresh perspectives and ideas that can challenge traditional thinking. This dynamic exchange of knowledge and experience leads to mentorship success and benefits all parties involved.

By nurturing cross-generational collaboration and creating meaningful connections, mentorship programs foster a sense of community and belonging. They allow individuals to leverage their technological advancements to enhance communication and knowledge sharing. Moreover, these programs challenge generational stereotypes and promote mutual understanding, ultimately cultivating a culture of mentorship that extends beyond organizations and communities.

In conclusion, intergenerational mentorship programs offer a wealth of opportunities for personal and professional development. The mentorship skills and best practices discussed in this article provide a solid foundation for establishing successful programs. As we look towards the future, the potential for growth and innovation through intergenerational mentorship is vast. By embracing the power of mentorship, we can bridge the age gaps and unlock the full potential of individuals across generations.

Chapter 39

Fifty and Fearless: Overcoming self-doubt and embracing challenges

Welcome to this empowering journey that will make you jump out of your skin. This is where we shall expose the power that lies in defeating self-doubt, overcoming challenges and inspiring women who are fifty years old or more. It doesn't matter how late you think it may be for personal growth when there are countless opportunities ahead.

Women at 50 often times struggle with self- doubt, questioning their capabilities, new daunting tasks among others. But please note that you are not alone whatsoever. Actually, this is a crucial point in your life from which you can reclaim your confidence, break free from limitation and unleash potentials.

Our mission is to direct you through the process of conquering self-doubt and embracing challenges with courage and determination. We will provide helpful tips on how to build confidence levels by providing practical insights, encouraging strategies and real life examples with clear set goals that can help develop our minds towards growth.

Step into Your True Self: Fifty is Fearless

This fearless journey for personal development empowers women who are 50 years old to become themselves; dare to face problems they meet in their lives every day seeking fulfillment. Are you bold enough to embrace fearlessness at fifty? Let's overcome self-doubt together.

Power of Self-Doubt

Self-doubt can hold us back from realizing our full potential and taking up new challenges in life. It creeps into our thoughts creating barriers that hinder our personal development as well as shattering our confidence too. However what causes it? How does one learn how to deal with it?

The reasons behind self-doubt vary greatly from past experiences plus negative internal dialogue up until external sources including societies' expectations among others (Restarick et al., 2013). One can start doubting himself/herself due to things like fear of failure or lack of self-belief or due to constant comparisons with others. The first step in dealing with self-doubt is understanding what causes it.

Overcoming self-doubt requires the development of strategies that enhance our confidence and resilience. Negative thoughts can be challenged through replacing them with positive affirmations for example. When we reframe our self-talk, focusing on strengths and accomplishments, we gradually create a more positive mindset.

Another powerful method is stepping outside our comfort zones and embracing new fearsome challenges. By so doing, we are able to discover our real abilities and strength as well. Pushing ourselves beyond the barriers of doubt enables us to realize how confident we can get as well as why we do not know the true potential within ourselves unless put into action.

Building a network of support around ourselves also helps us overcome self-doubt (Bettinger & Baker, 2011). We can seek encouragement or advice from family members, close friends or even mentors who will give us ultimate reason for pushing out of your personal doubt towards facing new chances.

" To overcome the journey of doubting oneself requires persistence and self-reflection. It means finding our value while recognizing fearfulness then working consistently to see that we build up trust over time." Faces in every direction: Overcoming Self-Doubt

Embracing Challenges as Opportunities

At fifty, life is full of possibilities and it's time to embrace challenges with a fearless spirit. Embracing challenges opens the door to personal growth and paves the way for new experiences and opportunities It might be scary to step out of your comfort zone and take on challenges at this stage, but the rewards are immense. It is an opportunity to push the limits you set for yourself, discover latent talents, and learn more about who you are.

So how can you embrace challenges and embrace personal growth? Below are some practical tips:

1. Set objectives:

Setting aims allows one to move in a certain direction; it also helps focus oneself. Thus, decide what you want to achieve by breaking it down into smaller manageable bits which will enable you maintain motivation and remain focused while attempting new things.

2. Develop a growth mindset:

A growth mindset means believing that one can always learn better or improve. Hence, see challenges as opportunities to acquire fresh skills and widen your understanding. When faced with failure, see it as a chance for personal growth.

3. Stretch beyond your own limits:

Do not fear trying out new things or venturing into uncharted territories. Take risks that have been carefully thought through and do things that scare you most. This will help broaden your perspective and realize your true potential.

4. Seek assistance:

Therefore, make friends with people who can support you whenever difficulty arises; connect with family members who understand what's going on in your life; keep seeking advice from those who have overcome similar obstacles; these people will give moral strength through their wisdoms thus enhancing self-confidence while maintaining motivation.

Embracing Challenges: Personal Growth at Fifty

Stepping outside of comfort zones and without any fear indulging in new experiences is an opportunity for endless possibilities awaiting discovery.

Building Confidence at Fifty

Many women find confidence building as an irresistible endeavor once they reach fifty years old; empowering them involves boosting their self-esteem levels so that they come to believe in themselves more than ever before during this time of their lives. Luckily there are many techniques as well as exercises aimed at boosting confidence levels hence enabling individuals deal away with self-doubt.

Positive Self-Talk offers a great way of boosting confidence. Individuals can replace negative thoughts with affirmative ones to rewire their thinking and become more confident. Besides, setting goals that are achievable and moving towards them always gives one an impression of having achieved something important thus boosting the self-confidence.

Another useful tool for building confidence includes embracing personal strengths and celebrating achievements. Accepting and appreciating one's special talents and skills creates self-esteem. Moreover, having encouragement from close individuals or joining empowering groups serves as a basis for supportive networks.

Building confidence is a process requiring patience and compassion for oneself. Therefore, confidence building involves undertaking activities that give oneself joy; stepping out of your comfort zones while taking care of yourself.

Hence women at fifty can overcome self-doubt, embrace their full potential by incorporating these confidence-building practices into their lives every day. They will be able to face life challenges with grace and resilience thus experiencing growth in their character as well as fulfillment.

Overcoming Fear of Failure

In addition to self-doubt, fear of failure is another common stumbling block people face. For instance, it makes us unable to take on new challenges leading to stagnation in our personal development processes. However we can conquer this fear and beat back all doubts by recognizing every failure as an opportunity to learn better through reframing it in this manner.

It is by seeing failures as opportunities to learn that people can view failure in a positive way. Each setback or mistake offers valuable lessons and insights, which can enable growth and improvement. The acceptance of challenges becomes simpler when we recognize that failure is an essential part of the journey.

One approach to mitigating fear of failure is to concentrate on the process rather than the outcome. This shift in mindset will liberate us from striving for perfection and instead encourage us to value progress and efforts made. If we allow ourselves some room for personal development and learning, then embracing challenges becomes less intimidating.

Another useful technique would be to stay around individuals who have your back all of the time. Trusting mentors' advice or getting into groups with similar goals helps one get over any fears that may be holding them back. A strong support network lifts us up during times when we doubt ourselves and keeps us motivated on our quests towards self-realization.

Fearlessness is needed in order to overcome self-doubt and embrace challenges head on. Thus, redefining failure, focusing on the process, asking for help can definitely eliminate fear of failing consequently open one's potentiality fully therefore let's take these obstacles with open arms thus embark into personal growth fearless journey.

Building a Growth Mindset

This becomes a step towards empowering women at fifty years old through personal development which is very vital for women aged 50 years old who want to make themselves empowered at this age. In fact; being able to look forward more easily helps us accept that our talents are not fixed but can be developed with determination, effort and experience of setbacks which are seen as opportunities for growth improvements in life as reflected by this quote by Henry Ford "Whether you believe you can do this or not, you are right" means that it all depends what attitude we have about things happening around us.

Embracing challenges is an opportunity for continuous learning at fifty; hence involve change habitually and for the better. Therefore, instead of looking at setbacks as failures in life, a growth mindset perceives them as stepping stones for personal development. Every obstacle provides an opportunity to learn something new and acquire skills that are useful for building stronger resilience.

Consider these practical tips when cultivating a growth mindset:

1. Have a Learning Mindset:

Be curious and willing to learn from challenges. Focus on what can be learned from mistakes rather than how bad they were. Value ongoing learning over immediate success.

2. Challenge Negative Thoughts:

Replace negative thoughts about yourself with positive affirmations and constructive self-talks. View obstacles as temporary challenges that can be overcome by grit and determination.

3. Seek Opportunities for Growth:

Step out of your comfort zone and actively seek opportunities to expand your knowledge base or skill set. Pursue new interests or hobbies that align with personal goals and lead to growth.

4. Surround Yourself with Supportive People:

Find people who believe in you and encourage your progress. Look for mentors, coaches, or friends who share similar aspirations, provide support, and hold you accountable.

Consequently, women at fifty years old can get rid of self-doubt by fostering a growth mindset which will enable them face all sort of challenges fearlessly throughout their lives leading them into the path of discovering themselves completely.

Goal Setting

Achievement of goals is crucial in personal development as well as conquering oneself hence empowerment of females at age fifty centers on understanding the power behind setting goals to rise above self-doubts thus making major strides in their lives through this process according to the following quotation:

The process of goal setting starts with the identification of meaningful and attainable objectives. The goals for women at fifty should be made clear and specific so as to give them a sense of direction and purpose in life. These goals must be crafted to accommodate their likes, dislikes and personal dreams.

Once goals have been set it is important to create strategies on how to stay motivated and overcome obstacles along the way. This can help maintain momentum by breaking larger goals into smaller components that can be handled one at a time. By doing this, it will not only encourage, but it will also reinforce self-belief in oneself.

Staying motivated and overcoming obstacles

In most situations when pursuing self-development at the age of fifty, challenges are likely to appear thereby leading to self-doubt. It is important however to find ways that can keep you going strong even during these hard times. Such people like family members, friends or those similar minded ones forms a support system around someone hence helping them up.

Also required is fostering positivity in attitude and resilience. Reframing obstacles as stepping stones rather than setbacks keeps hope alive for these women above 50 years enabling them persevere through tough times because they know where they come from too well by now who they are today Remembering what has been achieved so far can also work as evidence of their potential.

Women aged fifty years old surpass their doubts by setting significant objectives, maintaining motivation throughout the journey, and overcoming hindrances. By embracing the importance of goal setting towards women over 50 have always wished for more than what was given to them thus redefining their limits which unlock their full potential for each one among them. The path towards empowerment and bravery start with step one taken upon achieving any aim stated out above.

Seeking Support & Accountability

Overcoming self-doubt may sound scary especially when facing challenges for women above 50 years old. Hence, seeking support network plays an imperative role in empowering women and promoting personal development. To overcome self-doubt and become the best version of yourself, you need to surround yourself with a positive people.

There are various avenues you can explore to find the support you need. Joining community groups or organizations that cater to women at fifty can provide a safe space to share experiences, learn from others, and gain valuable insights. These groups often offer mentorship opportunities that serve as a source of guidance and encouragement, allowing you to navigate your journey with confidence.

Alternatively, seeking professional guidance from coaches or therapists who specialize in personal growth and empowerment can provide personalized support tailored to your specific needs. These professionals can offer tools, strategies, and techniques to help you overcome self-doubt, set goals, and hold yourself accountable. With their expertise, you can gain clarity, resilience, and the resilience to face challenges head-on.

Remember it is not weakness rather than strength that makes one seek for support system as well as being accountable of what he/she does. Encouragement comes through when one surrounds oneself with positive people while getting professional guidance where applicable creates an atmosphere where one becomes courageous enough in accepting any challenge that comes his/her way without fear such levels of belief. Together we will celebrate happiness at fifty which comes through personal growth beyond this stage.

Embracing Fearlessness at Fifty

Throughout this article, we have examined the journey of becoming fearless at fifty. It is a journey that requires grappling with challenges, defeating your weak self and undergoing personal development. When one takes the risk of stepping outside their comfort zone, you open yourself to a whole world of infinite possibilities and prospects.

Overcoming challenges is another important part of this process. It means going forward despite fears and getting involved in other activities that will help person grow. By challenging them head-on, you will discover abilities and powers that were unknown to you before now. Do not have doubts and always remember that you can overcome anything.

Remember also that personal growth is an ever ongoing process. For each fear faced and challenge surmounted, it makes one bolder until at last he/she becomes fearless at fifty. Embracing fearlessness at the age of fifty does not imply reaching a destination; rather it is about progress made along the way as well as journey itself.

So, keep pushing on, embracing more challenges and growing further up. With every new experience, self-confidence transforms into resilience resulting in fearlessness with time. The path may not always be simple but the results are invaluable. This is what fearlessness looks like when one hits fifty years; it turns life around beyond recognition.

Chapter **40**

The Digital Leap: Staying relevant in an ever-evolving tech landscape

Technology is constantly evolving, and it can be challenging to keep up, especially for individuals over 50. However, staying relevant in the digital age is crucial for career growth and personal development. Adapting to technology changes after 50 requires acquiring and honing tech skills that are in demand. In this article, we will explore strategies and skills required to stay competitive in a rapidly changing tech landscape. Whether you're looking to advance in your current role or explore new opportunities, this guide will provide insights on how to navigate the ever-evolving tech industry.

From embracing the digital age and assessing your tech skills to identifying gaps, leveraging your experience, and overcoming ageism, we've got you covered. We'll also share tips for work-life integration and show you how to future-proof your tech skills to ensure long-term success.

So, if you're ready to embark on the digital leap and stay relevant in an ever-evolving tech landscape at 50 and beyond, let's dive in!

Embracing the Digital Age

As technology continues to advance at a rapid pace, it's important for individuals over 50 to stay current and embrace the digital age. By embracing the latest technology trends, older adults can navigate tech advancements and stay connected in today's digital world.

One of the key aspects of staying current in tech after 50 is keeping up with the technology trends that are relevant to older adults. From mobile devices to smart home technology, there are numerous innovative solutions that can enhance the lives of seniors. By staying informed about these trends, older adults can make informed choices about the technology they incorporate into their daily lives.

However, navigating tech advancements can sometimes be challenging, especially for those who may not be as familiar with new technology. That's why it's important for seniors to seek guidance and support. Whether it's through tech classes, online tutorials, or personalized assistance, there are resources available to help older adults navigate the digital world with confidence.

Additionally, staying connected is crucial for older adults in the digital age. From communicating with loved ones through video calls to accessing online resources for health and wellness, technology offers a wealth of opportunities for seniors to remain connected to their communities and lead fulfilling lives. Embracing the digital age doesn't mean completely transforming your lifestyle overnight. It's about finding the right balance that works for you, incorporating technology into your daily routine in a way that enhances your life and keeps you connected.

In the following sections, we will delve deeper into specific strategies and skills that can help individuals over 50 adapt and navigate the ever-changing tech landscape. We will provide practical tips, resources, and insights on how to stay current in tech, embrace technology trends for older adults, and confidently navigate tech advancements as a senior.

Assessing Your Tech Skills

As a person over 50, it is crucial to assess your current tech skills to ensure you stay current in the ever-changing tech landscape. Enhancing your tech literacy is essential for staying competitive and relevant in the digital age.

To assess your tech skills, start by identifying the areas where you feel less confident or knowledgeable. Are there specific technologies or tools that you struggle with? Are there concepts or terms that are unfamiliar to you? Taking note of these areas will help you prioritize your learning and development.

Once you have identified the areas for improvement, explore the abundance of resources available to enhance your tech skills. Online tutorials, webinars, and e-learning platforms offer convenient and accessible ways to learn and practice new technologies. Additionally, consider enrolling in courses or workshops specifically designed for older adults to ensure a comfortable learning environment.

Don't be afraid to ask for help or seek guidance from tech-savvy friends, family members, or colleagues. They can offer valuable insights, share their experiences, and provide support as you navigate the world of technology.

Remember, staying current in tech after 50 is not about becoming an expert overnight, but rather a consistent effort to learn, adapt, and stay curious. Embrace the journey of improving your tech skills, and you'll find that technology can become a powerful tool in your personal and professional life.

Identifying Technology Gaps

As a person over 50, it's essential to identify any technology gaps you may have to stay current in the tech industry. Recognizing areas where you may need improvement is the first step towards bridging those gaps and keeping up with tech as a senior.

To identify technology gaps, start by assessing your current tech skills and knowledge. Evaluate your proficiency in areas such as digital literacy, programming languages, software applications, and emerging technologies. Consider the specific tech skills that are in demand in your field or industry.

Recognizing technology gaps:

Look for tasks or challenges in your work or personal life where technology hinders efficiency or productivity. Identify areas where you feel less confident or knowledgeable compared to your peers. Pay attention to trends and advancements in the tech industry that you may not be familiar with.

Bridge the gaps:

Once you've identified your technology gaps, it's time to bridge them. Start by seeking learning opportunities and resources that cater to your specific needs. Online courses, webinars, and tutorials can provide valuable knowledge and training. Join tech communities and professional networks to connect with experts who can offer guidance and support.

If you prefer a more structured approach, consider enrolling in a tech education program or attending workshops that focus on the specific skills you need to develop. Additionally, don't hesitate to reach out to colleagues or mentors who can provide mentorship and share their expertise.

Remember, staying current in tech after 50 is a continuous process. Embrace lifelong learning and be open to adapting to technology changes. By identifying and bridging your technology gaps, you can confidently keep up with tech as a senior and remain competitive in the ever-evolving digital landscape.

Lifelong Learning for Tech Success

In today's rapidly evolving tech industry, staying current and competitive is crucial, regardless of age. For individuals over 50, it is important to adapt to technology changes and continuously learn to remain relevant in this digital age.

Adapting to technology changes after 50 is not only possible but also essential for professional growth and success. By staying current in tech after 50, you can expand your skill set, increase your marketability, and seize new opportunities.

To stay competitive in tech at 50 and beyond, embracing lifelong learning is key. Continuous learning allows you to keep up with the latest technological advancements, trends, and best practices. It enables you to enhance your existing skills and acquire new ones, ensuring that you are well-equipped to tackle emerging challenges and contribute to the industry.

There are various strategies that can help you stay current in tech after 50. One effective approach is to enroll in online courses, webinars, and workshops that focus on technology and its applications. These resources provide valuable insights, industry knowledge, and practical skills that can help you adapt to technology changes and stay competitive.

Additionally, staying connected with professional networks and communities is essential for continuous learning. Engaging with like-minded individuals, attending industry conferences, and participating in online forums can expose you to new ideas, trends, and perspectives. It also provides opportunities for collaboration and knowledge sharing.

Another way to stay current and competitive is by exploring mentorship programs. Mentors can provide guidance, support, and share their experiences, helping you navigate the ever-changing tech landscape effectively.

Continuously honing your tech skills and staying informed about industry trends are critical components of adapting to technology changes after 50. By embracing lifelong learning and adopting a growth mindset, you can stay competitive in tech at 50 and beyond, opening doors to new opportunities and challenges in the digital era.

Seeking Tech Support and Resources

As a person over 50 navigating the ever-evolving tech landscape, staying up-to-date with technology is crucial. Fortunately, there are numerous resources available to help you enhance your tech literacy and keep pace with tech advancements.

To begin, consider reaching out to tech support professionals or specialists who can assist you in understanding and troubleshooting any tech-related issues you may encounter. Whether it's learning how to use a new device or overcoming a software problem, seeking expert guidance can save you time and frustration.

Additionally, there are various online platforms and communities specifically designed to cater to seniors' tech needs. These platforms offer helpful tutorials, forums, and Q&A sessions where you can ask questions and receive assistance from other users who have navigated similar challenges.

Furthermore, staying current with tech trends and developments can be achieved through newsletters, blogs, and technology-focused publications. Subscribing to credible sources will help you stay informed about the latest advancements, tips, and tricks, ensuring you are always in the loop.

Remember, tech literacy is a lifelong journey, and it's never too late to learn and adapt. By utilizing available tech resources and seeking support when needed, you can confidently stay up-to-date with technology as a senior, empowering yourself to fully participate in the digital age.

Building a Professional Network

In the tech industry, building a professional network is crucial for staying competitive and up-to-date, regardless of age. As a person over 50, creating meaningful connections with colleagues, industry experts, and mentors can greatly enhance your career prospects.

Networking offers numerous benefits, including access to job opportunities, industry insights, and valuable advice. By expanding your network, you increase your chances of staying current in tech, acquiring new knowledge, and discovering innovative trends.

To build a successful network, begin by attending industry events, conferences, and workshops. These gatherings provide opportunities to meet fellow professionals, exchange ideas, and forge partnerships. Additionally, consider joining online communities and forums related to your field, where you can engage in discussions, seek advice, and share your expertise.

When networking, it's essential to approach every interaction with authenticity and a willingness to learn from others. Be proactive in initiating conversations and building relationships. Remember, networking is not just about receiving, but also giving. Offer assistance, share insights, and be supportive of your network contacts.

Networking Tips:

- Attend industry events and conferences to meet like-minded professionals.
- Join online communities and forums to engage with experts in your field.
- Be proactive in initiating conversations and building relationships.
- Offer assistance, share insights, and provide support to your network contacts.
- Stay visible and active on professional networking platforms.
- Continuously expand and diversify your network for maximum benefits.
- By building a strong professional network, you can stay competitive, current, and up-to-date with the latest tech advancements, ensuring a successful and fulfilling career as a person over 50 in the tech industry.

Leveraging Experience and Transferable Skills

As a person over 50 in the tech field, your experience and transferable skills can be invaluable assets in staying competitive and adapting to technology changes. By leveraging your unique strengths, you can navigate the ever-evolving tech landscape and stay current in the industry.

One way to highlight your experience is by showcasing your successful track record and highlighting specific projects or achievements that demonstrate your expertise. This will not only demonstrate your capabilities to potential employers or clients but also show your ability to adapt to technology changes.

Additionally, your transferable skills can play a significant role in staying current in tech after 50. Transferable skills are those that can be applied across various roles or industries. For example, skills like problem-solving, communication, leadership, and adaptability are highly valued in the tech field. Emphasize these skills in your resume, cover letter, and interviews to showcase your versatility and ability to excel in the tech industry.

Furthermore, staying current in tech after 50 requires a willingness to continuously learn and upskill. Recognize the value of lifelong learning and seek opportunities to expand your knowledge and stay up-to-date with the latest technology trends. Online courses, workshops, industry events, and professional certifications can help you acquire new skills and demonstrate your commitment to staying competitive. It is also important to stay connected with others in the tech industry. Building a strong professional network can provide access to valuable resources, mentorship, and job opportunities. Attend industry conferences, join professional associations, and engage in online communities to expand your network and stay updated on industry trends.

In conclusion, by leveraging your experience and transferable skills, continuously learning, and building a strong professional network, you can stay competitive in tech at 50 and beyond. Embrace the opportunities that technology offers, adapt to its changes, and showcase your unique strengths to remain current in the tech field.

Balancing Work and Personal Life in the Tech Industry

As a person over 50 in the tech industry, finding the right balance between work and personal life can be a challenge. However, it is crucial for maintaining your tech skills, staying current in the field, and remaining competitive.

One effective strategy for balancing work and personal life is to prioritize your time and set boundaries. Determine your most productive hours and allocate them to focused work, while also making sure to schedule time for personal activities and relaxation. This will help you maintain a healthy work-life integration.

Another important aspect is managing your workload effectively. Learn to delegate tasks, set realistic expectations, and communicate with your team or clients about your availability. By doing so, you can avoid overloading yourself and create space for personal commitments.

Additionally, staying organized and efficient is key. Take advantage of productivity tools and software that can help you streamline your work processes and save time. This will allow you to accomplish tasks more efficiently, leaving room for personal pursuits.

Remember to establish healthy work-life boundaries, such as avoiding work-related emails or calls during personal hours. It is crucial to disconnect from work from time to time in order to recharge and maintain mental well-being.

Lastly, don't forget to make time for self-care and personal development. Engage in activities that bring you joy and rejuvenation, whether it's pursuing a hobby, exercising, or spending quality time with loved ones. By nurturing your well-being, you will not only enhance your overall satisfaction but also boost your productivity in the tech industry.

Balancing work and personal life in the tech industry can be demanding, but with the right strategies, it is possible to thrive both professionally and personally. Prioritize your time, set boundaries, and take care of yourself to maintain your tech skills, stay current in the field, and remain competitive at 50 and beyond.

Overcoming Ageism and Stereotypes

In today's rapidly evolving tech industry, individuals over 50 often face the daunting challenge of ageism and stereotypes. However, it is important to recognize that age does not define one's ability to adapt to technology changes or stay competitive in the field.

One way to overcome ageism and stereotypes is by showcasing the unique value and perspective that older generations bring to the tech landscape. With years of experience and wisdom, individuals over 50 possess a wealth of knowledge that can greatly contribute to innovation and problem-solving in the digital age.

It's crucial to stay proactive and continuously navigate tech advancements to demonstrate adaptability and competence. By actively embracing new technologies, older professionals can prove that age is not a barrier to staying relevant and competitive.

Moreover, networking and seeking support within the tech community can help to break down age-related biases. Building connections with colleagues, attending industry events, and participating in online communities can foster collaboration and provide opportunities for growth.

Conclusion: Overcoming ageism and stereotypes is essential for individuals over 50 to thrive in the tech industry. By highlighting their unique value, adapting to technology changes, and building a strong professional network, seniors can navigate the tech landscape with confidence and continue to make meaningful contributions.

Future-Proofing Your Tech Skills

As a person over 50, keeping up with technology trends and maintaining tech literacy is more crucial than ever. The ever-evolving tech landscape offers a multitude of opportunities for older adults to learn, grow, and stay connected. By future-proofing your tech skills, you can confidently navigate the digital age and embrace the latest advancements.

One key aspect of future-proofing is staying informed about technology trends specifically tailored to older adults. From wearable health trackers to smart home devices, there is a wide range of innovations designed to enhance the lives of seniors. By staying updated and exploring these trends, you can leverage technology to its full potential and make your daily life more convenient and enjoyable.

To ensure you remain relevant in the tech industry, continuous learning is essential. Embrace online courses, workshops, and tutorials to expand your knowledge and acquire new skills. Platforms like Coursera, LinkedIn Learning, and Udemy offer a wealth of resources to assist you in enhancing your tech literacy. By continuously updating your skillset, you can adapt to technology changes and confidently navigate the digital landscape.

Lastly, connecting with like-minded individuals who share your passion for technology can provide invaluable support and insights. Join tech-focused communities, attend conferences, and engage in online forums to build a network of peers and mentors. By collaborating and sharing experiences, you can gain valuable information and stay motivated on your journey to future-proofing your tech skills.

Chapter **41**

The Network Effect: Cultivating professional and personal connections

Welcome to an exciting stage of life where opportunities abound and connections are key. In this article, we delve into the power of networking at the age of 50 and beyond, exploring how cultivating professional and personal connections can transform your career and personal growth.

At 50, networking takes on a whole new meaning. It's about building relationships later in life that will not only open doors professionally but also enrich your personal life. Whether you're looking to advance your career, seek new collaborations or simply connect with like-minded individuals, nurturing robust networks becomes paramount.

Networking at age 50 offers unique advantages. It allows you to tap into a wealth of knowledge, experiences, and resources that your peers possess. By connecting with individuals who share similar goals and passions, you can expand your opportunities and gain access to valuable insights and support. However, as with any endeavor, networking in midlife comes with challenges. Limited time, energy, and adapting to new digital platforms can be daunting. But fear not! In this article we will equip you with effective strategies overcoming these obstacles while creating meaningful connections that last.

Join us as we explore the art of building professional relationships that go beyond business transactions. From networking events through mentorship opportunities we'll provide practical tips for expanding your professional network as well as advancing the career path.

But it's not all about work; cultivating personal connections is equally important. We'll guide you through strategies for developing meaningful friendships, finding common interests, keeping healthy work-life balance while building network that supports your own growth.

Technology has revolutionized the networking landscape hence with our help you'll learn how to leverage its power over here below. From social media platforms throughout virtual networking events learn about tools plus techniques which connect you to industry professionals colleagues prospective mentors among others.

In networking reciprocity creates a powerful bond; find out how giving back support within ones network establishes one as a valuable resource in their industry. This article will therefore illustrate the impact of reciprocity in creating and maintaining solid relationships for a lifetime.

Building long-term connections is a journey. We'll guide you through strategies for nurturing these relationships, staying in touch, and leveraging collaboration opportunities for personal and professional growth.

Finally, we'll explore how cultivating professional and personal connections at 50 and beyond empowers you to thrive in a networked world. Discover how networking can help you adapt to changes, seize opportunities, and thrive in a constantly evolving professional landscape.

So let's embark on this networking adventure together. Get ready to unlock new doors, forge valuable relationships, and cultivate professional and personal connections that will enrich your life at 50 and beyond.

The Value of Networking in Midlife

Networking is not just for young professionals starting their careers. In fact, it is just as essential for individuals in their fifties and beyond. Cultivating professional and personal connections at this stage of life can bring unique benefits, opening up a world of opportunities and resources.

Notwithstanding, another important aspect of networking at 50 is access to critical resources. Knowledge, insights, contacts are among the things that your associated members can help you with. From directions on certain work issues or tips on potential learning programs, your connections can provide an incomparable level of support.

Additionally, networking provides a chance for like-minded people to connect. These friendships with individuals who are in life stages similar to yours could be immensely helpful. Such ties can give verification, solace and fellowship. They are also a good source of advice and perspectives on how to navigate through challenges and choices at this stage of life.

In conclusion, networking for older adults should not only be appreciated but also be taken as a necessary evil. It is an efficient tool for connecting with other peers aged 50 and above hence expanding opportunities, gaining access to valuable resources and getting support from those who think alike. In the subsequent part we will analyze some of the obstacles that individuals may come across when networking in midlife as well as strategies that would help them overcome these barriers.

Overcoming Challenges in Midlife Networking

Networking during middle age comes with unique difficulties; however it is possible to use effective methods in order to cope with this situation (and build meaningful connections). Some of the most efficient ways that one can apply include juggling multiple responsibilities or navigating unfamiliar digital platforms such as:

1.Time and Energy Constraints

Midlife is a time when many people face challenges due to limited time and energy. Between employment duties, family commitments or personal responsibilities finding time for networking proves harrowing task (Davies et al., 2018). Nonetheless by prioritizing upon networking activities whilst effectively managing time it is possible to create distinctive periods for building relationships. Perhaps one could consider attending industry events or joining professional bodies along with organizing themselves virtual coffee meetings so as utilize their available hours optimally.

2.Digital Platform Navigation

As technology advances daily making networks available on online platforms is becoming a way of life among older individuals. This should not demoralize you since there is always a first time for everything. Take up the initiative to learn how to use popular social media platforms, career networking sites and web communities. Alternatively, register for webinars or seek out some guidance from younger colleagues on how best to navigate the spaces.

3.Breaking the Ice

Starting conversations and breaking the ice can be challenging especially when one wants to connect with new people during their midlife stage (Yong, 2015). It is important to know that everyone has insecurities and desires interaction with others. Begin by having informal discussions, asking open-ended questions as well as being an active listener when engaging someone in discourse. Develop rapport through finding areas of common interest shared by both of you.

4.Building Trust and Credibility

However, trust and credibility between professionals does not just come under any circumstances; it requires a lot of commitment (Tembo et al., 2016). If you want others to view you as an authority within your field then involve yourself in chats touching various industries where you provide appropriate insights or supporting other persons in need of guidance. In Midlife, consistency and dependability will make people see you as a reliable source thus making it easy for them to establish meaningful relationships with you.

5.Embracing Continuous Learning

In a business world that is evolving rapidly, it is important to be continuously learning for success in networking. It is relevant to be up-to-date with industry trends, attend workshops or seminars and search for chances of personal and professional growth. Demonstrating your willingness to learn and adapt will make you a more attractive connection in midlife networking.

By overcoming these challenges and implementing effective strategies, you can create a strong and diverse network that will support you both personally and professionally in midlife. Embrace the opportunities to connect and thrive at this stage of your life.

Building Professional Relationships

As professionals in our 50s and beyond, building and nurturing professional relationships becomes increasingly important. Whether you're seeking career advancement, counsel from seasoned colleagues or working together on new projects; networking is critical for connecting with like-minded individuals as well as remaining relevant within one's field.

One practical strategy toward professional networking over 50 years old involves attending networking events. These forge opportunities for interactions with industry practitioners, potential clients, as well as possible mentors. Active involvement during such events allows you to associate with people who share common interests with you therein sharing insights while forging invaluable connections.

Another option that one might consider entails joining industrial associations or organizations. Often times such groups provide specific opportunities for networking related activities consisting of industry-based resources along fellow same interest professionals. By taking part in these societies actively, they promote individual visibility within the occupational area thereby opening an even greater pool of information as well as backing.

Seeking Mentorship

Mentorship is significant not only at the beginning of one's career but also in their fifties or later years. This may involve finding mentors who offer advice, fresh perspectives plus directions through new experiences. Find senior people who have achieved what you are aspiring to achieve so that they mentor you on how things go about until then when the next step happens within your profession.

Furthermore, consider offering mentorship to others. Offering one's knowledge and understanding to budding professionals does not only help them succeed but also expands networks and builds connections that are lasting. The mentoring can be a two-way process in which both the mentor and the mentee learn from each other.

It is important for you to maintain regular communication and follow up with your connections as you cultivate professional relationships. Schedule regular check-ins, share relevant industry updates, and offer assistance whenever possible. Through these relationships you build, there are chances of collaboration, referrals, and growth in the job.

Remember that professional networking is not just about collecting business cards or making surface contacts. It's about forming genuine relationships based on trust, shared interests, and mutual support. By investing time and effort into building professional connections, you can create a robust network that supports your career trajectory, opens doors to new opportunities, and fosters long-term success.

Cultivating Personal Connections

While building professional connections is crucial, it is equally important to cultivate personal relationships in midlife. At 50 and beyond, finding common interests and developing meaningful friendships can contribute to your overall well-being and happiness.

Making connections in midlife may require some effort but it is always worth it because of what comes out of it. You will be able to share experiences with other people who are at this stage of their lives too hence giving each other emotional support as well as offering companionship.

Finding Common Interests

An effective way to develop personal connections is by identifying common interests that bring people together, such as joining a book club, starting a new hobby or volunteering for what you believe in. Participating in activities that align with your passions like joining group activities or attending events related to those passions can help one connect with others.

By engaging in group activities and attending events related to your interests, you can meet new people and share common experiences. These links may give rise to deep friendships and create community spirit.

Work-Life Balance

While creating personal connections it is important to maintain a well-balanced work-life. Prioritize spending time on yourself, maintaining relationships, and self-care contribute happiness and wellbeing in totality.

Try incorporating social activities into your routine like organizing regular meet-ups with friends or even joining community associations. Spend quality time with loved ones like never before for amazing memories. Find room between job and personal life making sure that you have room for both professional as well as personal connections.

Bear in mind that developing personal relationships requires time and effort but is an invaluable investment in one's general sense of bliss and joy. By prioritizing these friendships, one can have more fulfilling life throughout their midlife years till the end of their lives.

Aging 50 plus Technology Networking

In order for those who are above age 50 to network effectively today's connected world necessitates leveraging technology. Social media platforms including online communities as well as virtual networking events are some of the things that make this possible where different sorts of connections can be created both personally & professionally

LinkedIn, Facebook and Twitter serve as social media platforms that provide accessible means through which individuals could connect with peers, industry professionals or mentors-to-be easily. Build an impressive profile while actively participating within relevant groups if you wish to attract similar minded individuals, gain insights from them while establishing useful contacts.

Online communities; forums along special interest groups facilitates networking at convenience of your fingertips. Children also get to participate in these discussions, share ideas, ask for advice and connect with those who can assist them professionally or talk about their hobbies. They are a rich source of materials that are useful, supportive environments and collaboration platforms for initiatives as well as projects.

Participate in virtual networking events

Virtual networking events have gained significant traction in recent years, and they provide a convenient way to connect with professionals from around the globe. From webinars and conferences to industry-specific events, virtual networking offers a host of benefits. Without the limitations of physical distance, you can engage with experts, attend panel discussions, and connect with potential mentors, all from the comfort of your own home.

It is important to come prepared with a clear objective when participating in virtual networking events. Do some preliminary research on the speakers, topics covered during the event as well as attendees so that you can benefit from it. Be actively participating during live sessions by contributing to discussion points then follow up later after it has all ended so that connections made become more meaningful.

In conclusion, the networking power of technology has been revolutionized. It allows those in their 50s and beyond to connect with people from all walks of life. This is made possible by social media, online communities and virtual networking events. You can tap into a vast network of professionals, expand your expertise and break down geographical barriers that may exist. Age should not be a barrier; instead, take advantage of technology and unlock the potential for networking which will drive your success.

The Power of Reciprocity in Networking

Reciprocity has very great significance when it comes to networks for senior adults involving connections among peers at 50 years old. In order to maintain strong relationships, it is crucial to have mutually beneficial associations in place. By rendering assistance to your contacts as well as establishing yourself as an asset within your field you could create an active thriving professional community.

Reciprocity does not mean giving each other favors only but rather appreciating trust and respect between them that eventually foster meaningful relationships. A foundation for long-term connections benefiting everyone involved can be laid by genuinely assisting others and adding value.

One way of leveraging reciprocity is seeking opportunities where you can support those who rely on you. For example, guiding them or making industry introductions or links with important persons could be part of this effort. This ensures that you become an accountable trustworthy partner by sharing information freely about what you know best or even providing expertise at no cost.

Additionally, reciprocity is not just limited within one on one interactions but it goes further even in group settings also . When networking with peers at 50 understand that it's a give and take situation within the larger community as well . Engage in conversations , make contributions that add value to others including sharing insights , feedbacks etc . By doing so , you get known more and more respected thereby creating room for collaboration through which partnerships thrive .

Nurturing Long-Term Connections

For instance if you are in midlife and professional networking over 50, building long-term relationships is essential. These relationships require ongoing effort and nurturing to thrive. This section will explore effective strategies for staying in touch with your network, maintaining regular communication, and leveraging opportunities for collaboration and personal growth.

The Power of Communication

Stronger and more sustainable connections are created by regularly communicating with your networks. Engaging with your networks on a regular basis helps in building stronger bonds. Make it a priority to reach out to your network regularly, whether through phone calls, email or social media platforms like Facebook etc., as well as face-to-face meetings if possible. Listen actively and show genuine interest in the lives and achievements of those you associate with . Keep responding promptly even when nothing major is happening so that trust can be built thereby keeping the connections alive.

Stay Informed

Stay updated about what is going on within your network by knowing any recent developments or milestones they have made . You can follow them on social media platforms such as LinkedIn , join their industry newsletters or attend industry conferences where they are speaking so that you can remain up-to-date regarding their professional development process . Not only will this enable you to have meaningful conversations but it could also present opportunities for offering support when needed .

Offer Value and Support

Networking is two way traffic hence creating long term associations requires giving back some value to one's contacts. Hence sharing helpful resources , proffering advice / guidance or introducing those who may need help are all part of this kind of approach (Cite?). Being a valuable resource means that people know they can rely on you for anything thus developing trust in you professionally. This reciprocity strengthens your relationships and increases the likelihood of receiving support when you need it.

Collaborate And Grow

Always look for chances to work with your connections on different projects, initiatives or areas of shared interest. Not only does collaboration strengthen relationships but it also allows one to benefit from the knowledge and skills of others, thereby expanding his/her own. Consequently, by working together you can realize incredible results while deepening your professional as well as personal ties.

In conclusion, fostering long-term connections is a crucial part of networking at midlife and post 50 professional networks. By staying in regular communication, being informed, offering value and support and looking for opportunities to collaborate will enable you build strong and impactful relationships that will be beneficial both personally and professionally.

Flourishing in a Connected World

Networking becomes even more important as individuals grow older than fifty years because friends help in maintaining professionalism. It is all about coping with changes, taking on opportunities and striving in the constantly changing business world.

Through active participation in networking activities one can keep abreast with industry trends, access new learning sources thus widening his/her scope of thinking. This fosters an environment where individuals that share common objectives are able to offer support for each other thus enabling them reach greater heights through motivation.

Moreover, networking exposes you to amazing possibilities that otherwise you might not have been exposed to. Creating a diverse network comprising professionals from different backgrounds and sectors helps leverage rich expertise, experience and resources available therein.

So, don't underestimate what networking can do for you when you hit 50s. Networking at the level of building professional as well as personal relationships can help an individual adapt themselves even thrive in this world which operates on a network basis since collaboration is its lifeblood.

Chapter 42

Midlife Transitions: Navigating changes in career, lifestyle, and relationships

We are glad to have you here as we have put together a well-rounded chapter for midlife transitions! In this chapter, we will explore some of the changes that take place during this important stage of life and give you helpful tips on how to manage them. Midlife transitions include everything from changes in careers to shifting lifestyles and evolving relationships.

Midlife brings about different types of anticipated and unanticipated changes. Careers could go a different direction, lifestyles might need to be adjusted, or relationships changed drastically. It is a moment of growth, reflection and reassessing our priorities.

Nevertheless, navigating these transitions can sometimes become difficult. Hence our presence at such times. We intend to help you get through it smoothly by offering practical guidance, strategies, and support services for you during this transformational phase whether you are transiting career paths or adjusting to new lifestyle realities.

Our professionals put together insights on stress management, cultivating good relationships and planning for a secure future financially. There is also an exploration of self-care methods that can help develop resilience with personal growth being an integral part towards achievement at this time full of endless possibilities.

Therefore if you are ready for such an amazing experience lets start off today by entering into midlife transition where you will find advice on handling change in your career(s), life style(s)and relationship(s). Together let us make this period in life worth having fun while feeling empowered because it's all up-to-us!

Understanding Midlife Transitions

It is not easy going through midlife without any significant changes occurring especially when they affect everyone equally both internally & externally too. During these moments people tend to undergo diverse transformations within their jobs as well as changing lives among other things related with marriage or even friendship circles thus understanding the complexities involved with such movements may prove crucial since achieving success will be dependent on this knowledge.

Many emotions and challenges are experienced as a result of midlife transitions. Most people feel uncertain, lost, and question the choices they have made in their lives. It's important to keep in mind that these feelings are normal and part of the process. Gaining an understanding of what is going on can help individuals navigate through difficult situations and take advantage of personal growth opportunities brought about by mid-life crises.

A typical life transition event during this phase involves reconsidering one's career choice. Current job satisfaction might be questioned by many people while others may think about different professional ways to go after all. Such introspection usually leads to renewed sense of meaning and fulfillment. By doing so, new passions can easily be discovered leading one towards pursuing a career which aligns with his or her genuine aspirations.

Lifestyle adjustments are another vital area addressed during midlife transitions. At such phases, personal values have to be re-looked at including priorities & goals too. People may find themselves having to adjust to new obligations, shifting family dynamics or even exploring more activities in their spare time. Consequently, embracing lifestyle changes makes it easier for someone to lead a better life that is more balanced.

In addition, relationships change significantly during middle age passage period. Some people start questioning their existing relationships while trying to establish deeper connections with someone who they feel could understand them better than anyone else does; family structures also get altered such as from being parents involved directly into empty nesters' situations when adult children move out on their own for good though there is still those who would prefer staying home longer than necessary but need full time care due in large part because now they become caregivers themselves instead of being taken care off any further under any circumstances whatsoever.

Self-reflection

However, others consider these transitions as an opportunity for self-actualization and discovery about themselves. An individual, who spends time to learn his or her aspirations that are in line with their values can make informed decisions during this period of life. Valuable insights from self-reflection exercises such as meditation and journaling may offer insights into personal growth.

In examining midlife transitions as a concept and delving into the problems and feelings involved in the stage, it is important to do so with a sense of empathy and compassion. Everybody's way is different from any other approach. This process may involve seeking support, embracing experiences that lead to personal development as well as cultivate resilience which enable people go through midlife transition stages ready for new beginning.

Career Changes: Adapting to Change

When it comes to navigating midlife transitions, one of the most significant areas of change is often seen in our careers. Moving to another career; changing the task we perform at work or even getting a completely different profession all together are some of the examples on how you can adapt to career changes.

One important strategy for managing career transitions is adopting change as a chance for growth. Instead of refusing the move, think about exploring other businesses or roles that match your interest or skill set best. This shift in mindset might also bring forth unknown professional paths along with fresh obstacles to be tackled.

Moreover, being flexible and constant learning are fundamental parts of transitioning between careers by adapting yourself accordingly. Enhance your employability by taking courses online or engaging in networking events while participating in professional development programs since this will also boost your confidence towards success in future career undertakings.

Developing resilience is yet another critical part when adapting yourself into your new job setting after changing careers. Recognize that setbacks are normal and commonly happen within those early days. Stay committed on long-term goals regardless any frustrations encountered during early stages coupled with flexibility.

During periods such as these when you are moving from one job to another, it is essential to get guidance from mentors and career coaches or other people who have gone through similar situations. If you happen to meet such professionals along your way, they will guide you accordingly in order to avoid making costly mistakes.

Finally, embrace the opportunity for professional growth that career transitions bring. Discover and explore your passions during this period while equally maximizing your strengths based on what makes you happy as well as defining personal values on which goals should be set. Remember, change can create an avenue for both individual growth and job development resulting into a more satisfying career path.

Lifestyle Changes: Adapting to New Realities

Often lifestyle adjustments accompany midlife transitions when people need to adapt themselves according to changed habits, duties and priorities. At this stage of transformation, it becomes important for us to create a fulfilling and balanced lifestyle as per our changing needs and aspirations.

Willingness To Change

However, adapting new realities starts by accepting change as part of our midlife journey. These changes may come in form of career changes, shifts in family dynamics among others. By embracing these changes we can establish a foundation for personal growth and fulfillment.

Redefining Priorities

While this happens, it is not unusual to have a change in focus. Therefore, we should find what really matters and make deliberate choices. This way, we can lead meaningful and purposeful lives once we identify our guiding values and align our actions with them.

Establishing new habits

To adapt to these new times, one has to establish many different habits. This can mean starting an exercise program, for example, or taking up mindfulness meditation or even allotting time to hobbies such as painting. By including some positive routines in our everyday life we become more resistant and feel better.

Requesting Help

Sometimes people look for support during the periods of change from friends, family or professional resources who could offer important insights and motivate them. Support system development enables sharing experience; asking for assistance; discussing other's mistakes which have been done by people who are going through similar changes in lifestyle.

Self-Care as Priority

Throughout improvements made into our lifestyles self-care should be at the top of the list. This includes exercising the body right and feeding it properly; building mental wellness via meditation and self-reflection; acknowledging personal needs as well as establishing boundaries.

Midlife transitions call for adapting to new realities which may pose challenges but also provide opportunities for growth and self-discovery. Change is embraced so that priority can be refocused creating new habits looking for support while caring about oneself thus navigating through this phase with resilience leads us to a satisfying balanced life style hat coincides with personal values and goals.

Relationship Growth: Sustaining Bonds

In mid-life transition periods, relationships might undergo major transformations. Relationships require nurturing when individuals go through their own personal growths transforming themselves while ensuring healthy communication patterns exist among loved ones Understanding how relationships progress during this period helps manage its changes effectively without weakening ties between partners.

An important element of relationship evolution lies in recognizing how each partner has changed over time. Midlife transitions may cause changes in interests , priorities, and personal goals that influence how a relationship unfolds. It is important to be open-minded and adaptable to let these changes take place as they lead to personal growth and new experiences for both partners.

Cultivating contacts during this phase necessitates fostering an atmosphere of open communication. Taking time out to listen, therefore, enhances the foundation of a relationship. Additionally, having open dialogues where feelings are expressed without losing respect or empathy towards each other should be encouraged.

Managing Change and Challenges

Change management requires flexibility and compromises in relationships. Couples going through midlife transitions may need to adjust what they do everyday or redefine their roles or responsibilities according to the new changes taking place in their lives. Openly discuss your expectations with one another about particular matters such as time spent together so that you are sure about boundaries that will work for both of you.

This period may come with some difficulties but at the same time it's an opportunity for people who want to grow closer together. Challenging situations should be approached together by couples focusing on solutions and providing support for each other along the way. In addition, couple counseling can help navigate tough times when things appear bleak for them including professional guidance or even seeking therapy services aimed at helping couples cope up with difficult times while reinforcing intimacy bonds between them.

Promoting Healthy Communication

Midlife transitions require healthy communication that nurtures relationships. Active listening, empathy and validation of feelings can lead to understanding and strengthen the emotional connection between two people. Moreover, one should set aside specific quality time for meaningful conversations and shared activities in order to feel connected to each other.

Creating a supporting atmosphere where the needs of each partner are taken into account and emotional closeness is prioritized can make it possible for the relationship to flourish. In addition, checking in regularly with one's spouse and showing appreciation may also make a remarkable impact on their partnership during this transformative phase.

Managing Stress and Self-Care

Increased stress levels accompanied by anxiety often occur when individuals are going through midlife transitions. One has to concentrate self-care by using good ways towards managing stress so as to ensure that they stay in optimum physical, emotional, and mental health throughout this phase of life.

A major aspect of dealing with stress involves recognizing some key factors causing tension in your life. It could be something like having a new job or adapting to a different life style either way understanding what triggers you will help you take control measures aimed at reducing stress.

Exercise is another effective way of curing anxiety disorder. When you engage yourself in physical exercises, it increases your mood as well as helps in alleviating stress. This may include jogging round or near your house compound or doing yoga among others since whichever exercise routine best works for you can significantly lower your stress level.

Mindfulness practices such as deep breathing exercises; meditation; engaging yourselves into things that makes you happy including reading books; listening music; hobbies etc., also enhances relaxation techniques within daily program too support proper management of personal strain level.

Besides, you can also seek professional financial advice from a certified financial planner or advisor who may provide valuable insights and guidance. They can help you maneuver complicated money matters such as tax implications and investment strategies to ensure that whatever financial decision you make is aligned with your long-term goals.

It is equally instrumental to mention that financial considerations go beyond the immediate. This often calls for retirement planning during midlife transitions and ensuring one's financial security in later years. For instance, proper retirement planning may involve making contributions into retirement accounts, reviewing insurance policies, as well as considering estate planning so as to protect your future financially.

In conclusion, midlife transitions present an opportunity for personal growth and professional development but require careful consideration and planning when it comes to finances. In this way, whether by actively participating in what happens there or seeking counsel from professionals whenever necessary, we can navigate through this transition with ease and reach a point of stability over the long run.

Seeking Support & Building Resilience

At times negotiating midlife transitions can be difficult and transformative experience. During these stages of life having a strong support system is crucial; they assist in guiding us through changes as well as uncertainty. As such seeking support and building resilience are critical elements when going through the middle age shift successfully.

When faced with significant life changes like this it is good to have someone close like friends or family members or even support groups whom one could rely on for emotional support which facilitate easy passage along these paths. Sharing experiences, asking for advice from others who have already gone through similar experiences will comfort you greatly when facing a major change.

Building Resilience

Also, another important facet of mid-life transition is building resilience since resilience refers the ability to recover quickly after setbacks occur adapt change effectively overcome obstacles among others. It's a characteristic that can be groomed into existence over time.

Developing a positive mindset helps create resilience. Accepting changes towards growth while experiencing challenges as part of learning process helps build resilience. Other activities that assist in building one's resilience include taking care of one's body and mind through exercise, demonstrations of mindfulness, and self-care practices.

In addition, strong social connections also contribute to resilience. Supportive friendships or family bonds or community involvements foster meaningful connections among people; providing them with a sense of belongingness when things change.

Remember that midlife transitions can be periods of self-discovery, growth, and new opportunities. Thus, although it may seem natural to feel uncertain or overwhelmed during these phases, seeking support and building resilience is vital for navigating the changes successfully.

Embracing Growth & New Beginnings

These are mixed emotions that an individual will feel when he/she reaches the midlife considering what lies on their path. Despite this fear of the unknown which is natural during midlife transitions it is important to embrace chances for personal expansion as well as new beginnings.

Embracing growth means pushing ourselves out of our comfort zones and being open to new experiences. It means pursuing our passions and dreams even if they don't turn out according to how we had thought initially.Taking up a new business venture or learning a skill outside your area of expertise can be examples of embracing growth. This way we shall always broaden our knowledge scope while at the same time discovering other aspects about ourselves.

One can be thrilled and scared by new beginnings. It may involve a career change, moving away or just a change of attitude. We give ourselves permission to grow and carve out lives that are truly satisfying when we welcome these new beginnings.

Periods of midlife transition are complicated too, so as we traverse through them, let us maintain an optimistic approach full of excitement. Viewing every alteration as self-development opportunities and chances to start afresh will help in unlocking our potential for the future which is characterized by joy, satisfaction and numerous options.

Chapter **43**

Continued Education: The value of lifelong learning and skill acquisition

Welcome to our chapter on the importance of continued education at the age of 50! In today's fast-changing world, embracing lifelong learning and adult education has never been more important. Whether you are looking for personal growth or professional development, educational opportunities are vast.

Several advantages accrue from continuing in school at this age. It facilitates personal growth thereby allowing an individual to explore new areas and widen their sphere of knowledge. Moreover, it is a crucial tool for professional development that equips individuals with current knowledge and skills necessary for thriving in today's job market which is characterized by intense competition.

Lifelong learning plays a vital role in skill acquisition. Advanced study and participation in continuing education (CE) programs can keep such people relevant as well as adaptable no matter what range they may be in.

If you're wondering about educational opportunities available for adults out there, worry no more. There are many programs ranging from degree programs to online platforms or even community developmental initiatives targeting specifically adult learners.

Not only does continued education foster personal growth as well as professional development; it also promotes healthy aging and supports social inclusion within aging societies .This moreover leads to fulfillment and continuous growth path hence enabling one achieve his full potential .

In the following sections we will go deeper into each aspect stated here tackling issues of balancing continued education with other commitments and exploring the wider impact on society. Thus let us embark on this interesting journey of continued Education at 50 years old onwards!

The Benefits of Continued Education at 50

Continued education does not have an age limit. Indeed, seeking further education at fifty offers various benefits towards self-development and career progression. However, as the world rapidly evolves it becomes imperative to remain updated thus becoming adaptable .Continuing education provides the perfect venue whereby individuals can expand their knowledge base, acquire new skills sets while embracing lifelong learning.

One major benefit associated with pursuing continued education at 50 is self-growth. It enables one to become more intelligent and be fulfilled by pursuing new interests and passions. Moreover, participation in academic pursuits may bring on new perspectives which can help shape an individual's character through challenges that arise from various situations.

On the other hand, continuous education contributes immensely towards professional development as one grows old. Therefore, lifelong learning ensures success in today's competitive labor market. In addition, people are able to update their skills, acquire new knowledge or keep abreast of the industry trends enhancing their professional competencies and keeping them apace with the changing needs of their respective professions .To enhance employability among workers leading to career advancements; it becomes important for them to enroll into college.

There is also the possibility of continuing your education at 50 in order to widen your network and meet like-minded people. By taking part in study programs, these individuals can engage each other or collaborate on projects thereby developing relationships amongst learners and professionals within a certain field of work. As such connections often result into valuable partnerships as well as mentorship opportunities that foster sustained growth and development within communities despite age demographics.

At age 50, continued education is a golden opportunity for growth and development. By embracing lifelong learning, individuals can unleash their potential, keep relevant in an ever changing world and keep on acquiring knowledge that grow them as people.

Lifelong Learning for Skill Acquisition

In today's fast paced world, seeking knowledge and learning new skills are critical for personal and professional development. Lifelong learning offers continuous education which plays a vital role in helping individuals to stay relevant in the job market that is always evolving.

Individuals who are fifty years old and above have access to more advanced learning opportunities. Continuing education programs are designed with specific needs of individuals in mind who may want to acquire new skills or develop existing ones. Such courses offer learners a means of acquiring knowledge independent of traditional academic settings.

Continuing education courses on the other hand provide a wide range of subjects and approaches which enable an individual to gain various skills. Some of these courses could involve foreign languages, information technology or arts training among others which offer specialized resources plus instructions aimed at assisting people throughout their lives' educational journeys.

Through adopting life-long learning practices accompanied by advanced studies through continuing adult education, individuals open up their minds to endless possibilities besides having a competitive edge over others in the labor market hence living fulfilled lives. It actually provides lifetime avenues for adapting change, discovering new worlds as well as grabbing any personal or professional opportunities that come our way.

Exploring Educational Opportunities for Adults

For adults seeking further education there are multiple avenues of pursuing it successfully. If you need formal degree programs, online flexible e-learning platforms or community-based education projects specifically made for adults like you these choices are within your reach.

Formal degree programs give structure and detail to adult education initiatives. In addition, universities and colleges organize a variety of courses as well as other kind of undertakings which target adult learners' interests and requirements where they can be pursued on part time basis while allowing students achieve balance between their education and other commitments.

In case you are looking for flexibility, online learning platforms offer an easy access to educational resources and courses from the comfort of your home. The subjects and disciplines vary widely on these platforms so people can choose what they want to learn at a pace that suits them best.

Continuing Education Courses

In most instances community education programs have continuing education courses for adult learners. Such courses are usually designed to be practical so as to provide hands-on activities that can help acquire new skills or deepen knowledge in one particular field.

By exploring diversity in these forms of educations, you can find a match that is compatible with your interests and objectives. Whether you would like to expand your horizons, pursue alternative career paths or engage with lifelong learning, there will always be an appropriate option that matches your aspirations. Accessing numerous adult education resources can enable one embark on a personal journey towards achieving individual's goals both in life and professionally.

The Impact of Continued Education on Personal Growth.

Individuals who are learning always undergo change in their lives, and this impacts their life's fulfillment. Lifelong learning programs and courses present an opportunity for a transformative journey of self-discovery and development.

Lifelong learning is not solely about gaining knowledge or skills; it is about cultivating curiosity, flexibility, as well as a mindset for growth. In the process of continuing education people get to learn new things, take risks on unfamiliar subjects so that they can understand better the world around them.

Continuous education has the advantage of personal growth among others. It allows people to continue to learn new ideas even if they are not young any more or at different stages of life. At the age of 50 years and above people may find their full potential by grabbing advanced learning opportunities that will help them discover fresh interests.

Additionally, confidence and self-esteem get improved through continued education. Therefore, such individuals may feel proud when acquiring skills and knowledge that help them tackle various situations successfully with zeal. Personal growth goes beyond classrooms affecting all aspects of one's life- relationships, hobbies, general health.

The impact of continued education on personal growth cannot be overstated. It equips individuals with necessary tools and helps in developing a mindset for dealing with constant change in a digital technological era where there is need for lifelong learning institutions. Prioritizing personal development via further education can make your existence rich with meaning hence aiming towards a purposeful life which thrives on continuous learning experiences.

Professional development through Continued Education

Continued education provides a path toward achieving personal goals while enhancing professional competence. Through higher level trainings as well as ongoing course enrollment; some have gained relevance into potential career pathways.

Professionals can stay abreast with trends by continuously pursuing further studies in their areas of specialization which also ensures they keep relevant in the job market place over time. With advanced studying comes expertise as well as mastery over competitive landscapes that enhance chances of promoting career-wise and meeting professional objectives.

Continuing education courses aim at addressing specific industry requirements. They provide applied knowledge that a person can use directly in the workplace leading to better job performance and increased job satisfaction.

Moreover, it offers an opportunity for professionals to remain updated about current trends, technological advances, and best practices in their respective industries. New skills acquired coupled with information gathered by individuals make them valuable resources through which organizations can shine.

Professional development through continued education does not only apply to certain industries or occupations. Whether you are a healthcare professional seeking to learn the latest medical advancements or a business executive looking to develop strategic leadership skills, there are continuing education courses available to suit your needs.

Investing in continued education is an endorsement of lifelong learning valued by employers today. It shows a proactive approach towards career growth as well as commitment of going beyond one's limitations. In most cases, employers regard people who are pursuing further studies as committed members of staff serving their teams with enthusiasm.

For professionals to open up new opportunity windows, expand their knowledge magnitude and develop long-term career path, they must welcome advanced learning as well as continuing education courses. Lifelong learning is not only a means of reaching higher levels but also an enjoyable journey.

Striking a Balance between Continued Education with Other Commitments

It gets harder to balance educational pursuits with other responsibilities as we grow older. Striking a balance between work, family duties and personal commitments while pursuing lifelong learning requires effective time management and planning skills.

This makes it one of the benefits of adult education through its flexibility that allows individuals to fit it into their existing schedules. Institutions are offering evening and weekend classes so that people could acquire the necessary skills without affecting their jobs or family life. Moreover, online platforms have made studying more accessible than ever before enabling you to learn at your own pace while at home.

In order not to get lost in other activities when studying for continued education, it is crucial to prioritize tasks and set achievable objectives. Having specific days or hours each week dedicated for studies or attending lessons can help establish a routine thus avoiding any distractions from learning due to other engagements. Further breaking down complex tasks into smaller portions facilitates monitoring progress continuously.

Moreover there is another approach which entails using technology and productivity tools in order to simplify processes and increase output. These may be calendar apps, do-lists on excel sheets or project management software among others which will enable them be always near deadlines. Moreover taking care of oneself by participating in relaxation exercises is very important for mental soundness purposes hence preventing burnouts too.

Lastly, it is important that the student involves his/her family members, friends and employer in the whole process of training. This way they will understand both what one wants to achieve in this area as well as why continuous learning matters so much making it easier for them whenever some conflicts arise along the way towards achieving these goals. In addition an employer might allow free working conditions or even introduce scholarship programs for his/her staff.

In summary, effective time management, open communication and proactive planning are essential to balancing continued education with other commitments. By taking advantage of the flexibility that adult education programs have to offer and prioritizing learning, individuals can successfully incorporate lifelong learning into their busy lives thus taking advantage of the new doors of educational opportunities and self development.

The Role of Continued Education in Ageing Societies

In ageing societies, continued adult education has deep meaning. Thus, as people reach 50 years old pursuing educational opportunities is not only beneficial for them but also for the whole community.

This is where continued education plays a significant role in supporting healthy aging. In this way, adults engaging in lifelong learning keep their minds active, maintain cognitive abilities or minimize risks of age-related cognitive decline. It implies that schooling ensures mental stability and happiness since it helps maintain emotional well-being.

Furthermore, it promotes social inclusion through continuing education. When they decide to get into schools once more despite their age differences, such individuals come together thereby establishing groups of learners. This helps foster a sense of belongingness and reduces the effects of social isolation observed among elderly people in different parts of the world.

Intergenerational learning is another significant advantage of adult education. The older members bring their experience and knowledge in life to the classroom, making learning more meaningful for both the young and old. This uniqueness sets up one where people of all ages can share knowledge and ideas leading to a talking point, mutual understanding, and empathy.

The changing face of society, along with its demographics demands an understanding of the role that continual education plays in aging populations. Making sure that individuals over 50 years old have access to various educational programs allows them lead full lives, contribute significantly to their neighborhoods as well as continuing growth until death.

Lifelong Learning: A Route to Fulfillment and Growth

When we hit 50 years old, lifelong learning becomes a key component in our personal and professional journey. It offers us a chance to keep growing which no doubt will help us open new doors or find fulfillment at a personal level.

This process may be facilitated through lifelong learning activities by which our minds are given intellectual nutrition; horizons are expanded and it creates a deeper sense of purpose. As opposed to pursuing what we love most at different points in time or studying new things about it from other angles around us all the time. Whether through taking higher level classes, attending seminars or engaging in online courses among others this builds a mindset of being curious thought seeking.

Further still when it comes to professional development lifelong learning is very vital. In such rapidly changing work environment today's dynamic labor market requires constant acquisition of new skills and know-how. By enrolling for extension programs or taking available educational opportunities we can keep up with emerging trends so as remain competitive improve career future prospects (Bhola & Taylor 1999). Lifelong learning has empowered workers like me who have had to change jobs frequently because my current occupation did not feel challenging anymore; I am able stay ahead professionally by continuously gathering new information about industries I want be part of just before they come up.

Lifelong learning is at the core of our careers. Acquiring new skills and knowledge becomes increasingly important in a rapidly changing job market. Staying competitive, adapting to emerging trends and improving future career prospects are some of the reasons why people engage in continuing education programs and seize educational opportunities for themselves. As such lifelong learning makes one more agile and relevant, thereby ensuring that I have always been able to meet professional challenges confidently.

Basically, lifelong learning is about transformational journey where both personal and professional growth are concerned. It provides an opportunity to keep changing, pushing oneself beyond limits to achieve the intended purpose. At 50 years or above, as we embrace this course of action it can be said that we have embarked on a lifetime search for information, wisdom as well as self-improvement. Hence all let us enjoy the love we get from life-long studying after which you will be suprised by its impact upon our lives because it gives us insight into many other aspects making life exciting and meaningful (Watson & Liyimba 1995).

Chapter **44**

Financial Freedom at Fifty: What to do for Money Stability and Growth.

We present you this all-inclusive chapter on how to achieve financial freedom in your 50s. For that reason, it is vital that as you approach this important stage of life, you should consider saving money for the future and make sure you are financially independent. Employing proper techniques and having solid financial habits will ensure solid economic state today and further than that.

Planning for retirement after crossing fifty needs thorough thought and proactive action to guarantee a safe and comfortable future. In this article, we shall be discussing several means which may contribute to your prosperity by the time you are fifty years old. These shall range from assessing your current financial situation, creating an exhaustive budget, maximizing retirement contributions, diversifying investment portfolios, managing debts as well as exploring other income streams. This way, readers would have practical insights into achieving independence from their finances.

Moreover, it should be noted that the significance of keeping one up-to-date with regard to the prevailing trend in finance vis-à-vis those targeting persons aged 50years plus could not go unmentioned. For instance if it is about staying updated on investment strategies or understanding the newest forms of retirement planning financial education plays a key role towards meeting personal finance targets.

On one hand while we encourage taking control of our own money matters; we also acknowledge professional assistance's worth.

The knowledge provided by Tax professionals accountants specialists in wealth management provides invaluable advice that can help make these plans more successful through complex finances situations such as personalized suggestions about choosing different paths.

Come along with us in quest for financial freedom at fifty years old.time to dwell on strategies and steps that will allow you attain economic stability retired confidently endowed with wealth in fifties.

What is Your Current Financial Status?

Before heading off on a quest for financial freedom it must be remembered crucially that it is necessary to evaluate what state one has got to. You should take an inventory of your retirement savings, investment portfolio and existing debts in order to figure out where you are right now. This will enable you make a realistic plan consistent with your goals that will set you up for a bright future.

Begin by examining the state of your retirement nest egg. Find out how much you've saved and whether these savings can afford the kind of lifestyle you want when retired. Consider projected retirement age, estimated life expectancy as well as any pension or social security benefits for which one might be eligible. By doing this, one is able to identify the gaps in terms of his/her retirement saving plans thus making necessary corrections.

You should also assess your investment portfolio apart from your retirement savings. Review the performance and diversification of your investments and determine their suitability to your risk tolerance level and long-term objectives. Seek assistance if required to ensure that they are optimized for growth and stability.

Lastly, appraise what indebtedness currently exists in your name. Sum up the total sum due along with interest rates plus repayment duration specifics concerning it being secured or unsecured in nature. Prioritize the payment of high-cost loans so as to lower borrowing costs overall during this period of low-interest rates on loans as some people do prefer closing off costly lines faster than others just like them while offering would develop a debt reduction program which frees up more money for saving/investment purposes.

If you look at your financial situation thoroughly, you will gain valuable insights into what steps you need to take to become financially free. With this knowledge, proceed confidently and create a tailor-made financial plan that would direct you towards a safe and prosperous future.

Developing A Comprehensive Budget

Creating an extensive budget is an important step toward achieving financial freedom and security in one's fifties. This will ensure that your basic expenses are met, savings are prioritized, and debts are actively reduced. The next section will walk you through the process of building a budget which suits your financial plans.

Step 1: Evaluate Your Income and Expenses

Start by assessing where your income comes from including salary, returns on investment (ROI) among other revenue streams.Gauge them against varied fixed costs as well as variable ones. Fixed expenses like rent /mortgage payments or insurance premiums stay unchanged each month while variable costs such as groceries and entertainment fluctuate.By truly understanding how much you make versus how much it takes to run your life better ,savings for retirement and debt repayments can be calculated more accurately .

Step 2: Prioritize Essential Expenses

Ensure that your budget accounts for essential expenses such as housing, utilities, transportation, healthcare, and food – the vital aspects of daily life that must be given highest priority.Spend enough on these items so that there isn't any fat left in the budget.

Step 3: Allocate Savings

Saving for unexpected expenditures or retirement should therefore form a significant part of the budget . You should put aside some amount from every paycheque into yet another special account for retirement purposes . Set specific saving goals to remain motivated.

Step 4: Repay Debts Strategically

In case there are outstanding debts such as credit card balances or loans , develop a strategy which outlines how they would be paid off over time.First you need to prioritize paying off high interest debts because it saves money in long term. As you repay your debts, continue to cover basic expenses and make contributions to savings.

Step 5: Track Your Spending and Make Adjustments

The importance of keeping a close eye on how we spend can never be overstated as it helps us to remain focused on our budgets which in turn supports our financial goals. Regularly review your spending, making any necessary adjustments. Look for areas where you could reduce discretionary spending or cut costs, freeing up more money for savings and debt repayment.

By creating a detailed budget and actively managing your finances, taking control of your financial future is possible – this should be the aim for every person who wants to have financial security in their fifties.

Maximize Retirement Contributions

Planning for life after retirement becomes increasingly crucial as people approach their 50s; thus, this section will provide guidance on how individuals can minimize their tax bills while securing their retirement incomes from the Social Security Administration.

Another way of boosting one's retirement savings is through catch-up contributions. These are extra funds that those aged fifty years old or above may contribute. By increasing your contribution rate towards retirement accounts, you can help speed up your saving process and fill any preparedness gaps there might be in place.

Also, it is very important to explore different retirement account options. Traditional IRAs, Roth IRAs, 401(k)s and other employer-sponsored plans come with distinct benefits and taxation rules. Consult a financial professional for the best retirement accounts that fit your plans and situation.

Your investment choices can also increase your retirement contributions. Diversify your portfolio with stocks, bonds, and alternative investments. By investing in different asset classes you diversify your risk and may earn higher returns over long time frames.

In conclusion, boosting your retirements contributions by making use of catch-up contributions; learning about various types of IRA's; exploring other job-provided pension plan products as well as optimizing investment alternatives will ensure that one has a financially stable life even after retiring.

Diversify Your Investment Portfolio

When considering how to guarantee long-term financial stability one of the most crucial strategies for fifty-year-olds is spreading out risks across many fronts in their portfolios. This involves investing in stocks from different sectors and countries.

When you diversify your portfolio, market volatility may have less impact on your investments. If one asset class or sector goes down another may go up which could cancel any losses.

Asset allocation forms part of diversification process. It is possible to strike a balance through strategic allocation of assets across various categories like equities, fixed income securities such as bonds or debentures issued by governments/corporations, real estate among others depending on desired risk level/return expectations.

Rebalancing your portfolio is another way to do this kind of diversification occasionally. This allows you to ensure that your portfolio remains at its target resource mix and risk profile going forward. Rebalancing helps maintain desired levels of diversification while taking into consideration the investor's risk tolerance.

It is important to talk with a financial advisor who can evaluate investors' risk tolerance levels, time horizons as well as goals when considering investment alternatives. They will assist in determining appropriate investments and creating a diversified portfolio based on an investor's personal circumstances.

Reduce Debt and Manage Expenses

When it comes to achieving financial independence in your 50s, managing debt and reducing expenses are crucial steps. By implementing effective strategies, you can pay off high-interest debts, renegotiate loans, and trim unnecessary expenses so that more monies go into savings and investment.

Pay Off High-Interest Debts

The first thing that you should do to cut down on your overall liabilities is to pay back the most expensive ones initially. Credit cards loans with high interest rates will be the initial point of focus. Merge various debts into one which has less annual percentage rate of interest hence saving money from interest payments.

Renegotiate Loans and Mortgage Terms

Go back to your loans as well as the mortgage terms. Call your lenders for better interest rates; prolonging the repayment period or even aiming at reducing monthly installments. Refinancing/restructuring of the unpaid balance may be another way for lowing costs or easing pressure from monthly budgets.

Trim Unnecessary Expenses

Review all monthly expenses looking for ways to reduce expenditures in different areas. Analyze what services you currently subscribe to such as cable connections which you may no longer use or need anymore. For instance, consider downsizing by changing contracts like cable television subscription deals that are costing too much in relation to their competitors' packages or decreasing internet plans or insurance coverage packages among many others when seeking ways of reducing expenditure.

Also, ensure that you take note of your daily expenses to know where your money is going. This will enable you to make informed spending decisions while also indicating areas where further cuts can be made.

By reducing the debt and controlling expenditure, one can have a hold over financial conditions paving way for financial independence at the age of 50s.

Explore Other Ways of Income

To become rich in one's fifties, one has to explore for other ways of earning money faster. The next chapter addresses creating passive incomes which help diversify earnings and lead to accelerated freedom from finances.

One popular option is real estate investments. By investing in rental properties or Real Estate Investment Trusts (REITs), individuals can earn rental income or receive dividends from their estate holdings. This helps generate an ongoing cash flow while building wealth over time

Another idea would be part-time work which could entail taking on a part-time job or freelancing in your field of expertise. This does not only give an extra source of income but also offers an opportunity to use skills and experience when remaining flexible with time table in place.

If you have any talents or passions others pay for, you might want to find out how to monetize them. It may encompass selling handcrafted items, conducting workshops, teaching lessons or offering digital content such as e-books and online courses.

For instance, they say that it is important to invest in real estate so as to keep yourself busy with jobs that would not consume too much time like partime one work or turning hobbies into businesses by utilizing them online.

Insure Yourself against Sudden Losses

Safeguarding your financial future is crucial especially when you start getting older thus; it becomes necessary for people above fifty years old (50+)to consider having insurance plans which help secure their earned monies against possible risks that would come up at these stages until their deaths.Let's talk about insurance importance in retirement planning for people aged 50 and over.

Life Insurance

Life insurance is a crucial element of retirement planning for people above fifty years old (50+). This protects the financial interests of your family in case you die prematurely. With life insurance, you can be certain that your loved ones are protected and will have the means to maintain their current lifestyles, pay off any debts or loans as well as cater for funeral expenses. Consult an established insurer who will help identify what amount of coverage suits your unique needs.

Health Insurance

As you grow older, health care becomes more important. Good medical coverage is necessary for managing medical bills and making sure patients can get quality healthcare when needed. Individuals aged sixty-five years and above qualify to receive Medicare, a government-run health insurance scheme which covers hospital stays, outpatient visits, drugs among others. Look at all Medicare options available to see which one best fits your healthcare requirements.

Long-Term Care Insurance

Long-term care insurance helps to pay for the costs of extended care services such as nursing homes, assisted living facilities and home care. Long-term care should be considered and planned for when you are thinking about retirement because it can have serious financial consequences for both yourself and your family. Your retirement savings can be safe if you buy long-term care insurance and this will give you peace of mind.

It is important that these policies are reviewed periodically in order to ensure that the beneficiaries named therein are still relevant and that they reflect the testator's wishes. If you need help picking out a policy or determining how much coverage is appropriate, talk to an insurance professional who can help guide your choices based on what would work best with your retirement plans.

Never Stop Learning

Continued education is essential to achieving financial freedom at 50 years old since knowledge about the latest trends in finance as well as possible strategies are all bound to change. By educating yourself continually, you increase your chances of making informed decisions about various investments amidst changing economic situations.

You have to stay current with investment trends, retirement planning tactics, wealth building strategies etc. It's worth looking for resources specifically designed for persons in their fifties which will offer valuable insights.

Investment Fads

Stay ahead of trends by monitoring investment portfolios closely so that your choices would be guided by information rather than guesswork. You could also subscribe to financial magazines or do some research on authoritative websites dedicated to investments or even follow renowned economist for guidance on investments. Updating yourself continuously on investment trends ensures that whenever opportunities arise, you can shift the direction of your money accordingly.

Tactics in Retirement Planning

To achieve financial liberty, one must take into account numerous aspects including retirement planning among others. Stay updated with such issues like contributing towards retirement saving options in order to realize comfortable post-retirement period in your early 50s onwards . For instance, attend a webinar workshop with leading expert speakers who could guide you through the maze of your retirement plan offering practical advice.

Strategies for Creating Wealth

Even in your fifties, wealth creation is a journey. Search resources and educational materials on methods for creating wealth appropriate for people in this age group alone. You will learn what real estate investments are, passive incomes or other ways to make money that can lead you to financial independence faster.

Ongoing Financial Education

Educating yourself continuously is essential because it enables you to make informed decisions about finances, adapt to changing economic circumstances and confidently pursue whatever plans you have towards becoming financially free by the time you are fifty years old.

Use Experts

Seeking professional advice can be decisive as far as navigating through complex issues of retirement planning after 50 years is concerned. There are many professionals available who include tax advisors, financial planners and even retirement consultants who could help optimize your plans so that they can meet your desired goals of achieving financial freedom at age 50.

Furthermore, an advisor can provide valuable insights for individual needs. They will scrutinize where one stands in terms of money matters before identifying goals with intentions of developing a comprehensive plan meant to maximize savings towards retirement. An expert's counsel on asset allocation strategies, investment choices and risk management enables wise decision making concerning one's finances.

In addition to these professionals, tax specialists may provide assistance in understanding difficult taxation issues. This may entail finding out deductions; credits received together with strategies which may minimize taxes thus allowing more retention of acquired cash. Revamp saving during your working days by fine tuning how much income that is taxable due to optimizing tax situation resulting into earlier retirements.

The retirement planners specialize in the planning of retirements for individuals who are aged fifty years and above and may offer useful advice on how to maximize one's savings after one has stopped working. They will look at what you want to do, your expenditures and your major financial sources like pensions before they come up with an individual retirement plan that takes into consideration aspects such as life expectancy, inflation as well as health care expenses among others. With their insight, you can be sure that your plans for retiring will be carefully thought through to ensure a good retirement life.

Chapter **45**

Launching into the Next Decade: Preparing for and welcoming your sixties

Welcome to the next chapter of your life! Turning 60 is a milestone that signifies the beginning of an exciting new decade filled with possibilities. It's a time to reflect on your past achievements and embrace the future with open arms. In this guide, we will provide you with valuable insights and tips on how to navigate your 60s, including preparing for retirement and welcoming the opportunities that lie ahead.

As you approach this new phase of life, it's essential to prepare yourself both mentally and financially. We'll explore strategies for financial planning, ensuring that you make the most of your resources and lay a solid foundation for the future. Additionally, we'll discuss how to maintain physical and mental well-being, prioritize your relationships, and pursue new passions and hobbies that bring you joy.

Life is full of transitions, and your 60s may bring significant changes. From adjusting to an empty nest to finding purpose in retirement, we'll guide you through these transitions and show you how to embrace the opportunities they bring. We'll also delve into the importance of leaving a lasting impact and creating a meaningful legacy that extends beyond your 60s.

So, get ready to embark on this exciting journey with confidence and optimism. Your 60s can be a decade of growth, exploration, and fulfillment. Join us as we delve into the art of launching into the next decade and welcoming your sixties with open arms. Let's make these the best years of your life!

Reflecting on the Past and Embracing the Future

As you turn sixty and enter the exciting decade of your 60s, it's natural to take a moment to reflect on the journey you've traveled so far. This is a time to celebrate your accomplishments, cherish memories, and learn from the experiences that have shaped you.

Reflecting on the past allows you to gain valuable insights and wisdom that will guide you as you embrace the possibilities that lie ahead. It's an opportunity to let go of any regrets or missed opportunities and focus on creating a fulfilling future.

Entering the 60s is a milestone that signifies a new chapter in your life. It's a time to embrace the future with optimism, curiosity, and a sense of adventure. Instead of dwelling on the past, look forward to the exciting opportunities and adventures that await you.

This is your time to rediscover yourself, pursue new passions, and set new goals. Whether it's learning a new skill, starting a business, or traveling the world, the possibilities in your 60s are endless.

Embracing the future means letting go of any self-imposed limitations and embracing change with open arms. It's about pushing your boundaries and stepping out of your comfort zone to discover new horizons.

As you embark on this journey, remember that age is just a number. Your 60s can be a time of personal growth, self-discovery, and fulfillment. Take this opportunity to shape your future and create the life you've always dreamed of.

Navigating Physical Changes and Health

As we enter our 60s, it's important to acknowledge and understand the physical changes that occur as part of the aging process. Our bodies undergo various transformations, and taking proactive steps to prioritize our health becomes essential in this new phase of life.

Maintaining an active lifestyle is one of the key strategies to stay fit and healthy. Engaging in regular physical activity not only helps to keep our bodies strong, but it also contributes to our overall well-being. Whether it's going for a brisk walk, participating in low-impact exercises, or trying out new activities like yoga or swimming, finding a form of exercise that suits your preferences and abilities is crucial.

Additionally, it's vital to address common health concerns that may arise in our 60s. Regular check-ups with healthcare professionals, such as annual physical exams and recommended screenings, can help detect any potential health issues early on. Maintaining a nutritious diet, rich in fruits, vegetables, whole grains, and lean proteins, is another important aspect of staying healthy as we age.

Furthermore, staying socially connected and nurturing our relationships contributes to our overall well-being. Engaging in activities and hobbies that bring us joy and fulfillment not only provides cognitive stimulation, but it also helps to promote a sense of purpose and self-worth.

While navigating physical changes can sometimes feel challenging, it's important to approach this new phase of life with a positive mindset and a commitment to self-care. By prioritizing our health through maintaining an active lifestyle, addressing health concerns proactively, and nurturing our social connections, we can enter our 60s with confidence, embracing this next decade with vitality and well-being.

Financial Planning for the Next Decade

As you enter your 60s, it's crucial to prioritize your financial planning and prepare for retirement. This new decade of your life brings unique challenges and opportunities, and by implementing effective financial strategies, you can ensure a secure and fulfilling future.

One of the key aspects of financial planning in your 60s is preparing for retirement. It's important to assess your current financial situation, including your savings, investments, and retirement accounts. Consulting with a financial advisor can help you navigate this process and develop a personalized retirement plan that aligns with your goals and aspirations.

Retirement Savings

Building a robust retirement savings account should be a top priority. Consider maximizing your contributions to retirement plans, such as employer-sponsored 401(k) or individual retirement accounts (IRAs). Additionally, explore catch-up contributions, which allow individuals aged 50 and above to contribute additional funds to their retirement accounts.

It's also crucial to review your investment portfolio and ensure it aligns with your risk tolerance and long-term financial goals. As you enter your 60s, it may be prudent to shift your investment focus towards more conservative options that prioritize capital preservation.

Social Security and Pension Benefits

Understanding your Social Security and pension benefits is essential for comprehensive financial planning. Research the eligibility criteria, payment amounts, and claiming strategies for Social Security benefits. Exploring the potential benefits of delaying your Social Security claim can result in higher monthly payments.

If you have a pension, review the terms and conditions, and consider consulting with a financial advisor to determine the most optimal payout options.

Estate Planning

Estate planning is crucial when preparing for the next decade of your life. Review and update your will, trust, and other legal documents to ensure they reflect your current wishes. Consider working with an estate planning attorney to address any potential tax implications and ensure a smooth transfer of assets to your beneficiaries.

Don't forget to review your insurance coverage, including life, health, and long-term care insurance. Evaluating your insurance needs can protect you and your loved ones from unexpected financial burdens.

Financial planning in your 60s requires careful consideration and strategic decision-making. By investing time and effort in this aspect of your life, you can confidently embrace the next decade with peace of mind, knowing that you have a solid foundation for a secure and fulfilling future.

Reinventing Yourself in the 60s

Your 60s mark a significant milestone in life, presenting a prime opportunity for self-discovery and reinvention. Embracing this new chapter with open arms allows you to explore new passions and make the most of the exciting opportunities that come your way.

As you enter your 60s, it's essential to remember that age is just a number. This is your chance to redefine yourself, break free from old limitations, and embrace a renewed sense of purpose and fulfillment. Whether you've retired or are still working, this is your time to shine.

One way to reinvent yourself in your 60s is to explore new hobbies and interests. Perhaps there's a passion you never had the time to pursue before or an activity that has always intrigued you. Now is the perfect moment to immerse yourself in these experiences and uncover hidden talents.

Consider taking up painting, learning a musical instrument, or even trying your hand at writing. The possibilities are endless. Embrace your creativity and allow it to guide you toward a fulfilling and satisfying journey of self-expression.

Another avenue for self-reinvention is personal style. This is the time to experiment with different fashion choices and explore new looks. Update your wardrobe, try out new hairstyles or experiment with a fresh makeup routine. Discovering your personal style in your 60s can be liberating and empowering, allowing your outer appearance to reflect the vibrant spirit within.

Additionally, your 60s can be a time for personal growth and self-improvement. Consider enrolling in classes, workshops, or seminars that align with your interests and goals. Expand your knowledge and skills while connecting with like-minded individuals who share your enthusiasm for continuous learning.

Reinventing yourself also means embracing a positive mindset. Let go of any self-doubt or limiting beliefs that may hold you back. Cultivate self-confidence and embrace the wisdom and experiences you've accumulated throughout your life. Your 60s are a time to celebrate the person you've become and the potential for further growth.

So, as you step into this new chapter of life, remember that it's never too late to reinvent yourself. Embrace the opportunities that come your way, explore new passions, and live your life to the fullest. Your 60s can be a time of incredible self-discovery and transformation. Embrace the journey and watch as your reinvented self blossoms.

Maintaining Mental Well-being

As you enter your 60s, maintaining your mental well-being becomes even more crucial. This new decade brings with it a host of challenges and joys, and taking care of your mental health is essential for overall well-being and happiness. Here are some strategies to prioritize your mental health and cultivate a positive mindset:

1. Prioritize Self-Care

Make self-care a priority in your daily routine. Engage in activities that bring you joy and relaxation, such as meditation, reading, or pursuing hobbies. Taking time for yourself allows you to recharge and maintain a healthy mental state.

2. Stay Active & Engaged

Physical activity has been shown to have a positive impact on mental health. Engage in regular exercise or activities that keep you active, such as walking, swimming, or yoga. Additionally, staying socially engaged by participating in community groups, volunteering, or joining clubs can help enhance your sense of well-being.

3. Manage Stress

Stress is a part of life, but it's important to manage it effectively. Find healthy coping mechanisms that work for you, such as deep breathing exercises, journaling, or talking to a trusted friend or therapist. Prioritize stress management techniques that help you find balance and peace.

4. Cultivate Positive Relationships

Building and maintaining positive relationships with friends and family can greatly contribute to your mental well-being. Surround yourself with people who uplift and support you. Take the time to connect regularly, whether through phone calls, video chats, or in-person meetings.

5. Seek Professional Help When Needed

If you're struggling with your mental health, don't hesitate to seek professional help. Mental health professionals can provide valuable guidance and support tailored to your individual needs. Reach out to a therapist or counselor who specializes in geriatric mental health.

By prioritizing your mental well-being in your 60s, you can navigate the challenges and joys of this new decade with clarity, resilience, and happiness.

Relationships and Social Connections

Building and maintaining strong relationships is vital at any age. As you enter your 60s, nurturing and prioritizing your relationships becomes even more important.

Family and friends play a significant role in our lives, providing love, support, and companionship. It is essential to invest time and effort in strengthening these bonds, as they bring immense joy and contribute to our overall well-being.

Take the opportunity to reconnect with family members, especially those you may not have been able to spend as much time with in the past due to various commitments. Rekindle those connections by organizing family gatherings, planning vacations together, or simply reaching out for a heartfelt conversation.

Additionally, maintaining social connections beyond your inner circle is equally important. Participating in community events, joining clubs or organizations, and volunteering can help you form new friendships and expand your social network. Engaging in activities or hobbies you enjoy can lead to meeting like-minded individuals who share your passions.

Having a strong support system is crucial as you navigate the various transitions and challenges that can arise in your 60s. Surrounding yourself with positive and supportive individuals can provide comfort, advice, and encouragement when needed. These relationships can help reduce stress, enhance your sense of belonging, and contribute to a higher quality of life.

Remember, forming and maintaining relationships is a two-way street. Actively invest in the lives of others by being present, listening, and offering support. Small gestures like sending a heartfelt message, making a phone call, or scheduling regular get-togethers can strengthen bonds and demonstrate your commitment to the important people in your life.

Nurturing relationships and creating a robust social network can enrich your 60s in numerous ways. Whether it's sharing laughter, celebrating milestones, or providing a shoulder to lean on during challenging times, strong relationships and social connections contribute to a fulfilling and well-rounded life.

Pursuing New Passions and Hobbies

Your 60s can be an exciting time of exploration and self-discovery. It's a chance to embrace new passions and hobbies and find joy in activities that bring you fulfillment. Whether you have a lifelong interest you want to dive deeper into or you're looking to try something completely new, there are countless opportunities waiting for you.

Engaging in hobbies and pursuing new passions in your 60s has numerous benefits. It can provide a sense of purpose, enhance your mental and physical well-being, and foster personal growth. The key is to listen to your heart and follow your interests.

Trying new activities: Consider exploring activities you've always been curious about but didn't have the time or opportunity to pursue before. Maybe it's painting, playing a musical instrument, or learning a new language. Trying new things can be invigorating and open up new avenues of creativity and self-expression.

Rediscovering old passions: Your 60s can also be a time to reconnect with hobbies and interests you may have abandoned or put on hold during earlier stages of life. Revisiting old passions can reignite feelings of joy and enthusiasm and provide a sense of familiarity and comfort.

Finding community: Pursuing new passions and hobbies can also introduce you to a community of like-minded individuals who share your interests. Joining clubs, groups, or classes can provide opportunities for social interaction and meaningful connections, enhancing your overall well-being and sense of belonging.

Finding balance: While exploring new passions and hobbies, it's important to find a balance that suits your lifestyle and priorities. Don't overwhelm yourself with too many commitments or rush into activities that may not align with your interests. Take the time to explore and experiment, and allow yourself the freedom to adjust your pursuits as you go.

Embracing your 60s means embracing the chance to pursue activities that bring you joy and fulfillment. So, don't hesitate to step outside your comfort zone, try new things, and immerse yourself in the incredible world of passions and hobbies that await you.

Life Transitions and Adjustments

Life is full of transitions, and your 60s can bring about significant changes. As you enter this new phase of life, it's important to embrace the opportunities that come with it and navigate the adjustments that may be required.

One of the major transitions that individuals in their 60s face is adjusting to an empty nest. As children grow up and move out, it can be a time of mixed emotions. It's essential to focus on finding new purpose and creating a fulfilling life for yourself as you navigate this change.

Retirement is another significant adjustment that many people encounter in their 60s. Transitioning from a busy career to a life of leisure can be both exciting and challenging. It's important to plan for this phase and consider how you'll fill your days with activities that bring you joy and a sense of fulfillment.

Navigating Empty Nest Syndrome

Empty nest syndrome is a common experience for parents whose children have left home. It can be a time of mixed emotions, as feelings of sadness and loss may arise alongside newfound freedom and opportunities. To navigate empty nest syndrome:

Focus on self-care: Use this time to prioritize your own well-being and pursue activities that bring you fulfillment.

Stay connected: Maintain open communication with your children and find ways to stay connected, such as regular phone calls or video chats.

Explore new hobbies and interests: Take this opportunity to discover new passions and explore activities that you've always wanted to try.

Finding Purpose in Retirement

Retirement offers the chance to embark on a new chapter of life, free from the constraints of work. Here are some tips for finding purpose in retirement:

Set goals: Identify personal goals and aspirations for your retirement years, such as pursuing a new career, volunteering, or traveling.

Plan your finances: Ensure you have a solid financial plan in place to support your retirement lifestyle and help alleviate any financial stress.

Stay socially engaged: Cultivate social connections with others, whether through joining clubs, participating in community activities, or volunteering.

Remember, life transitions in your 60s can bring about new opportunities for personal growth and fulfillment. Embrace these changes and approach them with a positive mindset, knowing that this is a chance to create a life that reflects your passions and desires.

Travel and Adventure in Your 60s

Your 60s are an exciting time to embark on new adventures and explore the world. With more time and freedom on your hands, you can indulge in travel experiences that you've always dreamed of. Whether you're an avid adventurer or looking to try something new, there are plenty of opportunities to satisfy your wanderlust and seek thrilling experiences.

Safe and Enjoyable Travel Tips

When planning your travels in your 60s, it's essential to prioritize safety and comfort. Here are a few tips to ensure your journey is enjoyable:

Consult with your healthcare provider before embarking on any travel plans to ensure you are in good health and receive any necessary vaccinations.

Invest in travel insurance that covers medical emergencies and trip cancellations.

Pack wisely and include essentials such as medications, comfortable clothes and shoes, and any necessary documents.

Research the destination's COVID-19 safety protocols and travel restrictions to ensure a smooth and safe trip.

Stay hydrated, eat nutritious meals, and prioritize rest to keep your energy levels up during your adventures.

Recommended Destinations and Activities

The world is full of incredible destinations that offer unique experiences for travelers in their 60s. Here are some recommendations:

Exploring the historical sites and cultural treasures of Europe, such as Rome, Paris, or Athens.

Embarking on a wildlife safari in Africa to witness awe-inspiring wildlife up-close.

Indulging in a tropical getaway to Bali, Hawaii, or the Caribbean, where you can relax on pristine beaches and enjoy breathtaking sunsets.

Embracing the natural wonders of the world by visiting iconic landmarks like the Grand Canyon, the Great Barrier Reef, or the Amazon rainforest.

Engaging in adventurous activities like hiking, kayaking, or hot air ballooning to add an extra thrill to your travels.

Remember, age is just a number, and your 60s are the perfect time to add a dash of adventure to your life. Whether you prefer leisurely exploration or adrenaline-pumping activities, there's something for everyone to enjoy during this stage of life. So, pack your bags, broaden your horizons, and embrace the excitement of travel and adventure in your 60s!

Legacy and Leaving a Lasting Impact

As you enter your 60s, it's natural to reflect on the mark you've left on the world and consider the legacy you want to create. Leaving a lasting impact and making a difference in your community can bring a deep sense of fulfillment and purpose. Whether it's through philanthropy, mentorship, or sharing your knowledge and expertise, there are countless ways to leave a positive mark that extends beyond your 60s.

Creating a Meaningful Legacy

One way to leave a lasting impact is by creating a meaningful legacy. This can involve identifying causes or issues that resonate with you and dedicating your time, resources, and expertise to making a difference. Consider volunteering with local organizations, donating to charities, or even starting your own initiative to address a specific need in your community. By contributing to causes that align with your values, you can create a legacy that reflects your passions and leaves a positive impact on future generations.

Making a Difference in your 60s

Don't underestimate the power of your experiences and expertise gained over the years. Your 60s can be a time to share your knowledge and make a difference in the lives of others. Consider becoming a mentor or coach, offering guidance and support to younger individuals who can benefit from your wisdom. Additionally, you can explore opportunities to teach or give talks in your community, sharing your expertise and inspiring others to pursue their passions. By leveraging your skills and knowledge, you can leave a lasting impact on those around you.

Engaging with your Community

Engaging with your community is another powerful way to leave a lasting impact. Attend local events, join community organizations, and participate in activities that align with your interests. By actively contributing to the community, you can foster connections, build relationships, and create a positive environment for everyone. Your involvement can inspire others to take action, leading to a ripple effect of change and leaving a lasting impact on the community as a whole.

By focusing on leaving a lasting impact and making a difference in your 60s, you can ensure that your life continues to have meaning and purpose. Embrace opportunities to create a meaningful legacy, share your knowledge, and engage with your community. Your efforts have the potential to make a lasting impact that extends far beyond your 60s, leaving a positive mark on the world.

Embracing the Next Decade with Confidence

As you approach your 60s, it's crucial to recognize the importance of embracing the next decade with confidence and optimism. This final section of our guide reinforces the lessons learned throughout the article, empowering you to step into this new chapter of your life with enthusiasm and joy.

Reflect on the knowledge and insights gained from exploring topics like preparing for retirement, reinventing yourself, and maintaining physical and mental well-being. Use this reflection to build confidence in your abilities to navigate the challenges and embrace the opportunities that lie ahead.

Embracing the next decade means fully embracing who you are and the experiences that have shaped you. By embracing your 60s with confidence, you open yourself up to endless possibilities and the chance to create a meaningful legacy. So, step forward with assurance, knowing that this is your time to shine and make a difference.

"Turning 60 is not about counting years; it's about embracing the melody of memories, the rhythm of wisdom, and the dance of dreams yet to unfold."

References and Additional Reading

References

Bly, R. (1990). Iron John: A Book about Men. Reading, MA: Addison-Wesley.

Carstensen, L. L. (2006). The influence of a sense of time on human development. Science, 312(5782), 1913-1915.

Erikson, E. H. (1963). Childhood and society. New York: Norton.

Jung, C. G. (1933). Modern man in search of a soul. New York: Harcourt Brace Jovanovich.

Levinson, D. J. (1978). The seasons of a man's life. New York: Ballantine Books.

Peck, M. S. (1978). The Road Less Traveled, 25th Anniversary Edition: A New Psychology of Love, Traditional Values and Spiritual Growth. New York: Touchstone.

Additional Reading

Buckingham, M. and Coffman, C. (1999). First, Break All the Rules: What the World's Greatest Managers Do Differently. Simon & Schuster.

Evans, P. (2014). The Verbally Abusive Relationship, Third Edition: How to Recognize It and How to Respond. Broadview Press.

Frankl, V. E. (2006). Man's Search for Meaning. Beacon Press.

Gottman, J. and Silver, N. (1999). The Seven Principles for Making Marriage Work. Three Rivers Press.

Kingsolver, B. (1998). The Poisonwood Bible. HarperPerennial.

May, R. (1975). The Courage to Create. W. W. Norton & Company.

Plath, S. (2006). The Bell Jar. Harper Perennial.

This section provides references cited in the book as well as additional recommended reading on related topics of personal growth, relationships, meaning and wisdom that may be of interest to readers.